THE REVELS PLAYS

Former editors
Clifford Leech 1958–71
F. David Hoeniger 1970–85

General editors
David Bevington, E.A. Honigmann, J.R. Mulryne
and Eugene M. Waith

CAMPASPE
SAPPHO AND PHAO

MANCHESTER
UNIVERSITY PRESS

THE REVELS PLAYS

THE REVELS PLAYS

JOHN LYLY

CAMPASPE
edited by G. K. Hunter

SAPPHO AND PHAO
edited by David Bevington

MANCHESTER
UNIVERSITY PRESS

Manchester and New York

*Distributed exclusively in the USA
by* St. Martin's Press

Introduction, critical apparatus, etc.
Campaspe © G.K. Hunter 1991
Sappho and Phao © David Bevington 1991

Reprinted 1999

The right of G.K. Hunter and David Bevington to be
identified as the editors of this work has been asserted
by them in accordance with the Copyright,
Designs and Patents Act 1988.

First published by Manchester University Press 1991

This edition published by Manchester University Press
Oxford Road, Manchester M13 9NR, UK
and Room 400, 175 Fifth Avenue, New York, NY 10010, USA
http://www.man.ac.uk/mup

Distributed exclusively in the USA by
St. Martin's Press, Inc., 175 Fifth Avenue, New York,
NY 10010, USA

Distributed exclusively in Canada by
UBC Press, University of British Columbia,
6344 Memorial Road,
Vancouver, BC, Canada V6T 1Z2

British Library Cataloguing-in-Publication Data
A catalogue record for this book is available from the British Library

Library of Congress Cataloging-in-Publication Data applied for

ISBN 0 7190 3100 1 *paperback*

06 05 04 03 02 01 00 99   10 9 8 7 6 5 4 3 2 1

Typeset in Hong Kong
by Best-set Typesetter Ltd
Printed in Great Britain
by Bell & Bain Ltd, Glasgow

Contents

TO EUGENE WAITH
scholar, colleague, friend

General Editors' Preface

Clifford Leech conceived of the Revels Plays as a series in the mid-1950s modelling the project on the New Arden Shakespeare. The aim, as he wrote in 1958, was 'to apply to Shakespeare's predecessors, contemporaries and successors the methods that are now used in Shakespeare editing'. The plays chosen were to include well known works from the early Tudor period to about 1700, as well as others less familiar but of literary and theatrical merit: 'the plays included,' Leech wrote, 'should be such as to deserve and indeed demand performance.' We owe it to Clifford Leech that the idea became reality. He set the high standards of the series, ensuring that editors of individual volumes produced work of lasting merit, equally useful for teachers and students, theatre directors and actors. Clifford Leech remained General Editor until 1971, and was succeeded by F. David Hoeniger, who retired in 1985.

The Revels Plays are now under the direction of four General Editors, David Bevington, E.A.J. Honigmann, J.R. Mulryne and E.M. Waith. Published originally by Methuen, the series is now published by Manchester University Press, embodying essentially the same format, scholarly character, and high editorial standards of the series as first conceived. The General Editors intend to concentrate on plays from the period 1558–1642, and may include a small number of non-dramatic works of interest to students of drama. Some slight changes have been forced by considerations of cost. For example, in editions from 1978, notes to the introduction are placed together at the end, not at the foot of the page. Collation and commentary notes will continue, however, to appear on the relevant pages.

The text of each Revels play, in accordance with established practice in the series, is edited afresh from the original text of best authority (in a few instances, texts), but spelling and punctuation are modernised and speech headings are silently made consistent. Elisions in the original are also silently regularised, except where metre would be affected by the change; since 1968 the '-ed' form is used for non-syllabic terminations in past tenses and past participles ('-'d' earlier), and '-èd' for syllabic ('-ed' earlier). The editor emends, as distinct from modernises, the original only in instances where error is patent, or at least very probable, and correction persuasive. Act divisions are given only if they appear in the original or if the structure of the play clearly points to them. Those act and scene divisions not in the original are provided in small type. Square brackets are also used for any other additions to or changes in the stage directions of the original.

Revels Plays do not provide a variorum collation, but only those variants which require the critical attention of serious textual students. All departures of substance from 'copy-text' are listed, including any relineation and those changes in punctuation which involve to any degree a decision between alternative interpretations; but not such accidentals as turned letters, nor necessary additions to stage directions whose editorial nature is already made clear by the use of brackets. Press corrections in the 'copy-text' are likewise collated. On later emendations of the text, only those are given which as alternative readings still deserve attention.

One of the hallmarks of the Revels Plays is the thoroughness of their annotations. Besides explaining the meaning of difficult words and passages, the editor provides comments on customs or usage, text or stage-business—indeed, on anything judged pertinent and helpful. Each volume contains an Index to the Commentary, in which particular attention is drawn to meanings for words not listed in *OED*, and (starting in 1996) an indexing of proper names and topics in the Introduction and Commentary.

The Introduction to a Revels play assesses the authority of the 'copy-text' on which it is based, and discusses the editorial methods employed in dealing with it; the editor also considers the play's date and (where relevant) sources, together with its place in the work of the author and in the theatre of its time. Stage history is offered, and in the case of a play by an author not previously represented in the series a brief biography is given.

It is our hope that plays edited in this fashion will promote further scholarly and theatrical investigation of one of the richest periods in theatrical history.

DAVID BEVINGTON
E. A. J. HONIGMANN
J. R. MULRYNE
E. M. WAITH

Preface

This edition of two plays by Lyly has had a long gestation, often interrupted and only made possible by generous help from many sources. David Bevington received a publishing subvention from the Division of Humanities, University of Chicago, and George Hunter was given a generous matching grant from the Hilles Fund at Yale. To both of these institutions the editors are deeply grateful. George Hunter was enabled to finish his work on the Introduction when he was a Fellow at the Center for Advanced Study in the Behavioral Sciences in Stanford. For help with the proof-reading he thanks Mary Bly, and—especially—Shelagh and Ruth Hunter. The edition is, above all, the product of continuous exchange between the two editors. We have read one another's words many times, offering corrections, supplements, rephrasings, and pondered together the queries that one or another raised. We venture to hope that the results are better than either of us could have managed on our own. Outside this state of mutual support the person to whom we owe most is our dedicatee, who read our Introductions with that special quality of sceptical alertness that Maynard Mack has referred to as 'charitable severity'. We hope that he will approve of what we have learned from him and accept a gift tendered with respect and affection.

The editors would like to thank Leah Scragg for corrections included in this paperback edition.

Abbreviations

(A) ANCIENT TEXTS

Wherever possible, Graeco-Roman texts are cited by the standard reference to book, chapter and paragraph for prose texts, and by book and line (for Homer, Virgil, etc.) or by book, poem and line number (for Horace, Ovid, etc.) The Loeb Classical Library (L.C.L.) offers a convenient edition for the following classical authors, unless otherwise indicated.

Aelian   Claudius Aelianus, *De Natura Animalium* (*On the Characteristics of Animals*), L.C.L.

Aelian   *Varia Historia*, ed. Mervin R. Dilts (Leipzig, 1974). English translations are from Abraham Fleming, *A Register of Histories* (1576).

Aeschylus   Fragments, in *Tragicorum Graecorum Fragmenta*, ed. Augustus Nauck (Leipzig, 1856).

Apuleius   *The Golden Ass*, L.C.L.

Aulus Gellius   *Noctes Atticae*, L.C.L.

Bidpai   *The Moral Philosophy of Doni [The Fables of Bidpai] . . . first compiled in the Indian Tongue*, trans. Sir Thomas North (London, 1601).

Boethius   *The Theological Tractates and The Consolation of Philosophy*, L.C.L.

Catullus   *Poems*, L.C.L.

Cicero   *Works* (*De Inventione, De Oratore, In Catilinam*, etc.), L.C.L.

Quintus Curtius Rufus   *The History of Alexander the Great*, L.C.L.

Herodotus   *The Histories*, L.C.L.

Hesiod   *The Theogony*. In *The Homeric Hymns and Homerica*, L.C.L.

Homer   *Iliad*, L.C.L.

Homer   *Odyssey*, L.C.L.

Horace   *Satires, Epistles, Ars Poetica*, L.C.L.

Jerome   *Letters* of Saint Hieronymus, trans. Charles C. Mierow (Westminster, Md., 1963–. In progress).

Laertius   Diogenes Laertius, *Lives of Eminent Philosophers*, L.C.L.

Lucian   *Works*, L.C.L.

Ovid   *Amores*, L.C.L.

Ovid   *Ars Amatoria*, L.C.L.

Ovid   *Fasti*, L.C.L.

Ovid   *Heroides*, L.C.L.

Ovid   *Metamorphoses*, L.C.L.

Plato   *Works*, L.C.L.

Pliny   Gaius Plinius Secundus, *Natural History*, L.C.L. References are to book and paragraph. References to 'Holland' are to *The History of the World, Commonly Called The Natural History of C. Plinius Secundus*, trans. Philemon Holland, two parts (London, 1601).

Plutarch, *Lives*   *The Lives of the Noble Grecians and Romans*, L.C.L. English translations are those of Sir Thomas North, 1579. Tudor Translations edition, 6 vols. (London: 1895–6).

Plutarch, *Moralia, L.C.L.*
Propertius Poems, L.C.L.
Publilius Syrus *Sententiae,* In *Minor Latin Poets,* L.C.L.
Seneca *Tragedies,* L.C.L.
Seneca *Moral Essays,* L.C.L.
Statius *Thebiad,* L.C.L.
Terence *Plays,* L.C.L.
Tertullian *Apology,* L.C.L.
Valerius Maximus *Factorum et Dictorum Memorabilium Libri Novem.* Modern edition (Stuttgart, 1966).
Virgil *Aeneid,* L.C.L.
Virgil *Georgics,* L.C.L.

(B) OTHER ABBREVIATIONS

Adams   Joseph Q. Adams, ed., *Chief Pre-Shakespearean Dramas* (Boston, 1924).

Alciati   Andrea Alciati, *Emblemata* (1531, 1534 and innumerable subsequent editions.)

Bacon, *Promus   The Promus of Formularies and Elegancies (being private notes, circ. 1594, hitherto unpublished) by Francis Bacon,* ed. Mrs Henry Pott (Boston, 1883).

Bailey   See *Erasmus, Colloquia.*

Bartholomew (Berthelet)   *Bartholomaeus de Proprietatibus Rerum* (London, Thomas Berthelet, 1535). References are to book, chapter and page. Later editions of this book are often referred to as *Batman upon Bartholome.*

Bond   *The Complete Works of John Lyly,* ed. R. Warwick Bond, 3 vols. (Oxford, 1902). Citation is by volume and page.

Burton   *The Anatomy of Melancholy,* by Robert Burton, ed. A. R. Shilleto (London and New York, 1893).

Chambers   E. K. Chambers, *The Elizabethan Stage,* 4 vols. (Oxford, 1923).

Chaucer   *The Riverside Chaucer,* 3rd ed., gen. ed. Larry D. Benson (Boston, 1987).

Croll   See *Croll and Clemons.*

Croll and Clemons   *Euphues: The Anatomy of Wit; Euphues & His England,* by *John Lyly,* ed. Morris William Croll and Harry Clemons (London, 1916). This edition is cited for its commentary; references to the text of *Euphues* are to Bond's edition, cited above.

C.W.E.   The Collected Works of Erasmus; see *Erasmus.*

Daniel   *The Plays of John Lyly,* ed. Carter A. Daniel (Lewisburg; London and Toronto, 1988).

Dekker   *The Dramatic Works of Thomas Dekker,* ed. Fredson Bowers, 4 vols. (Cambridge, 1953–61).

Dent, *P.L.E.D.   Proverbial Language in English Drama Exclusive of Shakespeare, 1495–1616: An Index,* R. W. Dent (Berkeley, 1984).

Dent, *S.P.L.   Shakespeare's Proverbial Language: An Index,* R. W. Dent (Berkeley, 1981).

Dodsley *A Select Collection of Old English Plays*, originally published by Robert Dodsley in the year 1744; 4th edition by W. Carew Hazlitt, 15 vols. (London, 1874–6). The textual collation for *Campaspe* refers to the Dodsley editions of 1744, 1780 and 1825.

Erasmus Latin texts refer to the *Opera Omnia*, ed. J. Leclerc, 10 vols. (Leiden, 1703–6).

Erasmus, *C.W.E. The Collected Works of Erasmus* (Toronto, 1978–. In progress).

Erasmus, *Adagia* The *Adagia* are in process of being edited in *C.W.E.*; English versions, where available, are those translated and edited by M. M. Phillips and R. A. B. Mynors in vol. 31 of *C.W.E.*

Erasmus, *Parabolae* English versions of the *Parabolae* (*Similia, or Parallels*) are cited by page from R. A. B. Mynors's translation in vol. 23 of *C.W.E.*

Erasmus, *Apophthegmata* The Apophthegms are cited by speaker and number, except in the case of Diogenes, where only the number is given. English translations of the *Apophthegmata* are from Nicholas Udall, *The Apophthegmes of Erasmus*, 1564; rpt. (Boston, England, 1877). The Udall number is only cited in cases where it differs from the Erasmus number.

Erasmus, *Colloquia* English translations of the *Colloquia* are from Nathan Bailey, *All the Familiar Colloquies of Desiderius Erasmus of Rotterdam* (Glasgow, 1733).

Euphues References are by volume, page and line to Bond's edition.

Fairholt *The Dramatic Works of John Lilly*, ed. F. W. Fairholt, 2 vols. (London, 1858).

Feuillerat *John Lyly*, Albert Feuillerat, Cambridge, 1910; reissued (New York, 1968).

Fleay *A Biographical Chronicle of the English Drama*, Frederick Gard Fleay (London, 1891).

Fleming Translator of Aelian, *Varia Historia*; see *Aelian*, under Classical Texts.

Gosson Stephen Gosson, *The School of Abuse*, 1579, In *English Reprints, John Milton, Aeropagitica*, etc., ed. Edward Arber (Birmingham, 1868).

Greene *The Life and Complete Works of Robert Greene*, ed. Alexander B. Grosart, 15 vols. (London, The Huth Library, 1881–6).

Greg W. W. Greg, *A Bibliography of the English Printed Drama to the Restoration*, 4 vols., London, for the Bibliographical Society at the University Press (Oxford, 1939–59).

Heywood *John Heywood, Dramatic Writings*, ed. John S. Farmer, Early English Text Society, 1905 (*Witty and Witless, c.* 1530), and *A Dialogue Containing the Number of the Effectual Proverbs in the English Tongue*, ed. John S. Farmer, Early English Text Society (1906).

Holland Translator of Pliny's *Natural History*; see *Pliny*.

Hunter *John Lyly: The Humanist as Courtier*, G. K. Hunter (London, 1962).

Kyd *The Works of Thomas Kyd*, ed. Frederick S. Boas (Oxford, 1901).

Lilly William Lilly and John Colet, *A Short Introduction of Grammar* (1549 and subsequent dates).

Lyly See *Bond* and *Croll* above, and *Euphues*. Page and act-line-scene refer-

ences are to Bond's edition except for *Campaspe* and *Sappho and Phao*,
in which case the references are to this present edition.

Marlowe   *The Complete Works of Christopher Marlowe*, ed. Fredson T. Bowers,
2 vols. (Cambridge, 1973; 2nd ed., 1981).

Materialien   Materialien zur Kunde des älteren englischen Dramas. A series
featuring various titles.

M.L.N.   *Modern Language Notes.*

M.L.R.   *Modern Language Review.*

M.S.R.   Malone Society Reprints.

Mustard   W. P. Mustard, 'Notes on John Lyly's Plays', *S.P.*, XXII (1925),
267–9.

McKerrow   See *Nashe.*

N.&Q.   *Notes and Queries.*

Nashe   *The Works of Thomas Nashe*, ed. R. B. McKerrow, 5 vols., London,
1904–10; rpt. with supplementary notes by F. P. Wilson (Oxford,
1958).

O.E.D.   *The Oxford English Dictionary.*

Otto   August Otto, *Die Sprichwörter und Sprichwörtliche Redensarten der
Römer* (Leipzig, 1890).

P.Q.   *Philological Quarterly.*

Peele   *The Life and Works of George Peele*, Charles T. Prouty, gen. ed. (New
Haven, 3 vols., 1952–70).

Pettie   George Pettie, *A Petite Pallace of Pettie His Pleasure*, 1576, ed. Israel
Gollancz (1908).

P.L.E.D.   See *Dent.*

R.E.S.   *Review of English Studies.*

Scott   Sir Walter Scott, ed., *The Ancient British Drama*, 3 vols. (London and
Edinburgh, 1810).

S.P.   *Studies in Philology.*

S.T.C.   *A Short-Title Catalogue of Books Printed in England, Scotland, and
Ireland . . . 1475–1640*, by A. W. Polland and G. R. Redgrave, 1st ed.
(London, 1926), 2nd ed. rev. enl. (1976 and 1986).

Stowe   *The Annals of England*, by John Stowe, London, 1592 and later dates;
Annals, or, A General Chronicle of England (London, 1631).

Taverner   *Proverbs or Adages, with new additions gathered out of the Chiliades
of Erasmus*, Richard Taverner (London, 1539); see *Erasmus.*

Tilley   *A Dictionary of the Proverbs in England in the Sixteenth and Seventeenth
Centuries*, Morris Palmer Tilley (Ann Arbor, 1950).

Tilley, *Elizabethan Proverb Lore   Elizabethan Proverb Lore in Lyly's Euphues
and in Pettie's Petite Pallace*, Morris Palmer Tilley (London and New
York, 1926).

Udall   See *Erasmus, Apophthegmata.*

Walther   *Proverbia Sententiaeque Latinitatis Medii Aevi, Lateinische Sprichwörter und Sentenzen des Mittelalters*, Hans Walther, 5 vols. (Göttingen,
1963–7).

This Edition

Spellings for both of Lyly's plays in this edition have been modernised in accordance with the principles of the Revels series and with an eye also to Stanley Wells's *Re-editing Shakespeare for the Modern Reader* (Oxford, 1984) and to Stanley Wells and Gary Taylor's *Modernizing Shakespeare's Spellings* (Oxford, 1979). Some names of the characters, most specifically in *Sappho and Phao*, appear here in modern forms instead of the archaic spellings that are usually encountered: Sappho instead of Sapho, Sibylla for Sybilla, Callipho for Calypho. Spelling has been modernised as well in quotations in the Introductions and Commentary, except for the reproduction of original title pages and entrances from the Stationers' Register. In a similar vein, the punctuation of this edition is in accord with modern conventions, not those of Elizabethan authors and compositors. The attempt has been to reproduce Lyly's text for today's reader by finding the modern equivalent as precisely as possible. If this runs the risk of misinterpreting the text, such is the editor's responsibility. To rely extensively on Elizabethan conventions of punctuation is to present the reader with signals that are often misleading today and that are apt to be compositorial in many instances.

Editorial additions to the original stage directions are marked by square brackets, so that the reader can know when the stage directions are original and when they are not. Lyly's convention of massing the names of all the characters who appear in any given scene in one head-list, in imitation of the printed form of Roman comedy current in the Renaissance, has been altered to the more familiar convention today of indicating when each character actually seems to enter. There is little difficulty in establishing such entrances, since Lyly usually gives a clear textual indication ('But here cometh ...', or some such words). Exits can pose more of a problem, since indications in the dialogue are not always informative and since many exits are unmarked in the original; the present edition of *Campaspe*, for example, provides some twenty-one exits not given in the copy texts. There are some traces of a system, but the traces do not cohere. Thus in *Campaspe* the Page's exits are never marked; of seven exits for Diogenes only one is marked, at II.i.56.1 (which may be con-

nected with 'entrances' and 'exits' out of a tub, as discussed in the
Introduction to this play); and no exits are marked where the scene
ends with a song, whether in Blount, where the songs are printed,
or in the quartos, where they are omitted. This edition records all
changes in the stage directions in the collation.

It also silently expands some abbreviations and regularises speech
headings and other indications of characters' names in the stage directions. Elisions have been expanded except where metrically required.
In particular, words like *lov'd* are expanded to *loved* with the expec-
tation that the modern reader will pronounce the word in one syllable;
where a sounded last syllable is required, as in *entertainèd*, a grave
accent marks the vowel.

The excellence of the copy texts for both plays means that there
is little scope for conjectural emendation, and the history of the textual transmission has few if any of the quirks that charm and dismay
editors of Shakespeare. Nonetheless we have studied the issue of
emendation with care and have provided a few new readings. We
have checked every aspect of each other's work at every stage.

The collation is selective. It records all substantive departures from
Q1, giving attribution to the first edition to use the adopted reading;
it also selectively mentions a small number of emendations that are
worthy of serious consideration. Mere typographical and spelling variants are not normally recorded. No attempt has been made in the present edition to provide a historical conspectus of readings in editions
between 1584 and the present. There have not been many of these.
Campaspe was included in Dodsley's *Select Collection of Old Plays*
(1744) and was reprinted in that series in 1780 and 1825. The first
Dodsley edition seems to have been based on Q4, omitting the songs;
these were supplied from Blount in the 1780 edition, together with
a growing amount of modernisation (entries, exits, grammatical
smoothing). *Campaspe* was also included in Sir Walter Scott's *The
Ancient British Drama* (1810, closely following Dodsley), in J. S. K.
Keltie's *Works of the British Dramatists* (1870) and in F. W. Fairholt's
The Dramatic Works of John Lilly (the Euphuist) (1858, closely reprinting Blount's *Six Court Comedies*). During this same period down to
1900, *Sappho and Phao* was reprinted only in Fairholt's edition,
closely based on Blount.

The first critical edition of *Campaspe* is that of R. W. Bond, in
his *The Complete Works of John Lyly* (1902), supplied with extensive notes and an elaborate apparatus criticus, and still the standard

edition. Bond's text is, however, flawed by the inaccessibility to him of the First Quarto of *Campaspe*—the Huth copy, the only one known to him, had been removed 'into the country'—and by his reliance on a single British Library copy of *Sappho and Phao* that now turns out to be of the second rather than the first edition. These disadvantages were further compounded by Bond's error in taking the Third Quarto of *Campaspe* to be the second and his choice of that for his copy text. In plays that were as accurately printed as *Campaspe* and *Sappho and Phao*, these errors did not produce the textual disasters they might have done under other circumstances. Still, the collations will show that Bond's errors can mislead and indeed produce wrong readings in a number of important points. In an old spelling edition such as Bond's there are numerous errors in 'accidentals' arising from the wrong choice of copy text that do not however impinge upon modern spelling editions such as the texts presented in this volume.

Since the editorial work on this edition was completed, the editors have been able to consult Carter Daniel's *The Plays of John Lyly* (Lewisburg; London and Toronto, 1988). This is a modern spelling edition and thus avoids the mistakes that appear in Bond because of that editor's reliance on the accidentals of his wrongly chosen copy texts. But Daniel's is not a critical edition: his avowed purpose (a welcome one) is to provide an accessible reader's edition with a minimum of scholarly apparatus. His brief 'Bibliographical Notes' say only that the plays 'have been completely re-edited from microfilm copies of the printed quartos of the 1580s and 1590s and the collected *Six Comedies* of 1632' without specifying which early editions he has chosen for his copy texts and without providing any collation to indicate his departures from whatever texts were chosen. Carter's texts appear to be 'conservative' to the point of occasionally preserving misreadings in the original (see *Sappho and Phao*, I.ii.75, for instance, where Q1 was corrected by Q2). At other points he adopts readings that appear in later quartos (for example at *Sappho and Phao*, II.i.140 and II.iv.73) but without giving reasons for the change, since his procedures do not allow for textual comment. This is not to say that his choices are not usually defensible. In *Sappho and Phao* he generally seems to be relying on what we have identified as the First Quarto, but not always. In *Campaspe* his text is clearly based on Qq2, 3 (it does not seem possible to decide which). In every case where there is a substantive variation between the First Quarto and these later editions, Carter follows the later ones.

All surviving copies of the copy texts for the plays in this present volume (the First Quartos as here described) have been collated for press variants. No significant variants were discovered in *Sappho and Phao*; those in *Campaspe* have been recorded in the collations.

GEORGE HUNTER and DAVID BEVINGTON

Biography of Lyly[1]

John Lyly was born about 1554, probably in Rochester, Kent. His grandfather was William Lily, colleague of Erasmus and Dean Colet in setting up the first institution of Humanist education in England, St Paul's school in London. Lily was the first headmaster of the school and the author of 'Lily's Grammar', the standard Latin Grammar used in English schools into the nineteenth century. John Lyly's father was a minor ecclesiastical functionary, first in Rochester and subsequently in Canterbury. It is likely that Lyly was educated at the King's School, Canterbury. At some date between 1569 and 1570 he matriculated at Magdalen College, Oxford, where he supplicated for the B.A. in 1573. We have a letter from him to Lord Burghley, written in 1574, asking Burghley to recommend him for a Fellowship at Magdalen, but nothing came of this and he remained in Oxford, taking the M.A. in 1575. Like other literary hopefuls he soon migrated to London: we hear that between 1576 and 1578 he was 'hatching the eggs' that led to his first and most successful work, *Euphues, the Anatomy of Wit*, published in 1578, and followed in 1580 by a sequel, *Euphues and his England*. By 1582 Lyly was 'servant' to Edward de Vere, the seventeenth Earl of Oxford. It was the Earl of Oxford who gave him the opportunity to produce plays, passing to him the lease of the Blackfriars Playhouse and a troupe of boy actors to perform in it. In 1584 Lyly took his troupe to Court to perform *Campaspe* and *Sappho and Phao*. But the combination of interests that supported this venture seems to have broken up soon after this, and *Gallathea*, evidently meant for performance shortly after *Sappho*, was played at court by another company (the Paul's boys). It was not printed until 1591, when the Paul's company in its turn was 'dissolved', making its texts available to the bookseller. *Endymion* and *Midas* (which must be later than 1588 since it refers to the defeat of

---

1. The information in this section is derived from Albert Feuillerat, *John Lyly: Contribution à l'histoire de la Renaissance en Angleterre* (1910)—list of *Pièces Justicatives*; G. K. Hunter, *John Lyly: the Humanist as Courtier* (1962); and Mark Eccles, *Brief Lives: Tudor and Stuart Authors* (*Studies in Philology* Texts and Studies, 1982).

the Spanish Armada) were printed at the same time, and for the same reason.

The suppression of the boys' companies denied Lyly an outlet for his talents and (more important) a route to preferment. It was probably about this time that the Queen encouraged him (he alleges) 'to aim all [his] courses at the Revels', that is, to think of himself as a candidate for the post of Master of the Revels. He did become an 'Esquire of the Body', an honour, however, without emolument. In 1589 he wrote a pamphlet *Pap with a Hatchet* to defend the cause of the bishops against the satirical campaign appearing under the name of 'Martin Marprelate'; and it seems possible that he also wrote an anti-Martinist play for the boys, and that this caused the offence that drove the authorities to suppress them.

Three more Lyly plays were printed after 1591—*Mother Bombie* in 1594, *The Woman in the Moon* in 1597, *Love's Metamorphosis* in 1601. *The Woman in the Moon* (his one play in verse) may have been written to be performed by adult actors, but the other two clearly belong to the boys. Under what auspices they were performed, in London or the provinces, and in what years, remains unknown. Lyly was a member of Parliament in 1589, 1593, 1597–8 and 1601, for one pocket borough after another. He had married in 1583 one Beatrice Browne, an heiress of Mexborough, Yorkshire, and in 1592 he left London to live on his wife's property. But he was back in the capital by 1595, soliciting help from his many powerful friends. His begging letters to the Queen were copied into commonplace books as models of rhetoric, but they seem not to have secured the financial ends they were aimed at. He died in 1606. *Euphues* however continued to be reprinted for the next thirty years, and in 1632 six of the plays were resurrected as the work of 'old John Lyly . . . whom Queen Elizabeth heard, graced, and rewarded . . . a witty companion' who will 'be merry with thee in thy chamber'. The hope by which he had lived thus reappeared as the myth by which he was remembered.

Introduction to *Campaspe*

Campaspe was published in the first place without any previous entry being made in the Stationers' Register. It was printed with the date 1584 in three separate editions (Greg 84a,b,c):

[Q1:] A / moste excellent Co-/*medie of Alexander,* / Campaspe, and Dio-/ genes, / Played beefore the Queenes Ma-/iestie on twelfe day at night, by / *her Maiesties children, and the* / children of Poules. / [ornament] / *Imprinted at London for* / Thomas Cadman. / 1584.

The printer, Greg tells us, was Thomas Dawson.

There are copies of this edition in the Lilly library in Bloomington, Indiana, in the Houghton Library at Harvard (imperfect – lacking F4 and F4v), in Dulwich College, in the Pforzheimer Library and in the Huntington Library.

The running title in this and in all the subsequent quartos is 'A tragicall Comedie of / Alexander and Campaspe'.

[Q2:] Campaspe, / Played beefore the / *Queenes Maiestie on* / newyeares day at night, by / *her Maiesties Childrē, and / the Children of Paules.* / [ornament] / *Imprinted at London* / for Thomas Cadman. / 1584./

There are copies in the British Library, the Bodleian Library and the Folger Shakespeare Library (imperfect—lacking A1–4).

[Q3:] Campaspe, / Played beefore the / *Queenes Maiestie on* / newyeares day at night, by her / *Maiesties Children, and the* / *Children of Paules.* / [ornament] / *Imprinted at London* / for Thomas Cadman. 1584.

The only surviving copy is in the Dyce Collection in the Victoria and Albert Museum. It is imperfect—the final gathering is supplied from Q4.

Cadman, the publisher of Qq1-3, published no more books after 1589. The copyright may have seemed derelict, for in 1591, without any transfer being noted, the play was published again, under new auspices:

[Q4:] Campaspe / *Played beefore the* / Queenes maiestie on twelfe day / at

I

night, by her Maiesties / *Children, and the Chil-/dren of Paules.* / [ornament] /
Imprinted at London by *Thomas* / *Orwin*, for *William Broome*. / 1591.

There are copies of Q4 in the British Library, the Dyce Collection,
the Bodleian Library, the Huntington Library and Yale University.

William Broome died in 1591. In 1597 his widow regularised the
situation, her claim to several books (including *Campaspe*) being
recognised by the company ('The which copies were Tho Cadmans').
By 1601 Mrs Broome in her turn was dead, and rights in five of Lyly's
plays were taken up by George Potter. It was not until 1632, however,
that a new edition was forthcoming. In that year Edward Blount
printed six Lyly plays, whose copyright he had registered in 1628, as
Sixe Court Comedies, *Campaspe* being the second play in the sequence:

[Bl.] SIXE / COVRT / Comedies. / Often Presented and Acted / *before*
Queene ELIZABETH, / by the Children of her Ma-/iesties Chappell, and the
/ Children of Paules. / *Written* / By the onely Rare Poet of that / Time, The
Wittie, Comicall, / *Facetiously-Quicke and* / vnparalleld / IOHN LILLY,
Master / *of Arts*. / Decies repetita placebunt. / [ornament] / *London* / Printed
by *William Stansby* for *Edward* / *Blount*. 1632. /
[sig. G2] CAMPASPE / *Played before the Queenes* / *Maiestie* on *Twelfe* / day
at Night: / *By her* MAIESTIES / Children, and the Chil-/dren of *Paules*. /
[ornament] / LONDON, / Printed by *William Stansby*, / for *Edward Blount*.
/ 1632.

Many copies of Blount's edition are extant, for example in the British
Library, the Bodleian, Harvard, Yale, Folger and Huntington.

The order of the three 1584 editions remained for some time in
doubt, and false information may still be derived from excellent
authorities. Chambers and Bond gave the order as Q1, Q3, Q2. The
first edition of the *Short Title Catalogue* by Pollard and Redgrave
listed the three editions in Q2, Q3, Q1 order. It was not until W. W.
Greg's 1934 Malone Society edition of the play, followed up by W. A.
Jackson's Pforzheimer catalogue (1940) and Greg's own *Bibliography
of the English Printed Drama* (1939–59), that sufficiently rigorous
analysis produced clear evidence. Qq1–3 are, in the main, reprints of
one another, page for page and commonly line for line. Such changes
as there are (not mere corruptions) are often modernisations of more
archaic forms. But Q2 (at least) cannot be written off entirely as a
mindlessly derivative text. The change in the title page from 'twelfe
day at night' to 'newyeares day at night' is confirmed by court records
as a genuine correction (see below under 'Date'). Lyly was paid the
fee for that performance at court. His play text thus had a different

status from those of Shakespeare (say) or of any dramatist who sold his text to an acting company. Lyly had sold his play only to himself, since he himself controlled the acting company, and since (therefore) the power to release it to be printed it lay exclusively with him. He seems to have decided to print *Campaspe* (and *Sappho and Phao*) soon after their court performances (to advertise that success, I assume). The publisher was thus made directly responsible to a somewhat formidable court figure; and this no doubt imposed a more than usual meticulousness in the printing. Certainly these quartos are well printed, and require little emendation. I have found no convincing evidence of authorial emendation in Q2; but the conditions of publication were such that the possibility must be entertained. Bevington's Introduction to *Sappho and Phao*, below, similarly finds no evidence that the 1584 Q2 edition of that play offers any authorial corrections.

The status of Q4 offers further traps to students of Lyly. The date of this quarto makes its position in the succession quite clear; but it is also clear that the copy for the printer of Q4 was not (as one would normally expect) Q3, but the original Q1. (Q3 of *Sappho and Phao*, 1591, is similarly reprinted from Q1 of that play.) The connection is unusual enough to raise the question whether Broome and Orwin had any special reason to go back to the original text. The evidence tends to discount this possibility; it looks as if the connection was fortuitous. For one thing, the title page reverts, it will be noticed, to the erroneous 'twelfe day', which Q2 corrected, even though it keeps the Qq2–3 title *Campaspe* instead of copying the Q1 *A moste excellent Comedie of Alexander, Campaspe, and Diogenes*.

The text of *Campaspe* in Blount's collection is derived from Q4, with further minor changes, often modernisations. The startling new feature of the text of *Campaspe* (and other plays) in Blount's volume is the printing of texts for the songs, which were only indicated in the quartos by stage directions ('song', 'sing'). The issue raised by the songs is not, however, primarily a bibliographical one; the 'authenticity' that is in dispute is an authorial not a textual authenticity. Of course the answer to the authorial question affects our sense of the seriousness of Blount's publishing enterprise. If Blount undertook a search to discover Lyly's original songs (or at least the songs sung in the original performances) then we have discovered a degree of conscience we have not any other reason to expect. But the main arguments to be rehearsed here are non-textual, and it seems better to postpone them till a later point. See Appendix.

2. DATE AND AUTHORSHIP

It would seem as if the dating of *Campaspe* does not require us to pile up the dizzying ziggurats of speculation that characterise this exercise in most Elizabethan plays. There is, in fact, a simple and coherent story to be told. Yet the two most strenuous students of Lyly have conducted arguments of quite an opposite kind. Bond (II.310) offers us the improbable interpretation that the 'newyeares day at night' on the Q2 title page is a mistake for 31 December, and fixes on 31 December 1581 as the most probable date for the first performance (the Master of the Children of the Chapel Royal in London was paid for a performance on that date); and in this he is followed by Feuillerat (pp. 572–5). The reasons Bond gives for his choice are far from compelling. He takes it that the phrase 'Apelles [loved] the counterfeit of Campaspe', found in *Euphues and his England* (II.59, 21–2), tells us that Lyly had already by that date sketched out the plot of *Campaspe*, for Pliny does not say so much. He finds supporting evidence in another phrase from the same work. In the Preface 'to the Gentlemen Readers' (II.11, 6–8) Lyly explains the delay in publication by reporting that Euphues himself 'loitered, tarrying many a month in Italy viewing the ladies in a painter's shop, when he should have been on the seas in a merchant's ship'. Bond supposes that this is written to tell us that Lyly had spent 1579 writing *Campaspe* (= loitering in a painter's shop) instead of finishing *Euphues and his England*. The evidential force of such an interpretation is very slight, however. Pliny's statement that Apelles came to love Campaspe by painting her portrait can very quickly shade into an assumption that Apelles loved the portrait he had made. And Lyly regularly develops his sources in just this way.

If we leave the dangerous ground of interpreted quotations and turn to the listing of externally attested dates, we quickly find ourselves committed (if we are ever to make connections) to the assumption that Lyly wrote his plays to be performed and not as speculative literary exercises. The comments on staging below suggest, moreover, that *Campaspe* was written with precise forms of staging in mind. It seems safe, therefore, to use the history of Lyly's connection with the stage as the history of his playwriting.

In 1580 Richard Farrant, Master of the Children of the Chapel Royal at Windsor and lessee of the Blackfriars Theatre, died. The lease passed first to Farrant's widow and then to William Hunnis, Master of the Children of the Chapel Royal in London, who took out his sub-lease in December 1581. Hunnis was working as a theatrical entrepreneur as late as December 1582. Meantime the landlord of the Blackfriars was moving against the lessees. Subsequently (and therefore probably in 1583) Hunnis transferred the lease to Henry Evans, who used 'many delays' to keep the landlord from foreclosing, eventually transferring the lease to the Earl of Oxford who gave it to Lyly. So Lyly is unlikely to have got control of a theatre and a troupe of actors before the middle of 1583. On 'newyeares day at night' 1584 and on Shrove Tuesday of the same year he was paid for taking his troupe to court. It seems safe to assume that *Campaspe* and *Sappho and Phao*, stated on their title pages to have been performed at court on those days, are the plays for which Lyly was paid. The writing and theatrical preparation of *Campaspe* must belong, for these reasons, to 1583.

The First Quarto of *Campaspe* does not have an author's name on the title page or anywhere else in the volume. There is no entry in the Stationers' Register to aid us in our search. But there is sufficient converging evidence to put the matter beyond any reasonable doubt. The most palpable reassurance is to be found in Blount's issue of *Six Court Comedies*, where 'witty, comical, facetiously quick and unparalleled John Lyly' is acknowledged as the author of all six plays in the volume. It is only a mild irritant, not a counter-claim, that the entry for Blount's edition calls the author 'Peter Lyly'; John's brother Peter was a press censor, and his name was in consequence much on the minds of those in Stationers' Hall. The stylistic and theatrical evidence set out elsewhere in this edition all points in the same direction. Would that all attributions of authorship in Elizabethan drama were equally simple!

3. SOURCES AND TRADITIONS

The historical occasion for the action of *Campaspe* was found by Lyly most probably in a source he employed several times in his play: Plutarch's life of Alexander, used apparently in the translation by Sir Thomas North (see I.iii.95–113nn. below). Plutarch tells us of Alexander's savage destruction of the city of Thebes and of the shock waves this event sent through the Greek world, felt particularly strongly in Athens. In this aftermath, we are told:

> Then the Grecians having assembled a general council of all the states of Greece within the straits of Peloponnesus, there it was determined that they would make war with the Persians. Whereupon they chose Alexander

general for all Greece. Then divers men coming to visit Alexander, as well
philosophers as governors of states, to congratulate with him for his elec-
tion, he looked that Diogenes Sinopian (who dwelt at Corinth) would
likewise come as the rest had done; but when he saw he made no reckoning
of him, and that he kept still in the suburbs of Corinth at a place called
Cranium, he went himself unto him . . .[1]

The occasion of the play is thus set in a moment of peace between two
destructive wars—Theban and Persian. Of the fear or the political
calculation that may have driven the Greek city-states into this improbable harmony Lyly betrays no consciousness. The antithesis
between peace and war, arts and arms, is central to Lyly's presentation; but he declines to consider the political nature of their
interaction. The moment of peace is a moment when power relaxes
and warriors play games—whether these be the 'authentic' Greek
games of philosophy and art or the more modern diversions of courtly
(or at least gentlemanly) love.

The love story that Lyly used was one that was already well known
in art as in literature. By 1565/6 it had reached far enough down
through the social classes to be entered in the Stationers' Register as
the subject of a ballad: the 'history of Alexander, Campaspe, and
Apelles, and of the faithful friendship between them'.[2] The ballad
itself, like most of its fellows, has not survived. One must assume,
however, that it was not the vernacular spread of the story that
attracted Lyly. On the contrary it was rather the fact that the story
and its environment allowed him to draw (as he did) on a wide range
of classical sources.

The thirty-fifth and thirty-sixth books of the *Natural History* of
Pliny the Elder are concerned with the methods and personalities of
the great Greek painters—Zeuxis, Parrhasius, Protogenes, etc.—
among whom, says Pliny, 'Apelles surmounted all that either were
before, or came after.'[3] Within his elaborate and detailed account of
Apelles, Pliny devotes two paragraphs to his relationship to Alexander the Great. He tells us of Apelles: 'Very courteous he was and fair
spoken, in which regard King Alexander the Great accepted the
better of him, and much frequented his shop in his own person.'[4] In
my book on Lyly I have tried to elaborate on the general problem for
Renaissance artists (like Lyly) writing primarily for the world of court
manners (or 'courtesy'). I suppose that Lyly saw the reported
interchange between the 'king' (as he is called in Philemon Holland's
translation of 1600) and the courteous artist by the light of this general
problem. Pliny describes Apelles as a royal favourite: 'he [Alexander]

gave straight commandment that no painter should be so hardy to make his picture but only Apelles';[5] and his story may be taken as a model of the constraints and opportunities afforded by such a role. Against the strain of sycophancy that might be expected to attach to Apelles' being so 'courteous and fair spoken', Pliny allows a certain freedom or capacity to assert oneself that attaches to the artist as a craftsman professing his own 'mystery'. When Alexander 'being in [Apelles'] shop would seem to talk much and reason about his art, and many times let fall some words to little purpose, bewraying his ignorance, Apelles after his mild manner would desire his grace to hold his peace, and said, "Sir, no more words, for fear the prentice boys there, that are grinding of colours, do laugh you to scorn"'.[6] The key phrase here, for the court artist, is probably 'after his mild manner' (translating Pliny's *comitas*, the actual word that Lyly read). Apelles is said to have been able to exert his own sovereignty, in the area of his special expertise, without giving offence to his prince: 'So reverently thought the king of him, that being otherwise a choleric prince yet he would take any word at his hands in that familiar sort spoken in the best part, and be never offended.'[7] The dangers of being a prince's favourite artist are not concealed here. In his reference to 'choleric prince' Pliny was no doubt remembering the murders of Philotas, Clitus and Parmenio, and especially that of Callisthenes—a case raised by Lyly himself (I.iii.79ff. below)—who gave his prince wholesome philosophic advice, but not with the accomplished courtier's mild manner or familiar wit, and suffered torture and death as a consequence. The dangers for the Elizabethan artist were usually less drastic; but Pliny's emphasis on the manner or rhetoric by which a court artist can succeed must have seemed exemplary.

Pliny's next paragraph gives a specific instance of the reward that may come to a court artist whose independence is rendered tolerable by courtesy and fair language. Alexander, 'having among his concubines one named Campaspe[8] whom he fancied especially above the rest . . . he gave commandment to Apelles for to draw her picture all naked: but perceiving Apelles at the same time to be wounded with the like dart of love as well as himself, he bestowed her upon him most frankly'. Pliny is, of course, making a point about the magnanimity of Alexander: 'In this act of his he won as much honour and glory as by any victory over his enemies, for now he had conquered himself.'[9] But Pliny is also indicating the means by which Alexander, however 'great a commander and high-minded a prince he was otherwise', has

been eased into acting magnanimously to a commoner; both prince
and commoner have learned by the methods of 'courtesy' to allow
the space occupied by the other. This is certainly the moral that
Castiglione takes from the story:

> I believe Apelles conceived a far greater joy in beholding the beauty of
> Campaspes than did Alexander, for a man may easily believe that the love
> of them both proceeded of that beauty, and perhaps also for this respect
> Alexander determined to bestow her upon him that (in his mind) could
> know her more perfectly than he did. . . . And let them think that do enjoy
> and view the beauty of a woman so thoroughly that they think themselves in
> Paradise, and yet have not the feat of painting: the which if they had, they
> would conceive a far greater contentation, for then should they more
> perfectly understand the beauty that in their breast engendereth such heart's
> ease.[10]

Lyly stays close to the story that Pliny tells; but the difference that
time and temperament have imposed on the meaning of the story is
equally obvious. Campaspe is not, in Lyly's play, one of Alexander's
favourite concubines ('*dilectam sibi ex pallacis suis praecipue*'); for an
Elizabethan audience the love story could not be allowed to conform
too closely to these antique manners. What is interesting here is less,
however, the revision itself than the method by which Lyly throws
his revisionary light on to the material. By a technique which recurs
in his work—I shall discuss below its further use in the presentation
of Diogenes and Apelles—Lyly brings into close proximity different
aspects of behaviour, not so much, however, to achieve contrast as to
suggest more central though paradoxical positions. We first meet
Campaspe not as a concubine but as a humble Theban captive (and so
likely enough to become a concubine). But she is not alone when we
meet her: she is in the company of another lady whose condition she
seems to share. This is Timoclea, the sister of Theagenes, the Theban
general. It is she who does all the talking, while Campaspe stands by.
And the talk of this formidable *grande dame* displays her military/
aristocratic background. Timoclea's confrontation with Alexander is
not that of captive with captor, but closer to that of Porus, the
defeated Indian king, who told Alexander that he expected to be
treated 'princely': for ' "I comprehend all", said he, "in this word
princely" '.[11] Lyly here is obviously compressing into a few sentences
the whole ethical import of the story Plutarch tells about Timoclea's
conduct during the destruction of Thebes. A certain Thracian
company, Plutarch tells us, 'spoiled and defaced the house of

Timoclea, a virtuous lady of noble parentage'. Their captain, having raped Timoclea, demanded to know where he could find whatever gold and silver she had hidden. Timoclea pretended compliance and took the captain to a well where she said her treasure was stored. But when 'the barbarous Thracian stooped to look into the well she standing behind him thrust him in, and then threw stones on him and so killed him'.[12] For this crime Timoclea was carried before Alexander; he was so impressed by her 'noble answer and courageous deed' that he set her free. Timoclea had appeared at the English court in her own play ten years before *Campaspe*;[13] presumably Lyly could draw on residual memories of this earlier and fuller presentation.

But his purpose here is not to revive admiration for the paragon; Timoclea is in this play only to affect our attitude to Campaspe. When Alexander has heard and admired Timoclea he turns to his second captive: 'But what are you, fair lady, another sister to Theagenes?' Campaspe denies that she is a duplicate Timoclea: 'No sister to Theagenes, but an humble handmaid to Alexander, born of a mean parentage but to extreme fortune' (I.i.81–5). Campaspe's humility and disposability take her close to the concubine status that Pliny describes; but the twinning with Timoclea in this scene (Timoclea never appears again) is sufficient to guarantee her a share of dignity. Lyly is in search of a paradoxical effect compounded of compliance and independence. The story requires Campaspe to appear both as a chattel and as an honourable individual with freedom of choice; and so Alexander responds immediately to Campaspe's statement of humility by conflating her status with that of Timoclea; both are equally 'ladies' in terms of 'virtues', 'whatsoever your births be' (ll. 86–7).

I have already spoken about the relationship between Alexander and Apelles as a balance between freedom and constraint. Here again the achievement of the paradoxical balance arises from the combination of divergent sources. Pliny's account of Apelles' freedom of speech could hardly be reproduced by Lyly in the form in which he found it. Pliny speaks of Apelles' 'courtesy' and of his 'mild manner', as I have noted, but his account of Apelles' 'mild' rebuke to Alexander in the paint shop strikes the modern reader as something short of total complaisance. Certainly it is hard to imagine any such exchange between Elizabeth and a Tudor artist. And so Lyly's version of the scene places a further limitation on the artist's freedom of speech. There is now no reference to the paint boys laughing at the prince. Instead, we are given criticism which is evasive by its very brevity.

When Lyly's Alexander tries to paint and then says to Apelles, 'But how have I done here?' Apelles is tight-lipped enough to reply only 'Like a king', leaving it for the magnanimous Alexander to turn the point against himself explicitly: 'but nothing more unlike a painter' (III.iv.126–8).

In taking away some of Apelles' freedom of speech Lyly might seem to have unsettled the balance between independence and duty which elsewhere he takes as his central point. It is perhaps with the aim of restoring this balance that he introduces into Pliny's story another figure, whose well-documented dealings with Alexander illustrate independence and freedom of speech with a total absence of awe—Diogenes. Diogenes of Sinope is probably the most famous free-speaker of antiquity, and the accounts of his sharp refusals to compromise with authority came to Lyly from every side of the Humanist tradition.[14] The fullest list is in the *Lives of Eminent Philosophers* by Diogenes Laertius, the source of most subsequent material. Laertius' biographies are more gossipy than analytic, at least as much concerned with smart sayings as with deep thoughts. And so the Life of Diogenes rivals that of Plato in length, but is little more than a string of epigrams, of sharp and unpalatable exposures of social custom and social hypocrisy, setting the sufficiency of self-denial against the greed, pride and ambition of the social world: 'He was great at pouring scorn on his contemporaries. The school of Euclides he called bilious, and Plato's lectures a waste of time, the performances at the Dionysia great peep-shows for fools, the demagogues the mob's lackeys.'[15] His home in a tub, his one cloak folded for a bed, his lamp held up by daylight to look for an honest man—these famous characteristics or eccentricities have kept Diogenes in the sights of anecdotists and collectors of apophthegms, as in the medieval *Dictes and Sayings of the Philosophers* (among the earliest books printed in English) and in the widely read collections of Erasmus.

Erasmus's *Apophthegmata*, whence Lyly derived most of his Diogenes material, was careful in the dedication of the first edition to stress the morality of the form of the apophthegm, as one which (as it were) set a perpetual Diogenes against a perpetual Alexander, philosophic independence against the assumptions of authority. The one-liner is seen, that is, as having a necessary political function, 'none other kind of argument or matter [being] found more fit for a prince, especially being a young man, not yet broken in the experience of the world'.[16] And again:

The principal best sort of Apophthegms is that saying which in few words doth rather by a colour signify than plainly express a sense not common for every wit to pick out, and such a saying as no man could lightly feign by study and which the longer ye do consider it in your mind, the more and more it doth still delight you . . . most fit for princes and noble men, who for the urgent causes and busy matters of the commonwealth have not leisure to spend any great part of their life in study or in reading of books . . . no men's sayings are more taken up and used than those which be sauced with a certain grace of pleasant mirth[;] undoubtedly Socrates, Diogenes and Aristippus would serve better for teaching and training young children than either Xenocrates or else Zeno.[17]

Erasmus gives more space to Diogenes than to any other philosopher, and the social situation which recurs most often is that in which Diogenes' quick answers denote his fearless independence of Alexander. The situation is given plausibility by revealing at the same time the other side of this Humanist ideal: Alexander's magnanimous allowance of Diogenes' refusal to conform. In this case the king's magnanimity cannot be explained by the courtesy and fair speaking of the interlocutor, since these are the qualities Diogenes is most resolute not to possess.

It is not difficult to understand the element of wish-fulfilment in this image of the glory that was Greece. The Humanists (and particularly the northern Humanists) were anxious to assert the importance of education in Greek texts and imitation of Greek culture as routes to a morality that was free of superstition and illiberal obedience. But the world in which they lived was a world of jealous warring principalities and nascent nation states. The histories of the Greek sophists, the orators and the paradoxical sages showed, though with a teasing fragmentariness, the possibility of a social role for learning and wisdom which was not simply to be absorbed into the life of the court but to be held in tension against it. Lyly's Diogenes is presented, of course, with all the comic exaggeration of an extreme instance, but that left aside, he represents well enough one side of the Humanist dream. Erasmus, with different rhetoric but similar aims, spent much of his life avoiding, eluding and declining the stultifying commitments of court or curial honour. The life of his coadjutor, Sir Thomas More, revealed the other side of the coin: commitment killed him.

The literary consequence of these attitudes also points towards Diogenes. Erasmus and More began their literary collaboration with translations and imitations of Lucian, and Lucian seemed in this period an obvious twin to Diogenes. Like Lucian and Diogenes, Erasmus and More chose, in their major literary works—the *Utopia* and *The Praise of Folly*—to use forms that combined philosophy and comedy, to 'play the fool', as it were, with matters too serious to be allowed a straightforward statement. Lyly's Diogenes likewise lives on the knife-edge of the same paradox. Clearly he pays his way theatrically by the knockabout farce he provides in his encounters with a series of low-life characters. In this sense he is the Clown of the piece. But the Athenian context frees the 'allowed fool' from the nervous jokiness of a household entertainer who can be whipped into obedience. In the Greek context his not belonging can be given the full force of a rational choice. It is a choice whose natural consequence is poverty and contempt, just as the natural consequence of Apelles' choice lies in the uneasy compromise he has to maintain between the hope of pleasing and the fear of falling. Lyly is not concerned to indicate a preference between these alternatives but rather, it would seem, to stress their co-existence as inevitable elements in court culture.

The use of Apelles and Diogenes to embody complementary alternative responses to princely authority (leaving the mid-point between them to appear equally desirable and unrealisable) imposes certain features on the conduct of the play. As alternatives they are normally presented alternately. Several scenes (II.ii; III.iii; V.iv) show Alexander dealing first with one and then the other, so that their different attitudes to the same royal power are brought into an obvious comparative relationship; but, understandably enough, they are never allowed to meet—what would they speak about? The artist's love of beauty places him in the direct line of court tastes and court rivalries, giving him immediate access to the centre of power but rendering him vulnerable to military and aristocratic contempt. The thinker or scholar, on the other hand, may claim exemption from such involvement. His pursuit should render him free from flattery or fashion; but his freedom is bought by the sacrifice of comfort and approval. Within the fiction of the play the magnanimity of Alexander allows both responses to achieve success. In the end the 'king' takes up his true role as a military leader; with careless generosity he simply abandons the effort to make Diogenes a court philosopher and, condemning love as unfit for princes, he abandons Campaspe to Apelles. The very arbitrariness of these decisions reminds us, however, that magnanimity cannot be relied on and that the dilemmas of the court artist may then have a crueler conclusion.

In his presentation of Diogenes and the other philosophers Lyly was following the example set by one of his predecessors as a court entertainer and entrepreneur of child acting, Richard Edwards. Edwards's one surviving play, *Damon and Pithias*, of 1565, takes us to the court of Dionysius the tyrant of Syracuse. We are introduced to this world by Diogenes' fellow-philosopher, Aristippus, here the resident court philosopher and favourite. But Dionysius is no Alexander and so Aristippus can have no space to act like Diogenes. Aristippus makes the difference between them quite explicit in his opening speech:

> Some philosophers in the street go ragged and torn
> And feeds on vile roots whom boys laugh to scorn;
> But I in fine silks haunt Dionysius' palace
> Wherein with dainty fare myself I do solace.
> . . . I profess now the courtly philosophy,
> To crouch, to speak fair, myself I apply,
> To feed the king's humour with pleasant devices,
> For which I am called *Regius canis*.
> But wot ye who named me first the king's dog?
> It was that rogue Diogenes, that vile grunting hog.
> Let him roll in his tub to win a vain praise.[18]

The course of the play reveals the limitations on this 'courtly philosophy'. Aristippus wishes to differentiate himself from the rogue Diogenes at one end of the scale; he hopes equally to differentiate himself from mere parasites and flatterers at the other end. And that, as it turns out, is where the shoe really pinches. The court's ethical standards serve the whims of the tyrant, and the philosopher can maintain his balance only as long as he is permitted to do so. Aristippus is caught between his knowledge that Dionysius is wrong (and Damon and Pithias right) and the need to keep up with his principal rival for favour, the total flatterer Carisophus. And so Aristippus can neither speak out nor act well. True ethical standards have to be carried by the Athenian tourists, Damon and Pithias, who, though 'addicted to philosophy' (l. 444), offer no theories, proffer no advice, but act with such transparent virtue and unflinching self-sacrifice that the cruelty of the tyrant is at last overcome. As each of them in turn claims the right to die for his friend, Dionysius' 'spirits are suddenly appalled' (l. 1651). Even the executioner feels the effect: 'My hand with sudden fear quivereth' (l. 1660). These extraordinary effects, comparable to those that Plato describes as a consequence of the vision of The Good, show us that kings, though not amenable to philosophic instruction, may be changed by a real-life experience similar to Christian conversion. Aristippus seems to be in the play principally to reveal the dilemma of courtly philosophy, and once he has done so he is allowed to vanish. His false theory makes him useless in practice; the summing-up devolves upon a less contaminated figure, Eubulus, the king's chief counsellor, who can take the practical steps to rescue Damon and Pithias as soon as the king's conversion allows it. In his mouth the doctrine that ideal friendship is a guiding star for kings' courts is plausible as it would not have been if spoken by the self-interested professional philosopher, Aristippus.

A comparison of Lyly's handling of this theme with Edwards's allows us to calculate the degree of indirection that Lyly employs. Lyly does not offer us anything as drastic as a threat of death or a religious conversion. Nevertheless, the strange and apparently dead-end scene of the philosophers' feast (I.iii) provides a cameo view of some of the harsher realities which, though evaded by Apelles and Diogenes, are undoubtedly part of the world in which they live. The scene should also be appreciated as a typical courtly 'show' of famous figures from the past. The 'Seven Sages' are represented here by philosophers from the various Greek schools (spread across several centuries) who engage in philosophic conversation of the type found in Cicero's *De Natura Deorum*, a principal source of the matter discussed. At the same time the context seems also designed to show up a natural contradiction between authority and thought, military obedience and freedom of speculation.

The scene begins with the summoning of the seven philosophers to attend their ruler. At the end of Alexander's previous appearance he had been hailed as Plato's ideal philosopher-king. Yet in this scene the attempt to realise the ideal is shown to be fraught with difficulties. Chrysippus is the first person invited; but he is too caught up in his thoughts to even notice the messenger, and this summoning has to be reported as a failure: as the messenger says, 'seeing bookish men are so blockish and so great clerks such simple courtiers, I will neither be partaker of their commons nor their commendations' (I.iii.10–12). Chrysippus' failure to notice the invitation (in fact he turns up later in the scene as a member of Alexander's 'academy') is only a preparative for the more self-conscious and principled refusal of 'an old obscure fellow who, sitting in a tub turned towards the sun, read Greek to a young boy' (ll. 14–16), a 'fellow' we are expected to recognise as Diogenes.

All the philosophers save only he—Aristotle, Plato, Cleanthes,

Crates, Anaxarchus, Chrysippus—do what they are told and perform
as they are instructed. 'They were not philosophers', says Hephestion
in his blunt soldierly way, 'if they knew not their duties.' This is an
interpretation of *de officiis* which reduces philosophy to panegyric.
'My court shall be a school wherein I will have used as great doctrine
in peace as I did in war discipline', announces Alexander, though the
very next point he makes shows how far soldierly discipline continues
to dominate peace no less than war. The case of Callisthenes is raised,
'whose treasons against his prince shall not be borne out with the
reasons of his philosophy'. This is a reply to Aristotle's flattering
account of what 'literature' (books, reading, knowledge) can do to
exalt a king. Alexander points to Callisthenes, Aristotle's relative, a
philosopher-courtier whose love of truth did not (or rather will not)[19]
lead him to exalt the king but to 'seek to destroy' him. Such truth is
not permissible, for 'in kings' causes I will not stand to scholars'
arguments' (ll. 89–90). The philosophers have been summoned to
court to speak acceptable truths or they may suffer punishment:

> 'This meeting shall be for a commandment that you all frequent my court,
> instruct the young with rules, confirm the old with reasons. Let your lives
> be answerable to your learnings, lest my proceedings be contrary to my
> promises.' (I.iii.90–4)

To illustrate what he means Alexander then makes the philosophers
jump through the hoops of 'philosophic questions', one snappy question to each philosopher to be followed by an equally snappy answer.
Lyly took this royal quiz-show from Plutarch's account of Alexander's
dealings with his enemies the Gymnosophistae of India, where the
questions were in fact court-martial issues of life and death: 'He did
put them (as he thought) many hard questions, and told them he
would put the first man to death that answered him worst, and so
the rest in order.'[20] In the event he spared them all; and in any case
Lyly makes no reference to the life and death issue. But the example
of Callisthenes, inserted into the dialogue, keeps something of the
flavour of answering for dear life rather than for truth, as an important ingredient of this as of all court performances.

The absorption of the philosophers into court entertainment and
their acceptance of this absorption make a point about the moral
integrity of these sages, but it does not devalue philosophy itself. The
sages enter discussing a central Humanist issue: the relationship
between the philosophical conception of a First Mover and the
religious conception of a personal God. This is a subject more

Oxfordian than Athenian, but still indicative (and surely meant to seem so) of their concern with serious intellectual issues. Their subsequent decline into quiz-show contestants points up by contrast the philosophic integrity of the sage who is not present, Diogenes. The other philosophers visit Diogenes immediately after their interview with Alexander, and Lyly treats us then to a debate where the problem is very clearly set out. The duty of citizen Diogenes is to obey Alexander as the properly constituted authority (I accept without comment Lyly's quite un-Hellenic idea of the political arrangements), and this is what the other philosophers tell him. The duty of Diogenes as a seeker after truth and goodness is, however (as his answer indicates), quite separate: the role of the philosopher is to be on guard against courtly flattery and to protect the integrity of virtue by clowning and scorn and plain rudeness when required. And yet this unrelenting posture of rejection is shown to drive Diogenes into a narrow and even mechanistic response to the world. It is characteristic of Lyly's method that integrity here is balanced against a concomitant rigidity of attitude, whether the conversation be with Chrysus, the rival Cynic (III.iv), the performing family of Sylvius (V.i), the courtesan Laïs and her bullies (V.iii), the assembled philosophers (I.iii), or Alexander himself (II.ii; V.iv). In these terms we can see integrity as not the good alternative to courtly flattery but only as an antithetical kind of limitation.

In *Campaspe* Lyly shows us the contrasting problems of painting and philosophy, art and thought, in the context of the court. He does not speak about literature. Still, it is easy to see that literary art straddles the two difficulties he does talk about. Literature involves conceptual thinking, like philosophy, while the social responsiveness of its content draws it into the orbit of court entertainment and so of royal flattery, like painting. The writer is thus involved in a search for both the independence of thinking and the intimacy of shared cultural communication. Are these compatible? As a court artist Lyly had to hope they were; but *Campaspe* shows his powerful awareness that only exceptional circumstances could make them so.

4. DRAMATURGY

David Riggs in his *Shakespeare's Heroical Histories* discusses the cult of the apophthegm, which I have mentioned above in another context, to argue the point that drama which draws on the aesthetic of the apophthegm 'is free to disregard the temporal priorities that control

the movement of ordinary narrative history'.[21] He quotes Erasmus's
Preface to his collection of Apophthegmata:

> But in the speeches of the parts in comedies (that is, merry interludes) and
> in tragedies (that is, sad interludes, which we call stage plays) there is some
> more life and pith [than in philosophical dialogue] and a great grace they
> have, being set in an apt and fit place, albeit the name of apophthegms no
> sayings can have except the speaker, out of whose mouth they doen proceed
> be a person of great name, and the words purposely applied to some matter
> being even at that present hour in communication.
>
> (trans. Udall (1564); 1877 rp. p. xxi)

Riggs's analysis of the relevance of such ideas to English drama
focuses on such primitive morality-play structures as *King Darius*
(1565) and *Patient Grissil* (1559). At first view there seems to be little
in common between the clumsy discontinuity of such plays and the
fluent and easy movement of *Campaspe*. Peter Saccio uses, however,
a very similar set of ideas and applies them to the plays of Lyly and
to *Campaspe* in particular. Saccio sees the separate scenes, and indeed the 'main action' of *Campaspe*, as *anecdotal* in mode, and assumes in consequence that 'Lyly is avoiding the development of
plot'.[22] From yet another point of view M. R. Best has reached a
similar conclusion, setting Lyly's dramatic method against the 'dramatic equation': 'motivation leads to a situation of conflict which is
resolved in action'.[23] Jocelyn Powell discusses 'the interplay . . . of
several distinct modes of being' and again arrives at the perception
that 'the effect of this variety of movement is one of stasis. This is
Lyly's great dramatic discovery.'[24]

The unusual critical agreement on this point is, fortunately for all
concerned, shared by Lyly himself. Several persons have pointed to
the Epilogue to *Sappho and Phao* for a statement of this aesthetic:

> They that tread in a maze walk oftentimes in one path, and at the last come
> out where they entered in. We fear we have led you all this while in a
> labyrinth of conceits, divers times hearing one device, and have now
> brought you to an end where we first began.

Even earlier, in calling his first work *Euphues: The ANATOMY of Wit*,
Lyly provided a clear indication of his method of work. His aim
is to 'anatomise' or open up an area of life by exploring its divergent
inter-related elements—the more divergent the elements, the more
entertaining the anatomy lesson. *Euphues* has, of course, only a very
rudimentary plot (though based, I have argued elsewhere,[25] on
Terentian play-structure): Euphues, disregarding advice, prefers love

to friendship, is jilted in love, repairs his friendship and retires from the world. What is interesting here is the extent to which anatomy has led to circularity and indeed to that particular form of the circular plot which Best characterises as 'the acceptance of imperfection' (p. 80). This type of plot, in other words, offers an unfolding ethical perspective which was implicit from the beginning, given the variousness and divisiveness of the material, but which needs the understanding that five acts bring before we can see its inevitability.

This use of plot to defeat the progressivist assumptions of plot seems even stranger in drama than in a proto-novel of the type of *Euphues*. The example of Shakespeare has led us to look for dramatic characters who develop through time, absorbing the variety of experience and rendering it to us as a progression in personal outlook. In Lyly, the separate experiences of people are kept separate, not accumulated as facets of personality. They are organised for our attention in patterns which raise general moral questions and intellectual dilemmas. We are expected to notice and enjoy the extent to which differences can be turned into similarities; but we are not meant to suppose that the skill with which this is done deals with more than hypotheses. In the end, the contradictions remain and are accepted. The plot structure thus reflects the quality of the style, as in the recurrent similes that offer dazzling 'proof' that bizarre variety can be resolved into simple repetition: 'Ermines have fair skins but foul livers, sepulchres fresh colours but rotten bones, women fair faces but false hearts' (II.ii.65–7). But the absurdity of the conjunctions is evident, and no doubt meant to be evident: we are entertained by the possibility but never convinced of its truth.

Campaspe can thus be seen to make its effect by both separating and interconnecting its elements, Alexander's love for Campaspe being set against Apelles' love for her and also against Diogenes' total rejection of self-indulgence and the servant boys' obsession with girls, food and fun. Different ethical perspectives accumulate, but without causing any conflict of action between them. The world depicted is one whose static nature becomes increasingly evident as the play unfolds, but this does not cause us to lose interest in the shifting contours of attraction and opposition. At the end of the play the connections dissolve. Alexander must retreat from love (so that he can advance into Persia); Apelles and Campaspe are given happy love as a reward for passive humility; Diogenes can keep his philosophic independence by embracing a life of deprivation and isolation. To describe it in this way is, of course, to over-moralise the material;

Lyly's wonderful stylistic control gives to these options more an air of games to be played than any *Rasselas*-like 'choice of life' seriousness. But, as Powell has pointed out, the difference between such designations is liable to be exaggerated.

In thus anatomising and differentiating, but at the same time holding the material in a unity, Lyly can be seen to be balancing himself between two competing styles of drama evident, even today, among the surviving remnants of the court repertory of the 1580s. On the one side there existed a tradition of romantic adventures— chivalric tales of distressed love between princesses in disguise and noble orphans lost at birth by careless landowners, usually set in forest glades inhabited by shepherds and hermits or on pirate-infested seashores, and continuously alternating threats of disaster against unexpectable discoveries. In stylistic terms such worlds inevitably demanded for their expression a great variety of linguistic registers, styles and metrical forms; and this indeed is what we notice very quickly in the plays of this repertory.

The anonymous *Rare Triumphs of Love and Fortune* (probably performed at court on 30 December 1582) may serve as a pertinent example of such dramaturgy among Lyly's immediate predecessors. The action arises, we are told, from disorder on Olympus, where Venus fights with Fortune (here the daughter of Pluto) for control over human affairs. After a series of exemplary 'shows' the play settles down to a lengthy exposition of this instability in a plot that closely resembles that of Shakespeare's *Cymbeline*—though the material is less unified and the telling less coherent. It takes a series of recognition scenes much more complex than those in *Cymbeline* (and a direct intervention by the Olympian hierarchy) to wrench the play-world back to continuity, restoring speech to the bewitched prince, sanity to the magician responsible for his dumbness (a nobleman in exile), status to the exiled royal favourite, love to the self-exiled princess, family concord to the king and forgiveness to parasite and clown. *Love and Fortune* has a number of highly effective theatrical moments; unfortunately, nothing in it lasts long enough to build on the effects already made, and in such a consecutive plot this is a fatal weakness. The versification, veering between heroic couplets, hexameters, poulter's measure, fourteeners, blank verse and prose (for madness), augments the general confusion by concentrating our attention on the power of particular effects—and one must allow that they show considerable power.

Such a gallimaufry has a clear appropriateness for a court occasion in which the spectators are at least as interested in one another as in the play. Lyly too, we should notice, took care not to tire his audience with too-long concatenations of events. Yet even in 1582 the old-fashioned and quasi-medieval quality of such entertainment must have been obvious to some spectators at least. Another and more 'modern' dramaturgy was making headway in these same years, characterised by tighter plotting, realistic setting and bourgeois ethics.

The neo-classical comedy of the Italian courts and academies did not travel to England with any speed. Ariosto's (prose) *I Suppositi* of 1509 fathered what is probably the first English version of a play of this kind, George Gascoigne's *Supposes*, performed first at Gray's Inn, not long before its publication in 1566. The taste had reached Cambridge about 1579, when the anonymous *Hymenaeus* was performed at St John's College, and from then on the Italian form provided the standard version of classical comedy in the universities, whether shown intramurally or performed for a royal visit.

One play of this kind demands more than passing attention. Some time between 1580 and 1583 St John's College produced a Latin translation of Luigi Pasqualigo's *Il Fidele* by Abraham Fraunce, given the title of *Victoria*. The play exhibits the formula much as usual. Still, it is of special interest here, since only a short time later the same original was given in another (apparently independent) translation, this time into English, and performed at court, probably in the same year as *Campaspe*, 1584. The play of *Fedele and Fortunio. The Deceits in Love: Excellently Discoursed in a Very Pleasant and Fine Conceited Comedy of Two Italian Gentlemen. Translated out of the Italian, and set down according as it hath been presented before the Queen's most excellent majesty* (printed 1585) has been plausibly argued to be the work of Anthony Munday and further conjectured to have been performed at court by the same boy players as were responsible for *Campaspe*, under the same patron, the seventeenth Earl of Oxford.[26]

The story told in *Il Fedele* is of a type familiar to readers of the novelle of Bandello and Boccaccio: the daughter (or young wife) of citizen A loves and is loved by gentleman B while pursued at the same time by undesirable C and by other undesirables (*ad lib.*) who often have claims on family gratitude or respect. A maid or nurse has similar entanglements, though often more grotesque in kind; the suitors also tend to be surrounded by servants with overlapping interests. Such plays are tissues of urban intrigue conducted between characters with close and long-standing social relations though with sharply differentiated specialties—boastful soldiers, oppressive fathers, lubricious nurses, sprightly pages, pedantic doctors, eager *amorosi*—so arranged that no part of the plotting can move forward without engaging the simultaneously revolving gear wheels of other elements in the intrigue. Such plays bring before our minds the image of society as a kind of fairground machine in which the whole population is set spinning round the dilemmas created by the simultaneous pursuits of sex and money. And so, as the machine turns, we see the harried characters alternately groaning and singing, despairing and enraptured, sympathetic and absurd.

Plays of this kind share the chivalric romance's differentiation from Lyly in one respect at least: they are the very opposite of static. In Italianate comedy the characters can never stop running, for their intrigues are always on the point of collapse; in the romances the search for stasis is constantly interrupted by new discoveries and unexpected reappearances. Lyly's plays are close to the romantic repertory in their subject matter and their overall focus, their acceptance of love as more than socially endorsed appetite, as the kind of ennobling experience that animates the lovers in *Rare Triumphs of Love and Fortune*. But Lyly's plays offer us more than the romantic contemplation of love. They also offer us, by a witty and distancing treatment, a release from identifying with its power that reminds us of the Italian mode. They are able to balance themselves between the extremities of these other genres because their stasis allows a poised co-existence between their opposite schemes of priority. In the Italianate plays the pursuit of love inside an economically organised and anti-romantic context expresses the idealism of passion chiefly as an aspect of animal spirits in youth. Lyly, on the other hand, presents his material without suggesting any pattern of cause and effect: idealism and cynicism are each allowed their equal and opposite powers. The romance of love in *Campaspe* and *Sappho and Phao* thus comes to rest not on fulfilment but on the denial of love as a sufficiently heroic value; and such denial is given particular force throughout *Campaspe* by what we are shown of the philosophical cynicism of Diogenes and also the populist cynicism of the servant boys.

Everywhere in Lyly emotions are brought to our attention as matters to be discussed rather than acted upon, but *Campaspe* is probably the most concentrated example in this mode; it is above all a play of commentary. Clitus and Parmenio are present only as commentators on Alexander; by the context of their remarks they prepare us to understand the few actions we see. Similarly, Melippus is introduced at the beginning of I.iii with the sole function of preparing us for the appearance of Diogenes and the other philosophers. Once Alexander has registered the force of Campaspe's charms he avoids anything like a direct response (he never speaks to her alone); instead, he shares a long and brilliantly ornamented excursus on the event with Hephestion, while Clitus and Parmenio analyse his love from a more distant viewpoint. The servant boys talk all the time about their masters, especially about Diogenes. In consequence, our interest is focused less on what happens than on the different ways it can be represented. Lyly is not interested, it would seem, in the shock of the unexpected development. He arranges things so that we can scrutinise what we already anticipate for details of technique rather than accessions of human understanding. This is a characteristic his plays share with other exemplars of the courtly arts—imperial ballet, for example, or opera seria.

Lyly's reduction of romantic passion to a contemplative analysis largely derives, as I have indicated, from his uniquely static way of both allowing and controlling the potential conflicts in his plots. Behind the success of this technique lies (as so often in Lyly) the matter of stylistic power, and here the parallel of Italianate comedy permits us to attach what he is doing to some larger currents in the period. The connections between Lyly and Italian drama, when talked about, have usually been overstated; the particular correspondences that have been put forward have all been unconvincing. Yet if we place *Campaspe* side by side with its courtly neighbour, *Fedele and Fortunio*, we notice that the two plays, though totally different in general effect, share many points of technique. As I have already pointed out, both plays display the pursuit of love in a context predominantly anti-romantic. Both aim to give pleasure by showing us the transparent neatness of the dramatic construction, the fine dovetailing of the role to the plot and of one level of plot to another. Most importantly for my purposes, both plays (*Il Fedele* more obviously in the Italian prose than in the verse translation) employ a deliberately restricted verbal style, which functions to limit the range of emotional intensity in the speakers. Munday's translation (in which the effect is hardly apparent) is quite explicit about this as an ideal, describing the play as one in which the translator 'used no thund'ring words of state, / But clipped his wings to keep a meaner gait'. Munday's clodhopping fourteeners seem to the modern ear to be *meaner* less in the musical/rhetorical sense no doubt intended (i.e., middling in range as in *sermo mediocris*) than in a social sense (i.e., vulgar) so that we miss the effect. Yet even through Munday's jerky and unresonant versification we can see that the speech of this play is closely tied to the norms of real practical speech, aphoristic and laconic, a communal dialect designed to deal effectively with the surface of life's business.

In the obviousness of its rhythmical and conceptual organisation, Lyly's prose is certainly pushed far beyond the limits of realism and cannot be thought to reflect the business language of any particular community. The Athens of Campaspe must be considered (unlike the Florence of Pasqualigo) as an intellectual rather than a social construct. Yet the intellectual matters that appear in its discussions are treated in the same sharp dry way as appears in the witty business dialect of Italian prose comedy, equally unindulgent to long-drawn-out individual emotion. Since Jonas Barish first pointed it out,[27] it has become a received opinion that the structure of Lyly's prose does not simply reveal (as had been supposed) his taste for superficial ornament, but reflects rather the perceptions of a hyper-logical mind, distinguishing, defining, parallelling, and so presenting ideas as elements in a conceptual structure rather than as expressions of an individual temperament. Lyly's characters are not, like those of Pasqualigo, pursued by the imagination of disaster, and we, as witnesses, are not held in continual suspense to know who will win. The conflicts, such as they are, are not about actions but about general images of the self, the world, the other. In these somewhat rarefied terms we see that Lyly's style too can be called a 'business language', the language proper to something like the modern 'business simulation game', which seeks to expose the logic of decisions and non-decisions: how does Alexander choose between war and love? How does Campaspe compare ambition and contentment?

The structure of *Campaspe* is that of a triangle drama; but this is a triangle, we might say, without sharp corners, since here self-knowledge and self-control turn the sharpness of opposition into compromise; the effort is to produce a formulation equally appropriate for all sides, always allowing, of course, that social decorum inside hierarchy is accepted as natural limitation on the disruptive power of desire. The intellectual opposition of Alexander and Diogenes is presented similarly as a matter of shared forms used to convey antithetical perceptions. The intellectual community of Lyly's Athens, like the social community of Pasqualigo's Florence, is built on a structure of antithetical values which the comedy yet allows to be naturally co-existent. The Athenian antitheses lie not between (personal) love and (social) money but rather along the cracks of the war-philosophy-love nexus (the values of camp-academy-court). The incompatibles along these lines are explored less in a sequence of plot confrontations than in a series of witty exchanges and contrasting poses (Diogenes with the other philosophers, Campaspe with Timoclea, Hephestion with Alexander, Diogenes with Laïs, Alexander with the philosophers), arranged in terms of variation rather than development. The natural end of *Campaspe* is a structured separation, not any move towards absorption or unification: the love of Campaspe is replaced by the love of Bucephalus; Alexander leaves for Persia; Diogenes retreats into tub and self-sufficiency; Apelles and Campaspe are dismissed to a bourgeois happiness that the play does not care to bring into focus.

Campaspe, Lyly's first essay in dramatic form, picks up many of the techniques that he had already used in his narrative 'anatomy', *Euphues, the Anatomy of Wit* of 1578. The play, like the earlier work, is presented mainly as a series of dialogues, soliloquies and alternating orations. What Lyly has changed is the proportion of the elements. Though soliloquies of lovers (Apelles in III.v; Campaspe in IV.ii and IV.iv) still have an important place, the short sharp snip-snap exchanges between speakers have now become the staple mode. This does not mean, of course, that the play is simply a series of person-to-person dialogues. Only six of the nineteen scenes are of this kind— four of these being love-dialogues between Apelles and Campaspe. Even so, apparent departure from a simple dialogue pattern is often due to concealment rather than absence. Lyly's straight dialogues make very short scenes, and it is difficult to see how he could have extended them without risking monotony. His longer scenes (of over a hundred lines—I.i; I.iii; II.ii; III.iv; V.iv) all involve Alexander and are extended to this length because they show him engaged in a series of dialogues with a variety of persons—with the Theban captives in I.i, with different philosophers in I.iii, with Hephestion, with Diogenes and then with Apelles in II.ii; III.iv; V.iv. Even in scenes with greater equality among the persons speaking, Lyly normally leads the dialogue from the side of one dominant character, who distributes his demands for response among the other persons present. Thus, among the servant boys, Manes clearly dominates Psyllus and Granichus who are always placed, singly or together, in the position of respondents.

Campaspe is a short play (1518 lines of text, plus thirty-nine or fifty

lines for Prologue and Epilogue—the distinction being that between
the Court and the Blackfriars versions). It is thus shorter than any
Shakespeare play;[28] moreover it is divided into more scenes (nineteen in all) than any comparable play by Shakespeare. In typical
Elizabethan fashion adjacent scenes deal with different groupings of
characters, the play thus moving regularly from the concerns of one
group to the (overlapping) interests of another—from the Alexander
group of generals (Alexander, Hephestion, Clitus, Parmenio) to the
lovers, Apelles and Campaspe, to the servant boys, to Diogenes.
Thus in Act I: scene i establishes Alexander and introduces Campaspe; scene ii establishes the servant boys and talks about Apelles
and the philosophers; scene iii establishes the philosophers and
defines Diogenes' relation to the others. In Act II these separate
elements begin to interact: Diogenes talks to the servants, Alexander
interviews Diogenes and (finally) Apelles.

   T. W. Baldwin has indicated how closely *Campaspe* is tied to the
Terentian formula for comedy, taught in Tudor grammar schools.[29]
The general point is clear beyond question, though the details of
Baldwin's formulation are open to doubt. By the end of Act II the
protasis, indicating the diagrammatic relations of the characters, has
been set up. Act III gives us the *epitasis*, the complications which
arise when the separate pieces begin to conflict with one another:
Apelles is now in love with Campaspe (III.i), thus setting himself
into rivalry with Alexander, while the generals grow suspicious of
Alexander's behaviour. Act IV, the *summa epitasis* of the theorists,
the crisis point of the complication, increases the pressure on characters, since Campaspe also is now a consenting lover; Apelles becomes
desperate to protect at least his picture of Campaspe; the generals
tell us that time is passing and press for a beginning to the Persian
campaign. As is proper, the last episode in Act IV prepares us for the
catastrophe or dénouement in Act V: Apelles is ordered to take his
picture to the court; the king has grown impatient with the secret
opposition represented by his delays. Act V, however, manages to
delay the confrontation still further. Diogenes displays his humour;
Apelles tells us that a first interview with Alexander went badly;
Diogenes appears again to tell us how corruptingly love and war
are mixed together. Only in the fourth scene of the fifth Act does
Alexander himself reappear (after an absence of eight scenes)[30] and
only then are the fears that the others have been expressing finally laid
to rest: with transcendent geniality he unites Apelles and Campaspe
and sets off on his Persian expedition.

   Campaspe follows the Terentian plot formula with some fidelity;

yet, as I have noted above, this is not a play whose interest is closely tied to the progressive question of what will happen to whom. It is more centrally concerned with ethos (or pervading moral atmosphere) than with mythos (or structure of events): it creates an 'Athenian' world which is exactly the same at the end as at the beginning, whose features have not been changed by anything that has happened. It is for the purpose of filling in this picture of a 'world' (what Baldwin, caught in the idea that the Terentian pattern must be a pattern of active progression, calls 'padding') that most of the twenty-nine named characters are introduced. As commonly in Elizabethan dramaturgy, a high proportion of the characters are on stage for one appearance only (eighteen out of the twenty-nine).[31] The casting method by which an acting troupe of possibly no more than fifteen persons was able to populate the stage with such a variety of representative types also seems to be traditional.[32] It corresponds to that described for 'popular drama' in David Bevington's ground-breaking *From Mankind to Marlowe* (1962): the major actors move through the play by meeting one representative group after another; the minor actors appear in one peripheral role after another as old groups vanish and new groups are formed. Thus in I.iii we meet Melippus, a messenger, and six famous philosophers, who dispute first among themselves, then before Alexander, then in opposition to Diogenes, and thereupon disappear from the play. I assume that these same actors appear later as the corrupt soldiers in V.iii and as the performing family of V.i, more dispersedly as Timoclea or Chrysus or Solinus, and en masse as the 'Populus' in IV.i. A perfectly possible casting of the play for a troupe of fourteen is the following (the characters are arranged in order of the number of lines spoken, disregarding the number of characters any speaker performs):[33]

		lines
1.	Alexander for one	321
2.	Apelles for one	218
3.	Diogenes for one	148
4.	Campaspe + Melippus	143
5.	Psyllus + Sylvius + Cleanthes	141
6.	Hephestion for one	130
7.	Manes for one	102
8.	Granichus + Page + Trico + Chrysippus	73
9.	Parmenio for one	63
10.	Timoclea + Crates + Laïs	49
11.	Clitus for one	47

5. STAGING

To know the kind of staging for which *Campaspe* was written is impossible; but knowledge of the theatrical context may allow us to make guesses which are not entirely random. The title page to the play tells us that it was acted before the queen; and consultation of the records suggests that it was indeed performed at court 'on newyeares day at night' in 1584, probably in the Great Chamber at Whitehall.[34] The Prologues and Epilogues tell us that it was performed not only at court but also 'at the Blackfriars'—that is, in the first Blackfriars theatre, set up by Richard Farrant, Master of the Children of the Chapel Royal at Windsor, in 1576, as a commercial showcase for his boy actors. There patrons could be induced to pay good money to see the boys 'exercise' (so the fiction ran) in preparation for their performances at court. It would be convenient if these two venues could be shown to be compatible with one another; certainly it must have been convenient for the actors to 'rehearse' and perform in similar environments; and what we know about the outer dimensions of the rooms supports the idea. Leslie Hotson tells us that the Great Chamber in Whitehall measured sixty-two feet by twenty-nine[35]; Farrant's theatre in the Blackfriars probably measured forty-six by twenty-six.[36] If one removes from the floor space at court the room needed for the queen's chair of state and for the dais around it, room for an audience was probably quite comparable.

Auditorium space affects the amount of 'projection' required of the actors. But much more important in transferring a production from one auditorium to another is compatibility of stage space. And about this we know virtually nothing. The nature of the situation makes it probable that Farrant constructed his Blackfriars stage to conform to the mode at court, for it was the latter that was the determining factor in his whole precarious enterprise. As Glynnne Wickham has remarked (though apropos of a later period):

> Only madmen would deliberately prepare for Court performances in conditions totally different from those at Court; for not only would every move have to be reblocked to meet radically different stage and scenic conditions, but the loss of income to companies better prepared would be too serious to contemplate.[37]

We may begin then by raising the issue of performance at court. It seems probable that in the Great Chamber (or the Hall), in whatever palace was being used during the season of revels, the audience for performances sat on 'degrees' (benches banked up against the walls) on at least two sides of the room. The queen would sit on her stepped-up and canopied 'chair of estate' in whatever was considered 'the best position' to see and be seen, very likely in the middle of the hall. Leslie Hotson, in discussing a performance of Shakespeare's *Twelfth Night*, supposed to have taken place at Whitehall in 1602,[38] argues for an audience placed on all four sides of the room. He assumes (because on one occasion at least what he calls a 'grand ball' was followed by 'a mingled comedy with pieces of music and dances') that the actors performed on the floor of the hall, not on a raised stage. This would certainly make true arena staging more feasible. But there is much evidence against it. Among other testimonies[39] we hear from Hotson himself that in 1588 the Office of Works built, for the Great Chamber at Richmond, 'a new stage of fourteen foot square for the players to play on'.[40]

Hotson not only assumes that the audience was on all four sides of the stage, and that the 'stage' was only an area of the hall floor; he assumes also that the locations in the play (Olivia's house, Orsino's palace etc.) were represented on stage by custom-made 'mansions' of timber and canvas, set on either side of the stage and opened on all four sides (and so visible from all four sides) when in use by the play. It is entirely clear that such 'mansions' were a regular feature of staging at court. The Revels Office's accounts are full of statements about their building and transport. They are described there in 1571/2 as 'apt houses, made of canvas, framed, fashioned, and painted accordingly, as might best serve their several purposes'.[41] It seems likely that we must assume their use for the court (and so the Blackfriars) staging of *Campaspe*. But the acceptance of free-standing mansions does not commit one to floor-level performance or to arena staging. Hotson assumes that the actors sat on rushes at the side of the stage when they were not performing. But this is to ignore (among other factors) the exigencies of doubling. It is hard to see how the play could have been produced without some kind of private space at the back of the stage, to serve as a 'tiring house', prop store and entrance/exit facility, and to provide access underneath to the trap (when one was used). It is presumably to some such 'tiring house' that the Revels accounts make reference in 1574/5 when they speak of 'two ells of canvas to make fringe for the players' house in Farrant's play'.[42]

I am assuming (for reasons given above) that the staging arrangements in the first Blackfriars theatre followed the methods of the court so far as that was possible. We are, of course, once again without good evidence about the most important feature—the size of the stage. I have mentioned above the building of a stage fourteen foot square for the Great Chamber at Richmond. This seems, however, to be too small to accommodate the normal method of staging. To think of two 'mansions' large enough to allow persons to be 'discovered' inside them (say each one six foot square) is to notice that other action would be crowded off a stage only fourteen foot square. I assume therefore that the stage of the first Blackfriars was built all the way (or nearly all the way) across the twenty-six foot width of the hall (I do not suppose that a stage with two booths could afford to be less than twenty feet across). Irwin Smith offers an ingenious argument which leads us to the conclusion that the stage in Farrant's theatre was thirteen and a half feet deep.[43] The basis of the argument is dubious,[44] but the figure arrived at may be close enough for all that. Clearly Farrant was anxious to save as much space for seating as he could. But the Elizabethan stages we know about have dimensions which are within sight of the ratio traditionally known as the Golden Section (1/1.618). If the adult actors with stages of this shape shared court stages with the children, then we may suppose that Farrant (and Lyly) would not wish the child actors to be disadvantaged by 'exercising' on a stage very disproportionate. For such a reason Farrant may have been willing to build a stage nearer to fifteen feet in depth, even though that meant sacrificing two rows of seats.[45]

Campaspe is not a play which requires such stage features as an 'above' space, a 'within' recess, or a trap-door, which have been thought of as regular facilities in the adult playhouses. Of course there is no good reason why *Campaspe* should not be performed on a stage which possesses these features. Likewise the play does not require, if staged with 'mansions', two separate stage doors for simultaneous differentiated exits or entries. At a pinch one door will suffice for the action. It has been argued,[46] on the other side, that we can only make complete sense of the characters' movements on and off the stage if we have two doors, one to represent the route to the city, the other to the palace. This argument requires some special pleading, however, and rather tendentious interpretation of the action. For example, it is neither probable nor necessary that an audience should understand that Alexander (at I.iii.119.1) exits through 'the city' door (in order to release his Theban captives), and consequently must be understood to re-emerge from 'the city' at

II.ii.0. Of course spectators could be helped to see where he was
going by a sign-post on the door. But how many would bear this in
mind through the intervening scene, and connect his entrance with
his previous exit? For the continuity is not spoken about; no part of
the meaning depends on our noticing it. On the other hand, it was
no doubt a logistical convenience to have two doors, so that con-
gestion in the narrow spaces available could be avoided. It is certainly
more satisfying to imagine staging in these conditions.

The action of *Campaspe* is unified, in terms of place, by the city
of Athens,[47] where the philosophers of I.iii live and teach, where
Alexander and his generals recreate themselves between the destruction of Thebes (which provides the opening matter) and the Persian
expedition (the occasion of the ending), where Apelles has his workshop and Diogenes (for the purposes of the play) lives in his tub.
Most of the action must be understood to be taking place in the public spaces of that city, and indeed the action of the first two acts makes
no further demand on our localising imagination. Different groups of
people—soldiers, captives, servants, philosophers—co-exist by taking alternate possession of the open space. Diogenes' tub provides the
only obvious limitation on this openness. Bond's edition orders it to
be 'thrust' on and off the stage as required, but this seems an unnecessary piece of business. I take it that it was a permanent part of
the stage scene, even if marginally movable. The 'tub' is most easily
envisaged by thinking of it as a barrel standing on its end. In V.iii
Diogenes' entrance into the action is marked by 'But see Diogenes
prying over his tub.' This seems to mean that the actor who has been
crouching inside the tub suddenly stands up so that his head is visible
over the rim; and in this position, apparently, he conducts the conversation that ensues, for his exit is marked by 'Down, villain!' and
'Will you couch?' It seems probable, indeed, that Diogenes never
leaves the tub at all, unless at IV.i.23–4 where (as Manes tells us) 'my
master bustles himself to fly'. However, given the difficulty of getting
in and out of a tub placed in this position, probably we should assume
that even here Diogenes does not leave his 'home'. The well-attested
connection between a tub and a pulpit[48] ensures that Diogenes is well
placed for the sermon that follows.

For most purposes of the play there is no need to think of the tub
as positioned inside a 'discovery space', such as a curtained 'mansion'. But at one point the naked presence of the tub on the stage
seems to create a difficulty. In III.iv Alexander and Hephestion
occupy the stage for some twenty-seven lines before Alexander, at

l. 51, turns away from Hephestion and remarks, 'But behold
Diogenes talking with one at his tub.' I have added to my text here
the stage direction 'Diogenes is discovered in his tub, talking to
Chrysus.' How this discovery was effected remains, however, in
obscurity. When Alexander draws our attention to Diogenes' tub
Chrysus is already there. Has he been there throughout the scene?
It would be difficult to imagine him hiding out of the way, especially
on an open stage of the kind I have envisaged. The easiest solution
would be to have Alexander pull back a curtain, so revealing Chrysus
and Diogenes in the middle of their conversation. The difficulty is
that a curtain does not seem to be required anywhere else in the play.

I have spoken of the demands made on the stage by the first two
acts of the play. Act III, beginning the *epitasis* or complication of the
plot, introduces a new factor. At the end of Act II (in the *parasceue* or
preparatory move) Alexander has ordered Apelles to start painting
the portrait of Campaspe. By the beginning of Act III Apelles and
Campaspe have met; we see them either on their way to begin the
painting sessions in his workshop or taking a rest after the sessions
have started. In either case the emotional bond between them is
already visible. Apelles' workshop is thus established as a specific
theatrical polarity, a place where certain types of emotions and
relationships—the tentative and humble interdependence of 'two
loving worms'—appear naturally, in contra-distinction to other
polarities in the play, most specifically the imperious command of
Alexander, but also the severe mysogyny of Diogenes, the professional abstainer. After their conversation Apelles and Campaspe
make their exit into the workshop, which I take to be represented by
a wood and canvas 'mansion' on one side of the stage. Here, in the
space specifically associated with them, they are to be found again
two scenes later, the portrait-painting already some way advanced.
How far this entrance represents a 'discovery' is not clear. Current
thinking on Elizabethan staging inclines to the view that 'discovery
spaces' were too restrictive to allow more than initial tableaux to
be shown in them. Thereafter the characters have to move out and
conduct their conversation on the main stage. Certainly I believe this
must have been so in the cramped conditions of the first Blackfriars
theatre. They will not move far outside the workshop, of course.
Their presence on the main stage is not designed to establish any new
location, but simply to extend (as it were) the meaning of the inner
space in which they were first 'discovered'. At the end of the conversation they return again to the workshop. The curtain is drawn

and other matters take over the stage. Yet the workshop and its in-habitants (even with the curtains drawn) remain an important part of our understanding of what we see. The values of the workshop are present as an implicit commentary on the different things being spoken. The same is true, of course, of the tub of Diogenes, present (on the other side of the stage) as an antithetical statement of opposite values, reason against emotion, denial against acceptance.

Between these polarities, anchored in specific stage structures, moves the unanchored and undecided figure of Alexander. In my book on Lyly I thought of Alexander's palace as a third representative location on the stage. I now think that was wrong. Characteristically his supreme power makes him free in space as is neither Diogenes nor Apelles. In the recurrent pattern of his appearances Alexander enters first in debate with Hephestion, with whom he discusses the choice of life between love and war. Then he decides to visit Diogenes on one side of the stage, whose stability (as against Alexander's mobility) is a frequent matter for comment. The issue is primarily one of ethos, but the staging gives it physical particularity. At the end of the play, in Diogenes' final appearance, Alexander and Diogenes are both still making the same point:

> *Alexander*. Diogenes, I will have thy cabin removed nearer to my court, because I will be a philosopher.
> *Diogenes*. And when you have done so I pray you remove your court further from my cabin, because I will not be a courtier.   (V.iv.78–83)

The other (and contrasting) place to be visited by Alexander on his Athenian circuit is Apelles' workshop, which becomes established as another place where imperial command cannot be entirely successful. The central truth of this concerns Campaspe; but the point is made separately in one of those small emblematic scenes that are a recurrent feature of Elizabethan dramaturgy. As hegemon of Greece (soon to be master of the world) Alexander assumes that he can master the art of painting. His failure here, at the workshop, parallels his other failure, at the tub, and the magnanimity of his accepting failure here again parallels his magnanimity there, as well as anticipating his major magnanimity when he accepts the propriety of Campaspe's move from the palace back to the workshop. With considerable theatrical skill Lyly doubles the threat to the enclosed world of the workshop. At III.iv.129, Alexander declares the portrait-painting finished and orders Apelles to 'dismiss' Campaspe. In a rather unusual piece of stage business Lyly seems to require Campaspe to retire into the workshop and then (after last farewells perhaps) to re-emerge and walk slowly across the stage (towards the palace we must understand—see III.iv.139n.) while watched, and admired, by Alexander. This proves, however, to be only a temporary alienation. In the very next scene Apelles devises his scheme to give the portrait 'a blemish, that by that means she may come again to my shop'. In IV.ii we see Campaspe returning again for the second set of sittings; and the workshop structure again becomes a refuge for love under threat. Then the threat is realised a second time: in IV.v the page comes to tell Apelles that he 'must come away quickly with the picture'. In V.ii Apelles, detached from the workshop presumably, tells us how inadequately he behaved at court. He is full of foreboding. But Alexander's magnanimity turns out to be as extensive as his power; the idea of using the workshop as a refuge for love was unnecessary. In the final scene Alexander pretends that Apelles' shop has caught fire. The aim is to secure a spontaneous expression of values (as in the Judgement of Solomon). Apelles' reply reveals that he values Campaspe even more than his paintings. Mentally if not physically the workshop (as place of concealment) *has* been destroyed. (I assume that the audience were not too puzzled to see the stage booth still visible, unconsumed.) But it does not matter. Alexander turns his back on all these Athenian entanglements and marches off to Persia. It is presumably not unintentional that the stage picture at the end of the play is still dominated by the tub and the workshop, expressions both of Alexander's limitation and of his magnanimity in allowing for that limitation.

6. PERFORMANCE

The evidence available to us suggests that Lyly wrote most of his plays for particular companies of boy actors to perform, and that these were (in the cases of *Campaspe* and *Sappho and Phao* at least) companies over whom Lyly could exercise a considerable measure of control. The records supply us with a number of different titles for the companies involved—'Oxford's servants', 'the children of her Majesty's chapel', 'the children of Paul's'; but these groups seem to have existed in a relationship more fluid than the separate names would suggest. Richard Farrant, the great choir-boy impresario of the seventies, was officially Master of the Children of the Chapel Royal at Windsor, but he seems to have been able to deploy a company that drew on both the Windsor and the London Chapels

Royal, acting together in the 'private' theatre in Blackfriars that Farrant had set up in 1576. 'Lord Oxford's servants' were paid for the court performance of a play that most likely was *Campaspe* on 'newyeares day at night' 1584, and again on 3 March (Shrove Tuesday) for another play, most probably *Sappho and Phao*, John Lyly being the payee on both occasions. But the title pages of both these plays tell us that they were performed before the queen by 'her Majesty's children and the children [boys] of Paul's'. Under Oxford's protection Lyly seems to have aimed at the mantle of Farrant (who—as I have noted above, under 'Date'—had died in 1580), seeking the theatrical authority, even if not the other functions, of a choir-master. During the brief period when he held the lease of the Blackfriars theatre, Lyly must have had some power over both the chapel children and the Paul's boys,[49] both these choral organisations being, at that moment, somewhat disorganised; the Paul's Mastership had become vacant after the death of Sebastian Westcott in 1582, and William Hunnis, the Master of the Children of the Chapel Royal (who had earlier allowed Farrant to run the theatrical enterprise) was saved from bankruptcy only by Oxford's purchase of the Blackfriars lease.

However achieved, Lyly's command of a body of actors between some time in 1583 and May 1584 cannot be doubted. He had, presumably, the power to produce his own plays according to his own taste (with the Master of the Revels's permission). This does not mean of course, that *Campaspe* and *Sappho and Phao* show Lyly imposing an alien vision on his unfortunate servant-actors. These plays are written, it is evident, to exploit the talents the boys possessed by nature and training, drawing on their theatrical strengths and minimising their weaknesses. As actors the boys obviously possessed a highly disciplined talent for matching performances against one another, for team-work not dissimilar to that required for part-singing in elaborate polyphonic music—control over timing, volume, phrasing and the intonation patterns needed to display the vivacity of artificial speech forms. The age-range of the children involved is not clear;[50] presumably the point at which the treble voice begins to break is a *terminus ad quem*; the inconclusive evidence available suggests that the years between eleven and sixteen probably marked the peak of their theatrical usefulness. At such an age the dressing-up of children as adult men and women was, presumably, no longer offensively implausible. But the distance between the representation and the thing represented, which I take to be the key issue in the acting of children, was still entirely obvious. The enjoyment of child acting is largely dependent, I am suggesting, on the spectacle of the actors themselves enjoying the virtuosity involved in pretending to be someone unlike, self-consciously manipulating the symbols of femininity, senility, godlike authority or whatever. In such acting, as even today in the court-derived spectacles of opera and ballet, awareness of technical skill in the performer is matched for an audience of aficionados by appreciation of technique, so that the nature of the character being represented is distanced behind fascination with the means of representation.

In *Campaspe*, for example, the play sets up a range of contrasts between the shrinking Campaspe, the imperious Alexander, the pert Manes, the intransigent Diogenes. Yet each of these parts is being played by a boy who is only *playing* at being an adult of one kind or another, obviously collaborating with the others in keeping up the game of pretence. Contrast, tension, dispute are thus registered as part of the game, and can be expected to develop by way of the rules of the game, not by way of any psychological likelihood. With such actors, real opposition, like that between Shylock and Antonio, Don Pedro and Don John, Kate the Shrew and Petruchio, must be avoided; for each character in such a play as *Campaspe* is designed, like any single vocal line in a polyphonic texture, to provide contrast only within the limits of a total harmony; the price to be paid for this is that each separate vocal line tends to be individually inexpressive; the surprises and expressivenesses are provided by the clashes *between* the voices; the individual characters are not permitted to shift or develop in unpredictable ways as Shakespeare's characters usually do.

Self-consciously formal acting of the kind the children must have engaged in throws attention much more on the techniques of speech and much less on the feelings behind speech, in strong contrast to modern 'realist' theatre. Boys in grammar school were taught acting in order to encourage voice production and boldness of carriage; and the success of such methods is presumably demonstrated by the use of boys as Prologues (not only in plays, as in *Love's Labour's Lost* for example, where Shakespeare shows his reservations about the practice, but also in innumerable open-air shows, arches of triumph etc.). Paradoxically, Lyly's limitation of his dramatic language to prose (and to a special kind of prose) aids in this concentration on enunciative clarity. The emotional pressures that the rhythms of verse mimic are deflated in prose, and syntax is highlighted as representing the rhythm of thought. The cool impersonality of highly mannered prose thus turns its speakers into exponents of control, sceptical about the particular effects of passion or persuasion, and given to analysing the effects of what has already happened rather than seeking to influence the course of events that might happen. Let us look at some examples of Lyly's stylistic technique in the prose of *Campaspe*:

> *Parmenio.* Madam, you need not doubt; it is Alexander that is the conqueror.
> *Timoclea.* Alexander hath overcome, not conquered.
> *Parmenio.* To bring all under his subjection is to conquer.
> *Timoclea.* He cannot subdue that which is divine.
> *Parmenio.* Thebes was not.
> *Timoclea.* Virtue is.   (I.i.50–6)

The prose here moves under no less control than does stanzaic verse. The first three speeches are controlled by the polyptoton (i.e., the repetition of different forms of the same word) on *conquer*; towards one or another form of this word all three speeches move. The redefinitions of the word provide the logical substance of the exchange just as the different grammatical forms of the word control the rhythm. The sequence ends when Parmenio provides his declarative definition: to conquer is to create subjection. The next three lines then pick up the new base-word *subjection*: Parmenio's *subjection* is answered by Timoclea's *subdue* which is now redefined in terms of a new context which is signalled, once again, by the most important word in the line: the last one—*divine*. In terms of meaning at least, *divine* is the final word of each line of the second triplet, though in the second and third lines the actual word is suppressed.[51] Lyly seems to be aiming here to produce the effect of a *stretto* or narrowing of the syntactic space so that the effect of 'coming to a point' is marked in rhythm as well as meaning. The effect is also, of course, an effect of characterisation. Timoclea 'wins' the dispute with Parmenio by seizing the last and most compressed syntactic position; her definiteness and self-assurance are strongly asserted by means whose impact is stronger in terms of form than of content.

Consider, in contrast, the different kind of rhetoric deployed in longer speeches. Here is Hephestion concluding his argument that Alexander should not submit to the enervating impulses of love:

> Remember, Alexander, thou hast a camp to govern, not a chamber; fall not from the armour of Mars to the arms of Venus, from the fiery assaults of war to the maidenly skirmishes of love, from displaying the eagle in thine ensign to set down the sparrow. I sigh, Alexander, that where fortune could not

conquer, folly should overome. But behold all the perfection that may be in Campaspe—a hair curling by nature not art, sweet alluring eyes, a fair face made in despite of Venus and a stately port in disdain of Juno, a wit apt to conceive and quick to answer, a skin as soft as silk and as smooth as jet, a long white hand, a fine little foot, to conclude, all parts answerable to the best part—what of this? Though she have heavenly gifts, virtue and beauty, is she not of earthly mettle, flesh and blood? You, Alexander, that would be a god, show yourself in this worse than a man, so soon to be both overseen and overtaken in a woman, whose false tears know their true times, whose smooth words wound deeper than sharp swords. There is no surfeit so dangerous as that of honey, nor any poison so deadly as that of love; in the one physic cannot prevail, nor in the other counsel.   (II.ii.67–88)

Hephestion's persuasion depends, of course, on a basic antithesis between love and war, self-abandonment and self-control, which Lyly uses to generate an apparently infinite series of restatements and variations (what the age called *copia*). But the augmentations of the basic idea are not there simply to demonstrate fluency in discourse (as commentators on *copia* sometimes seem to imply). The passage breaks down into three paragraphs, each refocused by a direct reference to Alexander: 'Remember, Alexander . . .', 'I sigh, Alexander . . .', 'You, Alexander . . .', each screwing one notch tighter the assault on the king's dignity. The first paragraph is a reminder of practical duties; the second (more in sorrow than in anger) is a statement of the fall from perfection; the third is an assault on Alexander's self-image. The first paragraph plays to a repeated rhythm, restating the antithesis in its protean forms: camp/chamber, Venus/Mars, war/love, eagle/sparrow. The second paragraph offers us a cumulative *concessio*; let us concede that Campaspe has wonderful hair, eyes, port, wit, skin, hand, foot, everything (even the 'heavenly gifts'), yet in spite of all that she's only flesh and blood. The seesaw rhythm of antithesis has given way here to the slow accumulation and sharp decline of lengthy concession and quick refutation. The third paragraph returns us (with something like the symmetry of a *da capo* aria) to the antithetical mode. The explicitly stated relation of Alexander and Campaspe is now presented directly as an externally observable destruction of the higher form by the lower. The *coda* is self-consciousness: Hephestion knows that his speech cannot alter Alexander's passion. The reply speech of Alexander (which follows) is thus anticipated and prepared for; the relay-race baton is passed over smoothly; the one vocal line is 'tuned out' so that the next voice can 'tune in'.

Such musical analogies as I have been using seem inescapable when one is talking about the detail of Lyly's literary organisation, not simply because his actors were choir-boys, but rather more because of the ensemble nature of what he had to say—that experience can be given meaning only through the way it fits together, balancing the specificity of particular moments against the formality that is needed to articulate them. The musical analogy becomes more than analogical, of course, in the songs which appear or reappear (by whatever strange accident) in the text of the plays printed by Blount in 1632. I have discussed the songs in both *Campaspe* and *Sappho and Phao* in the Appendix. Here I need say no more than that I continue to suppose that Lyly wrote them.

The post-Elizabethan stage history of *Campaspe* is illuminated only by two widely separated and low-intensity items. This is perhaps less surprising than the fact that there is any post-Elizabethan stage history at all, *Campaspe* being a play so exactly matched to the circumstances of its early performance. R. W. Bond made known the first of these items, the notice in John Genest's *The English Stage 1660–1830* of a performance in 1731 of a play 'Never acted before, The Cynic or the Force of Virtue'. Genest gives an (abbreviated) cast list for the production and then goes on to say: '*The Cynic* was no doubt an alteration of *Alexander and Campaspe*, written by Lilly.' He then provides a summary of the plot of Lyly's play and notes: 'This play was printed in 1584—it had been acted at court and at Blackfriars—it is superior to the generality of Lilly's plays—the plot is slight but the dialogue is good, particularly as far as Diogenes is concerned.' Today we can piece out the information given by Genest by means of details given in *The London Stage 1660–1800*. There we learn that the play was performed on 22 and 23 February at Odell's Theatre in Aycliffe Street in Goodman's Fields—a theatre managed by Henry Giffard, who played Apelles; his wife played Campaspe and his brother, William Giffard (the elder), performed Alexander. The part of Diogenes was played by Philip Huddy, a veteran actor and regular member of the Goodman's Fields company. The cast list tells us something of the modifications imposed on the play: the philosophers of I.iii. have disappeared, as have Timoclea from I.i, Sylvius and his three sons from V.i and Laïs' military escort from V.iii. The play, thus shorn of its single-episode characters, was obviously concentrated on the love-story (referred to in the second title) played by the company's leading actors, and on the comic Diogenes who supplied the first title for the play. Two performances (the second

for 'the author's benefit') do not seem to have encouraged Giffard
to persevere with his experiment.

The second item in this brief and uneventful history springs out
of totally different circumstances. On 7, 8 and 9 December 1908 the
young ladies of Lady Margaret Hall in Oxford performed *Campaspe*
in Oxford's New Masonic Hall. The performance was noted in *The
Times* of 8 December (p. 12), which tells us that the performance was
in aid of the L.M.H. library and was under the direction of Miss
Hadow. From the same source we learn that the Epilogue at court
was performed 'with an adroit interpolation regarding Lyly's connection with Magdalen and the University'. Miss K. M. Lee, formerly
Vice-Principal of L.M.H., has generously provided me with further
information from 'The Brown Book', the college's annual record.
This tells us that

> In staging, the production was as nearly on the lines of the original per-
> formance as possible. It was opened by a pavan and a galliard danced by
> four ladies in Elizabethan costume—then the Prologue entered in the dress
> of the Paules boys of the period, and the play proceeded on a stage simply
> draped with dark curtains, with a recess at the back to represent Apelles'
> shop, while the only 'properties'—Diogenes' tub and a stool—were lifted
> on and off as the scene required.

The cast list from the extant programme suggests that the play was
performed without any radical cuts. The only names not represented
on the list are those of Laïs the courtesan and her military escort.

NOTES

1 Plutarch, *Lives*, IV.311.
2 See Hyder E. Rollins, *An Analytical Index to the Ballad Entries in the Stationers' Registers, 1557–1709* (rpt. 1967), no. 1119.
3 Pliny, *Natural History*, XXXV.36. Holland, II, p. 537.
4 *Ibid.*, XXXV.36. Holland, II, pp. 538.
5 *Ibid.*, VII.37; XXXV.36. Holland, II, p. 538.
6 *Ibid.*, XXXV.36. Holland, II, pp. 538–9.
7 *Loc. cit.*
8 It is too late now to do anything effective about Campaspe's name, but
  the form does seem to be inauthentic. The best manuscript of Pliny (the
  Bamburgensis) has 'pancaspe'—a form repeated in Aelian (*Varia Historia*,
  XII.34).
9 Pliny, XXXV.36. Holland, II, p. 539.
10 Castiglione, *The Courtier*, trans. Sir Thomas Hoby (1561). Tudor Translations edition (London, 1900), pp. 95–7.
11 Plutarch, *Life of Alexander*, IV.369.

12 *Ibid.*, p. 310. The same story of a heroic woman's revenge appears in the anonymous play *A Larum for London* (1599) where, during the sack of Antwerp, a burgher's wife tells Van End that her treasure is in the vault; when he looks down to find it she pushes him inside (M.S.R., ll. 311ff.).

13 Albert Feuillerat, *Documents Relating to the Office of the Revels in the Time of Queen Elizabeth* (Louvain, 1908), p. 206. The play was called *Timoclea at the Siege of Thebes*.

14 See J. L. Lievsay, 'Some Renaissance Views of Diogenes the Cynic', *J. Q. Adams Memorial Studies*, ed. J. G. McManaway et al. (Washington, D.C., 1948); Peter Paul, 'Shakespeare's Timon and Renaissance Diogeniana', *The Upstart Crow*, III (1980), 54–64. It is worth remembering that Diogenes' name appears on the title-page of the First Quarto, and that the only mention of *Campaspe* in Lyly's own lifetime refers to it as 'the silly interlude of Diogenes' (see N.W.'s Preface to Samuel Daniel's *The Worthy Tract of Paulus Jovius*, cited in Hunter, p. 280).

15 Diogenes Laertius, *Lives of Eminent Philosophers*, VI.24.

16 *The Apophthegmes of Erasmus*, trans. Nicholas Udall (1564); (Boston, England, 1877), p. ix.

17 *Ibid.*, xxii, xxvi.

18 Richard Edwards, *Damon and Pithias* (M.S.R.), ll. 14–26.

19 Chronologically speaking, Alexander's displeasure with Callisthenes (during the Persian campaign) comes *after* the present events in Greece.

20 Plutarch, *Life of Alexander*, IV.372.

21 Cambridge, Mass, 1971, p. 51.

22 Peter Saccio, *The Court Comedies of John Lyly* (Princeton, 1969), p. 30.

23 M. R. Best, 'Lyly's Static Drama', *Renaissance Drama*, n.s., I (1968), 75–86, esp. p. 76.

24 Jocelyn Powell, 'John Lyly and the Language of Play', *Elizabethan Theatre*, ed. John Russell Brown and Bernard Harris (London, 1966), pp. 147–67, esp. p. 158.

25 G. K. Hunter, pp. 54–7.

26 See *A Critical Edition of Anthony Munday's 'Fedele and Fortunio'*, ed. Richard Hosley (New York, 1981).

27 Jonas Barish, 'The Prose Style of John Lyly', *E.L.H.*, XXIII (1956), 14–35.

28 Relevant comparisons are with *The Taming of the Shrew* (2750 lines, 14 scenes); *Love's Labour's Lost* (2747 lines, 9 scenes); *The Comedy of Errors* (1763 lines, 9 scenes); *A Midsummer Night's Dream* (2222 lines, 9 scenes).

29 T. W. Baldwin, *William Shakspere's Five-Act Structure* (Urbana, Ill., 1947, pp. 496–7.

30 On Act IV absences see G. K. Hunter, 'Were there Act-pauses on Shakespeare's stage?', *English Renaissance Drama: Essays in Honor of Madeleine Doran and Mark Eccles*, ed. Standish Henning, R. Kimbrough, and R. Knowles (Carbondale, Ill., 1976), p. 30 and n. 14.

31 Saccio, in *The Court Comedies of John Lyly*, p. 30, speaks of this phenomenon as if it represented something special in the organisation of *Campaspe*. But compare, for example, Lodge's *The Wounds of Civil War* (1588), in which 27 characters, out of 47 in all, make only one apearance. Or take *Clyomon and Clamydes* (1570), which has 25 singletons out of 38, or *A Knack to Know a Knave* (1592) which has 17 out of 28.

32 See William A. Ringler Jr., 'The Number of Actors in Shakespeare's

Early Plays', *The Seventeenth-Century Stage*, ed. G. E. Bentley (Chicago, 1968), pp. 110–34. But compare Hunter, 'Act-pauses', p. 358, n. 15.

33 The line-counts are taken from the present edition, each printed line counting as one regardless of its length. The total number thus generated is 1518. The Malone Society edition, following the lineation of Q1, counts a total of 1510 (omitting the Prologues and Epilogues). The pattern I have outlined assumes that Apelles stays inside his 'workshop' booth till his first appearance in II.ii (and is therefore not at that time available for doubling). The arrangement adopted for the distribution of the philosopher roles in I.iii can be managed easily only if Cleanthes and Chrysippus leave the stage at I.iii.128, when the other philosophers go to visit Diogenes (Cleanthes and Chrysippus do not speak after this point). 'People' in IV.i could be played by actors 2, 3, 4, 5, 11, 13 or 14, or any selection from these. But see Ringler, *op. cit.*, p. 115: 'My experience in analyzing the casting of the plays indicates that a plural for mute "attendants," "soldiers," etc. should usually be interpreted as no more than two.'

34 See Glynne Wickham, *Early English Stages 1300 to 1660*, II.ii (London and New York, 1972), p. 221.

35 Leslie Hotson, *Shakespeare's Wooden O* (London, 1959), p. 297.

36 See Irwin Smith, *Shakespeare's Blackfriars Playhouse* (New York, 1964), chap. 6. In an unpublished paper John Astington estimates that the Great Chamber at Richmond measured 40 feet by 70.

37 Wickham, *op. cit.*, p. 29.

38 Leslie Hotson, *The First Night of 'Twelfth Night'* (London and New York, 1954).

39 In 1601–2 the Office of Works made out an account for 'framing and setting up a broad stage in the middle of the hall' (Hotson, *'Twelfth Night'*, p. 70, n. 1); in 1603/4 the Works charged for 'altering of a stage in the hall to bring it nearer the king' (*ibid.*, pp. 70–1). In 1580 the Revels Office used 'six single quarters' (2 by 4 inch studs) and 'two double quarters' (4 by 4 inch studs) 'to enlarge the scaffold in the hall on Twelfth Night'. The players on that occasion were Leicester's Men, the palace was Whitehall and the play was that referred in the Revels books as *The History of—* (Feuillerat, *op. cit.*, p. 327).

40 Hotson, *'Twelfth Night'*, p. 69, n. 1.

41 Feuillerat, p. 145.

42 *Ibid.*, p. 244.

43 Smith, *op. cit.*, pp. 141–4.

44 Smith draws on the clear use of a trap in Peele's *The Arraignment of Paris* 'presented before the Queen's majesty by the children of her chapel'— probably in 1581. But the text of Peele's play that has come down to us is tied precisely to its performance at court: 'she delivereth the ball of gold into the Queen's own hands'. If the play was performed not only at court but also in the Blackfriars it must have been modified in some ways. Those 'some ways' could well have included the use of the trap.

45 One of the few pieces of evidence we have offers its own contribution to puzzlement. In 1959 William E. Miller printed in *M.L.N.*, LXXIV, p. 2, a note from Abraham Fleming's translation of Virgil (1589) justifying the translation of '*scaena . . . versis . . . frontibus*' by references to Servius and

Vitruvius. These authorities described an ancient theatrical machine, the *machina versilis* or periaktos, which was a three-sided stage device that could be rotated to display different painted scenes. 'This device', says Fleming, 'was not unlike the motion of late years to be seen in the black friars' (compare *Shakespeare Quarterly*, xv, 1964, 61–5). The date of Fleming's book tells us that he must be referring to the first Blackfriars, so that we seem to be required to envisage a stage for *Campaspe* which accommodated not only mansions but also periaktoi. Unfortunately, for all the factuality of Fleming's comment, it is very hard to imagine a use for periaktoi in *Campaspe*. If we have a mansion for Apelles' workshop and a tub for Diogenes, what need is there in the play for a change of scene-painting? We seem to be reduced to the unsatisfactory assumption that periaktoi were available in the first Blackfriars playhouse, but that Lyly did not write *Campaspe* in such a way as to make use of the facility.

46 See Michael R. Best, 'The Staging and Production of the Plays of John Lyly', *Theatre Research*, IX (1968), 104–17, presenting material more fully set out in his University of Adelaide dissertation, 'The Development of Ideas and Techniques in the Drama of John Lyly'.

47 Compare D. Bevington below on the staging of *Sappho and Phao* (pp. 184ff.).

48 The connection arises presumably from Puritan preference for unornamented simplicity in church furnishings. The first reference in *O.E.D.* to link tub and pulpit is dated 1643 (*tub* sb. 4: 'applied contemptuously or jocularly to a pulpit, especially of a non-conformist preacher'). *Tub-preacher* is cited from the same year; *tub-thumper* from 1662; both are used with the same anti-Puritan emphasis. See also Pope's note on *Dunciad*, II.2: 'the pulpit of a Dissenter is usually called a Tub'. If the connection between Diogenes' tub and the pulpit of a Puritan preacher were to be allowed, then an intriguing possibility arises that Lyly's Diogenes may have been designed as a glance at the stiff-necked nonconformist preachers of Elizabeth's reign.

49 In 1589 Gabriel Harvey called Lyly 'the Vicemaster of Paul's' (as well as 'The Foolmaster of the Theatre'). W. Reavley Gair, *The Children of Paul's* (Cambridge, 1982), p. 96, has sought to reanimate a somewhat decayed theory that Harvey's words can be understood to refer to an actual post held by Lyly (Gair calls it a 'semi-official' post) as deputy to Thomas Giles, the almoner of St Paul's. The Paul's post would thus give Lyly powers over the Paul's boys parallel to those he seems to have acquired over the Chapel children. Elizabethan literary polemic, however, seldom provides terms that can be relied on as fact, even 'semi-officially'. 'Foolmaster of the Theatre' would appear to be a phrase without any factual basis whatsoever. Harvey is certainly playing on the theatrical meanings of *Vice* and *Fool*; and that may well be the whole justification of the remark. Certainly he would not be averse to drawing on the other meaning of vice, meaning sin. That *Vice* here also means deputy I am by no means convinced.

A more probable line of connection between Lyly and the Paul's boys is provided through Lyly's partner in the Blackfriars venture, Henry Evans, who was paid for a play acted at court by 'the children of the Earl of Oxford' on 27 December 1584. It thus appears that Evans (even if not Lyly) was still connected with the Blackfriars venture eight months after the lease for the Blackfriars theatre had been lost. Evans was also a legatee in the will of Sebastian Westcott, who had been master of the Paul's choir-boys for nearly thirty years before he died in April 1582. We do not know the nature of Evans's connection with Westcott, but that he had one is clear. Evans is one of those shadowy figures who flit through the labyrinths of Elizabethan theatrical litigation, usually seen last disappearing round a corner after some suspect negotiation. He later became a lessee for the second Blackfriars theatre, and is found suing and being sued as late as 1612. Such a skilled operator was no doubt a useful partner for Lyly in the perilous business of theatrical management.

50 We learn in the suit brought by Henry Clifton against the management of the Queen's Revels company (the successors to the Children of the Chapel Royal) that his son, abducted to be a player while he was on his way home from school, was aged thirteen at the time of the abduction. Saloman Pavy is said (in Ben Jonson's elegy on him) to have played on the stage between the ages of ten and thirteen. Nathan Field, born in 1587, was impressed into the Children of the Chapel Royal about 1600. Ostler and Underwood, Chapel boys in 1601, were adult actors about 1608.

51 I.e., 'Thebes was not [divine] / Virtue is [divine]'.

CAMPASPE

[CHARACTERS IN THE DRAMA,
IN ORDER OF APPEARANCE

CLITUS,
PARMENIO,   } *Macedonian officers.*

TIMOCLEA,
CAMPASPE,   } *Theban captives.*

ALEXANDER the Great, *King of Macedon.*
HEPHESTION, *his confidant.*
MANES, *servant to Diogenes.*
GRANICHUS, *servant to Plato.*
PSYLLUS, *servant to Apelles.*
MELIPPUS, *messenger from Alexander.*
PLATO,
ARISTOTLE,
CHRYSIPPUS,   } *Athenian philosophers.*
CRATES,
CLEANTHES,

CHARACTERS IN THE DRAMA, IN ORDER OF APPEARANCE] A list was first
supplied by Fairholt and was followed by Bond. Daniel arranges the names in
order of appearance.

The characters in *Campaspe* are some of them historical and others fictional.
The notes to the historical characters are designed only to indicate the range of
real time that Lyly drew on. For the fictional characters I have tried to indicate
precedents for the names chosen, with some suggestions of the implied
meanings.
    CLITUS] sometimes called a foster-brother to Alexander, killed by him
328 B.C.
    PARMENIO] Alexander's general, killed by him 330 B.C.
    TIMOCLEA] See I.i.36–49n. and Introduction, pp. 8–9.
    ALEXANDER] in 335 B.C., the period of the play, aged twenty.
    HEPHESTION] more properly HEPHAISTION, Alexander's closest
comrade. See II.ii.20–3n.
    MANES] See II.i.23–4n.
    GRANICHUS] named after the river in Asia Minor, site of a famous
victory in 334 B.C. where Alexander defeated the Persian host.
    PSYLLUS] presumably derived from Greek *psylla/psyllos*—a flea. In May's
Cleopatra (1626) there is a character called 'Psyll'.
    PLATO] d. 347 B.C.
    ARISTOTLE] d. 322 B.C.
    CHRYSIPPUS] See I.iii.2n.
    CRATES] Cynic disciple of Diogenes. d. 285 B.C.
    CLEANTHES] Stoic; pupil to Zeno. d. 232 B.C.

ANAXARCHUS, } *Athenian philosophers.*
DIOGENES,

Page *to Alexander.*

APELLES, *a painter.*

CHRYSUS, *a Cynic.*

SOLINUS, *an Athenian citizen.*

Athenian People.

SYLVIUS, *a father.*

PERIM,
MILO, } *his sons.*
TRICO,

MILECTUS, } *soldiers.*
PHRYGIUS,

LAÏS, *a courtesan.*

Captives.

SCENE: *Athens*]

ANAXARCHUS] accompanied Alexander on Persian campaign.

DIOGENES] d. 325 B.C.

APELLES] fl. 332 B.C.

SOLINUS] name of a Roman author of *Collectanea*; name for the Duke of Ephesus in Shakespeare's *The Comedy of Errors*.

SYLVIUS] 'A forester'—perhaps to suggest provinciality. Compare Shakespeare's *As You Like It*.

PERIM] There is a *Perimos* in the *Iliad* (XVI.695)—in a list of persons killed by Patroclus.

MILO] Milo of Crotona was a famous Olympian 'strong man'. This Milo is a 'tumbler' as befits a small boy with such a name.

TRICO] E. M. Waith points me to the *Oxford Latin Dictionary* where 'trico' is defined as 'one who practises evasion, a twister'.

PHRYGIUS] 'The Phrygian'—appropriately barbaric.

LAÏS] See V.iii.0.1n.

The Prologue at the Blackfriars

They that fear the stinging of wasps make fans of peacocks'
tails, whose spots are like eyes. And Lepidus, which could
not sleep for the chatting of birds, set up a beast whose head
was like a dragon; and we which stand in awe of report are
compelled to set before our owl Pallas' shield, thinking by her   5
virtue to cover the other's deformity. It was a sign of famine
to Egypt when Nilus flowed less than twelve cubits or more
than eighteen, and it may threaten despair unto us if we be
less curious than you look for or more cumbersome. But as
Theseus, being promised to be brought to an eagle's nest and   10
travelling all the day, found but a wren in a hedge, yet said,

---

3. chatting] *Qq1–3*; chattring *Q4*; chattering *Blount*; chanting *conj Bond.*   9.
curious] *Qq1–3*; courteous *Q4, Blount*.

---

1. *peacocks'*] There seems to be a reminiscence here of the fable of Argus,
whose hundred eyes were transferred by Juno to the tail of the peacock.

2. *Lepidus*] Bond cites Pliny, XXXV.38, who tells us that Lepidus, during his
triumvirate, was given lodging in a house buried in trees. He complained that
he had been robbed of sleep by the singing of the birds. The authorities had a
picture of a large snake (*draconem . . . depictum*) placed around the forest and
this at once frightened the birds into silence. Nashe, at the beginning of the
Prologue to *Summer's Last Will and Testament*, tells the same story, derived in
his case from Cornelius Agrippa (ed. McKerrow, IV.420: note on III.234). The
style of Nashe's Prologue suggests a deliberate parody of Lyly, and the
Lepidus reference may be part of the parody.

5. *set . . . shield*] i.e., use the queen's authority to defend our inadequate
work. The owl is, of course, a bird that flies by night and thus might be
thought to be ashamed to be seen by day. A further connection is provided by
the fact that the owl was the emblematic bird of Pallas Athene (and so of
Athens). Pallas' shield (more properly her aegis) carried the head of the
Medusa and so would provide a rather effective screen.

7–8. *when Nilus . . . eighteen*] from Pliny, V.10 and XVIII.47, quoted in
Erasmus, *Parabolae*, p. 270: 'The Nile brings famine to Egypt if it rises either
too little, less than eighteen feet, or too much, more than twenty seven'.

9. *curious*] attentive, taking care, skilled.

10. *Theseus*] The origin of this story is not known.

11. *wren*] the smallest of the English birds.

49

'This is a bird'; so we hope, if the shower of our swelling mountain seem to bring forth some elephant, perform but a mouse,
you will gently say 'This is a beast.' Basil softly touched yieldeth
a sweet scent, but chafed in the hand a rank savour. We fear   15
even so that our labours, slyly glanced on, will breed some
content, but examined to the proof, small commendation. The
haste in performing shall be our excuse. There went two nights
to the begetting of Hercules, feathers appear not on the Phoenix
under seven months, and the mulberry is twelve in budding;   20
but our travails are like the hare's, who at one time bringeth
forth, nourisheth and engendreth again, or like the brood of
trochilus, whose eggs in the same moment that they are laid
become birds. But howsoever we finish our work, we crave
pardon if we offend in matter and patience if we transgress in   25
manners. We have mixed mirth with counsel and discipline
with delight, thinking it not amiss in the same garden to sow
pot-herbs that we set flowers. But we hope, as harts that cast

---

13. seem] *Q1;* seeming *1744 (conj. Greg).*   16. slyly] *Q1;* slightly *conj. Bond.*

11–12. *yet . . . bird'*] Compare *Euphues*, 1.258, 6–7: 'The black raven [hath] .
the shape of a bird as well as the white swan.'
   12. *shower*] labour-pains (*O.E.D.*, sb., 1.5b).
   12–13. *our swelling . . . mouse*] A translation of Horace, *Ars Poetica*, 1.139:
'*parturient montes, nascetur ridiculus mus*'.
   14. *Basil*] *Euphues*, 11.69, 1, says that basil springs up when it is crushed.
   16. *slyly*] Bond suspects that the true reading is 'slightly'; *O.E.D.* (adv., 3)
indicates that the two words sometimes seem to converge. But a 'sly glance', a
covert or stealthy glance, seems appropriate enough.
   19. *Hercules*] Jupiter instructed Mercury to delay the sunrise while he was in
bed with Alcmena, the mother-to-be of Hercules. The labour of impregnating
Alcmena is usually said to have occupied *three* nights.
   Phoenix] mythical bird, only one of its kind, said to live five or six hundred
years.
   20. *mulberry*] Pliny's information (XV.27; XVI.34) is repeated in Erasmus,
Parabolae, p. 266: 'The mulberry breaks into leaf latest of all.'
   21. *like the hare's*] The point is made in both Plutarch's *Moralia* 829B ('On
Borrowing', X.325), and Pliny (VIII.81), and repeated in Erasmus, *Parabolae*,
p. 159: 'The hare at the same time brings forth young, suckles an earlier
offspring, and conceives a third.'
   23. trochilus] This bird (black plover) appears in *Euphues*, 1.193, 22 and
11.144, 12, but there, as in Erasmus, *Parabolae*, p. 250, and other sources, the
remarkable thing about it is its habit of cleaning the crocodile's teeth.
   26. *discipline*] instruction.
   28. *pot-herbs*] kitchen herbs.

their horns, snakes their skins, eagles their bills, become more
fresh for any other labour, so our charge being shaken off we   30
shall be fit for greater matters. But lest like the Mindians we
make our gates greater than our town and that our play runs
out at the preface, we here conclude, wishing that although
there be in your precise judgements an universal mislike yet we
may enjoy by your wonted courtesies a general silence.   35

28–30. *as harts . . . labour*] Mustard (S.P., XXII, 1925, p. 267) points out that
the harts and snakes here (but not the eagles) come from Ovid, *Ars Amatoria*,
III.77: '*Anguibus exuitur tenui cum pelle vetustas / Nec faciunt cervos cornua iacta
senes.*'

30–31. *our charge . . . matters*] The *charge* I take to be the command to write
this play. That being fulfilled (or *shaken off*), Lyly will be ready to engage in
greater (presumably administrative) tasks. See Hunter, *Lyly* (*passim*).

31. *the Mindians*] The classical form is 'Myndians'. Bond cites Laertius,
VI.57, and supposes (II.309) that this reference proves Lyly's direct knowledge
of Laertius. However, the point appears also in Erasmus, *Apophthegmata*,
no. 142 (Udall, no. 147).

34. *precise*] scrupulous.
an universal mislike] a dislike of everything in the play.

The Prologue at the Court

We are ashamed that our bird which fluttered by twilight, seeming a swan, should be proved a bat set against the sun. But as Jupiter placed Silenus' ass among the stars, and Alcibiades covered his pictures, being owls and apes, with a curtain embroidered with lions and eagles, so are we enforced upon a   5
rough discourse to draw on a smooth excuse, resembling lapidaries who think to hide the crack in a stone by setting it deep in gold. The gods supped once with poor Baucis; the Persian

---

1. fluttered] *Qq1–3;* fluttereth *Q4, Blount.*   6. resembling] *Q1 corr. (Indiana),*
Qq2–4, Blount; resbling *Q1 uncorr. (Harv., HN, Dulw., Pforz.).*

---

1. *our bird*] i.e., the play, seen in the Blackfriars Prologue, l. 5, as an *owl.*
   by twilight] i.e., in the social obscurity of the Blackfriars theatre, unlit by the presence of the queen.
   2. *swan . . . bat*] Even white looks black when seen against the sun. The fact that the swan flies in the day and the bat in the night is also a relevant point.
   the sun] i.e., the queen.
   3. *Silenus' ass . . . Alcibiades*] The collocation of Silenus and Alcibiades presumably comes from Plato's *Symposium* (216D), where Alcibiades compares Socrates to Silenus; presumably it reached Lyly through Erasmus's lengthy essay, 'Silenus Alcibiadis', in the *Adagia* (II.770C). The adage may be in Lyly's mind, since in it Erasmus discusses Diogenes as another Silenus figure and talks about his relation to Alexander. The ass (Silenus is regularly represented as sitting on an ass, because he is too drunk to be carried on his own legs) is said by mythographers to have been made into a star because he assisted Jupiter in his war against the giants. The idea appears in the *Phaenomena* of Aratus (892ff.), which speaks of two stars in the constellation of the Crab as *onoi* (or asses); see the Loeb Classical Library *Callimachus and Lycophron.* See also Natalis Comes, *Mythologiae* (1567), fol. 124. Bond refers the reader to Ovid, *Fasti*, VI.333ff.: the ass's braying saves Vesta from rape by Priapus. I am indebted to Thomas Hyde for the mythographic information here displayed.
   Alcibiades] Plutarch's Life of Alcibiades (II.106) tells us that he replaced the Athenian emblem on his shield by a picture of Cupid.
   4–5. *pictures . . . eagles*] In *Gallathea*, III.iv.42, we hear of 'Silenus' pictures: without, lambs and doves; within, apes and owls'. Pictures were often curtained.
   6–7. *lapidaries*] workers in gems.
   8. *The gods . . . Baucis*] Baucis and Philemon, poor cottagers, gave

52

kings sometimes shaved sticks; our hope is your Highness will
at this time lend an ear to an idle pastime. Appion, raising   10
Homer from Hell, demanded only who was his father; and
we, calling Alexander from his grave, seek only who was his
love. Whatsoever we present we wish it may be thought the
dancing of Agrippa his shadows, who in the moment they were
seen were of any shape one would conceive, or lynxes, who,   15
having a quick sight to discern, have a short memory to forget.
With us it is like to fare as with these torches which, giving
light to others, consume themselves; and we, showing delight
to others, shame ourselves.

---

hospitality to Jupiter and Mercury when they called, disguised as travellers.
See Ovid, *Metamorphoses*, VIII.

8–9. *the Persian . . . sticks*] On *Euphues*, II.213, 23–4, Bond quotes Aelian,
Varia Historia, XIV.12. Aelian tells us that this pastime of whittling was
designed to occupy them while travelling.

10–11. *Appion . . . father*] Reed in Dodsley 1780 quotes Pliny (XXX.6), who
tells us that Appion or Apion called up ghosts to ask Homer what was his
native country as also what were the names of his parents. Lyly appears to have
taken the information from Erasmus, *Parabolae*, p. 232: 'Apion . . . when he
had raised Homer from the dead, asked him nothing except the names of his
parents.'

12. *only*] only to know.

14. *Agrippa his shadows*] Agrippa's spirits. Henry Cornelius Agrippa of
Nettesheim (1486–1535) was a Humanist and reputed magician. He was in
London in 1510 in the heyday of the association of Erasmus, John Colet and
William Lilly, John's grandfather. See Frances Yates, *The Occult Philosophy in
the Elizabethan Age* (London and Boston, 1979). Compare Marlowe's *Doctor
Faustus*, I.i.144–5: 'Agrippa . . . Whose shadows made all Europe honour
him'.

15–16. *lynxes . . . forget*] Pliny (XXVIII.32) tells us only that the lynx has the
best sight of any animal. Lyly's double observation comes from Erasmus,
Parabolae, p. 234: 'The lynx has better sight than any living creature, but is
amazingly forgetful.'

17. *like*] likely.

17–18. *as with . . . themselves*] See Dent, *P.L.E.D.*, C39: 'A candle (torch)
lights others and consumes itself', where the second example is this from
Campaspe.

Act I

Actus Primus, Scaena Prima.

[*Enter*] CLITUS [*and*] PARMENIO.

Clitus. Parmenio, I cannot tell whether I should more commend in Alexander's victories courage or courtesy, in
the one being a resolution without fear, in the other a
liberality above custom: Thebes is razed, the people not
racked, towers thrown down, bodies not thrust aside, a   5
conquest without conflict, and a cruel war in a mild
peace.

Parmenio. Clitus, it becometh the son of Philip to be none
other than Alexander is. Therefore, seeing in the father
a full perfection, who could have doubted in the son an   10
excellency? For as the moon can borrow nothing else
of the sun but light, so of a sire in whom nothing but
virtue was, what could the child receive but singular? It
is for turquoises to stain each other, not for diamonds,
in the one to be made a difference in goodness, in the   15
other no comparison.

0.1.] *Bond; Clitus, Parmenio, Timoclea, Campaspe, Alexander, Hephestion. Q1.*
4. razed] *Q4, Blount;* raysed *Qq1–3.* 14. turquoises] *Turkies Q1 corr.*
(Indiana), Qq2, 3; Turkies *Q4, Blount;* Turkes *Q1 uncorr. (Harv., HN.,*
Dulw., Pforz.).

1–7.] Historically this account is quite untrue. Alexander's treatment of the
Thebans was famous for its savagery. Plutarch (*Life of Alexander,* IV.310) tells
us not only that the city was 'taken, destroyed, and razed even to the hard
ground', but also that six thousand were killed, the remaining thirty thousand
being sold into slavery.

    4. *Thebes*] Grecian city north-west of Athens, home of legendary heroes
(Laius, Creon, Oedipus, etc.), destroyed by Alexander in 335 B.C.

    5. *racked*] oppressed by extortions.

    13. *singular*] pre-unadulterated (virtue).

    14. *stain*] (1) throw coloured light on; (2) blemish the reputation of. Bond
compares *Euphues,* II.22, 35–6, on rubies.

    15–16. *in the one . . . comparison*] The transparency of the diamonds will
prevent any 'staining'; likewise the separate perfections of Philip and
Alexander make comparative judgements impossible.

Clitus. You mistake me, Parmenio, if, whilst I commend
Alexander, you imagine I call Philip into question,
unless happily you conjecture (which none of judge-
ment will conceive) that because I like the fruit there-   20
fore I heave at the tree, or coveting to kiss the child I
therefore go about to poison the teat.
Parmenio. Ay, but Clitus, I perceive you are born in the East
and never laugh but at the sun rising, which argueth,
though a duty where you ought, yet no great devotion   25
where you might.
Clitus. We will make no controversy of that which there
ought to be no question; only this shall be the opinion
of us both, that none was worthy to be the father of
Alexander but Philip nor any meet to be the son of   30
Philip but Alexander.

> [*Enter*] TIMOCLEA [*and*] CAMPASPE
> [*and other captives, with spoils*].

Parmenio. Soft, Clitus, behold the spoils and prisoners, a
pleasant sight to us because profit is joined with honour, not much painful to them because their captivity
is eased by mercy.   35
Timoclea. Fortune, thou didst never yet deceive virtue, because virtue never yet did trust fortune. Sword and fire
will never get spoil where wisdom and fortitude bears

31.1.] *Bond (subst.) after l. 35; not in Q1.*

19. *happily*] haply, perhaps.
21. *heave at*] *O.E.D.*, vb., 18b, glosses the phrase as 'threaten an attack on'.
But the meaning 'heave the gorge at . . . feel loathing' (vb., 16) seems more
plausible.
23. *born . . . East*] The remark is purely adventitious. Clitus was born in
Macedonia.
24. *and never . . . rising*] For this proverbial phrase, see Dent, *P.L.E.D.*
S979, and also *'plures adorant solem orientem quam occidentem'*, 'more people
worship the rising than the setting sun', in Erasmus, *Adagia*, II.786A.
31.2. and other captives, with spoils] The 'other captives' here matches the
reference to 'the rest', l. 47 below; 'spoils' seem to be indicated by ll. 32 and
69.
36–7. *Fortune . . . fortune*] Compare Dent, *P.L.E.D.*, F599: 'Fortune can
take from us nothing but what she gave us (our goods but not our virtue).'
36–49.] The story of Timoclea is told by Plutarch (*Life of Alexander*, IV.

sway. O Thebes, thy walls were raised by the sweetness
of the harp, but razed by the shrillness of the trumpet.   40
Alexander had never come so near the walls had Epaminondas walked about the walls, and yet might the Thebans have been merry in their streets if he had been to
watch their towers. But destiny is seldom foreseen,
never prevented. We are here now captives whose necks   45
are yoked by force but whose hearts cannot yield by
death. Come, Campaspe and the rest, let us not be
ashamed to cast our eyes on him on whom we feared
not to cast our darts.

Parmenio. Madam, you need not doubt; it is Alexander that is   50
the conqueror.

Timoclea. Alexander hath overcome, not conquered.

Parmenio. To bring all under his subjection is to conquer.

Timoclea. He cannot subdue that which is divine.

Parmenio. Thebes was not.   55

Timoclea. Virtue is.

Clitus. Alexander, as he tendereth virtue, so he will you; he
drinketh not blood but thirsteth after honour; he is
greedy of victory but never satisfied with mercy. In
fight terrible, as becometh a captain; in conquest mild,   60
as beseemeth a king. In all things, than which nothing
can be greater, he is Alexander.

---

40. razed] rased *Qq1, 2, 4, Blount;* raced *Q3.*   50. doubt; it] *Adams;* doubt, it
Q1.   50–1. Alexander that is the] *1744; Alexander,* that is, the *Qq1–3;
Alexander,* that is the *Q4, Blount.*

---

pp. 310–11) and appears also in 'The Bravery of Women', *Moralia,* 259D–
260D (III.561–7). See Introduction, pp. 8–9.

   39–40. *O Thebes . . . harp*] Amphion caused the walls of Thebes to rise by
playing on his harp.

   41–2. *had Epaminondas . . . walls*] Epaminondas was a famous general of
the Thebans (fl. 371 B.C.). Compare Plutarch, 'Sayings of Kings and Generals',
Moralia, 192C (III.139): 'No panic fear ever surprised the army of the Thebans
while Epaminondas was their general.'

   44. *watch*] guard.

   44–5. *destiny . . . prevented*] See Dent, *P.L.E.D.,* F82.11 (with quotations
from *Gallathea,* Sidney's *Arcadia,* Chapman and Webster).

   50–1.] Adams's repunctuation (see Collation) makes evident what I take to
be the true sense: 'do not fear; your conqueror is Alexander (famous for
magnanimity).' See *O.E.D., doubt,* vb. II.8(*intr.*): 'to be afraid'.

   57. *tendereth*] cherishes (*O.E.D.,* vb.[2], 3d).

   60. *terrible*] terrifying.

Campaspe. Then if it be such a thing to be Alexander, I hope it
shall be no miserable thing to be a virgin. For if he save
our honours it is more than to restore our goods. And   65
rather do I wish he preserve our fame than our lives,
which if he do, we will confess there can be no greater
thing than to be Alexander.

   [*Enter*] ALEXANDER [*and*] HEPHESTION.

Alexander. Clitus, are these prisoners? Of whence these spoils?
Clitus. Like your Majesty, they are prisoners, and of Thebes.   70
Alexander. Of what calling or reputation?
Clitus. I know not; but they seem to be ladies of honour.
Alexander. I will know.—Madam, of whence you are I know,
but who I cannot tell.
Timoclea. Alexander, I am the sister of Theagenes, who fought   75
a battle with thy father before the city of Chyeronie,
where he died—I say which none can gainsay—valiantly.
Alexander. Lady, there seem in your words sparks of your
brother's deeds, but worser fortune in your life than his
death; but fear not, for you shall live without violence,   80
enemies or necessity.—But what are you, fair lady,
another sister to Theagenes?
Campaspe. No sister to Theagenes, but an humble handmaid
to Alexander, born of a mean parentage but to extreme
fortune.   85

64. thing] *Qq1, 2, 4, Blount;* things *Q3.*   68.1.] *Bond; not in Q1.*   76.
Chyeronie] *Qq1–2,* Chyronie *Q3;* Chyeronte *Q4, Blount.*   77. valiantly] *Q2;*
valianly *Q1.*

---

66. *fame*] reputation for spotless purity.

70. *Like*] abbreviated form of 'If it like'.

75–7.] Lyly adapts this speech from North's Plutarch. There Timoclea is
carried before Alexander when it is discovered that she has murdered the
Thracian captain (see Introduction, p. 9). She 'followed the soldiers with such
a majesty and boldness. Alexander then asking her what she was, she answered
that she was the sister of Theagenes who fought a battle with King Philip
before the city of Chaeronea, where being general he was slain, valiantly
fighting for the defence of the liberty of Greece' (*Life of Alexander,* IV.310–11).

75. *Theagenes*] general of the Theban army, killed at the battle of Chaeronea
against Philip of Macedon, 338 B.C.

76. *Chyeronie*] I have preserved Q1's spelling for the sake of the prose
rhythm, though elsewhere (where this is not an issue) I have modernised Greek
names.

84. *mean . . . extreme*] moderate or middling . . . the worst possible.

Alexander. Well, ladies, for so your virtues show you, whatsoever your births be, you shall be honourably entreated.
Athens shall be your Thebes, and you shall not be as
abjects of war but as subjects to Alexander. Parmenio,
conduct these honourable ladies into the city; charge   90
the soldiers not so much as in words to offer them any
offence, and let all wants be supplied so far forth as
shall be necessary for such persons and my prisoners.

                    Exeunt PARMENIO *and captivi.*

Hephestion, it resteth now that we have as great care to
govern in peace as conquer in war, that whilst arms   95
cease arts may flourish, and joining letters with lances
we endeavour to be as good philosophers as soldiers,
knowing it no less praise to be wise than commendable
to be valiant.

Hephestion. Your Majesty therein showeth that you have as   100
great desire to rule as to subdue; and needs must that
commonwealth be fortunate whose captain is a philosopher and whose philosopher is a captain.   *Exeunt.*

Actus Primus, Scaena Secunda.

[*Enter*] MANES, GRANICHUS [*and*] PSYLLUS.

Manes. I serve instead of a master a mouse, whose house is a

---

87. *entreated*] treated.

89. *abjects*] persons abjected or cast down.

89–93. North's Plutarch says 'Alexander . . . commanded no man should
touch her [Timoclea] nor her children, and so freely let her go whither she
would' (*Life of Alexander*, IV.311).

93.1. and captivi] The 'captives' who go off with Parmenio may be only
Timoclea and Campaspe; but the reference to 'the rest' at l. 48 suggests that
mutes leave here as well as the two ladies.

94. *resteth*] remains.

101–3. *and needs . . . captain*] The famous Platonic dictum (*Republic*, 473D)
was well known in Humanist circles. See the note to Thomas More's *Utopia*
(Yale edn.), p. 86. Close to Lyly are the appearances of the sentiment in
Erasmus, *Adagia*, II.106C–111F (under *Aut regem aut fatuum nasci oportere*),
Sir Thomas Elyot's *The Governour* (London, 1531), I.12, and in William
Lilly's Latin Grammar (1542 edn., p. 11). See Dent, *P.L.E.D.*, P253.

1. *a mouse*] Compare Laertius, VI.22, and Erasmus, *Apophthegmata*,
no. 2. Diogenes admired the liberty of the mouse that ran about the city paying
no heed to social customs but intent only on its own good.

tub, whose dinner is a crust and whose board is a bed.

Psyllus. Then art thou in a state of life which philosophers
commend: a crumb for thy supper, an hand for thy
cup and thy clothes for thy sheets. For *Natura paucis*   5
contenta.

Granichus. Manes, it is pity so proper a man should be cast
away upon a philosopher; but that Diogenes that dog
should have Manes that dog-bolt, it grieveth nature
and spiteth art, the one having found thee so dissolute   10
(absolute I would say) in body, the other so single-
singular in mind.

Manes. Are you merry? It is a sign by the trip of your tongue

---

2. board is a bed] *Qq1–3;* bed is a board *Q4, Blount.*   10. thee] *Q2;* the *Q1.*
11–12. single-singular] *This ed.;* single singular *Q1;* single, singular *1744.*

---

2. *board is a bed*] The Q4 reading has been accepted by most modern
editors, but the Qq1–3 reading makes perfect sense: 'uses his table (i.e., the
floor) to sleep on'.

4–5. *an hand . . . cup*] Compare II.i.41–2 below.

5. *thy clothes . . . sheets*] See Laertius, VI.22: 'He was the first, some say, to
fold his cloak, because he was obliged to sleep in it as well.'

5–6. Natura paucis contenta] 'Nature is satisfied with only a few things.'
The phrase is proverbial; see Walther, *Sprichwörter*, no. 15924, Dent,
P.L.E.D., N45, and Nashe, ed. McKerrow, IV.424–5.

7. *so proper a man*] ironically spoken, 'so well-built or manly' (perhaps with a
pun on *Manes*).

7–8. *cast . . . philosopher*] Compare Edwards, *Damon and Pithias (M.S.R.)*
ll. 438f., where the servant complains, 'Your philosophical diet is so fine and
small / That you may eat your dinner and supper at once and not surfeit at all.'

8. *Diogenes that dog*] Here as throughout the play Diogenes is called a dog
because he belongs to the Cynic ('dog-like') school of philosophy, so called
because it barked against the unexamined proprieties of society.

9. *dog-bolt*] 'applied to a person as a term of contempt or reproach. Perhaps
originally = "a mere tool to be put to any use"' (*O.E.D.*, 2).

9–12. *it grieveth . . . mind*] Manes is absolutely dissolute by the nature of his
body; it brings art into contempt that a wit so unusual should belong to a mind
that lives in such a body. There may be a quibble on the logical and
grammatical senses of *absolute* and *singular*. The whole phrase is hard to be
certain about, for the *one . . . other* may refer to Manes and Diogenes as well as
to nature and art (equivalent to body and mind). The *absolute* I take to be that
which is properly capable of standing alone, the *single-singular* that which is
merely eccentric.

13. *the trip . . . tongue*] the way your tongue *trips* (or dances) through the
words you use.

and the toys of your head that you have done that today
which I have not done these three days.   15
Psyllus. What's that?
Manes. Dined.
Granichus. I think Diogenes keeps but cold cheer.
Manes. I would it were so; but he keepeth neither hot nor cold.
Granichus. What then, lukewarm? That made Manes run from   20
his master last day.
Psyllus. Manes had reason, for his name foretold as much.
Manes. My name? How so, sir boy?
Psyllus. You know that it is called *Mons, a movendo*, because it
stands still?   25
Manes. Good!
Psyllus. And thou art named *Manes, a manendo*, because thou
runnst away.
Manes. Passing reasons! I did not run away but retire.
Psyllus. To a prison, because thou wouldst have leisure to   30
contemplate.
Manes. I will prove that my body was immortal because it was
in prison.
Granichus. As how?
Manes. Did your masters never teach you that the soul is   35
immortal?

---

16. What's] whats *Qq1, 2, 4, Blount;* what is *Q3.*   21. last day] *Qq1–3;* the last
day *Q4, Blount.*

---

14. *toys*] foolish fancies, odd conceits (*O.E.D.*, sb. 4). See Dent,
P.L.E.D. T456.1.
20. *lukewarm*] By 'neither hot nor cold' Manes meant 'none at all';
Granichus twists the meaning to 'between hot and cold'.
21. *last day*] 'yesterday' (*O.E.D.*, 3b).
24. *Mons, a movendo*] This piece of comic etymology is based on the *lucus a
non lucendo* example of etymology by opposites (a grove is called *lucus* because
it excludes brightness [*lucendum*]). So the mountain (*mons*) is said to derive its
name from *movendum* (moving) because it does not move. Dent (*P.L.E.D.*,
Index) suggests a connection with F738: 'Friends may meet but mountains
never' where he cites *Mother Bombie*, V.iii.229ff. '. . . we four met, which
argued we were no mountains'.
27. *Manes, a manendo*] The same mode of derivation that named the
mountain 'mover' because it did not move (see l. 24n.) is used here to explain
that Manes, who is a runaway, takes his name from *manendum* (staying in
place) because he does not stay in place.
29. *Passing*] surpassing, excellent.

Granichus. Yes.

Manes. And the body is the prison of the soul?

Granichus. True.

Manes. Why then, thus: to make my body immortal I put it   40
   to prison.

Granichus. Oh, bad!

Psyllus. Excellent ill!

Manes. You may see how dull a fasting wit is. Therefore,
   Psyllus, let us go to supper with Granichus. Plato is the   45
   best fellow of all philosophers; give me him that reads
   in the morning in the school and at noon in the kitchen.

Psyllus. And me.

Granichus. Ah, sirs, my master is a king in his parlour for the
   body and a god in his study for the soul. Among all his   50
   men he commendeth one that is an excellent musician;
   then stand I by and clap another on the shoulder and
   say, 'This is a passing good cook.'

Manes. It is well done, Granichus, for give me pleasure that
   goes in at the mouth, not the ear; I had rather fill my   55
   guts than my brains.

Psyllus. I serve Apelles, who feedeth me as Diogenes doth
   Manes, for at dinner the one preacheth abstinence, the

---

40. thus: to] *Adams;* thus to *Qq1–4;* this to *Blount.*   41. to prison] *Qq1–3;* in prison *Q4, Blount.*

38.] Bond cites Plato, *Phaedo*, 82E–83B, but there is no real connection. Erasmus refers to the idea twice in the *Colloquia*, in the 'Religious Banquet' (1.680B) and in 'The Lying-in Woman' (1.770D): 'Some call it [the body] the prison of the soul.' See Dent, *P.L.E.D.*, B497. The medieval and Renaissance popularity of the idea probably derives from Macrobius's commentary on the *Somnium Scipionis* of Cicero (see William H. Stahl's edition, New York, 1952, pp. 71–2, 131–2). Compare Psalm cxli.7 and Isaiah xlii.7.

45–6. *Plato . . . philosophers*] A 'good fellow' is one who is easy-going and convivial.

46. *reads*] i.e., 'reads a lecture'.

49–53.] *Euphues*, 1.278, 33–4, says that Plato had 'a servant whose bliss was in filling of his belly'. This comes from pseudo-Plutarch, 'On the education of children' (*Moralia*, 10D, 1.49). Laertius' life of Diogenes tells a number of stories illustrating Plato's care for elegant living.

54–6.] Compare Erasmus, *Colloquia*, 'The Profane Banquet' (1.662C): 'Orators . . . tickle idle ears with a vain pleasure. But cookery feeds and repairs the palate, the belly, and the whole man' (Bailey, p. 68). The pairing of cookery and rhetoric presumably goes back to Plato's *Gorgias*, 463b ff.

other commendeth counterfeiting. When I would eat
meat he paints a spit, and when I thirst, 'O,' saith he, 'is   60
not this a fair pot?' and points to a table which contains
the banquet of the gods, where are many dishes to feed
the eye but not to fill the gut.
Granichus. What dost thou then?
Psyllus. This doth he then: bring in many examples that some   65
have lived by savours, and proveth that much easier it is
to fat by colours, and tells of birds that have been fatted
by painted grapes in winter, and how many have so fed
their eyes with their mistress' picture that they never
desired to take food, being glutted with the delight   70
in their favours. Then doth he show me counterfeits,
such as have surfeited, with their filthy and loathsome
vomits, and with the riotous bacchanals of the god
Bacchus and his disorderly crew, which are painted all
to the life in his shop. To conclude, I fare hardly though   75
I go richly, which maketh me, when I should begin to
shadow a lady's face, to draw a lamb's head, and some-
time to set to the body of a maid a shoulder of mutton,
for *semper animus meus est in patinis.*

---

61. *a table*] a painting.
62–3.] Compare *Euphues*, II.160, 35–6: 'they that live by the view of beauty
still look very lean'.
67. *to fat*] to grow fat.
67–8. *birds . . . grapes*] Psyllus glances at the story of Zeuxis, whose painted
grapes were pecked at by the birds. The story is told by Cicero, *De Inventione*,
II.i, by Pliny (XXXV.36), and in Erasmus, *Parabolae*, p. 276.
68–71. *and . . . favours*] Compare *Euphues*, II.59, 15–16: 'divers have lived
by looking on fair and beautiful pictures, desiring no meat'.
71–3. *Then . . . vomits*] Compare *Euphues*, I.188, 12–17: 'The Lacedaemon-
ians were wont to show their children drunken men . . . that by seeing their
filth they might shun the like fault. . . . The Persians . . . would paint an
epicure with meat in his mouth and most horribly overladen with wine.' The
Lacedaemonian example comes from Plutarch, 'Customs of the Spartans',
Moralia, 239A (III.441), or from his *Life of Lycurgus*, I.158. Bond notes that
the Persian example is 'perhaps of Lyly's invention'. By the time of *Campaspe*
the two ideas have combined into a single image.
77. *shadow*] portray.
78. *to set . . . mutton*] The fantasies of hunger lead into a reminiscence of
Horace, *Ars Poetica*, ll. 1–4: 'If a painter join to a human head the neck of a
horse . . . [or show] the top of a beautiful maiden to end in a loathsome fish
. . .'.
79. *semper . . . patinis*] 'my thoughts are always in the stewpan'. Bond

Manes. Thou art a god to me, for could I see but a cook's shop   80
    painted I would make mine eyes fat as butter. For I
    have nought but sentences to fill my maw, as *plures*
    occidit crapula quam gladius, musa jejunantibus amica,
    'repletion killeth delicately', and an old saw of absti-
    nence, Socrates' 'The belly is the head's grave.' Thus   85
    with sayings, not with meat, he maketh a gallimaufry.
Granichus. But how dost thou then live?
Manes. With fine jests, sweet air and the dog's alms.
Granichus. Well, for this time I will staunch thy gut, and
    among pots and platters thou shalt see what it is to serve   90
    Plato.
Psyllus. For joy of Granichus, let's sing.
Manes. My voice is as clear in the evening as in the morning.
Granichus. Another commodity of emptiness.

Song

---

81. I would] *Q1;* it would *conj. Greg.*   85. Socrates'] *This ed.; Socrates: Qq1, 2,
4, Blount; Socrates, Q3; by Socrates 1744; Socrates': Bond.*

---

points to the source in Terence, *Eunuchus,* IV.vii.46: '*Iamdudum animus est in
patinis*'. Compare Dent, *P.L.E.D.,* M971: 'His mind [is] on his meat',
exemplified, e.g., in *Euphues,* I.224, 31–2, and *Sappho and Phao,* III.ii.16–17.
    80. *Thou . . . to me*] i.e., compared to me you are without physical needs.
    81. *fat as butter*] proverbial; Dent, *P.L.E.D.,* B767.
    82. *sentences*] sententiae, wise sayings or proverbs.
    82–3. plures . . . gladius] surfeit kills more than the sword. Compare
Sappho and Phao, II.iii.19–20. Walther, no. 3605, gives various versions of
this proverb. Ecclesiasticus xxxvii.34 may be the original source. See also
Euphues, II.55, 26–7, and Dent, *P.L.E.D.,* G148.
    83. musa jejunantibus amica] The muse favours those who fast. See Dent,
P.L.E.D., D329: 'The sparing diet is the spirit's feast.'
    85. *Socrates' . . . grave*] The connection with Socrates is mysterious, but the
idea is commonplace. See Dent, *P.L.E.D.,* B293 and P123 (Erasmus, *Adagia,*
II.853D). The idea of *grave* (not the usual term) may come from Psalm v.9:
'their throat is an open sepulchre'—though the reference there is to the throat
as the organ of (blasphemous) utterance.
    86. *a gallimaufry*] a meal made of chopped-up scraps; a medley.
    88. *the dog's alms*] scraps of food thrown to dogs; with a further reference to
Diogenes as a dog (or Cynic).
    93. The implication is that fasting clears the voice. Compare ll. 80–6.
    94. *commodity*] advantage.
    94.1 *Song*] See Appendix for a general discussion of the songs in these plays.
The present example has the standard form of the 'three-man' or 'freeman'

Granichus. O for a bowl of fat canary, 95
    Rich Palermo, sparkling sherry,
    Some nectar else from Juno's dairy!
    O, these draughts would make us merry.
Psyllus. O for a wench (I deal in faces,
    And in other daintier things)! 100
    Tickled am I with her embraces,
    Fine dancing in such fairy rings.
Manes. O for a plump fat leg of mutton,
    Veal, lamb, capon, pig and coney!
    None is happy but a glutton, 105
    None an ass but who wants money.
Chorus. Wines, indeed, and girls are good,
    But brave victuals feast the blood.
    For wenches, wine and lusty cheer,
    Jove would leap down to surfeit here.   [*Exeunt.*] 110

Actus Primus, Scaena Tertia.

[*Enter*] MELIPPUS.

Melippus. I had never such ado to warn scholars to come be-
    fore a king. First I came to Chrysippus, a tall, lean,

95–110. *Granichus* ... here] *Blount; not in Q1.* 110. Exeunt.] *Bond; not in Q1.* 0.1.] *Bond; Melippus, Plato, Crisippus, Crates, Cleanthus, Anaxarchus, Alexander, Hephestion, Parmenio, Clytus, Diogenes. Q1.*

---

song, mentioned in *The Winter's Tale*, IV.iii.44, and in Dekker's *The Shoemaker's Holiday* (inserted songs). I take it that the three serving boys sing one stanza each. John E. Stevens (*Music and Poetry in the Early Tudor Court*, London, 1961), p. 286, suggests that 'three-man songs' may have consisted musically of two improvised parts added to a well-known tune. The food verse falls naturally to the hungry Manes, the girl verse to the painter's boy, Psyllus. The three boys together sing the final verse, which deals with all the pleasures.
    95. *fat*] 'fruity, full-bodied' (*O.E.D.*, adj., 7b).
    canary] canary wine.
    96. *Palermo*] wine from Palermo in Sicily.
    99–102.] Given that stanza 2 is about the charms of girls, one might expect that *other daintier things* and perhaps *fairy rings* have specific anatomical reference. Dictionaries of obscenities fail to uphold such imagination; but one should suppose that evidence in such matters will be oblique rather than direct.
    102. *fairy rings*] circles in grass (caused by the growth of certain fungi) of a different colour from the surrounding field. Popular superstition supposed that they were created by the dancing of the fairies.
    104. *coney*] rabbit.
    2. *Chrysippus*] Stoic philosopher of Tarsus (d. 207 B.C.). As Bond points out,

old, mad man, willing him presently to appear before
Alexander. He stood staring on my face, neither moving
his eyes nor his body. I urging him to give some answer,   5
he took up a book, sat down and said nothing. Melissa,
his maid, told me it was his manner, and that oftentimes
she was fain to thrust meat into his mouth, for that he
would rather starve than cease study. Well, thought I,
seeing bookish men are so blockish and so great clerks   10
such simple courtiers, I will neither be partaker of their
commons nor their commendations. From thence I
came to Plato and to Aristotle and to divers other, none
refusing to come saving an old obscure fellow who,
sitting in a tub turned towards the sun, read Greek to a   15
young boy. Him when I willed to appear before Alexander, he answered, 'If Alexander would fain see me,
let him come to me; if learn of me, let him come to me;
whatsoever it be, let him come to me.' 'Why,' said I,
'he is a king.' He answered, 'Why, I am a philosopher.'   20
'Why, but he is Alexander.' 'Ay, but I am Diogenes.'
I was half angry to see one so crooked in his shape to
be so crabbed in his sayings. So, going my way, I said,
'Thou shalt repent it if thou comest not to Alexander.'
'Nay,' smiling answered he, 'Alexander may repent it if   25
he come not to Diogenes; virtue must be sought, not

---

the same story appears in *Euphues*, I.276, 1–3. It comes eventually from
Valerius Maximus (VIII.vii.5), but told of Carneades. Lyly's version (referred
to Chrysippus) is told by Erasmus in his colloquy *Convivium Profanum*
(I.661D): 'Chrysippus is reported to have been so intent upon his logical
subtleties that he would have been starved at table unless his maid Melissa had
put the meat into his mouth' (Bailey, p. 67).

3 *presently*] immediately.

11. *simple*] simple-minded.

12 *commons*] provisions for a community.

15. *a tub . . . sun*] The *tub* is sufficiently an emblem for Diogenes to need no
further identification. Both Laertius, VI.38 (cited II.ii.145–8n., below) and
Plutarch (*Life of Alexander*, IV.311–12) speak of Diogenes sunning himself. So
also Erasmus, *Apophthegmata*, no. 46 (Udall no. 52).

19–21. *Why, said . . . Diogenes*] originally told by Laertius, VI.60: 'Alexander
. . . said, "I am Alexander, the great king." "And I," said he, "am Diogenes
the Cynic."' The story is repeated in Erasmus, *Apophthegmata*, no. 159. Udall
(no. 164) expands to read, 'I am that jolly fellow Diogenes the dog.'

24. *Thou . . . it*] Bond compares Laertius, VI.44, where Perdiccas
threatens Diogenes with death if he does not come to him. But the parallel is
very tenuous. Compare II.ii.163–4n., below.

offered.' And so, turning himself to his cell, he grunted
I know not what, like a pig under a túb. But I must be
gone; the philosophers are coming.   *Exit.*

[*Enter*] PLATO, ARISTOTLE, CHRYSIPPUS,
CRATES, CLEANTHES [*and*] ANAXARCHUS.

Plato. It is a difficult controversy, Aristotle, and rather to be   30
wondered at than believed, how natural causes should
work supernal effects.
Aristotle. I do not so much stand upon the apparition is seen in
the moon, neither the *demonium* of Socrates, as that I
cannot by natural reason give any reason of the ebbing   35
and flowing of the sea, which makes me in the depth of
my studies to cry out, '*O ens entium, miserere mei!*'

29.1–2.] Bond; *not in* Q1.   32. supernal] *Q1;* supernatural *Q2.*

29.1–2.] The collection of philosophers is anachronistic. Aristotle, Anaxarchus and Crates were alive in the reign of Alexander, but Plato had been
dead for sixteen years when Alexander came to the throne. Cleanthes (d. 240
B.C.) and Chrysippus (d. 207 B.C.) belong to the next century, and are in the
group only because they are speakers in one of the sources, Cicero's *De
Natura Deorum.*
33. *stand upon*] insist upon, emphasise, maintain (*O.E.D., stand,* vb.,
B.78 K).
33–4. *the apparition . . . Socrates*] The collocation of the two ideas may be
derived from Plutarch, who has two essays in the *Moralia,* one 'On the face in
the moon' (XII.34ff.), another 'On the demon of Socrates' (VII.373ff.). The first
of these discusses the apparent face as a sign of the existence of God above
nature, for the inexplicability of the face shows that the regularity of the face is
being disturbed by another and greater force. The existence of a 'demonium'
which accompanied Socrates and prompted his ideas is discussed not only by
Plutarch, but also in several Platonic dialogues, *Phaedrus,* 242C, *Apology,* 31D,
and at great length in the pseudo-Platonic *Theages* (128D–130E). Aelian refers
to it (*Varia Historia,* VIII.1) and Erasmus mentions it in the *Apophthegmata*
(Socrates, no. 81; Udall, no. 82) and the *Adagia* (under *Omnia Octo* – II.272C).
33. *is seen*] that is seen.
34–7. *I cannot . . . mei*] Bond compares *Euphues,* I.293, 10–12: 'Aristotle,
when he could not find out by the secrecy of nature the cause of the ebbing and
flowing of the sea, cried out with a loud voice, "O thing of things, have mercy
upon me!"' There are ancient sources – though not particularly reliable ones
—for the idea that Aristotle drowned himself because he could not understand
the tides of the Euripus; Ingemar Düring, *Aristotle in the Ancient Biographical
Tradition,* Göteborg, 1957, cites Gregory of Nyssa, Justin Martyr and Arabic
sources. The idea may be invoked in the present passage because in Cicero's
De Natura Deorum, a principal source, the tides are asserted to move for
natural rather than divine causes (III.x.24). The words put into Aristotle's

Plato. Cleanthes and you attribute so much to nature, by
searching for things which are not to be found, that,
whilst you study a cause of your own, you omit the   40
occasion itself. There is no man so savage in whom
resteth not this divine particle, that there is an omni-
potent, eternal and divine mover, which may be called
God.

Cleanthes. I am of this mind that that first mover, which you   45
term God, is the instrument of all the movings which we
attribute to nature. The earth, which is mass, swimmeth on the sea, seasons divided in themselves, fruits
growing in themselves, the majesty of the sky, the whole
firmament of the world and whatsoever else appeareth   50
miraculous—what man almost of mean capacity but
can prove it natural?

Anaxarchus. These causes shall be debated at our philosophers'
feast, in which controversy I will take part with Aristotle

---

mouth are the most mysterious element in the whole mixture. M. W. Croll, in
illustration of the *Euphues* passage, cites Nashe (ed. McKerrow, IV.335) and
Burton's *Anatomy* (ed. Shilleto, III.388). F. P. Wilson (addenda to McKerrow's
Nashe) adds *Greene's Mourning Garment* (ed. Grosart, IX.122–3): 'Aristotle
that all his life had been an atheist, cried out at his death "*Eris* [*sic*] *entium,
miserere mei.*" ' But no ancient sources for these words have been discovered.

40–1. *whilst . . . itself*] You study particular cases (*causes*) that
you find interesting but you do not think about the reason (*occasion*)
why particular things are as they are.

42. *particle*] Cicero in the *De Natura Deorum* (II.xiv.37) calls man *quaedam
particula perfecti*.

43–4. *which . . . God*] Chrysippus argues in the *De Natura Deorum*
(II.vi.16): 'What better name is there for this [superior being] than God?'

45–52.] Cleanthes' speech here is a variant of the speech in *Euphues*, I.293,
13ff., both being derived from the speech of Cleanthes in the *De Natura
Deorum* (II.v.13–15). The *Euphues* passage has Cleanthes speak of 'the fat-
ness of the earth, the fruitfulness of trees . . . the equality of moving in the
heaven, the course of the sun, the order of the stars, the bountifulness of
the Element (= Firmament)'; but there (as in Cicero) he is presenting this
evidence as proof of the existence of God. Here Lyly seems to have got it the
other way round: Cleanthes is asserting the primacy not of the miraculous but
of the natural, following the line of Cotta in Cicero's Book III, not that of
Balbus in Book II.

46. *the instrument*] the means by which nature's movings occur, so that the
First Cause is instrumental rather than transcendent.

51. *what man almost*] virtually no man. See *O.E.D.*, *almost*, 4.

53–7.] The 'philosophers' feast' will debate the issue of God's immanence or

that there is *Natura naturans*, and yet not God.   55
Crates. And I with Plato that there is *Deus optimus maximus*,
    and not nature.
Aristotle. Here cometh Alexander.

[*Enter*] ALEXANDER, HEPHESTION, PARMENIO [*and*] CLITUS.

Alexander. I see, Hephestion, that these philosophers are here
    attending for us.   60
Hephestion. They were not philosophers if they knew not their
    duties.
Alexander. But I much marvel Diogenes should be so dogged.
Hephestion. I do not think but his excuse will be better than
    Melippus' message.   65
Alexander. I will go see him, Hephestion, because I long to see
    him that would command Alexander to come, to whom
    all the world is like to come. — Aristotle and the rest,
    sithence my coming from Thebes to Athens, from a
    place of conquest to a palace of quiet, I have resolved   70
    with myself in my court to have as many philosophers as
    I had in my camp soldiers. My court shall be a school
    wherein I will have used as great doctrine in peace as
    I did in war discipline.
Aristotle. We are all here ready to be commanded, and glad we   75
    are that we are commanded, for that nothing better be-

---

56. *Crates*] *1744; Craterus Q1.*   58.1.] *Bond; not in Q1.*   61. were] *Qq1–3;* are
Q4, Blount.   knew] *Qq1–4;* know *Blount.*

---

transcendence. Lyly seems arbitrary about the positions he has assigned to his
minor philosophers. Though it is clear that Aristotle and Plato are on the
appropriate sides, it is not clear why Anaxarchus and Cleanthes argue for
Nature (with Aristotle) or why Crates and perhaps Chrysippus argue (with
Plato) for Godhead.

55. Natura naturans] that natural power from which all things in nature
proceed, as against *Natura naturata* or the nature created by that power. (The
language here is that of theological speculation.)

58.1.] Clitus and Parmenio do not speak when on the stage. Presumably
they are given an entry to underline Alexander's power.

63. *dogged*] See below, II.i.169.

64. *I do . . . but*] I can't help thinking that.

69. *sithence*] since.

73. *I will have used*] I wish to see practised.

76–8. *for . . . dignity*] Plutarch has a whole essay on a similar topic: 'That a

cometh kings than literature, which maketh them come
as near to the gods in wisdom as they do in dignity.

Alexander. It is so, Aristotle; but yet there is among you, yea,
and of your bringing-up, that sought to destroy Alex-   80
ander—Callisthenes, Aristotle, whose treasons against
his prince shall not be borne out with the reasons of his
philosophy.

Aristotle. If ever mischief entered into the heart of Callisthenes,
let Callisthenes suffer for it; but that Aristotle ever   85
imagined any such thing of Callisthenes, Aristotle doth
deny.

Alexander. Well, Aristotle, kindred may blind thee and affection me, but in kings' causes I will not stand to scholars'
arguments. This meeting shall be for a commandment   90
that you all frequent my court, instruct the young with
rules, confirm the old with reasons. Let your lives be
answerable to your learnings, lest my proceedings be
contrary to my promises.

Hephestion. You said you would ask every one of them a   95
question which yesternight none of us could answer.

---

92. rules] *Qq1–4;* rulers *Blount.* be] *Qq1, 2, 4;* by *Q3.*

---

philosopher ought to converse especially with men in power' ('*maxime cum
principibus philosopho esse disserendum*', *Moralia*, X.28–47).
    77. *literature*] book learning.
    79–83.] Compare Laertius, V.10: 'It is said that he [Aristotle] incurred
[Alexander's] displeasure because he had introduced Callisthenes to him.'
Alexander's 'displeasure' with Callisthenes came long after the ostensible time
of Lyly's action.
    80. *of your bringing-up*] 'Callisthenes had been brought up with him'
(Plutarch, *Life of Alexander*, IV.363).
    81 *Callisthenes*] See Introduction, p. 15. On the detail of his history, see
Laertius, V.5, Plutarch, *Life of Alexander*, IV.359ff. and Quintus Curtius,
VIII.vi–viii.
    82. *borne out with*] made allowances for.
    85–7. *but . . . deny*] Both Plutarch and Laertius tell us that Aristotle
rebuked Callisthenes for his free speech to Alexander.
    88. *kindred*] Plutarch tells us that Callisthenes was son to Hero,
Aristotle's niece.
    89. *stand to*] submit to (*O.E.D.*, 76a).
    95–113.] As Bond notes, the questions here come from Alexander's inter-
rogation of the Gymnosophists, as described in Plutarch's *Life of Alexander*,
IV.372–3. The wording shows Lyly following North's translation word for
word. But Lyly alters the order of the questions and omits question 1

Alexander. I will. Plato, of all beasts which is the subtlest?
Plato. That which man hitherto never knew.
Alexander. Aristotle, how should a man be thought a god?
Aristotle. In doing a thing unpossible for a man.   100
Alexander. Chrysippus, which was first, the day or the night?
Chrysippus. The day—by a day.
Alexander. Indeed, strange questions must have strange an-
    swers. Cleanthes, what say you, is life or death the
    stronger?   105
Cleanthes. Life, that suffereth so many troubles.
Alexander. Crates, how long should a man live?
Crates. Till he think it better to die than live.
Alexander. Anaxarchus, whether doth the sea or the earth
    bring forth most creatures?   110
Anaxarchus. The earth, for the sea is but a part of the earth.
Alexander. Hephestion, methinks they have answered all well,
    and in such questions I mean often to try them.
Hephestion. It is better to have in your court a wise man than
    in your ground a golden mine. Therefore would I leave   115
    war to study wisdom, were I Alexander.

('Whether the dead or the living were the greater number? He answered, "the
living. For the dead", said he, "are no more men"'), question 4 ('Why did he
make the Sabbas rebel? "Because", said he, "he should live honourably or die
vilely"') and question 6 ('How a man should come to be beloved? "If he be a
good man", said he, "not terrible"').

    97–8.] This is the third question in North's Plutarch: 'Which of all beasts
was the subtlest? "That", said he, "which man hitherto never knew"'.

    99–100.] This is the seventh question in North's Plutarch: 'How a man
should be a god? "In doing a thing", said he, "impossible for a man"'.

    101–4.] This is the fifth question (with following comment) in North's
Plutarch: 'Which he thought was first, the day or the night? He answered, "the
day, by a day". The king finding his answer strange added to this speech:
"Strange questions must needs have strange answers."'

    103–4.] Compare Dent, P.L.E.D., Q10: 'Like question, like answer'.

    104–6.] This is the eighth question in North's Plutarch: 'Which was the
stronger, life or death? "Life", said he, "that suffereth so many troubles"'.

    107–8.] This is the ninth question in North's Plutarch: 'How long a man
should live? "Until", said he, "he think it better to die than to live"'.

    109–11.] This is the second question in North's Plutarch: 'Whether the
earth or the sea brought forth most creatures? He answered, "the earth. For
the sea", said he, "is but a part of the earth."'

    115–17. *Therefore . . . Hephestion*] This is, as Bond notes, an adaptation of a

Alexander. So would I, were I Hephestion. But come, let
us go and give release, as I promised, to our Theban
thralls. ·

      Exeunt [ALEXANDER *and his train*].

Plato. Thou art fortunate, Aristotle, that Alexander is thy 120
scholar.

Aristotle. And all you happy that he is your sovereign.

Chrysippus. I could like the man well if he could be contented
to be but a man.

Aristotle. He seeketh to draw near to the gods in knowledge, 125
not to be a god.

Plato. Let us question a little with Diogenes, why he went not
with us to Alexander.

    [*Exeunt* CLEANTHES *and* CHRYSIPPUS.]

   [DIOGENES *is discovered in his tub*.]

Diogenes, thou didst forget thy duty that thou went'st
not with us to the king. 130

Diogenes. And you your profession, that you went to the king.

Plato. Thou takest as great pride to be peevish as others do
glory to be virtuous.

Diogenes. And thou as great honour, being a philosopher, to be
thought court-like as others shame, that be courtiers, to 135
be accounted philosophers.

Aristotle. These austere manners set aside; it is well known

---

118. promised, to] *Qq2, 3;* promised to *Qq1, 4, Blount.* 119. thralls] *Qq1–4;*
thrall *Blount.* 122. all you] *Qq1, 4, Blount;* you *Qq2, 3.* 128.1.] *This ed.; not
in Q1.* 128.2.] *1744* ('*Enter Diogenes*'); not in *Q1.* 137. aside;] *This ed.;*
aside, *Qq1;* a side, *Bond.*

passage in Plutarch's *Life of Alexander*, IV.332–3, on an occasion when Darius
offered ten thousand talents to Alexander if he would make a treaty. 'Parmenio
said unto him: "If I were Alexander", quoth he, "surely I would accept this
offer." "So would I indeed", quoth Alexander again, "if I were Parmenio." '
The story was also available in Erasmus, *Apophthegmata* (Alexander, no. 11),
and Quintus Curtius, IV.xi.44.

  128.1.] For an argument that the doubling pattern requires Cleanthes and
Chrysippus to leave the stage at this point, see Introduction, note 33.

  137. *set aside*] The punctuation adapted here from Q1 implies that *set aside* is
an imperative: 'stop being so moralistic; you are a criminal yourself'. But *set
aside* may equally well be participial: 'but leaving to one side your austerity, it

that thou didst counterfeit money.

Diogenes. And thou thy manners, in that thou didst not counterfeit money.   140

· *Aristotle.* Thou hast reason to contemn the court, being both in
  body and mind too crooked for a courtier.

Diogenes. As good be crooked and endeavour to make myself
  straight from the court as to be straight and learn to be
  crooked at the court.   145

Crates. Thou thinkest it a grace to be opposite against
  Alexander.

Diogenes. And thou to be jump with Alexander.

Anaxarchus. Let us go; for in contemning him we shall better
  please him than in wondering at him.   150

                    [DIOGENES *retires into his tub.*]

Aristotle. Plato, what dost thou think of Diogenes?

Plato. To be Socrates furious. Let us go.   *Exeunt* Philosophi.

150.1.] Adams ('*They walk away*'); not in Q1.

---

is well known . . .', implying that Diogenes' *manners* are the only austere thing
about him. In the latter case, Q1's comma need not be raised to a semi-colon.

  138. *thou . . . money*] See Laertius, VI.20, and Erasmus, *Apophthegmata*,
no. 140 (Udall, no. 145) for the same story (with a different ending).

  139–40.] Diogenes' point seems to be that it is not mere money that the
other philosophers have counterfeited by offering their services to Alexander;
they have counterfeited their morality (*manners*).

  141. *contemn*] scorn.

  144. *from the court*] away from the court. *Make myself straight from the court*
also suggests 'get away from the court as quickly as possible', with a play on
straight ('immediately') and *crooked*.

  146–8.] Compare the saying of Diogenes in Laertius, VI.45, and in
Erasmus, *Apophthegmata*, no. 81 (Udall, no. 87) where Callisthenes (or
Aristotle) is said to be happy because he is favoured by Alexander. No, says
Diogenes, he is wretched, because he can dine only when it pleases Alexander
to dine, but Diogenes dines when it pleases Diogenes.

  148. *jump*] exactly agreeing.

  152. *To . . . furious*] The remark is in Laertius, VI.54, and Aelian, *Varia
Historia*, XIV.33 (which provides the attribution to Plato). *Furious* is Latin
furiosus = mad (Greek *mainomenos*). I would be surprised to know that this
does not appear somewhere in Erasmus, but I have not been able to discover it.

Act II

Actus Secundus, Scaena Prima.

DIOGENES [*is discovered in his tub.*
To him enter] PSYLLUS, MANES [*and*] GRANICHUS.

Psyllus. Behold, Manes, where thy master is, seeking either
for bones for his dinner or pins for his sleeves. I will go
salute him.

Manes. Do so, but mum, not a word that you saw Manes.

Granichus. Then stay thou behind and I will go with Psyllus.   5

[*Psyllus and Granichus approach the tub.*
Manes stands aside.]

Psyllus. All hail, Diogenes, to your proper person.
                                    [*Diogenes holds up his light.*]

Diogenes. All hate to thy peevish conditions.

Granichus. O dog!

Psyllus. What dost thou seek for here?

Diogenes. For a man and a beast.   10

Granichus. That is easy without thy light to be found. Be not
all these men?

Diogenes. Called men.

Granichus. What beast is it thou lookest for?

Diogenes. The beast my man, Manes.   15

Psyllus. He is a beast indeed that will serve thee.

Diogenes. So is he that begat thee.

0.1–2.] *Adams (subst.); Diogenes, Psyllus, Manes, Granichus. Q1.*   4. word
that you] *Qq1, 4, Blount;* woord you *Qq2, 3.*   5.1–2.] *This ed.; not in Q1.*
6.1.] *Bond ('with a lantern'—at II.i.1); not in Q1.*

---

2. *pins . . . sleeve*] Bond says that Diogenes needs the pins 'because his
sleeves are in holes'.

6. *to . . . person*] to you yourself.

6.1. *his light*] Line 11 demands the property here. Bond cites Laertius
(VI.41): 'He lit a lamp in broad daylight and said, as he went about, "I am
looking for a man."' The story appears also in Erasmus, *Apophthegmata*,
no. 63 (Udall, no. 69).

73

Granichus. What wouldst thou do if thou shouldst find Manes?

Diogenes. Give him leave to do as he hath done before.

Granichus. What's that?   20

Diogenes. To run away.

Psyllus. Why, hast thou no need of Manes?

Diogenes. It were a shame for Diogenes to have need of Manes
      and for Manes to have no need of Diogenes.

Granichus. But put the case he were gone, wouldst thou   25
      entertain any of us two?

Diogenes. Upon condition.

Psyllus. What?

Diogenes. That you should tell me wherefore any of you both
      were good.   30

Granichus. Why, I am a scholar and well seen in philosophy.

Psyllus. And I a prentice and well seen in painting.

Diogenes. Well then, Granichus, be thou a painter to amend
      thine ill face, and thou, Psyllus, a philosopher to correct
      thine evil manners. [*Seeing Manes*] But who is that?   35
      Manes?

Manes. I care not who I were, so I were not Manes.

Granichus. [*To Manes*] You are taken tardy.

Psyllus. [*To Granichus*] Let us slip aside, Granichus, to see the
      salutation between Manes and his master.   40

                          [*Psyllus and Granichus stand aside.*]

Diogenes. Manes, thou knowest the last day I threw away my
      dish to drink in my hand, because it was superfluous.

---

35. *Seeing Manes*] *This ed.; not in Q1.*   38. *To Manes*] *This ed.; not in Q1.*   39.
To Granichus] *This ed.; not in Q1.*   40.1.] *Adams (subst.); not in Q1.*

23–4.] Originally told by Laertius (VI.55): 'advised to go in pursuit of a
runaway slave, he replied, "It would be absurd if Manes can live without
Diogenes [while] Diogenes cannot get on without Manes."' Also in Erasmus,
Apophthegmata, no. 133 (Udall, no. 138).

25. *put the case*] allow the supposition.

26. *entertain*] take into service.

31, 32. *well seen in*] skilled in, knowledgeable about.

37.] For the rhetorical form compare Shakespeare, *Troilus*, V.i.61–3: 'Ask
me not what I would be if I were not Thersites, for I care not to be the louse of
a lazar, so I were not Menelaus.'

38. *taken tardy*] caught unawares.

41–2. *thou . . . superfluous*] See Laertius, VI.37, and Erasmus, *Apophthegmata*
no. 41 (Udall, no. 47): Diogenes seeing 'a lad drinking out of the palm of his

Now I am determined to put away my man and serve
myself, *quia non egeo tui vel te.*

Manes. Master, you know a while ago I ran away; so do I mean   45
to do again, *quia scio tibi non esse argentum.*

Diogenes. I know I have no money; neither will I have ever a
man; for I was resolved long sithence to put away both
my slaves: money and Manes.

Manes. So was I determined to shake off both my dogs: hunger   50
and Diogenes.

Psyllus. [*Aside*] O sweet concent, between a crowd and a Jew's
harp!

Granichus. [*Aside*] Come, let us reconcile them.

Psyllus. [*Aside*] It shall not need, for this is their use; now do   55
they dine one upon another.

                    Exit DIOGENES [*inside his tub*].

Granichus. How now, Manes! Art thou gone from thy master?

Manes. No, I did but now bind myself to him.

Psyllus. Why, you were at mortal jars.

Manes. In faith, no; we brake a bitter jest one upon another.   60

---

47. will I have] *Qq1–4;* will have *Blount.*   52, 53, 54. Aside] *This ed.; not in
Q1.*   60. bitter] *Qq1, 3, 4, Blount;* better *Q2.*

---

hand . . . took out of his scrip a little treen tankard or dish . . . and the
same cast away from him . . . as a thing superfluous'.

44. quia . . . te] 'because I don't need you or [*by another construction*] you'.
The sentence is based, Bond notes, on the model in Lilly's Grammar for verbs
taking accusative or genitive: '*Egeo* or *indigeo tui vel te.*' The sentence occurs on
sig. DI of the 1567 edn.

46. quia . . . argentum] 'because I know you haven't any money'. Manes
caps Diogenes' quotation from Lilly's Grammar with a corresponding
quotation from the next page (sig. DIV), dealing with verbs which take the
dative.

50–1. both . . . Diogenes] Diogenes is a 'dog' for the usual reason: he is a
Cynic in philosophy. It is more difficult to know why hunger is a dog. Both
Latin and Greek, however, refer to hunger as making the stomach 'bark'
(*latrans stomachus / nēdus hulaktousa*) and this may supply the connection. On
the other hand, the reference may simply be to hunger and Manes both
'dogging' him, as David Bevington suggests to me.

52. concent] musical concord.

crowd] a fiddle (*O.E.D.*, sb., 1.b). Psyllus speaks ironically: Diogenes and
his servant are just about as much in harmony as two dissimilar instruments.

55. their use] their usual behaviour.

58.] Manes' point seems to be that quarreling is what binds him to
Diogenes.

59. at mortal jars] in deadly dispute.

Granichus. Why, thou art as dogged as he.

Psyllus. [*To Granichus*] My father knew them both little
    whelps.

Manes. Well, I will hie me after my master.

Granichus. Why, is it supper time with Diogenes?   65

Manes. Ay, with him at all times when he hath meat.

Psyllus. Why then every man to his home; and let us steal out
    again anon.

Granichus. Where shall we meet?

Psyllus. Why, at *Alae vendibili suspensa haedera non est opus.*   70

Manes. O Psyllus, *habeo te loco parentis*; thou blessest me.

                                          Exeunt.

                Actus Secundus, Scaena Secunda.

        [*Enter*] ALEXANDER, HEPHESTION [*and a*] Page.

Alexander. Stand aside, sir boy, till you be called.
                              [*The Page stands aside.*]
    Hephestion, how do ye like the sweet face of Campaspe?

62. To Granichus] *This ed.; not in Q1.*   70. Alae] *Bond; Ala Qq1–4, Blount.*
0.1.] *Bond (subst.); Alexander, Hephestion, Page, Diogenes, Apelles. Q1.*   1.1.]
Adams ('The Page withdraws'); not in Q1.   2. ye] *Qq1–3 (yee); you Q4,
Blount.*

---

61. *dogged*] See ll. 50–1 and n.

63. *whelps*] (1) puppy-dogs; (2) impertinent or ill-conditioned young
fellows.

66.] Bond compares Laertius, VI.40: 'To one who asked what was the
proper time for lunch he said, "If a rich man, when you will; if a poor man,
when you can."' The story is repeated in Erasmus, *Apophthegmata*, no. 60
(Udall, no. 66).

70. *at Alae . . . opus*] at the tavern, whose motto is 'when there is good wine
for sale there is no need to hang up a bunch of ivy' or (more colloquially) 'good
wine needs no bush'. Lyly offers us a comic variant on the proverb (Erasmus,
Adagia, II.589C), substituting the pseudo-Latin *ala* (= ale) for *vinum* (wine).
These Athenian servants are assimilated to their English counterparts and
drink ale, not wine. Dent, *P.L.E.D.*, W462.

71. *habeo . . . parentis*] 'I have you in place of a parent.' This comes from
Lilly's Grammar (1567 edn., sig. D4v), exemplifying the omission of the
preposition.

thou blessest me] It was the business of the father to give blessing to his
children. Psyllus, by setting up the meeting at the tavern, has blessed Manes,
and so may be thought of as a father.

Hephestion. I cannot but commend the stout courage of
    Timoclea.

Alexander. Without doubt Campaspe had some great man to   5
    her father.

Hephestion. You know Timoclea had Theagenes to her brother.

Alexander. Timoclea still in thy mouth! Art thou not in love?

Hephestion. Not I.

Alexander. Not with Timoclea, you mean, wherein you re-   10
    semble the lapwing, who crieth most where her nest is
    not. And so you lead me from espying your love with
    Campaspe: you cry 'Timoclea'.

Hephestion. Could I as well subdue kingdoms as I can my
    thoughts, or were I as far from ambition as I am from   15
    love, all the world would account me as valiant in arms
    as I know myself moderate in affection.

Alexander. Is love a vice?

Hephestion. It is no virtue.

Alexander. Well, now shalt thou see what small difference I   20
    make between Alexander and Hephestion. And sith
    thou hast been always partaker of my triumphs thou
    shalt be partaker of my torments. I love, Hephestion,
    I love; I love Campaspe, a thing far unfit for a Mace-
    donian, for a king, for Alexander. Why hangest thou   25
    down thy head, Hephestion, blushing to hear that
    which I am not ashamed to tell?

Hephestion. Might my words crave pardon and my counsel
    credit, I would both discharge the duty of a subject (for
    so I am) and the office of a friend (for so I will).   30

13. Campaspe: you] *Campaspe, you QI.*

---

3. *stout*] undaunted.

11. *lapwing*] proverbially described as running away from its nest in order to
mislead those who are searching for its eggs. See Dent, *P.L.E.D.*, L68.

14–15. *subdue ... thoughts*] Lyly may be remembering Pliny's praise of
Alexander (for giving away Campaspe): 'he won as much honour and glory as
by any victory over his enemies, for now he had conquered himself' (XXXV.36).
Plutarch makes a similar remark about Alexander's respect for the family of
Darius (*Life of Alexander*, IV.322).

20–3.] For the trust reposed in Hephestion see generally in Plutarch's *Life
of Alexander*, and in Erasmus, *Apophthegmata*, Alexander, nos. 14, 29, 62;
Udall, nos. 28, 60.

24–5. *Macedonian*] The Macedonians were characterised, as contrasted with
the Greeks, by dedication to war.

Alexander. Speak, Hephestion, for whatsoever is spoken,
  Hephestion speaketh to Alexander.
Hephestion. I cannot tell, Alexander, whether the report be
  more shameful to be heard or the cause sorrowful to be
  believed. What, is the son of Philip, King of Macedon,   35
  become the subject of Campaspe, the captive of Thebes?
  Is that mind whose greatness the world could not contain drawn within the compass of an idle alluring eye?
  Will you handle the spindle with Hercules when you
  should shake the spear with Achilles? Is the warlike   40
  sound of drum and trump turned to the soft noise of
  lyre and lute, the neighing of barbed steeds, whose
  loudness filled the air with terror and whose breaths
  dimmed the sun with smoke, converted to delicate
  tunes and amorous glances? O Alexander, that soft and   45
  yielding mind should not be in him whose hard and
  unconquered heart hath made so many yield. But you
  love. Ah, grief! But whom? Campaspe. Ah, shame, a
  maid forsooth, unknown, unnoble, and who can tell
  whether immodest, whose eyes are framed by art to   50
  enamour and whose heart was made by nature to enchant. Ay, but she is beautiful; yea, but not therefore
  chaste. Ay, but she is comely in all parts of the body;
  yea, but she may be crooked in some part of the mind.
  Ay, but she is wise; yea, but she is a woman. Beauty is   55
  like the blackberry, which seemeth red when it is not

50. art] *Qq1, 2, 4, Blount;* nature *Q3.*

37–8. *whose . . . contain*] Compare III.iv.21–3 below.
  39. *handle . . . Hercules*] Captivated by Omphale, Hercules consented to be
dressed as one of her maidens and to spin thread among the others. Used
generally as an image of the effeminising effects of love.
  40. *Achilles*] forms a natural antithesis to Hercules above. Disguised as a
woman by his mother (to save him from Troy and death), he yet revealed his
masculinity in both love and arms.
  40–5.] These standard symbols of the love/war antithesis reappear later in
the play at IV.iii.13–27 and are parodied at V.iii.19–24.
  42. *barbed steeds*] Compare *Richard III*, I.i.10 (in the context of the same
antithesis between love and war): 'instead of mounting barbèd steeds'.
  52–5. *Ay, but . . . Ay, but . . . Ay, but . . . yea, but . . .*] The figure of
altercatio displayed here is a favourite of Lyly's (see, for example, *Endymion*,
III.iv.116ff., *Euphues*, I.205, 20ff. and I.233, 3ff.) and appears also in the
proto-Euphuist Pettie's *Petite Palace* (ed. Gollancz), II.95. For other theatrical

ripe, resembling precious stones that are polished with
honey which the smoother they look the sooner they
break. It is thought wonderful among the seamen that
mugil, of all fishes the swiftest, is found in the belly   60
of the bret, of all the slowest. And shall it not seem
monstrous to wise men that the heart of the greatest
conqueror of the world should be found in the hands
of the weakest creature of nature—of a woman, of a
captive? Ermines have fair skins but foul livers, sep-   65
ulchres fresh cólours but rotten bones, women fair faces
but false hearts. Remember, Alexander, thou hast a
camp to govern, not a chamber; fall not from the armour of Mars to the arms of Venus, from the fiery assaults of war to the maidenly skirmishes of love, from   70
displaying the eagle in thine ensign to set down the

---

examples see Kyd, *The Spanish Tragedy*, II.i.19–28 (ed. F. S. Boas) and
Greene, *James IV*, I.i.166ff. and II.ii.192ff. (ed. J. A. Lavin).

57–9. *precious . . . break*] Bond cites Pliny, who indeed (XXXVII.74) refers to
precious stones being boiled in honey, but says nothing about breaking.

60–1. *mugil . . . slowest*] taken from Pliny (IX.67) by Erasmus, *Parabolae*,
p. 254: 'The turbot [*bret*] and . . . are the slowest moving of all fishes, but are
often found to have in their stomachs a grey mullet [*mugil*], the fastest fish of all.'

65. *Ermines . . . livers*] Bond compares *Euphues*, II.61–2, 38ff.: 'Beautiful
women are but like the ermine, whose skin is desired, whose carcase is
despised.'

65–6. *sepulchres . . . bones*] Bond compares *Euphues*, I.202, 10–11: 'in the
most curious sepulchre[s] are enclosed rotten bones'. Tilley, S225, cites Pettie:
'In goodly sumptuous sepulchres rotten bones are rife.' The eventual source
must be Matthew xxiii.27. See also Dent, *P.L.E.D.*, S225.

68–9. *fall . . . Venus*] The emasculation of the soldier by the power of love
has had a favourite representation since antiquity in the amours of Mars and
Venus. Compare nn. 39, 40, above. Spenser's Sir Verdant (*Faerie Queene*,
II.xii.72–80) is a good English example of literary imitations of such images of
Mars and Venus as are supplied (for example) by Botticelli's famous picture.
By an interesting coincidence, the Botticelli picture derives several of its details
from a picture of Alexander and Roxana painted by Aëtion and described by
Lucian in his *Herodotus and Aëtion*.

71. *the eagle . . . ensign*] As 'the king of birds' the eagle was early associated
with Jupiter and (as a portent) with success in battle (as at the battle of Arbela
between Alexander and Darius; see Plutarch, *Life of Alexander*, IV.338). As a
military ensign, the Roman legions' eagle naturally came to stand for Empire
and was adopted by a series of Roman and Holy Roman emperors, so that it
was easy to read it back into the imperial posture of Alexander. Albrecht
Altdorfer's painting of Alexander's victory at Issus seems to show the imperial
eagle on the flag of Alexander. D. J. A. Ross (*Illustrated Medieval Alexander-*

sparrow. I sigh, Alexander, that where fortune could
not conquer, folly should overcome. But behold all the
perfection that may be in Campaspe—a hair curling by
nature not art, sweet alluring eyes, a fair face made in   75
despite of Venus and a stately port in disdain of Juno, a
wit apt to conceive and quick to answer, a skin as soft as
silk and as smooth as jet, a long white hand, a fine little
foot, to conclude, all parts answerable to the best part—
what of this? Though she have heavenly gifts, virtue   80
and beauty, is she not of earthly mettle, flesh and blood?
You, Alexander, that would be a god, show yourself in
this worse than a man, so soon to be both overseen and
overtaken in a woman, whose false tears know their true
times, whose smooth words wound deeper than sharp   85
swords. There is no surfeit so dangerous as that of
honey, nor any poison so deadly as that of love; in the

Books in Germany and the Netherlands, Cambridge, 1971) has plates from two
MSS in The Hague which show Alexander displaying an eagle on his pennant
and on his shield.

72. *sparrow*] set against the eagle not simply as small against large, weak
against strong (see *Macbeth*, I.ii.35) but as an emblem of love (or lechery)
against war. Sparrows for their lechery were thought to be Venus' birds.

75–6. *in despite of*] cognate to *in disdain of* in l. 76. The phrase has probably
to be understood as 'able to scorn', 'in defiance of' (compare *O.E.D.*, *despite*,
sb., 5a). Campaspe seems formed to rival Venus.

76–7. *Venus . . . Juno . . . wit*] Behind the triad lies memory of the
goddesses involved in the Judgement of Paris – Venus, Juno, Minerva – *wit*
being substituted for Minerva (see *O.E.D.*, *Minerva*, 1b.). The submerged
implication is that had Campaspe been there, she would have won the prize.

77–9. *skin . . . hand . . . foot . . . all parts*] Lyly makes a gesture towards the
convention of the *blazon* or anatomical tour of the beloved. Compare Sidney,
'What tongue can her perfections tell' (*Arcadia*, 3rd Eclogue).

77–8. *soft . . . jet*] See Dent, *P.L.E.D.*, J49.01 and S449.

81. *mettle*] substance.

flesh and blood] See Dent, *P.L.E.D.*, F367: 'To be flesh and blood as others
are'.

83. *overseen*] deceived.

84–5. *whose . . . times*] who know the best time to turn on the waterworks.

85–6. *smooth . . . swords*] Compare Dent, *P.L.E.D.*, W839: 'Words hurt
more than swords.'

86–7. *no surfeit . . . honey*] Compare Erasmus, *Parabolae*, 237: 'nothing is
more insidious than poisonous honey' (taken from Pliny, XXI.44). Also
Laertius, VI.51: 'Ingratiating speech he compared to honey used to choke you.'
Dent, *P.L.E.D.*, H560: 'Too much honey cloys the stomach' points to

one physic cannot prevail, nor in the other counsel.

Alexander. My case were light, Hephestion, and not worthy
to be called love, if reason were a remedy or sentences   90
could salve that sense cannot conceive. Little do you
know, and therefore slightly do you regard, the dead
embers in a private person or live coals in a great prince,
whose passions and thoughts do as far exceed others in
extremity as their callings do in majesty. An eclipse in   95
the sun is more than the falling of a star; none can conceive the torments of a king unless he be a king, whose
desires are not inferior to their dignities. And then
judge, Hephestion, if the agonies of love be dangerous
in a subject, whether they be not more than deadly unto   100
Alexander, whose deep and not-to-be-conceived sighs
cleave the heart in shivers, whose wounded thoughts
can neither be expressed nor endured. Cease then,
Hephestion, with arguments to seek to refel that which
with their deity the gods cannot resist, and let this suf-   105
fice to answer thee, that it is a king that loveth and
Alexander, whose affections are not to be measured by
reason (being immortal) nor, I fear me, to be borne
(being intolerable).

91. salve] *1744;* salve, *Q1.*

Proverbs, xxv.27, as a source. Compare also *Euphues.*, II.191, 18–19: 'honey
taken excessively cloyeth the stomach, though it be honey'.

88. *physic*] medicine.

90. *if . . . remedy*] See Dent, *P.L.E.D.*, L517: 'Love is without reason', and
Euphues, I.231, 19: 'love gives no reason of choice'.

sentences] wise sayings.

91. *that*] that which. I do not accept Qq's comma after 'salve'.

91–3. *Little . . . prince*] One might have expected Alexander here to be
complaining that Hephestion is confusing the tepid love of a commoner with
the conflagration in a prince's heart. But the words used imply only a
parallelism.

92. *slightly*] As well as the current sense, see also *O.E.D.*, adv., 4:
'slightingly'.

104. *refel*] refute.

105. *with their deity*] with all their godlike might.

105. *the gods . . . resist*] The widely cited expression of this proverbial idea
is that of Publilius Syrus, *Sententiae*, 22: '*Amare et sapere vix deo conceditur.*'
See also Dent, *P.L.E.D.*, G275.01.

108. *being immortal*] After being saluted in Egypt as the son of Jupiter,
Alexander was given to assuming the status of a god.

Hephestion. I must needs yield, when neither reason nor   110
  counsel can be heard.

Alexander. Yield, Hephestion, for Alexander doth love and
  therefore must obtain.

Hephestion. Suppose she loves not you. Affection cometh not
  by appointment or birth, and then as good hated as   115
  enforced.

Alexander. I am a king and will command.

Hephestion. You may, to yield to lust by force; but to consent
  to love by fear you cannot.

Alexander. Why, what is that which Alexander may not con-   120
  quer as he list?

Hephestion. Why, that which you say the gods cannot resist,
  love.

Alexander. I am a conqueror, she a captive; I as fortunate as
  she fair; my greatness may answer her wants, and the   125
  gifts of my mind the modesty of hers. Is it not likely
  then that she should love? Is it not reasonable?

Hephestion. You say that in love there is no reason, and therefore there can be no likelihood.

Alexander. No more, Hephestion. In this case I will use mine   130
  own counsel, and in all other thine advice. Thou mayst
  be a good soldier, but never good lover. Call my page.
                    [*The Page comes forward.*]
  Sirrah, go presently to Apelles and will him to come to
  me without either delay or excuse.

Page. I go.   [*Exit* Page.]   135

Alexander. In the mean season, to recreate my spirits, being so
  near, we will go see Diogenes. And see where his tub is.
  Diogenes!

132.1.] *1744* ('*Enter Page*'); not in *Q1.*   135. *Exit* Page] *Bond (subst.); not in
Q1.*   137–8. Diogenes. And] *Qq1, 4, Blount; Diogenes,* and *Qq2, 3.*

110–32.] This type of exchange between a ruler in the grip of passion and a
counsellor representing reason is adapted from a convention of Senecan
tragedy much imitated in the Renaissance.
  114–16.] See Dent, *P.L.E.D.*, L499: 'love cannot be compelled'.
  122. *you say*] referring to l. 105 above.
  126. *modesty*] modest capacity.
  128. *You say*] referring to ll. 89–91 above.
  in love . . . reason] See Dent, *P.L.E.D.*, L517.
  129. *likelihood*] picking up and answering the *likely* in Alexander's
preceding speech.

DIOGENES [*is discovered in his tub*].

Diogenes. Who calleth?

Alexander. Alexander. How happened it that you would not　140
come out of your tub to my palace?

Diogenes. Because it was as far from my tub to your palace as
from your palace to my tub.

Alexander. Why then, dost thou owe no reverence to kings?

Diogenes. No.　145

Alexander. Why so?

Diogenes. Because they be no gods.

Alexander. They be gods of the earth.

Diogenes. Yea, gods of earth.

Alexander. Plato is not of thy mind.　150

Diogenes. I am glad of it.

Alexander. Why?

Diogenes. Because I would have none of Diogenes' mind but
Diogenes.

Alexander. If Alexander have anything that may pleasure Dio-　155
genes, let me know, and take it.

Diogenes. Then take not from me that you cannot give me, the
light of the world.

Alexander. What dost thou want?

Diogenes. Nothing that you have.　160

Alexander. I have the world at command.

Diogenes. And I in contempt.

Alexander. Thou shalt live no longer than I will.

Diogenes. But I shall die whether you will or no.

138.1.] *Bond* ('*The tub is thrust on*') *at 135.1; not in Q1.*　164. I shall] *Qq1, 4,
Blount;* I will *Qq2, 3.*

140–3.] Erasmus, *Apophthegmata*, no. 74 (Udall, no. 80) only has it that
'being spoken to and invited to come unto Alexander, he refused so to do'.

148.] Compare Nashe (ed. McKerrow, I.286): 'Kings are gods on earth.'
McKerrow says 'proverbial', and quotes Menander.

150.] The contrast between Plato's conformism and Diogenes' non-
conformity is made several times in Laertius and in Erasmus, *Apophthegmata*
(e.g., nos. 9, 11, 211; Udall, nos. 9, 11, 217).

155–8.] Bond points to Laertius, VI.38: 'Alexander . . . said, "Ask of me
any boon you like." To whom he replied, "stand out of my light." ' The story
is repeated in Erasmus, *Apophthegmata*, no. 46 (Udall, no. 52).

163–4.] This is in the spirit of the passage Bond cites from Laertius, VI.44
(repeated in Erasmus, *Apophthegmata*, no. 74, Udall, no. 80), but not close

Alexander. How should one learn to be content?   165
Diogenes. Unlearn to covet.
Alexander. Hephestion, were I not Alexander I would wish to
    be Diogenes.
Hephestion. He is dogged but discreet, I cannot tell how, sharp
    with a kind of sweetness, full of wit, yet too, too wayward.   170
Alexander. Diogenes, when I come this way again I will both
    see thee and confer with thee.
Diogenes. Do.   [*He retires into his tub.*]
Alexander. But here cometh Apelles.

              [*Enter*] APELLES.

    How now, Apelles? Is Venus' face yet finished?   175
Apelles. Not yet. Beauty is not so soon shadowed, whose
    perfection cometh not within the compass either of
    cunning or of colour.

---

169. how, sharp] *1744;* how: sharp *1780;* how sharpe *Qq1–4, Blount.*   173.
He . . . tub] *This ed.; not in Q1.*   174.1.] *1780; not in Q1.*

---

enough to require a connection. In Laertius Perdiccas threatens Diogenes with
death if he does not come to see him, to which Diogenes replies that he is
unimpressed, since a beetle or tarantula could do as much. The word *will* is
ambiguous here. In l. 164 it must mean 'exercise your will'. In l. 163
Alexander *could* be saying 'you will die as soon as me', but the context strongly
favours the meaning, 'I can decide to put you to death at any time.'

    165–6.] This sounds like a commonplace, but I have not found any
parallels.

    167–8.] Bond cites Laertius, VI.32: 'Alexander is reported to have said,
"Had I not been Alexander, I should have liked to be Diogenes".' The saying
is reproduced in Erasmus, *Apophthegmata,* no. 26 (Udall, no. 32).

    169. *dogged*] presumably means 'behaving like a Cynic' (not in *O.E.D.*),
sharp, mordant, bitter; as well as 'currish, crabbed' (*O.E.D.,* 2).

    169–70. *sharp . . . sweetness*] Laertius, VI.76, has 'so great was the magic
spell (*inux*) of Diogenes' words'. But (*pace* Bond) this seems rather remote
from the present passage.

    175. *Is . . . finished*] Lyly (introducing Apelles here for the first time) gives
him a background of work made plausible by what Pliny says. Apelles' most
celebrated picture, Pliny tells us (XXXV.36), was the Venus Anadyomene. He
also tells us that some say that 'by the pattern of this Campaspe, Apelles made
the picture of Venus Anadyomene'. Presumably the sight of Campaspe is
assumed to have released Apelles from the problems he describes in ll. 176–8.

    176. *shadowed*] portrayed, painted.

Alexander. Well, let it rest unperfect; and come you with me
      where I will show you that finished by nature that you   180
      have been trifling about by art.   [*Exeunt.*]

181. *Exeunt*] *1744; not in Q1.*

---

179. *unperfect*] incomplete, not finished.
180. *show you that*] i.e., show you Campaspe herself.

Act III

[Enter] APELLES *[and]* CAMPASPE *[attended by* PSYLLUS*]*.

Apelles. Lady, I doubt whether there be any colour so fresh
   that may shadow a countenance so fair.

Campaspe. Sir, I had thought you had been commanded to
   paint with your hand, not to gloze with your tongue;
   but, as I have heard, it is the hardest thing in painting   5
   to set down a hard favour, which maketh you to despair
   of my face, and then shall you have as great thanks to
   spare your labour as to discredit your art.

Apelles. Mistress, you neither differ from yourself nor your
   sex; for, knowing your own perfection, you seem to   10
   dispraise that which men most commend, drawing
   them by that mean into an admiration, where, feeding
   themselves, they fall into an ecstasy, your modesty being
   the cause of the one, and of the other, your affections.

0.1.] *Bond (subst.); Apelles, Campaspe. Q1.*

0.1.] I have represented this as a regular *Entry*. But there is some
likelihood that the *Entry* involves a *Discovery*. The opening dialogue suggests
that we first see Apelles actually engaged in painting Campaspe. I assume,
however, that the pair quickly move out of the 'workshop' and conduct the rest
of their dialogue on open stage.

1–2.] There is presumably an intended irony in Apelles' repetition to
Campaspe of the sentiments he has just expressed about his picture of Venus;
see II.ii.176–8.

2. *shadow*] portray, as at II.ii.176, but also set up in opposition to *fresh* and
fair.

4. *gloze*] comment (*O.E.D.*, 1b) or flatter (*O.E.D.*, 3).

5. *heard*] pronounced *hard* in the sixteenth century, so that the jingle with
hardest . . . hard is perfect.

6. *a hard favour*] an ugly face.

7–8. *then . . . art*] i.e., if you abandon the attempt to paint my ugly face you
will be thanked for not spending time on that; the thanks will be as great as
would be the discredit to your art if you persisted, for people would think the
painted face ugly because you lacked the competence to make it beautiful.

9–14.] Apelles sees Campaspe's 'typically feminine' technique as that of

86

Campaspe. I am too young to understand your speech though   15
    old enough to withstand your device. You have been so
    long used to colours you can do nothing but colour.
Apelles. Indeed the colours I see, I fear will alter the colour
    I have. But come, madam, will you draw near? For
    Alexander will be here anon.—Psyllus, stay you here   20
    at the window. If any enquire for me, answer *non lubet
    esse domi.*
                Exeunt [APELLES *and* CAMPASPE *into the shop*].

                Actus Tertius, Scaena Secunda.

            PSYLLUS [*remains outside the shop*].

Psyllus. It is always my master's fashion, when any fair gentle-
    woman is to be drawn within, to make me to stay with-
    out; but if he should paint Jupiter like a bull, like a
    swan, like an eagle, then must Psyllus with one hand
    grind colours and with the other hold the candle. But let   5

22.1] Bond (*subst.*); *not in Q1.*   0.1.] Adams (*subst.*); *Psyllus, Manes. Q1.*

affected self-dispraise, affected because she is, in fact, entirely self-conscious
about her own beauty. The combination of beauty and modesty draws men
into *admiration* (wonder) and eventually, encouraged to persist because of her
modesty, they fall into an ecstasy. Thus modesty causes admiration, and
affections (qualities, attributes) raise ecstasy.

    16. *device*] plot, trap.

    16–17. *You . . . colour*] As a painter you are so used to pigments that your
speech is composed of rhetorical *colores*, deceptive modes of rhetorical
persuasion.

    18–19. *Indeed . . . have*] The beautiful colour of your complexion will,
I fear, so affect me that I will turn pale (or blush). Lyly may be playing
with the catch-phrase 'fear no colours' (don't be afraid of anything), Dent,
P.L.E.D., C520.

    21. *window*] It is not clear if the *window* is a stage property or a piece of
imagination.

    21–2. non lubet esse domi] 'It does not please him to be at home.'

    2. *drawn*] (1) conducted; (2) depicted.

    2–3. *without*] (1) outside; (2) without participating.

    3–4. *bull . . . swan . . . eagle*] the forms in which Jupiter ravished Europa,
Leda and Ganymede.

    5. *hold the candle*] i.e., so that the painter can see his subject—a standard
phrase for unskilled help (*O.E.D.*, *candle*, 11.5c).

him alone; the better he shadows her face the more will
he burn his own heart. And now if a man could meet
with Manes! who I dare say looks as lean as if Diogenes
dropped out of his nose.

[*Enter*] MANES.

Manes. And here comes Manes, who hath as much meat in   10
his maw as thou hast honesty in thy head.
Psyllus. Then I hope thou art very hungry.
Manes. They that know thee know that.
Psyllus. But dost thou not remember that we have certain
liquor to confer withal?   15
Manes. Ay, but I have business. I must go cry a thing.
Psyllus. Why, what hast thou lost?
Manes. That which I never had, my dinner.
Psyllus. Foul lubber, wilt thou cry for thy dinner?
Manes. I mean I must cry, not as one would say *cry*, but *cry*,   20
that is, make a noise.
Psyllus. Why, fool, that is all one; for if thou cry thou must
needs make a noise.
Manes. Boy, thou art deceived. *Cry* hath divers significations
and may be alluded to many things, *knave* but one and   25
can be applied but to thee.

---

7. a man] *Qq1–3;* any man *Q4, Blount.*   9.1.] *Bond; not in Q1.*

6–7. *the better . . . heart*] The phrase is set up on the basis of the antithesis
between shadow and sunburn, but the primary meaning of *shadows* is
'portrays'.

9. *dropped . . . nose*] a proverbial phrase for hunger; see Dent, *P.L.E.D.*,
H813: 'Hunger drops out of his nose.'

10–13.] Manes announces his arrival by indicating that he has overhead
what Psyllus has just said. He confirms his leanness, but at the same time
wittily puts down his interlocutor: the absence of food in his gut (*maw*) is no
more remarkable than the absence of honesty in Psyllus' head. Psyllus
responds that the equivalence requires Manes to do without food, for Psyllus is
happy to do without honesty. Manes replies that the equivalence means he has
to be hungry.

14. *remember*] See II.i.67–70 above.

15. *to confer withal*] to converse with (*O.E.D.*, *confer*, vb., 6).

16. *cry a thing*] make a proclamation (especially about things lost and found;
see *O.E.D.*, *cry*, vb., 5c). Psyllus' reply assumes that *cry* means 'weep and
wail' (*O.E.D.*, vb., 9). The quibbling in ll. 17–25 depends on the alternation
of these meanings.

Psyllus. Profound Manes!

Manes. We Cynics are mad fellows. Didst thou not find I did
    quip thee?

Psyllus. No, verily; why, what's a quip?   30

Manes. We great girders call it a short saying of a sharp wit
    with a bitter sense in a sweet word.

Psyllus. How canst thou thus divine, divide, define, dispute,
    and all on the sudden?

Manes. Wit will have his swing; I am bewitched, inspired,   35
    inflamed, infected.

Psyllus. Well then, will not I tempt thy gibing spirit.

Manes. Do not, Psyllus, for thy dull head will be but a grind-
    stone for my quick wit, which, if thou whet with over-
    thwarts, *periisti, actum est de te.* I have drawn blood at   40
    one's brains with a bitter bob.

Psyllus. Let me cross myself; for I die if I cross thee.

Manes. Let me do my business. I myself am afraid lest my

---

30. what's] *Q1, Blount ('whats'); what is Qq2-4.*   34. sudden] *Qq1, 3, 4,
Blount; disdaine Q2.*   40. periisti] *Q4, Blount ('perijsti'); peristi Qq1-3.*

---

27. *Profound Manes*] an ironic acknowledgement of defeat in the wit contest.
28. *We Cynics*] Manes aligns himself with his master.
29. *quip*] very rare in a transitive use, with the sense 'make a joke against'.
31. *girders*] those who gird (scoff or jest).
33. *divine, divide, define, dispute*] The four capacities named seem intended
to suggest the process of scholastic logic: to infer the topic; to distinguish the
possibilities of argument; to define the particular issues; to dispute on that
basis.
35. *Wit . . . swing*] presumably equivalent to the proverbial 'Wit, whither
wilt thou?' (Dent, *P.L.E.D.*, W570). See also Y48: 'Youth will have its course
(swing)'.
35-6. *bewitched, inspired, inflamed, infected*] four mental states invoked to
correspond to the four capacities named above (l. 33). There seems to be
nothing precise in the connection. It seems probable that *infected* means only
'influenced' or 'overcome'.
39-40. *overthwarts*] i.e., contradictions, repartee (literally, cross-pieces).
40. *periisti . . . te*] 'Thou hast perished; thou art done for.' Bond points to
Terence, *Eunuchus*, I.i.9: '*actum est; illicet: Peristi*'. See also Terence, *Adelphoe
(The Brothers),* Act III, ll. 325-6.
41. *one's*] of a particular person.
    bob] jibe, taunt.
42.] I will bless myself in preparation, for I am certain to die if I contradict
you.

wit should wax warm, and then must it needs consume
some hard head with fine and pretty jests. I am some-   45
times in such a vein that for want of some dull pate to
work on I begin to gird myself.
Psyllus. The gods shield me from such a fine fellow, whose
words melt wits like wax!
Manes. Well then, let us to the matter. In faith, my master   50
meaneth tomorrow to fly.
Psyllus. It is a jest.
Manes. Is it a jest to fly? Shouldst thou fly so soon, thou
shouldst repent it in earnest.
Psyllus. Well, I will be the cryer.   55
Manes and Psyllus (one after another). Oyez, oyez, oyez. All
manner of men, women or children that will come
tomorrow into the market-place, between the hours
of nine and ten, shall see Diogenes the Cynic fly.
Psyllus. I do not think he will fly.   60
Manes. Tush, say *fly*.
Psyllus. Fly.
Manes. Now let us go; for I will not see him again till mid-
night. I have a back way into his tub.

---

53. so soon] *Q1;* so, soone *Bond.*

---

47. *gird*] scoff at; rare in the transitive use.
49. *melt . . . wax*] Psyllus picks up the *wax* from l. 44 and changes the
meaning.
52–3.] Psyllus says, 'you are joking'; Manes replies, 'flying is no joke'.
53–4. *Shouldst . . . earnest*] The antithesis seems imperfect: *in earnest* must
be set against *jest*, and one would expect *soon* to be answered by 'late' or 'at
leisure' (as in the proverbial 'marry in haste and repent at leisure'; Tilley,
H196). But the two possibilities seem to be compressed into one.
56. one after another] The s.d. leaves open a number of theatrical
possibilities. The repetition can be word-by-word, phrase-by-phrase or
sentence-by-sentence.
Oyez, oyez, oyez] (Q1: O ys, O ys, O ys) formal, three-part Law-French
introduction to a proclamation: hear ye, hear ye, hear ye.
61.] The point of this remark is, I take it, that Psyllus, in his repetition of
Manes' proclamation, has not been willing to bring out the last word *fly*.
Manes, who has no such inhibitions, urges him to complete the sentence.
64. *a back . . . tub*] Editors must be puzzled to know what this tells us about
the stage appearance of Diogenes' tub. Manes' explanation (l. 67) suggests that
the phrase may be present only to set up the joke.

Psyllus. Which way callest thou the back way, when every way   65
    is open?

Manes. I mean, to come in at his back.

Psyllus. Well, let us go away, that we may return speedily.

                                     Exeunt.

Actus Tertius, Scaena Tertia.

[*Enter*] APELLES [*and*] CAMPASPE [*from the shop*].

Apelles. I shall never draw your eyes well, because they blind
    mine.

Campaspe. Why then, paint me without eyes, for I am blind.

Apelles. Were you ever shadowed before of any?

Campaspe. No. And would you could so now shadow me that   5
    I might not be perceived of any.

Apelles. It were pity but that so absolute a face should furnish
    Venus' temple amongst these pictures.

Campaspe. What are these pictures?

Apelles. This is Leda, whom Jove deceived in likeness of a   10
    swan.

0.1.] *This ed; Apelles, Campaspe. Q1.*   3. blind.] *Qq2, 3, Blount;* blind? *Qq1,
4.*   10. Jove] *Qq1, 4, Blount (Ioue);* loue *Qq2, 3.*

68.] The line, directed towards the audience, could be making an obvious
stage reference ('see you soon'); inside the fiction it reminds us of the drinking
bout arranged.

0.1.] Bond and Adams assume that the following scene takes place *inside* the
workshop or stage booth. I assume that the booth provides only an initial point
of reference. See Introduction, pp. 31–2.

3. *I am blind*] It is not clear what Campaspe means by this, unless it is 'I too
am blinded by love'; but such a remark would seem insufficiently modest for
Campaspe. David Bevington suggests an oblique reference to the traditional
blindness of Cupid.

4. *shadowed*] painted. In the next line the word is picked up in the sense of
'conceal'.

7. *absolute*] perfect.

7–8. *furnish Venus' temple*] Pliny tells us that Apelles' picture of Venus
Anadyomene was hung in the shrine of Venus at Cos. But it may be that *Venus'
temple* is meant only metaphorically (Campaspe's picture will join the other
exemplars of female beauty).

8, 9. *these pictures*] Apelles and Campaspe gesture towards pictures hung in
his workshop, or Apelles may pick up individual pictures from a stack. There
is no requirement that the audience should be able to see them inside the
workshop.

10. *Jove*] Bond misreports that Q1 reads 'loue'.

Campaspe. A fair woman, but a foul deceit.

Apelles. This is Alcmena, unto whom Jupiter came in shape of
    Amphitrion her husband and begat Hercules.

Campaspe. A famous son, but an infamous fact.   15

Apelles. He might do it because he was a god.

Campaspe. Nay, therefore it was evil done because he was a
    god.

Apelles. This is Danaë, into whose prison Jupiter drizzled a
    golden shower and obtained his desire.   20

Campaspe. What gold can make one yield to desire?

Apelles. This is Europa, whom Jupiter ravished; this Antiopa.

Campaspe. Were all the gods like this Jupiter?

Apelles. There were many gods in this like Jupiter.

Campaspe. I think in those days love was well ratified among   25
    men on earth when lust was so full authorised by the
    gods in heaven.

Apelles. Nay, you may imagine there were women passing
    amiable when there were gods exceeding amorous.

Campaspe. Were women never so fair, men would be false.   30

Apelles. Were women never so false, men would be fond.

Campaspe. What counterfeit is this, Apelles?

Apelles. This is Venus, the goddess of love.

Campaspe. What, be there also loving goddesses?

Apelles. This is she that hath power to command the very   35

---

12. *foul*] Perhaps there is a pun on 'fowl'.

15. *infamous fact*] shameful crime.

17–18.] The gods ought to provide moral examples, and therefore their
lapses are more wicked than those of ordinary men.

19. *Danaë*] Apelles does not say that the gold was the cause of Jupiter's
success, but the possibility is allowed as in many treatments of the story.
Horace, *Odes*, III.16, is a famous example. It is cited by Erasmus, *De Copia*,
II.11 (*C.W.E.*, XXIV.611).

21.] Campaspe's question is not, I think, how much gold would be needed,
but rather 'Is it possible that any amount of gold should succeed?'

22. *Antiopa*] Antiope, or Antiopa (both forms seem to have been current),
was ravished by Jupiter in the shape of a satyr.

25. *ratified*] made valid, given consent to.

28–9. *passing amiable*] exceedingly worthy to be loved.

31. *fond*] (1) amorous; (2) foolish.

32. *counterfeit*] likeness. Presumably this is the picture referred to above,
II.ii.175.

this] Perhaps in this case at least the picture should be present on the stage,
able to be picked up and scrutinised by the speakers.

affections of the heart.

Campaspe. How is she hired? By prayer, by sacrifice, or
    bribes?

Apelles. By prayer, sacrifice and bribes.

Campaspe. What prayer?   40

Apelles. Vows irrevocable.

Campaspe. What sacrifice?

Apelles. Hearts ever sighing, never dissembling.

Campaspe. What bribes?

Apelles. Roses and kisses. But were you never in love?   45

Campaspe. No; nor love in me.

Apelles. Then have you injured many.

Campaspe. How so?

Apelles. Because you have been loved of many.

Campaspe. Flattered perchance of some.   50

Apelles. It is not possible that a face so fair and a wit so sharp,
    both without comparison, should not be apt to love.

Campaspe. If you begin to tip your tongue with cunning, I
    pray dip your pencil in colours and fall to that you must
    do, not that you would do.   [*Exeunt into the shop.*]   55

Actus Tertius, Scaena Quarta.

[*Enter*] CLITUS [*and*] PARMENIO.

Clitus. Parmenio, I cannot tell how it cometh to pass that in
    Alexander nowadays there groweth an unpatient kind
    of life: in the morning he is melancholy, at noon sol-
    emn, at all times either more sour or severe than he was
    accustomed.   5

Parmenio. In kings' causes I rather love to doubt than con-
    jecture, and think it better to be ignorant than inquisi-
    tive; they have long ears and stretched arms, in whose

51. It is] *Q2;* Is it *Q1.*   54. pray dip] *Qq1, 4, Blount;* pray you dip *Qq2, 3.*   55.
Exeunt into the shop] *This ed.; not in Q1.*   0.1.] *Bond; Clytus, Parmenio,
Alexander, Hephestion, Crysus, Diogenes, Apelles, Campaspe. Q1.*

37–45.] With this litany of Venus compare the passage in *Love's Metamorphosis* (II.i.104ff.) on 'the substance of love'.

1–23.] Lyly may have intended us to see in this conversation the irony that
both Clitus and Parmenio were murdered by Alexander during the Persian
campaign. The death of Parmenio in particular fulfilled the remark put into his
mouth here (ll. 8–10).

8. *long . . . arms*] Erasmus, *Adagia,* II.69E–70B, combines the idea of kings'

heads suspicion is a proof and to be accused is to be
condemned.   10

Clitus. Yet between us there can be no danger to find out the
cause, for that there is no malice to withstand it. It may
be an unquenchable thirst of conquering maketh him
unquiet. It is not unlikely his long ease hath altered his
humour; that he should be in love it is not impossible.   15

Parmenio. In love, Clitus? No, no, it is as far from his thought
as treason in ours. He, whose ever-waking eye, whose
never-tired heart, whose body patient of labour, whose
mind unsatiable of victory, hath always been noted,
cannot so soon be melted into the weak conceits of love.   20
Aristotle told him there were many worlds; and that he
hath not conquered one, that gapeth for all, galleth
Alexander. But here he cometh.

        [Enter] ALEXANDER *[and]* HEPHESTION.

Alexander. Parmenio and Clitus, I would have you both ready
to go into Persia about an embassage no less profitable   25
to me than to yourselves honourable.

Clitus. We are ready at all commands, wishing nothing else
but continually to be commanded.

Alexander. Well then, withdraw yourselves till I have further
considered of this matter.   30

                Exeunt CLITUS *and* PARMENIO.

18. tired] *Qq1, 4, Blount;* tried *Qq2, 3.*   23.1.] *Bond; not in Q1.*

---

long hands (from Ovid, *Heroides*, XVII.166; compare *Euphues*, I.221, 34–5:
'Kings have long arms') and reference to their eyes and ears: '*Multae regum
aures atque oculi.*' The two ideas are commonly combined in the Renaissance.
See Bacon, *Promus* (ed. Pott), no. 1115, and Sir William Alexander, first Earl
of Stirling, *The Tragedy of Julius Caesar*, l. 1936, with a significant emendation: 'Tyrants' ears hear much, their hands reach far.' Dent, *P.L.E.D.*, K87.

11–12.] *between us* may mean 'between Clitus and Parmenio' or 'between us
and Alexander'. They should be able to find out the cause of Alexander's
distemper since there is no *malice* (ill-will) between them to reject a plausible
explanation. Clitus in the following lines offers three independent possibilities.

21–3. *Aristotle . . . Alexander*] Both Plutarch, 'On Tranquility of Mind',
Moralia, 466D (VI.177–9), and Erasmus, *Apophthegmata* (Alexander, no. 58)
tell this story, but of Anaxarchus rather than Aristotle: 'When he had heard
the philosopher Anaxarchus holding opinion . . . that there were worlds out of
number . . . he fell on weeping. . . . Have I not, trow you, a good cause to
weep, in that whereas there be worlds innumerable, I am not yet come to be
full lord of one?' (Udall, no. 56).

22. *that gapeth for all*] he who longs to conquer all worlds.

Now we will see how Apelles goeth forward. I doubt me
that nature hath overcome art and her countenance his
cunning.

Hephestion. You love, and therefore think anything.

Alexander. But not so far in love with Campaspe as with   35
Bucephalus, if occasion serve either of conflict or of
conquest.

Hephestion. Occasion cannot want if will do not. Behold all
Persia swelling in the pride of their own power, the
Scythians careless what courage or fortune can do, the   40
Egyptians dreaming in the soothsayings of their augurs
and gaping over the smoke of their beasts' entrails. All
these, Alexander, are to be subdued, if that world be
not slipped out of your head which you have sworn to
conquer with that hand.   45

Alexander. I confess the labours fit for Alexander, and yet
recreation necessary among so many assaults, bloody
wounds, intolerable troubles. Give me leave a little, if
not to sit, yet to breathe. And doubt not but Alexander
can, when he will, throw affections as far from him as   50
he can cowardice. But behold Diogenes talking with
one at his tub.

DIOGENES [*is discovered in his tub,
talking to*] CHRYSUS.

Chrysus. One penny, Diogenes; I am a Cynic.

Diogenes. He made thee a beggar that first gave thee anything.

---

41. augurs] *Qq1, 4, Blount;* auguries *Qq2, 3.*   52.1–2.] *This ed.; not in Q1.*

31–3. *I doubt . . . cunning*] Alexander fears that Campaspe's beauty will have
overcome Apelles' artistic control (cunning).

36. *Bucephalus*] Bucephalus, Alexander's warhorse, here stands by
metonymy for the whole enterprise of war and conquest.

38.] If there is enough desire (*will*) there will be no lack of opportunity.

38–43. *Behold . . . subdued*] Lyly uses the advantage of hindsight to show us
Alexander poised on the brink of the conquests we know he later achieved.
The reference to the auguries of the Egyptians has no doubt, beyond the
general reference to that nation's attributes, a particular reminder of
Alexander's journey to the oracle at Siwa.

49. *to breathe*] to draw breath (as after exercise).

52.1–2.] See Introduction pp. 30–1.

52.2. *CHRYSUS*] I have Graecised Lyly's *Crysus*, even though no person
called Chrysus is known, supposing that Lyly intends a connection with *chrysos*
= gold.

Chrysus. Why, if thou wilt give nothing, nobody will give thee.   55
Diogenes. I want nothing till the springs dry and the earth
    perish.
Chrysus. I gather for the gods.
Diogenes. And I care not for those gods which want money.
Chrysus. Thou art a right Cynic, that will give nothing.   60
Diogenes. Thou art not, that will beg anything.

            [*He retires into his tub.*]

Chrysus. Alexander, King Alexander, give a poor Cynic a
    groat.
Alexander. It is not for a king to give a groat.
Chrysus. Then give me a talent.   65
Alexander. It is not for a beggar to ask a talent. Away!

            [*Exit* CHRYSUS.]

        Apelles!

    [*Enter*] APELLES [*and*] CAMPASPE [*from the shop*].

Apelles. Here.
Alexander. Now, gentlewoman, doth not your beauty put the
    painter to his trump?   70
Campaspe. Yes, my lord; seeing so disordered a countenance,
    he feareth he shall shadow a deformed counterfeit.

            [CAMPASPE *withdraws into the workshop.*]

Alexander. Would he could colour the life with the feature!

61.1.] *This ed.; not in Q1.*   66.1.] *This ed.; not in Q1.*   67.1.] *This ed.; not in
Q1.*   72.1.] *This ed.; not in Q1.*

---

60. *right*] true.

62–66.] The story is found in Seneca, *De Beneficiis* (II.16), contrasting
Alexander and Antigonus, and also in Plutarch, 'The sayings of kings',
Moralia, 182E (III.73). Lyly derived it from Erasmus, *Apophthegmata*,
(Antigonus, no. 15): 'Unto Thrasillus a cynic asking of him, in the way of a
reward, a groat or six pence: "That is no reward for a king to give" (quoth he).
The cynic eftsoons replying, "Well, then give me a talent": "Nay" (quoth he)
"that is no meet reward for a cynic to receive" ' (Udall's translation). Erasmus
tells a very similar story of Alexander and Perillus (*Apophthegmata*, Alexander,
no. 6) but the sums of money named there are different (ten talents and fifty),
so that we may judge the Antigonus version to be the true source.

70. *to his trump*] obliging the [card-player] to call on his highest resources.
See Dent, *P.L.E.D.*, T545.

73.] Would he could paint not only Campaspe's proportion and shape but
also the quality of life in her.

And methinketh, Apelles, were you as cunning as report saith you are, you may paint flowers as well with   75
sweet smells as fresh colours, observing in your mixture
such things as should draw near to their savours.

Apelles. Your Majesty must know it is no less hard to paint
savours than virtues; colours can neither speak nor
think.   80

Alexander. Where do you first begin, when you draw any
picture?

Apelles. The proportion of the face, in just compass as I can.

Alexander. I would begin with the eye as a light to all the rest.

Apelles. If you will paint as you are, a king, your Majesty may   85
begin where you please; but as you would be a painter
you must begin with the face.

Alexander. Aurelius would in one hour colour four faces.

Apelles. I marvel in half an hour he did not four.

Alexander. Why, is it so easy?   90

Apelles. No, but he doth it so homely.

Alexander. When will you finish Campaspe?

Apelles. Never finish; for always in absolute beauty there is
somewhat above art.

83. proportion] *Qq1, 2, 4, Blount;* proposition *Q3.*

74–5. *as cunning . . . you are*] Pliny (XXXV.36) says that Apelles could paint
unpaintable things, such as thunder and lightning.

75–80. *you may . . . think*] A similar point about the limitation of pictorial
representation is made in Marston's *Antonio and Mellida*, V.i, where the
foolish knight Balurdo has to be told that the painter cannot represent a song.
See also the 'Painter Scene' added to Kyd's *The Spanish Tragedy* (in F. S. Boas,
ed., *Kyd*, III.xiiA).

83. *just compass*] proper proportion (*O.E.D.*, sb., I).

85. *as you . . . king*] (1) as having the power to do what you please; (2) as
someone who has no professional skill in painting.

88.] The story comes from the pseudo-Plutarch 'On the education of
children' (*Moralia*, I.31), but without the name of the 'wretched painter'.
Pliny, XXXV.37, in a passage that follows a discussion of Apelles, describes the
painter Arellius as one who represented his mistresses as goddesses. This may
supply the origin of the name in Lyly.

91. *homely*] roughly, without refinement.

93–4. *for . . . art*] a commonplace most memorably articulated by Pope in
'snatch a grace beyond the reach of art' (*Essay in Criticism*, l. 155). Closer to
Lyly's own time, see Marlowe, *1 Tamburlaine*, V.i.172f. (Revels edn.): 'One
thought, one grace, one wonder at the least, / Which into words no virtue can
digest'. See Samuel Holt Monk, '"A Grace Beyond the Reach of Art"',

Alexander. Why should not I by labour be as cunning as   95
    Apelles?

Apelles. God shield you should have cause to be so cunning as
    Apelles!

Alexander. Methinketh four colours are sufficient to shadow
    any countenance, and so it was in the time of Phidias.   100

Apelles. Then had men fewer fancies and women not so many
    favours. For now, if the hair of her eyebrows be black,
    yet must the hair of her head be yellow; the attire of
    her head must be different from the habit of her body,
    else would the picture seem like the blazon of ancient   105
    armory, not like the sweet delight of new-found ami-
    ableness. For as in garden-knots diversity of odours
    make a more sweet savour, or as in music divers strings
    cause a more delicate concent, so in painting the more
    colours the better counterfeit, observing black for a   110
    ground and the rest for grace.

---

105. would] *Qq1, 4, Blount;* must *Qq2, 3.*

Journal of the History of Ideas, v (1944), 131–50. Pliny in his appraisal of
Apelles (XXXV.36) says that he excelled all other painters in *charis,* which
Philemon Holland's translation (1601) says is 'as one would say, the grace'.

    97–8.] Compare Erasmus, *Apophthegmata* (Philip, no. 29): when Philip
gave technical advice to a minstrel, the minstrel replied, 'God forfend, Sir
King . . . that ye should have more sight and knowledge in this gear than I'
(Udall's translation).

    99–100.] As Bond notes, this comes from Pliny (XXXV.32), who tells us that
the restriction to four colours belonged to the time of 'Apelles, Aetion [Echion
in some versions], Melanthius and Nicomachus'—that is, to the present of the
play. Lyly pushes it back to the time of Phidias (mid-fifth century B.C.).

    102. *favours*] qualities of appearance.

    105. *blazon*] a painting of a heraldic coat of arms (*armory*).

    106. *armory*] O.E.D. distinguishes *armory* from *armoury* (armour), and I
have conformed my spelling to this distinction.

    107. *garden-knots*] flower beds.

    108. *divers strings*] different pitches of string instruments.

    109. *concent*] harmony.

    110. *counterfeit*] representation (but with a suggestion also of deceptive
illusion).

    110–11. *black . . . ground*] As Bond notes, this seems to be a misreading of
Pliny XXXV.36. Holland translates: 'One secret he [Apelles] had himself . . .
and that was a certain black varnish [*atramentum*] which he used to lay upon his
painted tables when he had finished them.'

    111. *grace*] See ll. 93–4n.

Alexander. Lend me thy pencil, Apelles; I will paint and thou
        shalt judge.
Apelles. Here.
                    [*Alexander takes the charcoal and draws.*]
Alexander. The coal breaks.   115
Apelles. You lean too hard.
Alexander. Now it blacks not.
Apelles. You lean too soft.
Alexander. This is awry.
Apelles. Your eye goeth not with your hand.   120
Alexander. Now it is worse.
Apelles. Your hand goeth not with your mind.
Alexander. Nay, if all be too hard or soft, so many rules and
        regards that one's hand, one's eye, one's mind must all
        draw together, I had rather be setting of a battle than   125
        blotting of a board. But how have I done here?
Apelles. Like a king.
Alexander. I think so; but nothing more unlike a painter.
        Well, Apelles, Campaspe is finished as I wish; dismiss
        her and bring presently her counterfeit after me.   130
Apelles. I will.   [*Exit* APELLES.]
Alexander. Now, Hephestion, doth not this matter cotton as I
        would? Campaspe looketh pleasantly, liberty will in-
        crease her beauty, and my love shall advance her
        honour.   135
Hephestion. I will not contrary your Majesty, for time must

114.1.] *This ed.; not in Q1.*   130. and] *Q1* (&), *Q4, Blount; not in Qq2, 3.*
131. *Exit* APELLES] *This ed.; not in Q1.*

---

112. *pencil*] artist's brush or instrument of drawing; here, charcoal.
115. *coal*] charcoal used for writing or drawing (*O.E.D.*, sb., 4c).
125. *setting . . . battle*] settling the arrangement of (an army) for battle
(*O.E.D.*, set, vb.², 70).
126. *blotting*] painting coarsely, daubing (*O.E.D.*, blot, vb.¹, 2b).
a board] a panel used as a surface for a painting.
127. *Like a king*] as at l. 85.
129–30. *dismiss her*] end your painting sessions with her.
132. *cotton*] prosper, succeed (*O.E.D.*, vb., II.4).
136. *contrary*] contradict, gainsay.
136–7. *for time . . . wrought*] Compare Dent, *P.L.E.D.*, T340: 'Time wears
away love.' Hephestion's second formulation ('and reason . . . nursed'), if
taken literally, makes the judgement that Alexander's love or appetite is
infantile.

wear out that love hath wrought, and reason wean what
appetite nursed.

[*Campaspe comes out of the workshop*
and crosses the stage.]

Alexander. How stately she passeth by; yet how soberly; a
sweet consent in her countenance with a chaste disdain,   140
desire mingled with coyness and (I cannot tell how to
term it) a curst yielding modesty!
Hephestion. Let her pass.

[*Exit* CAMPASPE.]

Alexander. So she shall, for the fairest on the earth.   *Exeunt.*

138.1–2.] *Bond* ('*Campaspe comes from the studio*'); *not in Q1.*   143.1.] *Adams*
('*Campaspe leaves the studio and passes down the street*'); *not in Q1.*

---

137. *that*] that which.

139–42.] For a similar string of paradoxical observations see Hephestion
on Diogenes, II.ii.169–70 above.

139. *she passeth by*] See Introduction, pp. 32–3, for the theatrical issue
involved here. To deal with it I have been obliged to assume a number of stage
movements, at ll. 72.1, 138.1–2 and 143.1. I have caused Campaspe to
withdraw into the workshop while Alexander is having his drawing lesson,
quite arbitrarily placing her exit at l. 72.1. At l. 129 Apelles is told to 'dismiss'
Campaspe. I assume that he exits into the workshop, where presumably he
joins Campaspe. At l. 138 I have made Campaspe re-emerge from the
workshop; she has been given her 'dismissal' by Apelles, while they were
together in the workshop. She walks slowly (and sadly, perhaps) across the
stage, watched by Alexander and Hephestion. By l. 143 she must have passed
through the stage door.

140. *consent*] She is obeying Alexander's order even though she also *disdains*
or dislikes it.

142. *curst yielding modesty*] the most compressed form of the oxymoron
Alexander has been pursuing. The only appropriate sense of *curst* in *O.E.D.* is
4a: 'cantankerous, shrewish', and even this seems unlikely as a description of
Campaspe. The regular Shakespearean usage applied to women veers between
'shrewish' and 'resolutely resistant to men'—these two being, perhaps, only
two aspects of the same phenomenon, seen from different angles. Certainly
Campaspe's resistance is the point being discussed in this passage: whatever
yielding her modest behaviour suggests, she is too resolutely modest to yield in
fact. Fairholt defines her attitude as 'modesty tempered in yielding by a
contrary emotion' (1.289).

143–4.] Hephestion says, 'Let us stop talking about her' or 'Let her go';
Alexander picks up *pass* in the sense of 'surpass, excel'.

Actus Tertius, Scaena Quinta.

[*Enter*] PSYLLUS [*and*] MANES.

Psyllus. I shall be hanged for tarrying so long.
Manes. I pray God my master be not flown before I come.
Psyllus. Away, Manes, my master doth come.

[*Exit* MANES.]

[*Enter*] APELLES [*from his shop,
carrying his painting of Campaspe*].

Apelles. Where have you been all this while?
Psyllus. Nowhere but here.   5
Apelles. Who was here sithence my coming?
Psyllus. Nobody.
Apelles. Ungracious wag, I perceive you have been a-loitering.
    Was Alexander nobody?
Psyllus. He was a king. I meant no mean body.   10
Apelles. I will cudgel your body for it, and then will I say it was
    nobody because it was no honest body. Away! In!

Exit PSYLLUS [*into the shop*].

Unfortunate Apelles, and therefore unfortunate because
Apelles! Hast thou by drawing her beauty brought to
pass that thou canst scarce draw thine own breath? And   15
by so much the more hast thou increased thy care by
how much the more thou hast showed thy cunning.

0.1.] Bond; *Psyllus, Manes, Appeles. Q1.*   3.1–3.] *Bond (subst.); not in Q1.*
6. sithence] *Qq1, 4, Blount; since Qq2, 3.*   12. Away! In!] *Qq1–4, Blount*
('*Away in*'); *Away, in. 1744; Away in! Bond.*

---

   1. *tarrying so long*] i.e., tarrying at the tavern, as arranged at II.i.69–70 and
confirmed at III.ii.14–15, 68.
   2. *be not flown*] has not attempted to fly (as promised at III.ii.50ff.); with a
suggestion of 'has not departed hastily'.
   13–14. *Unfortunate . . . because Apelles*] For the rhetorical structure,
compare *Sappho and Phao*, II.iv.16–17: 'O divine love, and therefore divine
because love', and *Gallathea*, I.iii.1–2: 'fair Phillida, and I fear me too fair,
being my Phillida'. It is a trick much used by Robert Greene. See *Arbasto*, sig.
C3 (ed. Grosart, III.196), *Farewell to Folly*, sig. G4v (IX.299) and *Pandosto*, sig.
D4v (IV.279).
   15–17. *And . . . cunning*] a Latinate construction (*quanto . . . tanto*). The
more skilfully Apelles has represented Campaspe in his painting the more he is
oppressed by his love for her.

Was it not sufficient to behold the fire and warm thee
but with Satyrus thou must kiss the fire and burn thee?
O Campaspe, Campaspe, art must yield to nature, rea-   20
son to appetite, wisdom to affection. Could Pygmalion
entreat by prayer to have his ivory turned into flesh, and
cannot Apelles obtain by plaints to have the picture of
his love changed to life? Is painting so far inferior to
carving, or dost thou, Venus, more delight to be hewed   25
with chisels than shadowed with colours? What Pygmalion or what Pyrgoteles or what Lysippus is he that ever
made thy face so fair or spread thy fame so far as I?
Unless, Venus, in this thou enviest mine art, that in
colouring my sweet Campaspe I have left no place by   30
cunning to make thee so amiable. But, alas, she is the
paramour to a prince: Alexander, the monarch of the
earth, hath both her body and affection. For what is

18–19. *Was . . . burn thee*] Bond compares *Euphues*, II.42, 2–3: 'as Satirus,
not knowing what fire was, would needs embrace it and was burned', and cites
Aesop as a source; ed. Halm (Leipzig, 1889) no. 387. The earliest extant
source is in Plutarch, 'How to profit by one's enemies' (*Moralia*, II.7), whence,
no doubt, it appears in the Aesop Appendix and Erasmus, *Parabolae*, p. 189.
Compare Dent, *P.L.E.D.*, F281.

21. *Pygmalion*] In the well-known myth (Ovid, *Metamorphoses*, X)
Pygmalion falls in love with his ivory statue and prays to Venus (successfully)
that it be turned into human flesh.

23–4. *cannot . . . life*] The analogy with Pygmalion is defective unless we
suppose that Apelles, despairing of the living Campaspe because she belongs to
Alexander, wishes to have his painting turned into a second Campaspe.

25. *Venus*] The name has a double appropriateness: (1) as the goddess who
answered Pygmalion's prayer; (2) as the goddess Apelles has been painting,
perhaps using Campaspe as a model.

26–8. *What Pygmalion . . . as I*] Bond points to other adaptations of the
passage from Pliny (VII.37; compare XXXV.36) in *Euphues*, II.38, 16–17,
II.73, 15 and II.204, 9–11; compare Erasmus, *Apophthegmata* (Alexander, no.
35; Udall, no. 34) and *Parabolae*, p. 220. Pliny tells us that Alexander
commanded that only Apelles should paint him, that only Pyrgoteles should
sculpt him, and only Lysippus cast him in bronze. Lyly here makes Apelles
substitute the name of Pygmalion for his own name.

30–1. *I have . . . amiable*] Apelles has exhausted all the 'places' or methods
of his art in painting Campaspe and will therefore have no means left to
make his Venus picture so beautiful. Compare II.ii.175n. and III.iii.7–8n.

32–3. *Alexander . . . earth*] only proleptically true. At this point Alexander
was only *hegemon* of Greece.

33. *body and affection*] As her conqueror Alexander owns her *body*; as the
next sentence shows, Apelles presumes that Alexander has also won her love.

it that kings cannot obtain by prayers, threats and promises? Will not she think it better to sit under a cloth   35
of estate like a queen than in a poor shop like a house-
wife? And esteem it sweeter to be the concubine of the
lord of the world than spouse to a painter in Athens?
Yes, yes, Apelles; thou mayst swim against the stream
with the crab, and feed against the wind with the deer,   40
and peck against the steel with the cockatrice; stars are
to be looked at, not reached at; princes to be yielded
unto, not contended with; Campaspe to be honoured,
not obtained, to be painted, not possessed, of thee. O
fair face! O unhappy hand! And why didst thou draw it   45
so fair a face? O beautiful countenance, the express
image of Venus, but somewhat fresher, the only pattern of that eternity which Jupiter, dreaming of asleep,
could not conceive again waking! Blush, Venus, for I
am ashamed to end thee. Now must I paint things un-   50

48. dreaming of] *Qq1–3; dreaming Q4, Blount.*

35–8. *Will . . . Athens*] picking up the point made by Pliny (XXXV.36), as
translated by Philemon Holland: 'that being the concubine of a king she
should become the bedfellow of a painter'.

39–40. *swim . . . crab*] Bond notes the parallel with *Euphues*, I.208, 9–10:
'the sea crab swimmeth always against the stream'. Compare Dent, *P.L.E.D.*,
C784.11 and *S.P.L.*, S930.1. Apelles may strive against the way things are,
but he will not succeed.

40. *feed . . . deer*] See Dent, *P.L.E.D.*, D189.11 for parallels.

41. *cockatrice*] a fabulous animal, half cock, half serpent, usually in this
period identified with the basilisk, whose most notable characteristic was its
power to kill its prey by looking at it (see Pliny, VIII.33). One way to kill a
basilisk was to show it a mirror. In *The Wars of Alexander* (E.E.T.S. (E.S.) 47
(1886), ll. 4837–57) we learn that Alexander himself used this method. As a
cock the cockatrice will 'peck against the steel [mirror]', seeking to destroy the
mirrored cockatrice, but he is doomed already by the glance he has given
himself.

41–3. *stars . . . contended with*] Tilley, S825, cites *Euphues*, II.46, 28–9,
which links stars and princes in the same way. Compare *Sappho and Phao*,
II.ii.155n.

44–5. *O fair . . . hand!*] Apelles looks at his picture of Campaspe. The *face*
is that of Campaspe in the picture; the *hand* is his own hand, which drew the
face.

48–9. *which . . . waking*] It is possible that there may be a reminiscence here
of the seduction of Jupiter in Bk. XIV of the *Iliad*, contrived with the aid of
Venus, and to his disillusioned awakening in Bk. XV.

49. *Venus*] That is, the picture of Venus he was painting at II.ii.175.

50–1. *things unpossible*] See III.iv.75–80n. above.

possible for mine art but agreeable with my affections:
deep and hollow sighs, sad and melancholy thoughts,
wounds and slaughters of conceits, a life posting to
death, a death galloping from life, a wavering constancy, an unsettled resolution, and what not, Apelles?   55
And what but, Apelles? But as they that are shaken with
a fever are to be warmed with clothes, not groans, and
as he that melteth in a consumption is to be recured by
cullises, not conceits, so the feeding canker of my care,
the never-dying worm of my heart, is to be killed by   60
counsel, not cries, by applying of remedies, not by
replying of reasons. And sith in cases desperate there
must be used medicines that are extreme, I will hazard
that little life that is left to restore the greater part that
is lost; and this shall be my first practice, for wit must   65
work where authority is not. As soon as Alexander hath
viewed this portraiture I will by device give it a blemish
that by that means she may come again to my shop, and
then as good it were to utter my love and die with denial
as conceal it and live in despair.   70

Song

Cupid and my Campaspe played

56. but, Apelles] *This ed. (conj. Bond)*; but *Apelles Q1*.   70.1. Song] *The Song Q1*.   71–84. Cupid . . . me?] *Blount; not in Q1*.

---

53. *wounds . . . conceits*] i.e., heart-wounding, life-threatening thoughts.

56. *And what but, Apelles*] I have altered the punctuation and the sense from Q1's 'what but *Apelles*'. I take the meaning to be, 'And what but sighs, thoughts, conceits etc. will I be able to depict?'

59. *cullises*] strong broths used as restoratives for invalids.

feeding canker] a spreading sore or ulcer.

60. *worm*] 'a grief or passion that preys stealthily on a man's heart . . . (like a worm in a dead body)' (*O.E.D.*, sb., 11). Probably suggested here by *canker*, since 'cankerworm' is often used in this sense. The 'never-dying worm' was conceived of as one of the standard pains of hell (*O.E.D.*, sb., 6b.)

62–3. *in cases . . . extreme*] Bond compares *Euphues*, 1.213–14, 37ff.: 'a desperate disease is to be commited to a desperate doctor'. Taverner (1539) translates Erasmus's '*malo nodo malus quaerendus cuneus*' (II.70F) by 'a strong disease requireth a strong medicine'. See Dent, *P.L.E.D.*, D357.

65. *practice*] exercise of practical skill (in this case medicine).

68. *that by that means*] so that he can repair the blemish by a new sitting.

71–84.] See Appendix, pp. 301–3. This seems to be a solo song. Apelles is

At cards for kisses. Cupid paid:
He stakes his quiver, bow and arrows,
His mother's doves and team of sparrows,
Loses them too; then down he throws   75
The coral of his lip, the rose
Growing on's cheek (but none knows how),
With these the crystal of his brow,
And then the dimple of his chin;
All these did my Campaspe win.   80
At last he set her both his eyes;
She won, and Cupid blind did rise.
    O Love, has she done this to thee?
    What shall (alas) become of me?
                      [*Exit.*]

84.1. *Exit*] Bond; not in *Q1*.

---

alone on the stage, and in the last line he makes a direct reference to himself. The poetic form is close to that of a sonnet: fourteen lines concluded by an offset couplet. The musical form must have been non-stanzaic; the natural syntactic breaks are asymmetrically arranged: kisses/ paid/ too/ how/ chin/ win/ eyes/ rise/ thee/ me/. Bond points to an analogue in Philippe Desportes, *Les Amours de Diane* (1573), Bk. I, sonnet 15; and Ernst G. Mathews (*MLN*, LVI, 1941, 606–7) has shown that the Desportes poem is a translation of Gaspar Gil Polo's sonnet '*Probaron en el campo su destreza*' from the *Diana Enamorada* (1564). The *Diana* was translated into English by Bartholomew Yong and this sonnet with it (published in 1598, but probably in MS by 1583). Here it is (spelling modernised): 'Diana, Love, and my fair Shepherdess, / Did in the field their chiefest cunning try, / By shooting arrows at a tree nearby / Whose bark a painted heart did there express: / Diana stakes her beauty merciless, / Cupid his bow, Argia her liberty; / Who showèd in her shot a quicker eye, / A better grace, more courage and success; / And so she did Diana's beauty win, / And Cupid's weapons, by which conquered prize, / So fair and cruel she hath ever bin, / That her sweet figure from my wearied eyes, / And from my painful heart her cruel bow / Have stolen my life and freedom long ago.' The poem in *Campaspe* may be derived from any one of the three versions of this earlier sonnet; there seems no evidence which allows us to prefer one or another as the actual source.

72. *Cupid paid*] The verb here may mean that Cupid paid the forfeit (kisses) at the end of the first game. Then he went on to raise the stakes, and paid all these too. Or it may be that the forfeits were to be kisses only when Campaspe lost. But Campaspe never lost, so only Cupid paid. And so the poem goes on to enumerate the various stakes that Cupid laid against Campaspe's kisses, losing them one after the other. The punctuaton I have chosen points to the second line of interpretation.

Act IV

[Enter] SOLINUS, PSYLLUS *[and]* GRANICHUS.

Solinus. This is the place, the day, the time that Diogenes hath
    appointed to fly.
Psyllus. I will not lose the flight of so fair a fowl as Diogenes is,
    though my master cudgel my 'no body' as he threatened.
Granichus. What, Psyllus, will the beast wag his wings today?   5
Psyllus. We shall hear, for here cometh Manes.

[Enter] MANES.

    Manes, will it be?
Manes. Be! He were best be as cunning as a bee or else shortly
    he will not be at all.
Granichus. How is he furnished to fly? Hath he feathers?   10
Manes. Thou art an ass; capons, geese and owls have feathers.
    He hath found Daedalus' old waxen wings and hath
    been piecing them this month, he is so broad in the
    shoulders. O, you shall see him cut the air even like a
    tortoise.   15

0.1.] *Bond; Solinus, Psyllus, Granichus, Manes, Diogenes, Populus. Q1.* 6.1.
Bond; not in Q1.

---

3. *fair a fowl*] with a play on the antithesis of *fair/foul*.
4. *as he threatened*] See III.v.11–12 above.
8–9. *Be . . . bee . . . be*] The wordplay is suggested by Psyllus' 'will it be?'.
11. *capons, geese and owls*] Manes has chosen his birds for their despicable
associations: the eunuch, the foolish, the obscure.
12. *Daedalus' . . . wings*] Compare Dekker, *Old Fortunatus*, II.ii.200–1:
'Ambition . . . piecing Daedalus' old waxen wings'. Daedalus escaped from
Crete by constructing wings of feather and wax which he fastened on to himself
and so flew to Cumae. See Ovid, *Metamorphoses*, VIII.
13. *been piecing them*] been repairing or enlarging them by inserting new
feathers. If *he is so broad in the shoulders* has only a physical reference, then the
idea must be one of enlarging: Daedalus' wings are too small for Diogenes.
14–15. *like a tortoise*] The simile is used mainly, of course, to suggest
ungainliness. The idea of a flying tortoise had already appeared (as Bond notes)
in Bidpai's fable of the cranes who carried the tortoise to new water. There is

Solinus. Methinks so wise a man should not be so mad; his
    body must needs be too heavy.

Manes. Why, he hath eaten nothing this sevennight but cork
    and feathers.

Psyllus. Touch him, Manes.   20

Manes. He is so light that he can scarce keep him from flying
    at midnight.

Populus intrat.

DIOGENES [emerges from his tub].

Manes. See, they begin to flock; and, behold, my master
    bustles himself to fly.

Diogenes. Ye wicked and bewitched Athenians, whose bodies   25
    make the earth to groan and whose breaths infect the
    air with stench, come ye to see Diogenes fly? Diogenes
    cometh to see you sink. Ye call me dog; so I am, for I
    long to gnaw the bones in your skins. Ye term me an

22.2.] *Bond (subst.) at l. 24; not in Q1.*   25. Ye] *Qq1–3;* You *Q4, Blount.*

also the story of the flying tortoise that fell on Aeschylus and killed him,
referred to in Spenser's *Shepherdes Calendar*, July, ll. 221ff., and described in
Pliny, x.3; Valerius Maximus, *Factorum et Dictorum Memorabilium Libri
Novem*, IX.12, Ext. 2; and Aelian, *On the Characteristics of Animals*, VII.16.

18–19. *cork and feathers*] lightweight substances. Compare Dekker, *Old
Fortunatus*, II.ii.161, where Fortunatus has flown from Babylon to Cyprus.
His servant remarks, 'my old master's soul is cork and feathers'.

21–2.] I do not understand the function of the words used here, unless a
pun on 'light' is intended: 'he is lightest when there is no light'. Or perhaps
Diogenes is being compared to a ghost that appears at midnight.

22.1. *Populus* intrat] The people come in. Presumably Lyly used as many
actors as he could muster for this entry of 'the populace'. According to my
calculation (see above, pp. 26–7), Lyly should have had at least seven spare
actors available at this point.

25ff.] This device of Diogenes', to collect a crowd by promising some folly
and then berating it for its interest in folly, is close to instances given in
Erasmus's *Apophthegmata*. Thus in no. 14 Diogenes sings a song and seems to
be going to dance, and 'when a very great multitude of people had now
gathered together and swarmed about him' he then lectures them on their
levity and their indifference to wisdom. In no. 25 (Udall, no. 31) he calls men
around him in the market place and then when they come he drives them
away, calling them not men but beasts.

28. *sink*] primarily present to supply the antithesis to *fly*. The meaning (not
very precise) must be something like 'sink into stupidity'.

29–30. *hater of men*] On the assimilation of Diogenes and Timon in the

hater of men; no, I am a hater of your manners. Your   30
lives dissolute, not fearing death, will prove your deaths
desperate, not hoping for life. What do you else in
Athens but sleep in the day and surfeit in the night,
back-gods in the morning with pride, in the evening
belly-gods with gluttony? You flatter kings and call   35
them gods; speak truth of yourselves and confess you
are devils. From the bee you have taken not the honey
but the wax to make your religion, framing it to the
time, not to the truth. Your filthy lust you colour under
a courtly colour of love, injuries abroad under the title 40
of policies at home, and secret malice creepeth under
the name of public justice. You have caused Alexander
to dry up springs and plant vines, to sow rocket and

Renaissance, see Lievsay, 'Some Renaissance Views of Diogenes', *J. Q. Adams
Memorial Studies*, ed. J. G. McManaway *et al.* (Washington, 1948).

32. *desperate*] in religious despair, having given up hope of salvation or
eternal life.

34. *back-gods . . . pride*] Bond thinks this refers to the pride of wearing
splendid clothes on one's back (see *O.E.D.*, *back*, sb. 1, 2b for the sins of back
and belly). This may well be right; but the parallel antithesis of sleep/surfeit in
the day/night suggests that *back-gods* and *pride* should have something to do
with sleep, or at least with being in bed. *Back* also meant 'virility, sexual
energy' in this period (see Marston, *The Malcontent*, IV.v.58–9 and Webster,
The Duchess of Malfi, II.v.71–3)—as it still does; and *pride* also means
'erection' (neither of these in *O.E.D.*). In consequence the phrase may refer to
morning lust rather than morning ostentation.

38. *wax*] Compare ll. 18–20 in the Epilogue at the Court below. Wax is an
inappropriate substance to make religion of, for it can be moulded to taste, as
true religion cannot. The Athenians are condemned as 'politiques', suiting
their religious beliefs to the pressures of the time rather than the truth of their
profession.

40–1. *injuries . . . at home*] You defend the wrongs you do others by
describing them at home as political advantages.

43. *dry . . . vines*] This seems to be only an elaborate way of saying 'prefer
wine to water', that is, the sophisticated to the natural. The same antithesis
appears in IV.iii.4–5 below.

43–4. *sow . . . endive*] i.e., encourage the bad and destroy the good.
Euphues, I.222, 25–7, makes a distinction that seems appropriate to the
context here: 'Though thou have eaten the seeds of rocket, which breed
incontinency, yet have I chewed the leaf cress, which maintaineth modesty.'
Croll and Clemons gives ample authority for such beliefs, both about rocket
(*cruca*) and about cress (*nasturtium officinale*); but endive (*intibus*) is not
described as an anaphrodisiac in any of the usual sources. Nonetheless the
meaning of the antithesis given here in *Campaspe* seems to be clear, and one
must suppose that Lyly simply transferred to the endive what he knew about

weed endive, to shear sheep and shrine foxes. All conscience is sealed at Athens: swearing cometh of a 'hot   45
mettle', lying of a 'quick wit', flattery of a 'flowing
tongue', undecent talk of a 'merry disposition'. All
things are lawful at Athens. Either you think there are
no gods, or I must think ye are no men. You build as
though you should live for ever and surfeit as though   50
you should die tomorrow. 'None teacheth true philosophy but Aristotle, because he was the king's school-
master'—O times, O men, O corruption in manners!
Remember that green grass must turn to dry hay. When
you sleep you are not sure to wake, and when you rise   55
not certain to lie down. Look you never so high, your

---

cress. There is, however, one further complication. *O.E.D.* (*rocket*, sb.², 1)
quotes T. Tymmes's translation of Du Chesne's *Quersitanus* (1605), Preface,
vi: 'Like bad and unskilful herborists to sow rocket and weed endive'.
Tymmes may be quoting Lyly; but in that case what does he suppose that Lyly
means?

44. *shear . . . foxes*] i.e., despoil the innocent and sanctify the despoilers.

45. *sealed*] Two possible meanings for *sealed* attach to two variant
interpretations of *All conscience*. If *All conscience* means 'adapting conscience
to all contingencies', then *sealed* probably means 'given a charter or licence,
assented to' (*O.E.D. seal*, vb.¹, 1.1d and 4 *.*). This reading connects better
with ll. 45–6 following. On the other hand, *All conscience* may mean 'every
conscientious impulse', and then *sealed* will be *O.E.D.* vb.¹, II. 9 and 11:
'fastened, closed up'.

45–6. *hot mettle*] passionate temperament—one of the fancy names given to
justify or excuse unconscionable behaviour.

48–9. *Either . . . men*] Either your immorality derives from a belief that
there are no protectors of morality (*gods*) or else you are not *men* (subject to
the gods) at all. Compare V.i.21–4 below, where (again) the wickedness of
some (godless) men is taken as a proof that there are gods who justify virtue.

49–51. *You build . . . tomorrow*] Tertullian (*Apology*, XXXIX.14) put this
much-repeated remark into the mouth of Diogenes, who said of the
Megarensians that they 'feasted as if they would die tomorrow but built as if
they would never die'. Compare Jerome, *Epistles*, CXXIII.15 and CXXVIII.45,
and Plutarch, 'On love of wealth', *Moralia* 525B (VII.19). Laertius (VIII.63)
gives the remark to Empedocles, speaking to the Agrigentines; Aelian, *Varia
Historia*, XII.29, makes Plato say it to the Agrigentines. See Otto, no. 1080.

53. *O times . . . manners*] a reminiscence of the famous Ciceronian tag *O
tempora, O mores* (*In Catilinam*, I.i.2), and elsewhere.

54. *green . . . hay*] Compare *Euphues*, II.134, 20–1: 'such men . . . think
green grass will never be dry hay'. The origin of the imagery must be in the
biblical 'All flesh is grass' (1 Peter, i.24). See Dent, *P.L.E.D.*, G413 and
G415.11.

heads must lie level with your feet. Thus have I flown over your disordered lives, and if you will not amend your manners I will study to fly further from you that I may be nearer to honesty. 60

Solinus. Thou ravest, Diogenes, for thy life is different from thy words. Did not I see thee come out of a brothel-house? Was it not a shame?

Diogenes. It was no shame to go out, but a shame to go in.

Granichus. [*Aside to Manes*] It were a good deed, Manes, to 65 beat thy master.

Manes. [*Aside to Granichus*] You were as good eat my master.

One of the people. Hast thou made us all fools, and wilt thou not fly?

Diogenes. I tell thee, unless thou be honest I will fly. 70

People. Dog, dog, take a bone!

Diogenes. Thy father need fear no dogs, but dogs thy father.

People. We will tell Alexander that thou reprovest him behind his back.

Diogenes. And I will tell him that you flatter him before his 75 face.

People. We will cause all the boys in the street to hiss at thee.

Diogenes. Indeed I think the Athenians have their children ready for any vice, because they be Athenians.

[*Exit the people.*]

Manes. Why, master, mean you not to fly? 80

65, 67. S.Ds.] *This ed.; not in Q1.*   79.1.] *Adams; not in Q1.*

57–8. *flown over*] surveyed; with a reminiscence of his promise to *fly*, and making preparation for his *fly* = flee below (ll. 59, 70).

62–4. *Did . . . go in*] Compare Laertius, II.69, and Erasmus, *Apophthegmata* (Aristippus, no. 12). Being expected to feel shame when a young man saw him inside a whorehouse, Aristippus said, 'Young man, to enter into such a place as this is no shame at all, but not to be able to go out again indeed that is a foul shame.' Compare Tilley, W531; the quotation given there from Heywood's *Royal King and Loyal Subject* seems to be a direct borrowing from *Campaspe*. As Dent, *P.L.E.D.*, W531 indicates, the proverb variously attaches shame to going in or to not being able to leave.

70. *fly*] (1) flee; (2) travel through the air.

72.] I do not know what insult is intended here, but the general idea is that men bite more dangerously than dogs.

79. *because . . . Athenians*] The children are also Athenians and therefore prone to vice.

Diogenes. No, Manes, not without wings.

Manes. Everybody will account you a liar.

Diogenes. No, I warrant you; for I will always say the Athenians
    are mischievous.   [*He retires into his tub.*]

Psyllus. I care not. It was sport enough for me to see these old   85
    huddles hit home.

Granichus. Nor I.

Psyllus. Come, let us go; and hereafter when I mean to rail upon
    anybody openly it shall be given out I will fly. *Exeunt.*

Actus Quartus, Scaena Secunda.

[*Enter*] CAMPASPE.

Campaspe. (*Sola*) Campaspe, it is hard to judge whether thy
    choice be more unwise or thy chance unfortunate. Dost
    thou prefer—but stay! Utter not that in words which
    maketh thine ears to glow with thoughts. Tush, better
    thy tongue wag than thy heart break. Hath a painter   5
    crept further into thy mind than a prince, Apelles than

---

84. *He . . . tub*] Adams (*subst.*); *not in Q1.*   0.1.] Adams (*subst.*); *Campaspe,
Apelles. Q1.*   2. thy chance] *Qq1, 2, 4, Blount;* the chance *Q3.*

81.] i.e., not until I turn into a bird. No reference to 'Daedalus' old waxen
wings' (l. 12 above) is intended.

84. *mischievous*] most probably this is *O.E.D.*, adj., 2: 'designing mischief
or harm'. Diogenes will claim that the idea he is a liar arises from the malice of
the Athenians.

85–6. *old huddles*] *O.E.D.* seems to indicate that Lyly invented (and
virtually monopolised) this phrase, in the sense of 'miserable ancient persons'.
See *Euphues*, I.194, 9 and I.247, 4.

86. *hit home*] struck to the quick.

0.1.] Campaspe was last seen (III.iv.143) leaving the workshop for the
court. Her speech here reflects that change of venue. Apelles' entry from the
workshop re-establishes the earlier connection.

1. Sola] alone.

3. *prefer*—] The anacoleuthon presumably represents Campaspe's unwillingness to say out loud what Apelles has already articulated (III.v.35–8).

3–4. *Utter . . . thoughts*] Even to think such things make me blush. Let me
not speak them!

4–5. *Tush . . . break*] The common idea lying behind this is that griefs that
find vent in words are manageable. Those that cannot speak break the heart.
The much-quoted classical tag that encapsulates the idea is Seneca's '*curae leves
loquuntur, ingentes stupent*' (*Agamemnon*, l. 115).

Alexander? Fond wench, the baseness of thy mind
bewrays the meanness of thy birth. But alas, affection
is a fire which kindleth as well in the bramble as in the
oak, and catcheth hold where it first !ighteth, not where   10
it may best burn. Larks that mount aloft in the air build
their nests below in the earth, and women that cast their
eyes upon kings may place their hearts upon vassals. A
needle will become thy fingers better than a lute, and a
distaff is fitter for thy hand than a sceptre. Ants live   15
safely till they have gotten wings, and juniper is not
blown up till it hath gotten an high top. The mean estate is without care as long as it continueth without
pride. But here cometh Apelles, in whom I would there
were the like affection.   20

> [*Enter*] APELLES [*from the workshop*].

Apelles. Gentlewoman, the misfortune I had with your picture
     will put you to some pains to sit again to be painted.
Campaspe. It is small pains for me to sit still, but infinite for
     you to draw still.
Apelles. No, madam; to paint Venus was a pleasure, but to   25
     shadow the sweet face of Campaspe, it is a heaven.

11. aloft] *Qq1, 2, 4, Blount;* aloof *Q3.*   20.1.] *1780; not in Q1.*

---

7. *Fond*] Foolish.

8. *bewrays the meanness*] exposes the lowness.

9–10. *in the bramble . . . oak*] The *oak* (king of the forest) represents
nobility, strength, capacity to sustain a fire; the *bramble* is low, weedy, short-
lived, and will not support a fire. And yet both catch fire. See the anonymous
poem 'Compare the bramble with the cedar tree' printed in Bond (III.483).

11–12. *Larks . . . earth*] Compare Dekker, *The Whore of Babylon*, III.i.108–
10: 'the lark / . . . so they may mount high / Care not how base and low their
rising be', and Shakespeare, Sonnet 29: 'the lark . . . arising / From sullen
earth sings hymns at heaven's gate'.

15–16. *Ants . . . wings*] See Dent, *P.L.E.D.*, A256: 'The ant had wings to
do her hurt', and *Sappho and Phao*, II.i.147.

16–17. *juniper . . . high top*] The standard notion that the humble estate can
be represented by small shrubs which remain rooted when tall trees are blown
down is depicted variously by different trees. 'Cedrus cecidit' in the Appendix
to Erasmus' *Adagia* has the pine (*picea*) safe while the cedar is endangered.
Lyly uses a juniper/oak contrast in *Euphues*, II.219, 6–7.

21. *misfortune*] i.e., the deliberate blemish which Apelles predicted at
III.v.67–8.

23–4. *still . . . still*] without moving . . . constantly, continuously.

Campaspe. If your tongue were made of the same flesh that
your heart is, your words would be as your thoughts
are; but such a common thing it is amongst you to commend that oftentimes for fashion sake you call them   30
beautiful whom you know black.

Apelles. What might men do to be believed?

Campaspe. Whet their tongues on their hearts.

Apelles. So they do, and speak as they think.

Campaspe. I would they did.   35

Apelles. I would they did not.

Campaspe. Why, would you have them dissemble?

Apelles. Not in love, but their love. But will you give me leave
to ask you a question, without offence?

Campaspe. So that you will answer me another, without   40
excuse.

Apelles. Whom do you love best in the world?

Campaspe. He that made me last in the world.

Apelles. That was a god.

Campaspe. I had thought it had been a man. But whom do you 45
honour most, Apelles?

Apelles. The thing that is likest you, Campaspe.

Campaspe. My picture?

Apelles. I dare not venture upon your person. But come, let us
go in, for Alexander will think it long till we return.   50

> *Exeunt [into the shop].*

50.1. *Exeunt . . . shop*] Bond (*subst.*); *Exeunt. Q1.*

---

29. *you*] i.e., all you men.

31. *black*] The context requires that the word be antithetical to *beautiful* (or
'fair'), so the sense must be 'foul' or 'ugly'.

33.] *Whet* in the normal sense of 'sharpen' can hardly be intended here, for a
sharp tongue could be as easily deceptive as true. The phrase must have the
same general reference as ll. 27–8, i.e., 'bring the tongue into conformity with
the heart'.

38. *Not . . . their love*] Apelles explains l. 36 by stating that he does not wish
men to tell lies to those they love, but would like the power to conceal that he is
in love (since his suit to Campaspe is bound to be hopeless).

45. *I had . . . man*] Campaspe refers to Apelles' 'making' the picture of her.

49. *venture . . . person*] (1) venture to name you directly; (2) venture to be
your lover.

Actus Quartus, Scaena Tertia.

[*Enter*] CLITUS [*and*] PARMENIO.

Clitus. We hear nothing of our embassage, a colour belike to
blear our eyes or tickle our ears or inflame our hearts.
But what doth Alexander in the mean season but use for
tantara, sol-fa-la; for his hard couch, down beds; for his
handful of water, his standing cup of wine?   5
Parmenio. Clitus, I mislike this new delicacy and pleasing
peace; for what else do we see now than a kind of softness in every man's mind, bees to make their hives in
soldiers' helmets, our steeds furnished with footcloths
of gold instead of saddles of steel, more time to be re-   10
quired to scour the rust off our weapons than there was
wont to be in subduing the countries of our enemies?
Sithence Alexander fell from his hard armour to his soft

---

8. to make] *Qq1, 4, Blount;* do make *Qq2, 3.*   11. off] *1744;* of *Q1.*

1. *embassage*] discussed in III.iv.24–30 above.
colour] specious reason, pretext (*O.E.D.*, sb., 12).
1–5. *to blear . . . wine*] The three impositions on the senses, described in the
first sentence, are matched by three examples of sensory indulgence in the
second sentence. But only one of the relations (ears/tantara) is parallel.
3. *in . . . season*] in the meantime.
4. *tantara*] an echoic word for trumpet-call—the sound of war.
sol-fa-la] notes of the gamut or musical scale, used here to convey the idea of
written, elaborate, courtly, effete music.
5. *standing cup*] a cup with a stem and base (*O.E.D.*, *standing,* ppl.a.4.a).
8–9. *bees . . . helmets*] Bond points to *Euphues,* II.209, 36–7 'In whose
government the bees have made their hives in the soldiers' helmets'. The
famous emblematic picture which lies behind this widely used phrase appears
first in Alciati's *Emblemata.* It has a fine expression in English in Peele's poem
'His golden locks time hath to silver turned', in his *Polyhymnia* (*Works,* ed.
C. T. Prouty, 1.244).
9. *footcloths*] richly ornamented cloths laid over a horse's back and hanging
to the ground.
11. *scour . . . weapons*] The *rust* that accumulated on weapons and armour,
and which had to be *scoured* off before they could be used again, was a
traditional image of peacetime; with the ideological advantage that it suggested
the decay of shining vigour which was also said to be a consequence of peace.
Compare V.iv.6–8 below.
13–27.] With this series of contrasts between (manly) war and (effeminate)
peace, compare the opening soliloquy of *Richard III,* which offers a similar
list of topics: bruised arms set against wreaths, mounting . . . steeds against
caper[ing] nimbly, fright[ening] adversaries against court[ing] a looking-glass.

robes, behold the face of his court: youths that were
wont to carry devices of victory in their shields engrave   15
now posies of love in their rings; they that were ac-
customed on trotting horses to charge the enemy with
a lance now in easy coaches ride up and down to court
ladies; instead of sword and target to hazard their lives,
use pen and paper to paint their loves. Yea, such a fear   20
and faintness is grown in court that they wish rather to
hear the blowing of a horn to hunt than the sound of a
trumpet to fight. O Philip, wert thou alive to see this
alteration—thy men turned to women, thy soldiers to
lovers, gloves worn in velvet caps instead of plumes in   25
graven helmets—thou wouldst either die among them
for sorrow or confound them for anger.

Clitus. Cease, Parmenio, lest in speaking what becometh thee
not thou feel what liketh thee not; truth is never without a scratched face, whose tongue, although it cannot   30
be cut out, yet must it be tied up.

Parmenio. It grieveth me not a little for Hephestion, who
thirsteth for honour, not ease; but such is his fortune
and nearness in friendship to Alexander that he must
lay a pillow under his head when he would put a target   35
in his hand. But let us draw in, to see how well it becomes them to tread the measures in a dance that were
wont to set the order for a march.   *Exeunt.*

---

16. *posies . . . rings*] brief emblematic verses or mottoes engraved (in rings,
for example) and sent as tokens of love.

18. *easy coaches*] The epithet is transferred. Not the coaches but the riders
are *easy* (take their ease). According to Stowe's *Annals* (1631 edn., p. 867),
coaches were first introduced into England in 1564.

19. *target*] shield, used also as a pillow by a soldier in the field (see ll. 35–6).

20. *paint*] express. The pen and paper are presumably used for writing love-
sonnets.

23. *O Philip, . . . alive*] Philip of Macedon died in 336 B.C.

26. *graven*] engraved (or capable of being engraved); metallic rather than
velvet.

28–9. *Cease . . . not*] Do not utter these unbecoming treasons lest you incur
punishment.

29–30. *truth . . . face*] See Dent, *P.L.E.D.*, T572.

36. *draw in*] withdraw.

37–8. *measures . . . march*] Compare the opening speech of *Richard III* once
again: 'dreadful marches to delightful measures' (I.i.8).

Actus Quartus, Scaena Quarta.

[*Enter*] APELLES [*and*] CAMPASPE.

Apelles. I have now, Campaspe, almost made an end.
Campaspe. You told me, Apelles, you would never end.
Apelles. Never end my love, for it shall be eternal.
Campaspe. That is, neither to have beginning nor ending.
Apelles. You are disposed to mistake; I hope you do not   5
    mistrust.
Campaspe. What will you say if Alexander perceive your love?
Apelles. I will say it is no treason to love.
Campaspe. But how if he will not suffer thee to see my person?
Apelles. Then will I gaze continually on thy picture.   10
Campaspe. That will not feed thy heart.
Apelles. Yet shall it fill mine eye. Besides, the sweet thoughts,
    the sure hopes, thy protested faith, will cause me to
    embrace thy shadow continually in mine arms, of the
    which by strong imagination I will make a substance.   15
Campaspe. Well, I must be gone; but this assure yourself, that
    I had rather be in thy shop grinding colours than in
    Alexander's court following higher fortunes.
                            [*Exit* APELLES *into his shop.*]
    Foolish wench, what hast thou done? That, alas, which
    cannot be undone; and therefore I fear me undone. But   20

18.1.] *1744; Campaspe alone. Q1.*

4.] This is the scholastic definition of eternity. See Boethius, *De Consolatione Philosophiae*, V.vi, and Thomas Aquinas, *Summa Theologica*, quaestio x, art. iv: 'Aeternitas principio et fine careat.'

5. *disposed to mistake*] in the mood to misunderstand what I say.

14–15. *embrace . . . substance*] There is an elaborate play here on the philosophic concepts of *shadow* and *substance*. The *shadow* Apelles is talking about is at its most literal level the picture (or 'shadow') of Campaspe. Campaspe herself is the *substance* of which the picture is the shadow. But hope and faith and *strong imagination* (the power of forming concepts out of material not present) will enable him to make the picture (or shadow) into the substance. I do not know how far one should pursue the implicit parallel with the religious capacity to believe in an invisible *substance*. Apelles seems to have in mind the Pygmalion story, as at III.v.21ff.

16. *gone*] to Alexander's court, presumably.

17. *shop*] workshop, studio.

20. *and therefore . . . undone*] I fear I have betrayed my preference for Apelles and therefore must expect to be *undone* by the anger of Alexander.

content is such a life I care not for abundance. O Apelles,
thy love cometh from the heart, but Alexander's from
the mouth. The love of kings is like the blowing of
winds, which whistle sometimes gently among the
leaves, and straightways turn the trees up by the roots,   25
or fire, which warmeth afar off and burneth near hand,
or the sea, which maketh men hoise their sails in a flattering calm and to cut their masts in a rough storm. They
place affection by times, by policy, by appointment; if
they frown, who dares call them unconstant, if bewray   30
secrets, who will term them untrue, if fall to
other loves, who trembles not if he call them unfaithful?
In kings there can be no love but to queens; for as near
must they meet in majesty as they do in affection. It is
requisite to stand aloof from king's love, Jove and   35
lightning.   *Exit.*

Actus Quartus, Scaena Quinta.

[*Enter*] APELLES.

Apelles. Now, Apelles, gather thy wits together. Campaspe
is no less wise than fair; thyself must be no less cunning than faithful. It is no small matter to be rival with
Alexander.

[*Enter*] Page.

---

32. not if] *Adams, conj. Greg;* not, if *Q1.*   0.1.] *Bond (subst.); Apelles, Page.*
Q1.   4.1.] *Bond; not in Q1.*

---

21. *content . . . abundance*] Compare Dent, *P.L.E.D.*, C629: 'Contentment
is great riches.'
27. *hoise*] hoist.
27-8. *flattering*] delusively promising.
28. *cut their masts*] To cut down the mast was a desperate but quick way of
losing sails and so avoiding being capsized.
29. *appointment*] arrangement.
34-6. *It is . . . lightning*] A standard Renaissance formula urging
private men to stay private is '*procul [porro] a Jove atque fulmine*',
found in, e.g., Erasmus's *Adagia*, II.148f. Erasmus refers the idea to
'tyrants, that is, most princes' and brings up the example of Alexander and
Diogenes. The idea of *love* seems to be introduced into the commonplace by
Lyly so as to match the adage to what precedes it. See Dent, *P.L.E.D.*, J81.
1-4.] Apelles is here given sentiments parallel to those of Campaspe

Page. Apelles, you must come away quickly with the picture.   5
    The king thinketh that now you have painted it you
    play with it.
Apelles. If I would play with pictures I have enough at home.
Page. None perhaps you like so well.
Apelles. It may be I have painted none so well.   10
Page. I have known many fairer faces.
Apelles. And I many better boys.   *Exeunt.*

(IV.iv.19ff. above), but attuned to action rather than emotion. He is able to draw on the audience's awareness of the favourite Humanist theme of the poor scholar's rivalry with the rich suitor, shown in English in, e.g., Medwall's *Fulgens and Lucres.*

    5–7.] In III.iv.129–30 Alexander pronounced the picture of Campaspe to be finished and ordered Apelles to bring it to him. In III.v.66–8 Apelles planned to show the picture to Alexander and then blemish it. In IV.ii.21ff. we saw Apelles 'repairing' the self-inflicted blemish. Now Alexander has seen through the manœuvre and is calling for the final delivery.

    7. *play with it*] tinker with it. (But Apelles answers in the sense of idly entertaining oneself with a fantasy.)

    11. *fairer faces*] i.e., fairer than in the picture of Campaspe.

Act V

Actus Quintus, Scaena Prima.

DIOGENES [*is discovered in his tub*], MANES [*in attendance.*
Enter to them] SYLVIUS, PERIM, MILO [*and*] TRICO.

Sylvius. I have brought my sons, Diogenes, to be taught of
thee.

Diogenes. What can thy sons do?

Sylvius. You shall see their qualities. [*To Perim*] Dance, sirrah!
[*Music sounds.*] *Then Perim danceth.*

How like you this? Doth he well?   5

Diogenes. The better, the worser.

Sylvius. The music very good.

Diogenes. The musicians very bad, who only study to have
their strings in tune, never framing their manners to
order.   10

Sylvius. Now shall you see the other. [*To Milo*] Tumble,
sirrah!

Milo tumbleth.

0.1–2.] *Adams (subst.); Diogenes, Sylvius, Perim, Milo, Trico, Manes. Q1.*   4.
To Perim] This ed.; not in Q1.   4.1. *Music sounds] This ed.; not in Q1.*   11. *To*
Milo] This ed.; not in Q1.

1–2.] The bringing of children to be taught by Diogenes is mentioned
several times in Laertius. For many years Diogenes was tutor to the children of
Xeniades, to whom he had been sold in slavery (see Laertius, VI.30–31, 74).

6.] This paradox comes from Laertius, VI.46: 'A youth was playing cottabos
in the baths. Diogenes said to him, "The better you play the worse it is for
you."' The story reappears in Erasmus, *Apophthegmata*, no. 84 (Udall,
no. 90). The quotations in Tilley, and Dent, *P.L.E.D.*, B333, make it clear
that most Elizabethan authors thought Diogenes was referring to dancing. In
context here, Diogenes means, 'The better you dance, the more you corrupt
your moral being.'

8–10. *who . . . order*] This comes once again from Laertius (VI.65), repeated
in Erasmus, *Apophthegmata*, no 182: 'When he saw a certain minstrel . . . he
said, "Thou fellow, art thou not ashamed of thyself, that thou knowest the way
how to set tunes in true chord upon a piece of wood and canst [sc. knowest] no
skill to frame thy life by the rule of right discretion and reason?"' (Udall,
no. 188).

How like you this? Why do you laugh?

Diogenes. To see a wag that was born to break his neck by
destiny to practise it by art.   15

Milo. This dog will bite me; I will not be with him.

Diogenes. Fear not, boy; dogs eat no thistles.

Perim. I marvel what dog thou art, if thou be a dog.

Diogenes. When I am hungry, a mastiff, and when my belly is
full, a spaniel.   20

Sylvius. Dost thou believe that there are any gods, that thou
art so dogged?

Diogenes. I must needs believe there are gods, for I think thee
an enemy to them.

Sylvius. Why so?   25

Diogenes. Because thou hast taught one of thy sons to rule his
legs and not to follow learning, the other to bend his
body every way and his mind no way.

Perim. Thou dost nothing but snarl and bark like a dog.

Diogenes. It is the next way to drive away a thief.   30

Sylvius. Now shall you hear the third, who sings like a nightingale.

31. sings] *Q4, Blount;* signes *Qq1–3.*

14–15. *break . . . destiny*] Dent (*P.L.E.D.*) suggests that this is a variant on
Tilley, W232: 'Hanging goes by destiny.'

16–17.] From Laertius, VI.61, repeated in Erasmus, *Apophthegmata*, no. 79
(Udall, no. 85): the boys cry, 'dog, dog, dog' and run away, afraid, they say,
'lest thou shouldest bite us'. 'Be of good cheer', Diogenes replies; 'a dog eats
no beets.'

19–20.] Compare Erasmus, *Apophthegmata*, no. 159 (Udall, no. 165):
Diogenes is asked why he is called a dog. He replies, 'because that, on such as
give me aught I make much fawning . . . and such as be naught [wicked] I
bite'. Spaniels are noted for their fawning; Dent, *P.L.E.D.*, S704.

21–4.] This story comes from Laertius (VI.42, and also II.102). It is retold
in Erasmus, *Apophthegmata*, no. 72: 'Lysias . . . asked Diogenes whether he
believed there were any gods. To whom Diogenes answered: "How may it
stand with reason that I should not believe? Yes; since I am fully persuaded
that thyself art a fellow of the gods abandoned and accursed"' (Udall, no. 73).

22. *dogged*] currish, spiteful.

26–8.] This comes from Laertius (VI.70) and Erasmus, *Apophthegmata*,
no. 15: 'He rebuked men for that they . . . exercised themselves . . . to the end
that they might at length be . . . cunning therein, and not one of them all
would put himself to any pain that they might . . . prove well disposed and
honest men.'

31–3.] This is from Plutarch, 'The sayings of kings', *Moralia*, 191B

Diogenes. I care not; for I have heard a nightingale sing herself.
Sylvius. [*To Trico*] Sing, sirrah!

Song

Trico. (*Singeth*)	What bird so sings yet so does wail? 35
	O 'tis the ravished nightingale.
	Jug, jug, jug, jug, Tereu, she cries,
	And still her woes at midnight rise.
	Brave prick-song! Who is't now we hear?
	None but the lark so shrill and clear. 40
	How at heaven's gate she claps her wings,
	The morn not waking till she sings.

34. *To Trico*] *This ed.; not in Q1.*   35–47. Song What . . . Spring] *Blount; not
in Qq1–4.*   35. *Trico. (Singeth)*] *Trico Singeth (as s.d.) Q1; Tryco Singeth/ Song
Blount.*

(*Agesilaus,* III.131): 'Being exhorted to hear one that imitated the voice of the
nightingale, "I have often", said he, "heard nightingales themselves." '

35–47.] See Hunter, *John Lyly*, Appendix, especially pp. 368–70. The
description of this song as non-stanzaic which is given there (p. 369) seems to
be in error. Though printed continuously, the song falls into three four-line
sections (or stanzas). The first stanza deals with the nightingale. The second
stanza begins by referring us back to the nightingale ('Brave prick-song') but is
otherwise concerned with the lark. The third stanza is divided between the
robin and the cuckoo, and then the final line of the cuckoo couplet is repeated
to give a rousing finale. Each bird is given the standard poetical characteristics:
the nightingale recalls the ravished Ovidian Philomela; the lark (compare
IV.ii.11–12 above) beats at heaven's gate; the robin is *poor* (see l. 44n.); the
cuckoo heralds the spring. Compare the first three-man song in Dekker's *The
Shoemakers' Holiday*, another spring song with the nightingale treated in stanza
2 and the cuckoo in stanza 3.

37. *Jug, jug, jug, jug*] *O.E.D.* has quotations from Skelton (1523) and
Gascoigne (1576), showing the earlier use of this 'imitative representation' of
the nightingale's song.

Tereu] the vocative of 'Tereus' (i.e., 'O Tereus'). Tereus was the ravisher of
Philomela, whose cry, after she was metamorphosed into a nightingale, could
be heard as an outcry against Tereus. The idea does not appear in Ovid's
handling of the story.

38. *at midnight*] i.e., when the nightingale is most easily heard.

39. *prick-song*] (1) music written (or *pricked*) down on paper; (2) the song of
the nightingale, setting its breast against the thorn (see Tilley N183).

41–2.] The lark is seen as singing an *aubade*, waking up the heavens so that
the gate will open and the sun come out. She *claps* her wings not only because
she moves them up and down like hands clapping (*O.E.D.*, vb.¹, III.8), but
also because she *claps* (knocks) at the door (*O.E.D.*, vb.¹, II.3). The parallel
between this song and the *aubade* in *Cymbeline* II.iii.20–6 ('Hark, hark, the
lark') has been much remarked.

Hark, hark, with what a pretty throat
Poor robin red-breast tunes his note.
Hark how the jolly cuckoos sing   45
'Cuckoo' to welcome in the Spring,
'Cuckoo' to welcome in the Spring.

Sylvius. Lo, Diogenes, I am sure thou canst not do so much.
Diogenes. But there is never a thrush but can.
Sylvius. What hast thou taught Manes thy man?   50
Diogenes. To be as unlike as may be thy sons.
Manes. He hath taught me to fast, lie hard and run away.
Sylvius. How sayst thou, Perim? Wilt thou be with him?
Perim. Ay, so he will teach me first to run away.
Diogenes. Thou needest not be taught, thy legs are so nimble.   55
Sylvius. How sayest thou, Milo? Wilt thou be with him?
Diogenes. Nay, hold your peace; he shall not.
Sylvius. Why?
Diogenes. There is not room enough for him and me both to
tumble in one tub.   60
Sylvius. Well, Diogenes, I perceive my sons brook not thy
manners.
Diogenes. I thought no less, when they knew my virtues.
Sylvius. Farewell, Diogenes; thou needest not have scraped
roots if thou wouldst have followed Alexander.   65

59–60. both to tumble] *Qq1–3;* to tumble both *Q4, Blount.*

---

44. *Poor robin*] It is not clear why the robin redbreast is *poor*, unless it is
because the red is seen as blood. *Poor robin* had become a cant term before
1661 when *Poor Robin's Almanac* was first published. 'Poor Cock Robin'
appears in the last line of the nursery rhyme 'Who killed Cock Robin?' of
indeterminate date.

45–6.] The idea that the migratory cuckoo is the harbinger of spring in
England appears in song as early as evidence allows—in 'Summer is ycommen
in', the first part-song in English (13th century).

49. *thrush*] the same joke as referred to the nightingale above (ll. 31–3
and n.).

52. *lie hard*] (1) sleep on the ground; (2) tell powerful lies.

54.] *Run away* appeared last in Manes' list. Perim wishes it to precede
fasting and lying hard.

60. *tumble*] Milo is the tumbler (l. 12.1).

61. *brook not*] cannot endure.

64–7.] The story is told in Laertius (II.68) of Diogenes and Aristippus, in
Erasmus, *Apophthegmata*, (Aristippus, no. 1), of Aristippus and Dionysius,
and again (under Diogenes, no. 148, Udall, no. 153) of Diogenes and Plato.

Diogenes. Nor thou have followed Alexander if thou hadst
   scraped roots.   *Exeunt.*

Actus Quintus, Scaena Secunda.

[*Enter*] APELLES *alone.*

[*Apelles.*] I fear me, Apelles, that thine eyes have blabbed
   that which thy tongue durst not. What little regard
   hadst thou! Whilst Alexander viewed the counterfeit
   of Campaspe, thou stoodest gazing on her countenance.
   If he espy or but suspect, thou must needs twice perish,   5
   with his hate and thine own love. Thy pale looks when
   he blushed, thy sad countenance when he smiled, thy
   sighs when he questioned, may breed in him a jealousy,
   perchance a frenzy. O Love, I never before knew what
   thou wert, and now hast thou made me that I know not   10
   what myself am. Only this I know, that I must endure
   intolerable passions for unknown pleasures. Dispute
   not the cause, wretch, but yield to it; for better it is to
   melt with desire than wrestle with love. Cast thyself on
   thy careful bed; be content to live unknown and die   15
   unfound. O Campaspe, I have painted thee in my
   heart—painted? nay, contrary to mine art, imprinted;

3–4. thou! Whilst . . . Campaspe, thou . . . countenance.] *This ed;* thou,
whilst . . . *Campaspe,* thou . . . countenaunce? *Qq1, 2, 4, Blount;* thou, whilst
. . . *Campaspe?* thou . . . countenaunce. *Q3.*   11. I know] *Qq1, 3, 4, Blount;*
know *Q2.*   17. heart-painted] *This ed;* hearte, paynted *Q1;* heart, painted
Qq2, 4; heart: painted *Blount.*

---

   2. *regard*] probably 'observant attention or heed bestowed' (*O.E.D.*, sb., 6).
   3. *counterfeit*] picture.
   4. *countenance*] This could refer to her countenance in the picture or to her
real countenance as she stood there in the court, looking on at the event.
   5. *twiceperish*] i.e., metaphorically (from love) and physically (from
Alexander's hate).
   7. *blushed*] i.e., with pleasure, when he saw Campaspe's form in the picture.
   12. *unknown*] not experienced.
   13. *wretch*] i.e., Apelles himself (not Love, addressed in ll. 9ff.).
   15. *careful bed*] transferred epithet: the bed will hold the man who is *careful*
(full of cares).
   17. *contrary . . . art*] He is a painter and not a printer. (With a play on 'in my
heart' and 'contrary to mine *art*'.)

and that in such deep characters that nothing can raze it
out unless it rub thy heart out.   *Exit.*

Actus Quintus, Scaena Tertia.

[*Enter*] MILECTUS, PHRYGIUS [*and*] LAÏS.

Milectus. It shall go hard but this peace shall bring us some
pleasure.
Phrygius. Down with arms and up with legs; this is a world for
the nonce.
Laïs. Sweet youths, if you knew what it were to save your   5
sweet blood you would not so foolishly go about to spend
it. What delight can there be in gashing, to make foul
scars in fair faces and crooked maims in straight legs?
As though men, being born goodly by nature, would of
purpose become deformed by folly, and all forsooth for   10
a new-found term called *valiant*, a word which breedeth
more quarrels than the sense can commendation.
Milectus. It is true, Laïs, a feather bed hath no fellow, good

---

19. thy] *Q1;* my *1744.* 0.1.] *Adams (subst.); Milectus, Phrigius, Layis,
Diogenes. Qq1–4, Blount. (Lays, Qq2, 3).* 13. Laïs] *Blount, Q4 (Layis); Lays
Qq1, 2.*

18. *characters*] engraved marks.
19. *thy heart*] *my* heart, which the impression of *you* has made *yours.*
0.1. *LAÏS*] courtesan of Corinth, whose favours were sought by the most
celebrated orators and philosophers of Greece.
1. *It . . . but*] There will be problems if this does not happen.
3. *arms*] weapons (but with a play on the antithesis of *arms* and *legs. Legs* are
for dancing and lovemaking.)
3–4. *for the nonce*] for this one occasion; perhaps, for our purposes.
6. *spend*] shed.
11. *new-found term*] *O.E.D.* does not support any idea that the adjective
valiant was 'new-found' in 1584. But the use of the word as a substantive
(*valiant*, adj. and sb., 8) does seem to be novel. The first example given (1609)
is from the Douai version of Jeremiah xlvi.9, 'let the valiants come forth',
where *valiants* is equivalent to the Vulgate *fortes*, and is represented in the
Authorised Version by 'mighty men' and in the Revised Standard Version by
'warriors'. The second example is also biblical—from the heading to chapter
xxi of 2 Samuel in the Authorised Version (1611), 'four valiants of David slay
four giants'—and seems equally unidiomatic. Something of the same air of
fashionable neologism as appears in Lyly can be found in Donne's fifth
Paradox: 'If then the *valiant* kill himself, who can excuse the coward?'
13. *a feather . . . fellow*] This has a proverbial turn of phrase. Dent (*S.P.L.,*

drink makes good blood, and shall pelting words spill
it?   15
Phrygius. I mean to enjoy the world and to draw out my life at
the wire-drawer's, not to curtail it off at the cutler's.
Laïs. You may talk of war, speak big, conquer worlds with
great words; but stay at home, where instead of alarums
you shall have dances, for hot battles with fierce men   20
gentle skirmishes with fair women. These pewter coats
can never sit so well as satin doublets. Believe me, you
cannot conceive the pleasure of peace unless you despise
the rudeness of war.
Milectus. It is so. But see Diogenes prying over his tub.   25

DIOGENES [*is discovered in his tub*].

Diogenes, what sayst thou to such a morsel? [*He points
to Laïs*].
Diogenes. I say I would spit it out of my mouth because it
should not poison my stomach.

25.1.] *Adams ('They advance to Diogenes' tub'); not in Q1.*   26–26.1. *He points
to Laïs*] *Adams; not in Q1.*

F181.1) gives a list of Elizabethan '. . . has no fellow' locutions, but has no
other mention of a feather bed.
  13–14. *good . . . blood*] Dent, *P.L.E.D.*, W461.
  14. *pelting*] paltry, worthless.
  16–17. *draw . . . wire-drawer's*] elongate or stretch out my life.
  17. *curtail . . . cutler's*] have my life cut short (curt) with a sword made by a
cutler.
  18–24.] a negative version of the praise of war given above by Parmenio
(IV.iii.6–27 above), proceeding through the same topics.
  21. *pewter coats*] See *O.E.D.*, *pewter*, sb., 5: 'also humorously, in *pewter coat*
[citing the present passage as the sole example], a cuirass or coat of mail'.
Definition 2a is however virtually the same ('applied to armour'), separated
only because the use is more substantival. Compare Dekker, *Whore of Babylon*,
V.iii.39, and Barnes, *The Devil's Charter*, l. 2971 (ed. R. B. McKerrow,
Materialien, 1904).
  22. *sit*] fit, suit (*O.E.D.*, 16).
  24. *rudeness*] violence.
  25. *prying over*] with the clear implication that the tub is standing upright on
the stage.
  26. *morsel*] a choice piece (of flesh), girl. Diogenes replies, of course, to the
normal (food) meaning.
  28. *poison*] Compare Laertius, VI.61, repeated in Erasmus, *Apophthegmata*,
no. 162: 'Beautiful strumpets he avouched to be like unto bastard or
Muscadine tempered and mixed with deadly poison' (Udall, no. 168).

Phrygius. Thou speakest as thou art; it is no meat for dogs.

Diogenes. I am a dog, and philosophy rates me from carrion.   30

Laïs. Uncivil wretch, whose manners are answerable to thy
   calling! The time was thou wouldst have had my company, had it not been, as thou saidst, too dear.

Diogenes. I remember there was a thing that I repented me of,
   and now thou hast told it. Indeed it was too dear of   35
   nothing, and thou dear to nobody.

Laïs. Down, villain, or I will have thy head broken.

Milectus. [*To Diogenes*] Will you couch?

Phrygius. Avaunt, cur!

      [DIOGENES *retires into his tub.*]

   Come, sweet Laïs, let us go to some place and possess   40
   peace. But first let us sing; there is more pleasure in
   tuning of a voice than in a volley of shot.

Milectus. Now let us make haste lest Alexander find us here.

                Exeunt.

---

35. it. Indeed] *Adams;* it:indeed *Q4, Blount;* it, indeed *Q1; it indeed Q2.*
39.1.] *Adams (subst.); not in Q1.*   40 Laïs] *Lays Qq1, 2, 4, Blount.*

---

 29. *as thou art*] i.e., like a Cynic, currishly.

 30. *rates*] 'chides or drives away from' (*O.E.D.*, vb., 2); used technically of
dog-handling. *O.E.D.*, vb., 2, 1b, cites Stephen Gosson (1579): 'He rateth his
dog for wallowing in carrion.'

 31. *answerable*] conformable.

 31–2] *thy calling*] as a Cynic or dog.

 32–3. *The time . . . dear*] This story is told of Demosthenes and Laïs, and
appears in Erasmus, *Apophthegmata* (Demosthenes, no. 14): 'Demosthenes,
feared [i.e., appalled] with the greatness of the price [charged by Laïs],
changed his mind, saying, "I will not buy repentance so dear" ' (Udall no. 14).
In Lucian's *True History* Diogenes marries Laïs in the Islands of the Blest, and
'often would oblige the company with a dance'. See also Aulus Gellius, I.viii.

 35–6. *too dear of nothing*] too costly even at no price.

 36. *dear to*] beloved of.

 37. *Down*] Disappear down inside your tub. Such an exit corresponds to the
mode of entrance noted in l. 25.

 38. *couch*] crouch down (used mainly of animals).

 41. *let us sing*] It looks as if a song is missing at l. 42.0. See Appendix for
discussion of the appearance and disappearance of the songs in Lyly's plays.
It may be worth noting that the usual three-voice singing group is present
here.

Actus Quintus, Scaena Quarta.

[*Enter*] ALEXANDER [*and*] HEPHESTION, [*attended by*] Page.

Alexander. Methinketh, Hephestion, you are more melancholy
    than you were accustomed; but I perceive it is all for
    Alexander. You can neither brook this peace nor my
    pleasure. Be of good cheer; though I wink I sleep not.
Hephestion. Melancholy I am not, nor well content; for I know   5
    not how, there is such a rust crept into my bones with
    this long ease that I fear I shall not scour it out with
    infinite labours.
Alexander. Yes, yes; if all the travails of conquering the world
    will set either thy body or mine in tune, we will under-   10
    take them. But what think you of Apelles? Did ye ever
    see any so perplexed? He neither answered directly to
    any question nor looked steadfastly upon anything. I
    hold my life the painter is in love.
Hephestion. It may be, for commonly we see it incident in   15
    artificers to be enamoured of their own works, as
    Archidamus of his wooden dove, Pygmalion of his

0.1.] *Bond (subst.); Alexander, Hephestion, Page, Diogenes, Apelles, Campaspe.*
Q1. 6. how, there] *1744;* how there *Q1.*

1-4.] Hephestion's melancholy has been prepared for in the comments of
Parmenio, IV.iii.32ff.
    4. *wink*] keep my eyes shut; *not* the modern sense.
    6-7. *rust . . . scour*] See IV.iii.11n. above for the military associations of
these words.
    9. *conquering the world*] a clear sounding of the theme on which the play will
come to an end.
    10. *set . . . in tune*] restore our physiological humours to a proper balance,
thus curing the humoral imbalance of lovesickness and melancholy.
    13. *nor looked steadfastly*] Apelles himself described this condition in
V.ii.1-9.
    14. *hold*] bet (*O.E.D.*, 13).
    15. *incident in*] likely to happen in.
    17. *Archidamus . . . dove*] Bond refers to Lodowick Lloyd's poem 'The
Triumphs of Trophes' (1586), which he prints as Lyly's (III.428-32). Line 71
of this poem reads: 'These would make Architas' wooden dove to fly.'
Archytas of Tarentum is discussed in Laertius, VIII.79-83, though the wooden
dove is not mentioned there. It is mentioned, however, in Aulus Gellius,
X.xii.9. It is not clear why Lyly changed Archytas to Archidamus. The latter
name is known as that of several members of the royal house of Sparta.
    Pygmalion] See III.v.21n. above.

ivory image, Arachne of his wooden swan—especially
painters, who, playing with their own conceits, now
coveting to draw a glancing eye, then a rolling, now a   20
winking, still mending it, never ending it till they be
caught with it. And then, poor souls, they kiss the
colours with their lips, with which before they were
loath to taint their fingers.

Alexander. I will find it out.—Page, go speedily for Apelles.   25
Will him to come hither, and when you see us earnestly
in talk, suddenly cry out, 'Apelles' shop is on fire!'

Page. It shall be done.

Alexander. Forget not your lesson.

                                               [*Exit* Page.]

Hephestion. I marvel what your device shall be.   30

Alexander. The event shall prove.

Hephestion. I pity the poor painter if he be in love.

Alexander. Pity him not. I pray thee, that severe gravity set
aside, what do you think of love?

Hephestion. As the Macedonians do of their herb beet, which,   35
looking yellow in the ground and black in the hand,
think it better seen than touched.

Alexander. But what do you imagine it to be?

Hephestion. A word, by superstition thought a god, by use
turned to an humour, by self-will made a flattering   40
madness.

Alexander. You are too hard-hearted to think so of love. Let us
go to Diogenes.

29.1.] *Bond; not in Q1.*

---

18. *Arachne*] not known to history. Presumably Lyly invented the person
and the swan to complete the threesome. *Arachne* in mythology is of course the
Lydian woman who challenged Athene to a contest of weaving and was turned
into a spider—another artificer enamoured of her own works.

21. *still*] continually.

31. *event*] result.

33–4. *set aside*] having been set aside (past participle).

35. *beet*] Bond cites Pliny XIX.40, who tells us that the plant has cabbage-
like leaves above ground and a black root, and that 'some people scruple to
taste beets'.

39. *A word*] i.e., love. Compare Dent, *P.L.E.D.*, W781.11: 'X is but a
word', and 'John Lyly to the Author his friend', Bond, I.26: 'love, which
women account but a bare word'.

DIOGENES [*is discovered in his tub*].

Diogenes, thou mayst think it somewhat that Alexander
cometh to thee again so soon.   45

Diogenes. If you come to learn, you could not come soon
enough; if to laugh, you be come too soon.

Hephestion. It would better become thee to be more courteous
and frame thyself to please.

Diogenes. And you better to be less, if you durst displease.   50

Alexander. What dost thou think of the time we have here?

Diogenes. That we have little and lose much.

Alexander. If one be sick, what wouldst thou have him do?

Diogenes. Be sure that he make not his physician his heir.

Alexander. If thou mightst have thy will, how much ground   55
would content thee?

Diogenes. As much as you in the end must be contented withal.

Alexander. What, a world?

Diogenes. No, the length of my body.

Alexander. Hephestion, shall I be a little pleasant with him?   60

Hephestion. You may; but he will be very perverse with you.

43.1.] *This ed.; not in Q1.* 61. perverse] *Q1 corr. (Harv., HN, Indiana,
Pforz.), Qq2, 4, Blount;* peruese *Q1 uncorr. (Dulw.).*

44. *somewhat*] a thing worth considering (*O.E.D.*, 4).

48. *courteous*] The duplicity of the word allows Hephestion to mean well by
it ('mannerly, pleasant') and Diogenes to take it up in a bad sense ('courtier-
like, flattering').

51. *here*] in this life on earth.

52.] From Seneca, *De Brevitate Vitae*, 1.iii. The same passage is used in
Euphues, 1.284, 36, where Seneca is named.

54.] From Publilius Syrus, *Sententiae*, 373: '*Male secum agit aeger medicum
qui heredem facit.*' Dent, *P.L.E.D.*, F483, gives the *Campaspe* reference as his
first example.

55–9.] This apophthegm appears in Erasmus, *Apophthegmata* (Philip, no.
33): 'Philippus having on a time gotten a fall in the wrestling place, when in the
arising again he had espied the print and measure of his whole body in the
dust, he said: "O, the folly of man, how we to whom of nature a very small
portion of the earth is due, desire to have in our hands all the universal world"'
(Udall's translation). Erasmus notes that this sentiment was something
Alexander could well have taken to heart.

60. *pleasant*] jocular; but Hephestion appeals to the antithesis of *pleasant*
(agreeable) and *perverse* (ill-tempered).

Alexander. It skilleth not; I cannot be angry with him. Dio-
genes, I pray thee, what dost thou think of love?
Diogenes. A little worser than I can of hate.
Alexander. And why?   65
Diogenes. Because it is better to hate the things which make to
love than to love the things which give occasion of hate.
Alexander. Why, be not women the best creatures in the
world?
Diogenes. Next men and bees.   70
Alexander. What dost thou dislike chiefly in a woman?
Diogenes. One thing.
Alexander. What?
Diogenes. That she is a woman.
Alexander. In mine opinion thou wert never born of a woman,   75
that thou thinkest so hardly of women. But now cometh
Apelles who, I am sure, is as far from thy thoughts as
thou art from his cunning. Diogenes, I will have thy
cabin removed nearer to my court, because I will be
a philosopher.   80
Diogenes. And when you have done so I pray you remove your
court further from my cabin, because I will not be a
courtier.
Alexander. But here cometh Apelles.
                          [DIOGENES *retires into his tub.*]

---

62. skilleth] *Qq1, 2;* skills *Q4, Blount.*   77. thoughts] *Qq1, 2, Blount;* thogt
Q2.   78. cunning] *Q1 corr. (Harv., HN, Indiana, Pforz.), Qq2, 4, Blount;*
coming *Q1 uncorr. (Dulw.).*   84.1.] *This ed.; not in Q1.*

62. *It skilleth not*] It doesn't make any difference.
66–7. *make to love*] cause us to love.
76. *thou . . . women*] See Erasmus, *Apophthegmata,* no. 119 (Udall, no. 124)
and, in particular, Erasmus's comment (*apud* Udall): 'For Diogenes was one
that loved no women in no sauce, but hated them deadly'.
76–7. *But . . . Apelles*] This remark raises a question about the size of the
stage for which the play was designed. Is Apelles' approach visible at this point
though he is still approaching at l. 84? This seems improbable. The general
principles of Lyly's staging (see Introduction, pp. 31–2) suggest that he should
appear through the curtain hung in front of his 'workshop'. Alexander's
remark must therefore be interpreted as meaning no more than that he has
been sent for and will arrive shortly.
79, 82. *cabin*] The word can be used for any temporary shelter, a hovel, or
for the cell or cave of an anchorite.

[Re-enter Page with] APELLES.

Apelles, what piece of work have you now in hand?   85
Apelles. None in hand, if it like your Majesty. But I am de-
     vising a platform in my head.
Alexander. I think your hand put it in your head. Is it nothing
     about Venus?
Apelles. No, but something above Venus.   90
Page. Apelles, Apelles, look about you! Your shop is on fire.
Apelles. Ay me, if the picture of Campaspe be burnt I am
     undone!
                              [He starts for the shop.]
Alexander. Stay, Apelles, no haste. It is your heart is on fire,
     not your shop; and if Campaspe hang there I would she   95
     were burnt. But have you the picture of Campaspe?
     Belike you love her well, that you care not though all
     be lost so she be safe.
Apelles. Not love her. But your Majesty knows that painters in
     their last works are said to excel themselves, and in this   100
     I have so much pleased myself that the shadow as much

84.2.] *1780; not in Q1.*   85. now in hand] *Qq1, 4, Blount;* in hand *Q2.*   90.
above] *Q4;* about *Qq1, 2, Blount.*   93.1.] *This ed.; not in Q1.*

---

87. *platform*] plan, design, model.
88. *your hand ... head*] Perhaps 'your present mental state was in fact
produced by the exercise of your painting—you fell in love with Campaspe
through painting her'.
88–90. *Is ... Venus*] The Q4 reading here, though without textual
authority, restores some point to an exchange which otherwise is singularly
lacking in it. The two words involved are close graphically, only a common t/e
confusion separating one from the other.
92. *the picture of Campaspe*] In IV.v Apelles was told to cease delays and
bring the picture at once to Alexander's court. In V.ii we learn from Apelles
that this has happened, and Alexander (ll. 11ff. above) seems to be referring to
the same occasion, when he brought the picture to court. Why then is the
picture of Campaspe still in Apelles' studio? We must suppose either that
Apelles has taken it back once again for further retouching (which was
forbidden) or that he has painted a second picture—or that Lyly thought such
consistency unimportant.
95. *hang there*] i.e., in your heart.
99–100. *But ... themselves*] See Erasmus, *Colloquia* ('Puerpura', 1.767B):
'Artists are usually most exquisite in their later performances', '*solent artifices in
posterioribus se ipsos vincere*'. Lyly's wording seems to show that he was directly
following Erasmus's Latin.

delighteth me, being an artificer, as the substance doth
others that are amorous.

Alexander. You lay your colours grossly. Though I could not
    paint in your shop, I can spy into your excuse. Be not   105
    ashamed, Apelles; it is a gentleman's sport to be in
    love.—Call hither Campaspe.

                                 [Exit Page.]
    Methinks I might have been made privy to your affec-
    tion; though my counsel had not been necessary, yet my
    countenance might have been thought requisite. But   110
    Apelles forsooth loveth underhand, yea, and under
    Alexander's nose, and—but I say no more.

Apelles. Apelles loveth not so; but he liveth to do as Alexander
    willeth.

              [Re-enter Page *with]* CAMPASPE.

Alexander. Campaspe, here is news: Apelles is in love with   115
    you.

Campaspe. It pleaseth your Majesty to say so.

Alexander. Hephestion, I will try her too.—Campaspe, for the
    good qualities I know in Apelles and the virtue I see in
    you, I am determined you shall enjoy one the other.   120
    How say you, Campaspe? Would you say 'Ay'?

Campaspe. Your handmaid must obey if you command.

Alexander. Think you not, Hephestion, that she would fain
    be commanded?

Hephestion. I am no thought-catcher, but I guess unhappily.   125

107.1.] *Adams; not in Q1.*   114.1.] *1780 ('Enter Campaspe'); not in Q1.*   120.
the other] *Qq1, 2;* another *Q4, Blount.*

---

104. *You . . . grossly*] Your pretences are laid on too thick (hence, I don't
believe you).

104–5. *Though . . . shop*] See III.iv.112ff. above.

106–7. *it is . . . love*] Compare the Paul's Prologue to *Midas,* ll. 11–12:
'Courtiers [call] for comedies; their subject is love.'

110. *countenance*] patronage, moral support (*O.E.D.,* sb., 8).

117.] a polite way of avoiding either denial or confirmation. (Dent, *S.P.L.,*
P407.1.)

122.] Campaspe, as a prisoner of war, is at her conqueror's disposal.
Compare I.i.83–4 above.

125. *thought-catcher*] quoted but not glossed in *O.E.D., thought,* 7.

Alexander. I will not enforce marriage where I cannot compel
    love.

Campaspe. But your Majesty may move a question where you
    be willing to have a match.

Alexander. Believe me, Hephestion, these parties are agreed;   130
    they would have me both priest and witness. Apelles,
    take Campaspe. Why move ye not? Campaspe, take
    Apelles. Will it not be? If you be ashamed one of the
    other, by my consent you shall never come together.
    But dissemble not. Campaspe, do you love Apelles?   135

Campaspe. Pardon, my lord, I love Apelles.

Alexander. Apelles, it were a shame for you, being loved so
    openly of so fair a virgin, to say the contrary. Do you
    love Campaspe?

Apelles. Only Campaspe.   140

Alexander. Two loving worms, Hephestion. I perceive Alexan-
    der cannot subdue the affections of men though he con-
    quer their countries. Love falleth like dew as well upon

---

135. dissemble not. Campaspe] *Adams (subst.);* dissemble not *Campaspe Q1*.
142–3. he conquer] *Qq1–2;* conquer *Q4, Blount*.   143. like dew] *Qq1–2;* like
a dew *Q4, Blount*.

Presumably it refers to someone who can catch, i.e., apprehend, other people's
thoughts.
   unhappily] unfavourably—that is, in respect of Alexander's love.
   128. *move a question*] Presumably Campaspe is thinking, however anachron-
istically, of the question in the Marriage Service in the Book of Common
Prayer: 'Wilt thou have this man . . . '
   where] whether.
   130. *these . . . agreed*] the Marriage Service again: 'Forasmuch as N and M
have consented together in holy wedlock . . .'
   131. *both . . . witness*] In the Marriage Service the priest says, 'Who giveth
this woman to be married to this man?', and then the father or other person
signifies that he is *willing to have a match* (l. 129).
   135.] I change the punctuation in the Qq (as does Adams) because the
adjuration *dissemble not* seems intended to apply to both lovers, who have been
treated in parallel in the preceding lines. And in the following lines the
'Apelles, . . . Do you love Campaspe?' seems to demand a parallel 'Campaspe,
do you love Apelles?'
   141. *Two loving worms*] *O.E.D.*, sb., II.10c, glosses *worm*: 'a creature (used
with tenderness, playfulness, commiseration)'. Bond compares *Euphues*,
II.182, 3.
   143–4. *Love . . . cedar*] Compare IV.ii.8–10 above: 'affection is a fire which
kindleth as well in the bramble as in the oak'.

the low grass as upon the high cedar. Sparks have their
heat, ants their gall, flies their spleen. Well, enjoy one   145
another. I give her thee frankly, Apelles. Thou shalt see
that Alexander maketh but a toy of love and leadeth
affection in fetters, using fancy as a fool to make him
sport or as a minstrel to make him merry. It is not the
amorous glance of an eye can settle an idle thought in the   150
heart. No, no, it is children's game, a life for seamsters
and scholars; the one pricking in clouts have nothing
else to think on, the other picking fancies out of books
have little else to marvel at. Go, Apelles, take with you
your Campaspe; Alexander is cloyed with looking on   155
that which thou wonderedst at.

Apelles. Thanks to your Majesty on bended knee. You have
honoured Apelles.

Campaspe. Thanks with bowed heart. You have blessed
Campaspe.   160

     Exeunt [APELLES *and* CAMPASPE].

Alexander. Page, go warn Clitus and Parmenio and the other
lords to be in a readiness.

       [*Exit* Page.]

---

149. as a minstrel] *Qq1, 2; a minstrel Q4, Blount.*   156. wonderedst] *Q1;*
wondrest Qq2, 4, Blount.   160.1. APELLES *and* CAMPASPE] *Bond; not in Q1.*
162.1. *This ed.; not in Q1.*

144–5. *Sparks . . . spleen*] i.e., all creatures, however lowly, have
their own emotions. Allowing that the trees appear in the preceding
sentence, one can see that Lyly is here repeating *Euphues,* II.90, 22–3:
'low trees have their tops, small sparks their heat, the fly his spleen, the ant her
gall'. Compare *Endymion,* II.ii.19. Dent (*P.L.E.D.,* S714.11) has only Lyly
examples for the *sparks* adage; but Erasmus, *Adagia* (II.829F), attests to the
popularity of the later two ('*Inest et formica et serpho bilis*' and '*habet et musca
splenem*'). See also Dent, *P.L.E.D.,* F393.

151–4. *seamsters and scholars; the one . . . have . . . the other . . . have*] The
grammatical confusion between singulars and plurals here no doubt arises
from alternating assumptions about the *seamsters and scholars.* At one point
each is considered as a class, and so is singular; elsewhere each is seen to
comprise many individuals and so is plural.

152. *pricking in clouts*] sewing cloth.

156. *wonderedst*] The past tense presumably refers back to the point at
which Apelles fell in love.

Let the trumpet sound, strike up the drum, and I will
presently into Persia. How now, Hephestion, is Alexander able to resist love as he list?   165
Hephestion. The conquering of Thebes was not so honourable
as the subduing of these thoughts.
Alexander. It were a shame Alexander should desire to command the world if he could not command himself. But
come, let us go. I will try whether I can better bear my   170
hand with my heart than I could with mine eye. And
good Hephestion, when all the world is won and every
country is thine and mine, either find me out another to
subdue or, of my word, I will fall in love.   *Exeunt.*

163–4. *I will . . . Persia*] Alexander invaded the Persian domains in 334 B.C.

166–9. *The conquering . . . himself*] See Pliny XXXV.36: 'He showed [by
giving up Campaspe] that however great a commander and high-minded a
prince he was otherwise, yet in this mastering and commanding of his
affections, his magnanimity was more seen: and in this act of his he won as
much honour and glory as by any victory over his enemies; for now he had
conquered himself' (Holland's trans.). See also Dent, *P.L.E.D.*, C552.

170–1. *better bear . . . eye*] Perhaps this is a reference back to III.iv, where
Alexander could not paint because he could not match hand and eye; now as a
soldier he will match heart (courage) and hand (performance).

173. *thine and mine*] The comradeship of Alexander and Hephestion is
commented on by most of the historians. Quintus Curtius tells us that when
the wife and mother of Darius mistook Hephestion for Alexander the king
said, 'You committed no mistake. Hephestion is likewise Alexander' (Bk. III,
cap. xii, 31).

The Epilogue at the Blackfriars

Where the rainbow toucheth the tree, no caterpillar will hang
on the leaves; where the glow-worm creepeth in the night, no
adder will go in the day. We hope in the ears where our travails
be lodged no carping shall harbour in those tongues. Our
exercises must be as your judgement is, resembling water,   5
which is always of the same colour into what it runneth. In the
Trojan horse lay couched soldiers with children, and in heaps
of many words we fear divers unfit among some allowable. But
as Demosthenes with often breathing up the hill amended his
stammering, so we hope with sundry labours against the hair   10
to correct our studies. If the tree be blasted that blossoms, the
fault is in the wind and not in the root; and if our pastimes be

---

4. *in those tongues*] in the tongues of those whose ears have heard Lyly's
travails (efforts).

5. *exercises*] The convenient fiction was that performance in the 'private'
(that is, enclosed and expensive) theatres, such as the Blackfriars, was only an
exercise or preparation for the true performance at court before the queen. The
use of 'her Majesty's children' and other nominal choir-boys in what was in
fact a secular and commercial enterprise was thus made nominally defensible.

5–6. *resembling ... runneth*] from Erasmus, *Parabolae*, p. 144: 'flowing
water hath no definite colour, but always takes its colour from the ground over
which it flows'.

6–7. *In the Trojan ... children*] This appears to be one of Lyly's more bizarre
historical inventions. There is a possibility that he was misled by reading of
Neoptolemus (one of the heroes inside the horse) in Servius' commentary on
Aeneid, II.263. Servius speaks of his name: '*Neoptolemus, quia ad bellum ductus
est puer*' (so called because he was brought to the war as a boy). See *Servianorum
in Vergilii Carmina commentariorum editionis harvardianae*, II. (Cambridge,
Mass., 1946).

8–10. *But ... stammering*] Plutarch's *Life of Demosthenes* (V.290–1) tells us
that 'touching the stammering of his tongue ... he did help it ... And for his
small voice he made that louder by running up steep and high hills, uttering
even with full breath some oration or verses.' Mustard (*S.P.*, XXII, 267) cites
the same information from Cicero, *De Oratore*, I.61 (261).

10. *against the hair*] running against the natural grain. See Dent, *P.L.E.D.*,
H18.

11. *blasted*] stricken by a pernicious wind.

12. *pastimes*] Lyly's self-depreciating term for his own play (and others of its
kind).

misliked, that have been allowed, you must impute it to the
malice of others and not our endeavour. And so we rest in good
case if you rest well content.   15

---

13. *that ... allowed*] that have been approved for performance by the
Master of the Revels.

14–15. *in good case*] in good condition (*O.E.D.*, *case*, sb.¹, 5).

The Epilogue at the Court

We cannot tell whether we are fallen among Diomedes' birds
or his horses; the one received some men with sweet notes,
the other bit all men with sharp teeth. But as Homer's gods
conveyed them into clouds whom they would have kept from
curses, and as Venus, lest Adonis should be pricked with the   5
stings of adders, covered his face with the wings of swans, so
we hope, being shielded with your Highness' countenance,
we shall, though hear the neighing, yet not feel the kicking of
those jades and receive, though no praise (which we cannot
deserve) yet a pardon, which in all humility we desire. As yet   10
we cannot tell what we should term our labours, iron or bullion; only it belongeth to your Majesty to make them fit either

---

1–2. *Diomedes' . . . horses*] Bond points out that there are two different
Diomedeses involved here. Diomedes the Homeric hero was shipwrecked
between Troy and Italy, and Venus turned his companions into birds (Ovid,
Metamorphoses, XIV). Pliny (X.61) says that the birds remained friendly to the
Greeks though hostile to barbarians. The Thracian Diomedes was the owner of
man-eating horses; he was killed by Hercules. Erasmus describes him in the
Adagia, under the heading of *Diomedea necessitas* (II.335B).

3–5. *as Homer's . . . curses*] In the *Iliad* the gods frequently snatch away
their favourites from death (the usual form of *curse*) by wrapping them in
clouds. Thus Paris is rescued from Menelaus in Book III (380ff.) and Aeneas
from Diomedes in Book V (331ff.).

5–6.] Venus sought to protect Adonis from the boar hunt in which he was
killed. The idea that she *hid* him may be derived by contamination with the
source story for *Sappho and Phao* (cited below, p. 154) where she hides Phao in
long lettuce leaves. See also below p. 154 for the opinion that Adonis and Phao
are variant names for the same person. The association of Venus and swans is
amply documented (see F. Bömer, *Metamorphosen* (Heidelberg, 1980), Bk X,
pp. 225–7).

9. *jades*] Perhaps Lyly is still thinking of the horses of Diomedes. A *jade* is a
broken-down or ill-trained horse. The enemies of the author who backbite
against the play can only make a noise. They cannot harm him because he has
the *countenance* (support) of the Queen.

11–12. *bullion*] gold.

12. *only it belongeth*] it belongs only.

12–14. *fit . . . anvil*] Gold is appropriate to the *mint* where it will be made
into current coin by having the queen's countenance stamped on it. If it is not
true metal it will be treated like iron: broken on the blacksmith's anvil and
melted down in his forge (because it is a forgery).

for the forge or the mint, current by the stamp or counterfeit
by the anvil. For as nothing is to be called white unless it had
been named white by the first creature, so can there be nothing 15
thought good in the opinion of others unless it be christened
good by the judgement of yourself. For ourselves again, we are
like these torches' wax, of which, being in your Highness'
hands, you may make doves or vultures, roses or nettles, laurel
for a garland or elder for a disgrace. 20

FINIS

18. these torches' wax] *Qq1, 4* ('*these torches wax*'); those torches waxe *Q2;*
these Torches of Waxe *Blount;* these Torches, wax *1744;* those torches—waxe
Adams.

14–15. *nothing . . . creature*] Adam gave the proper names to all the
creatures in the Garden of Eden: 'and whatsoever Adam called every living
creature, that was the name thereof' (Genesis ii.19).

17. *For ourselves again*] Perhaps this means 'Coming back (after the general
remarks preceding) to the particular subject of the players, the play, and the
author'.

18. *these torches' wax*] The progressive changes in the readings in this
passage (see collations) indicate a progressive departure from Q1's implicit
gesture towards the actual torches in the actual hall. By the time of Blount
(1632) the phrasing has become generalised and purely literary.

19. *doves . . . nettles*] things innocent or predatory, beautiful or noxious.

19–20. *laurel . . . garland*] a crown of victory or of poetic triumph.

20. *elder . . . disgrace*] The bad reputation of the elder tree presumably
derived (as Bond notes) from the tradition that Judas hanged himself on an
elder tree.

Introduction to *Sappho and Phao*

This edition of *Sappho and Phao*, the first critical edition since R. Warwick Bond's three-volume edition of *The Complete Works of John Lyly* in 1902,[1] is based upon a first quarto of 1584 previously unidentified as such. The evidence that follows here is set forth in fuller detail in my article on 'The First Edition of John Lyly's *Sappho and Phao* (1584)'.[2] The play's publication history, as revised in the light of this new identification, is as follows.

The Stationers' Register for 1584 contains this entry:

> 6ᵗᵒ Ap'lis Tho cadman. Yt is graunted vnto him yᵗ if he gett yᵉ/cōmedie of sappho laufully alowed vnto him. Then nōne of this/cūpanie shall Interrupt him to enioye yt   vjᵈ.
> [*in margin* Lyllye *in a later hand*][3]

Earlier in 1584, Thomas Cadman had published *Campaspe* without entering the play in the Stationers' Register. On the present occasion, he evidently desired to provide himself with the legal protection afforded by such an entry before undertaking to publish a second play by Lyly. The wording of the entry, and the previous collaboration on *Campaspe*, suggest co-operation between Lyly and Cadman and a concern on Lyly's part to ensure the literary integrity of the published text.

Bond's edition of *Sappho and Phao* in 1902, the first edition in modern times to base its work on original texts, took for its copy text a single quarto of 1584 in the British Museum (now the British Library, C. 34. d. 17) bearing the following title page and colophon:

> Sappho and Phao, / *Played beefore the* / Queenes Maiestie on Shroue-/ tewsday, by her Maiesties / *Children, and the Boyes* / *of Paules.* / [ornament] *Imprinted at London* for Thomas Cadman. / 1584.
> [Colophon]
> *Imprinted at London by Thomas* / Dawson, for Thomas Cadman.

Bond identified this quarto (later numbered S.T.C. 17086 in A. W. Pollard and G. R. Redgrave's *Short Title Catalogue* of 1926) as Q1, and a subsequent quarto appearing in 1591 (S.T.C. 17087) as Q2.[4]

In 1939, however, W. W. Greg's *A Bibliography of the English*

Printed Drama to the Restoration identified not one but two quartos in 1584. Greg assigned the number 82a to the British Library copy and 82b to a quarto then known to exist in two copies, one in the Library of Worcester College, Oxford, and one in the Huntington Library in California. Greg noted a few variants, especially in the catchword on A3, and concluded from the fact that the speakers' names are not indented in 82a except in the A gathering whereas 82b extends the indenting of speakers' names to the outer forme of the B gathering that 82b was the reprint.[5] The S.T.C. catalogue, which in its first edition of 1926 wrongly assigned only one number, 17086, to all three of the copies named above, followed Greg's lead in its second edition of 1976, assigning number 17086 to the British Library quarto and 17086.5 to the other quarto, now represented in yet another copy at the National Library of Scotland at Edinburgh. This second edition of the S.T.C. catalogue thus accepted Greg's briefly stated case for 17086 (Greg's 82a) as the First Quarto and thereby implicitly confirmed Bond's choice of this edition for his copy text in his edition of 1902 (though Bond seems to have consulted no other).

The three extant quartos of 17086.5 (a fourth copy reported in the National Union Catalogue for the United States at the City University of New York turns out to be only a photographic copy of the Huntington quarto) are identical to one another and without press variants (though the Worcester Library copy is torn on C2-C2v, obliterating some text). All copies of 17086.5 bear a title page essentially like that of 17086 but vary the colophon as follows:

Imprinted at London by Tho-/mas Dawson, for Thomas Cadman.

This is the edition assumed until now to be the reprint of 17086, although the argument for such a determination of priority is contained in two sentences in Greg. What follows is a summary of the evidence (more fully laid out in the article in *Studies in Bibliography*, XLII, 1989) for my argument that 17086.5 is in fact the First Quarto and 17086 a reprint of the same year.

Physical similarities between the two quartos plainly suggest that whichever of the two texts came first sold out quickly and had to be supplemented by a second printing. Little of substance was changed. In both, the pagination is identical from A to G2v (A1v and G2v being blank) except for one variation in the catchword, as noted in Greg's *Bibliography* and the 1976 S.T.C. catalogue, on A3. Reprinting is line for line except for a total of about fifty scattered lines, and even in these instances it seems clear that the compositor of the reset copy was departing from the lineation of his copy only under the pressure of crowding and was eager to rejoin the lineation of his copy as soon as possible in order to continue with his line-by-line resetting. New initials, border decorations and ornaments on the title page and first three pages of text and on the last page visually distinguish the two quartos from each other but do not appreciably assist in the task of determining priority. Other physical differences are readily apparent: the page signature B4 is present in 17086.5 but missing in 17086, the *Exeunt* at the end of I.iii on B2 comes at the end of the line in 17086.5 but is dropped below the line in 17086, and so on. These differences are all reversible as evidence in the question of priority.

Various other kinds of evidence do, on the other hand, support the hypothesis that 17086.5 was printed first. One such kind of evidence has to do with the indentation of speech prefixes. The 17086.5 compositor indents his speech prefixes in his first gathering (with one exception owing to the presence of a block initial) and continues to do so in the outer forme (B1, B4V, B2V-B3) of his second gathering, but shifts to unindented speech prefixes thereafter for the remainder of the play. The 17086 compositor indents throughout the A gathering, as does 17086.5, but then uses an unindented format beginning with B1 and continuing through the rest of the play. Greg, as we have seen, takes the evidence on indented speech prefixes to confirm the identity of 17086.5 as the reprint, since it indents the speech prefixes through the outer forme of gathering B whereas 17086 shifts to unindented speech prefixes beginning with B. Certainly these quartos were set by formes. Yet the copy used by the compositor of the reprint edition was presumably a bound copy of the earlier quarto, and in this case we can best explain the consistency of 17086 by hypothesising that this compositor, seeing that his copy for the B gathering was apparently inconsistent (varying back and forth from page to page), decided to standardise practice from that point on with unindented speech prefixes. The reverse hypothesis fails to explain why the 17086 compositor, if he printed first, shifted to unindented speech prefixes after he had finished the A gathering, and has to suppose that the 17086.5 compositor, faced with a copy now perfectly consistent in the B gathering in its use of unindented speech prefixes, followed copy on the pages of the inner forme as he set gathering B but preferred instead to indent speech prefixes on the pages of the outer forme. (Greg implies that the outer forme of gathering B of 17086.5 was set before the inner forme, but this is not demonstrable, and in fact the order of printing seems to have been the other way around.)

In the matter of providing a period after abbreviated speech prefixes and none after unabbreviated ones, the 17086.5 copy follows a more random practice that is easier to account for by supposing that this quarto came first (perhaps setting from inconsistent or heavily abbreviated manuscript copy) and was then regularised in 17086 than to hypothesise that 17086 offered a regularised text which 17086.5 then proceeded to follow only haphazardly and inconsistently. Examples are on C1, C3 and E1 and following.

Variations in the spellings or abbreviated spellings of speech prefixes are similarly easier to explain if we suppose that the 17086 compositor, coming second in the sequence of printing, regularised what he saw in his copy. In I.iv, for example, the 17086.5 compositor prints *Lamia* in the opening stage direction and then *Lamya* for the prefix of her first speech; the 17086 compositor uses the same spelling for both. It is more likely that the variation was in 17086.5's manuscript copy or that the manuscript offered abbreviated speech prefixes than to suppose that, faced with consistency in a printed copy of 17086, the 17086.5 compositor varied the spelling arbitrarily. He might have done so carelessly, to be sure, but probability favours the first hypothesis when it is repeated in example after example. Variations in speech prefixes for *Trachinus* (*Trach.*, *Trachi.*), *Mileta* (*Mile.*, *Milet.*, *Mileta.*), *Criticus* or *Cryticus* (*Criti.*, *Cryti.*), and *Calypho* (*Caly.*, *Cali.*) all follow the same pattern of greater consistency in 17086 and a haphazard variation in 17086.5 that would have to have been produced in disregard of consistency in the copy if 17086.5 were second. The fact that both texts are generally careful in their printing militates against carelessness as an explanation for the variation seen in the speech prefixes of 17086.5.

Spelling preferences again point to 17086 as the reprint. A good example is in the spelling of 'deuill' and 'deuilles' in II.iii. The word is spelled thus eight times in 17086.5, along with one instance of 'deuil' and one of 'deuils'—never 'diuell' or 'diuells'. 17086, on the other hand, prefers *'diuell'* in its first three uses of the word and sporadically thereafter. Yet in the fourth appearance of the word, the 17086 compositor switches to 'deuill', and subsequently mingles this 'eui' spelling among his preferred 'iue' spellings. And where 17086 agrees with 17086.5 in the 'eui' spelling, it also concurs with 17086.5 in the choice of a single or double 'l' at the end of the word. It is not impossible to imagine that 17086 was printed first, if the manuscript copy was irregular, but the generally high quality of the text militates against this supposition; variations and abbreviations in speech prefixes in author's papers are often irregular, but spellings tend to follow a preferred choice. The hypothesis of 17086 as the second printing requires us only to suppose that this compositor was sporadically imposing his preferred spelling on his copy while at other times following the spellings he found.

Other spelling preferences point to a reprint by the 17086 compositor, and confirm that each quarto was set by a single compositor. The 17086 compositor seems to prefer to spell words like 'whom', 'sweet', 'how', 'pay', 'indeed' and 'think' without a final '-e', whereas the 17086.5 compositor strongly prefers the final '-e' when the spellings vary between the two texts: there are about forty-two instances where the 17086 compositor prefers no final '-e' and only sixteen instances where he adds a final '-e' not found in 17086.5. Common spellings, of which there are many, indicate a marked preference for the final '-e'. As a matter of probability, then, assuming that each compositor had a preferred way to spell such words and that the copy too was more or less consistent, we can assume that the author's manuscript preferred the final '-e' and that the 17086.5 compositor followed this pattern whereas the 17086 compositor sometimes imposed his own preference against his copy (17086.5). The hypothesis that 17086 was printed first must suppose that the compositor vacillated between final '-e' and the lack of it, or was following arbitrary spellings in his copy, whereas the hypothesis that 17086.5 was printed first assumes more simply that the compositor or his manuscript copy had a predilection for one spelling (final '-e') and that subsequently the 17086 compositor's preference for no final '-e' was at variance with his copy (17086.5).

Spellings involving the choice of final '-y' or '-ie' (as in 'ready', 'enemy', 'study', 'beauty', 'ferry') and of a final '-es' or '-s' ('stings', 'locks', 'kissings') follow a similar pattern with even stronger statistical confirmation: for example, the 17086.5 compositor adopts the '-ie' ending also preferred in common readings in twenty-five instances when the spellings vary between the two texts, and never goes in the other direction of preferring a final '-y'. Use of ampersands in the place of 'and' tends to support a similar hypothesis. These spelling tests are only probable, but cumulatively they are suggestive because they all point in one direction.

For one last mechanical bit of evidence, one that seems conclusively irreversible, I am indebted to Eric Rasmussen. An apparently stray mark appears on C2v of 17086.5 between ll. 14 and 15, caused perhaps by a space that has worked up and caught the inking. In

17086, the same space is filled by an unnecessary comma. It seems highly unlikely that a comma in 17086 would have been omitted and then fortuitously replaced by a stray mark, but entirely plausible on other hand that the 17086 compositor was attempting to rationalise what he took to be a punctuation mark. We have here, then, the kind of evidence that enabled Greg to distinguish conclusively between nearly identical editions of *The Elder Brother*.[6]

Concluding that the 17086 text represents Q2, we are in a position to judge whether any of its corrections and emendations point to authorial change. The reprint is a conservative one. There are a few predictable misprints, like 'teech' for 'teeth' at II.i.108, 'one' for 'on' at IV.iii.13, and 'though' for 'thought' at IV.iii.73. The Q2 compositor corrects a few obvious misprints like 'hearken' for 'yearken' at II.i.39. 'Ouerwatching' is probably a sensible correction of Q1's 'ourwatching' at IV.iii.60, even if 'ourwatching' might be regarded as a variant spelling of or error for 'o'erwatching'. The Q2 compositor emends when the context clearly requires a change, as in 'sir boy' for 'sir boyes' at I.ii.75 when only one page is being addressed, 'requireth no lesse' for 'requireth no losse' at II.iv.73, 'weane' for 'weave' at III.i.30 (in a sentence that continues with a metaphor of nursing), and 'croked' for 'crooked' at III.iii.62 (in a sentence about the night-raven).

Sometimes the compositor's changes sound like plausible but unnecessary guesswork, as at I.iii.2, where 'thy diet' is changed to 'the diet' to underscore a seeming antithesis between Athens and the court but which misses the point that 'thy diet' applies well to the page Molus in his new courtly environment. Q2's 'reare me vp, my bed, my head' at III.iii.81–2 is probably correct as an emendation of Q1's 'rear me vp, my bead, my head', although it is also possible that 'bead', an unusual form for 'bed', is a misprint for 'head'. Q2's reading of 'hearte' for Q1's 'heate' at III.iii.103 is inviting at first, since the phrase 'in the pride of thy heart' is so colloquially familiar, but the image of heat is thoroughly defensible in a description of the sun, or Phoebus. Again, Q2's emendation of 'binde' to 'blinde' at III.iv.9 is attractive but unnecessary, since the imagery of binding in swaddling bands continues in the same sentence. The Q2 compositor makes things worse rather than better when he changes 'the best friend with thy tatling' to 'the best friend with the tatling' at IV.iii.44–5; Q1 probably needs emendation to 'thy best friend with thy tatling'. Q2's 'withstanding' instead of Q1's 'withdrawing' at V.ii.4 would be a defensible reading if Q2 were the original text, but

Q1 makes sense as it stands and nothing points to authorial change. These instances, the strongest candidates for showing evidence of authorial involvement in the various emendations printed by Q2, are all explicable as commonsense corrections or as sophistications that should be resisted by an editor.

In summary, the Q2 compositor appears to have been a careful workman who corrected some errors while making others of his own and speculated intelligently about matters that did not seem to him quite right in his copy. Nothing points conclusively or even suggestively to his using marked copy or corrected proofs. Q2 is a useful text for the occasional sensible corrections it makes, but offers no authority.

The printer of both Q1 and Q2, Thomas Cadman, who also printed three separate quartos of *Campaspe* in 1584, published nothing after 1589. His rights in *Campaspe* and in *Sappho and Phao* may have passed by informal agreement to William Broome, or the copyright may have seemed derelict, for in 1591, with no record of transfer in the Stationers' Register, Broome issued quarto editions of Lyly's first two plays. Both were printed for him by Thomas Orwin. The title page of *Sappho and Phao* reads as follows:

[Q3] Sapho and Phao, / *Played beefore the* / Queenes maiestie on Shroue / tewsday, by her Maiesties / *Children, and the Boyes* / *of Paules.* / [ornament] / Imprinted at London by *Thomas* / *Orwin*, for *William Broome.* / 1591.

This quarto is a reprint of Q1 without recourse to Q2, just as Q4 of *Campaspe* in 1591 is a reprint of that play's Q1. At I.ii.75, I.iii.2, I.iii.23, II.i.154, II.ii.2, II.ii.29 and II.iii.25, for example, Q3 follows Q1 in reading 'sir boyes', 'thy diet', 'worldlings', 'vines', 'is', 'thy ferrie' and 'an' instead of Q2's 'sir boy', 'the diet', 'wordlings', 'vine', 'in', 'the ferrie' and 'a'. The first of these, as we have seen, is an error sensibly emended by the Q2 compositor; the others are correct in Q1 and in error in Q2. Q3's dependence on Q1 is correspondingly close throughout the text. The pagination is identical with that of Q1, and generally the resetting is line by line. A colophon is lacking.

Q3 does introduce a number of new readings, and some of them are undeniable improvements. Q1–2's erroneous or misleading 'needelesse' in l. 10 of the Prologue at the Court, for example, is corrected to 'needles' (i.e., 'needle's') in Q3. The question of authority thus arises once again, especially since Q3 is the last reprint during the author's lifetime. Taken as a whole, however, the new

readings in Q3 suggest no authorial involvement. The few improvements are commonsense, while most changes are instead arbitrary or
in error. See, e.g., 'the Theater of Athens' for 'The Theater at Athens'
in the Prologue at the Blackfriars, l. 12; 'that' for 'which' in the
Prologue at Court, l. 10; 'glaunce at others faces' for 'glaunce on
others faces' at II.i.106; 'will I' for 'I will' at II.i.136; 'a deuill' for 'the
deuill' at II.iii.52; 'Be they all deuilles that haue hornes' for 'Be they
all deuilles haue hornes' at II.iii.72; 'it is' for 'is it' at III.ii.10; 'gyue
your selfe leaue to slumber' for 'gyue your selfe to slumber' at
III.iii.30–1; and 'to be imaginatiue' for 'to be the imaginatiue' at
IV.iii.51. None of these emendations is more than uninspired guesswork or stylistic 'improvement', and cumulatively they provide no
evidence of authorial intervention. The situation thus parallels that
which Hunter describes in his Introduction to *Campaspe*, above:
the various quartos subsequent to Q1, even those following in 1584
(Q2 and Q3), contain no convincing demonstration of authorial
involvement.

As in the case of Q4 of *Campaspe* in the same year, the transfer of
Q3 of *Sappho and Phao* to Broome seems not to have involved Lyly.
Copies of Q3 (S.T.C. 17087) are to be found in the British Library,
the Bodleian, the Dyce Collection in South Kensington, the Folger
Shakespeare Library, Harvard University Library, Yale University
Library, the Huntington Library and elsewhere.

After William Broome's death in 1591, his widow Joan eventually
gained recognition of her rights in the books he had published, for a
Stationers' Register entry of 12 April 1597 (Greg, *Bibliography*, I.13)
entered both plays and two other books, 'The wch copies were Tho
Cadmans', to her. (*Gallathea*, *Endymion* and *Midas* had been entered
to her in the Stationers' Register on 4 October, 1591; Greg, *Bibliography*, I.7). On 23 August 1601 *Sappho and Phao* was transferred,
along with *Campaspe*, *Gallathea*, *Endymion* and *Midas*, from 'mystres
Brome Lately deceased' to George Potter (Greg, *Bibliography*, I.17).
No publication ensued, and it was not until 9 January 1628 that
Potter's five plays, together with *Mother Bombie*, were registered to
Edward Blount (Greg, *Bibliography*, I.36). His edition of six Lyly
plays (he did not include *The Woman in the Moon* and *Love's Metamorphosis*) appeared under the following title in 1632 (S.T.C. 17088):

[Bl.]　SIXE / COVRT / Comedies. / Often　Presented　and　Acted / *before
Queene* ELIZABETH, / by the Children of her Ma-/iesties Chappell, and
the / Children of Paules. / *Written* / By the onely Rare Poet of that / Time,
The　Wittie,　Comicall, / *Facetiously-Quicke　and* / vnparalleld / IOHN

LILLY, Master / *of Arts*. / Decies repetita placebunt. / [ornament] / *LONDON* / Printed by *William Stansby* for *Edward* / *Blount*. 1632. /

[sig. L2] SAPHO / AND / PHAO, / *Played before the Queenes* / *Maiestie on Shroue-/tuesday:* / *By her* MAIESTIES / Children, and the Chil-/dren of *Paules*. / [ornament] / LONDON, / Printed by *William Stansby*, / for *Edward Blount*. / 1632.

A variant title in the Huntington copy reads 'Witie' for 'Wittie'. *Sappho and Phao* occupies sigs. L2–O12v in duodecimo, and is a reprint from Q3 with minor changes (just as *Campaspe* in this volume is a reprint of Q4, 1591) except for the addition of the songs. Typical of readings that show the dependency of the 1632 reprint on Q3 are the following: Prologue at the Blackfriars, l. 12, 'at' Q1–2, 'of' Q3 Bl.; l. 16, 'bee from' Q1–2, 'bee free from' Q3, 'be free from' Bl.; II.i.70, 'read' Q1–2, 'red' Q3–Bl.; II.i.91, 'waxed' Q1–2, 'wexed' Q3–Bl.; II.i.82, 'suckered' Q1–2, 'succored' Q3, 'succoured' Bl.; II.i.106, 'on' Q1–2, 'at' Q3–Bl., etc. Copies of Blount's edition are available in the British Library, Yale University Library, the Huntington Library, the Library of Congress, Indiana University Library, the Boston Public Library, the University of Chicago Library and a number of others.

Blount's major contribution was to provide songs to the plays where in quarto they had only been indicated by stage directions. G. K. Hunter has argued cogently[7] that Blount may have had access to the music library of the Paul's boys. Songs may have been written out for the boy actors on separate sheets, rather than being included in the prompt-book, and were perhaps withheld from publication as an important part of the boys' stock in performance. A contrasting view, urged among others by Greg and John Robert Moore,[8] is that Blount may have used or adapted songs by Dekker and other early seventeenth-century writers on suitable themes. The issue is much debated, and is in any event a question of authorship rather than of textual authority.

The editorial implications of this textual history of *Sappho and Phao* seem clear. Q1 is the authoritative text. Lyly seems to have had nothing to do with the minor changes successively introduced into Q2, Q3 and the Blount edition of 1632, though Q2 and Q3 (especially Q2) both introduce some sensible emendations that commend themselves to the editor. The songs are properly included in modern editions, although it should be understood that the authority for Lyly's authorship of them is not the same as for the Q1 text. The only modern editions prior to the present one are F. W. Fairholt's edition

(1858),[9] based on the Blount edition of 1632 and including the numerous unauthorised changes that had crept into the text by that time; Bond's *Lyly*, based on Q2 in the mistaken assumption that it was the First Quarto; and Carter A. Daniel's *The Plays of John Lyly*,[10] which appears to have consulted Q1, although its lack of indication as to what early text was chosen as copy text and the absence of any collation make it hard to trace what the editor has done. See 'This Edition' (p. xvii, above) for further comment on Daniel's editing of this play.

2. DATE AND AUTHORSHIP

Although Lyly's names does not appear on the title pages of Qq1–3, the name is mentioned in the Stationers' Register entry of 6 April 1584 in a later hand. He is named as the recipient of payment in November 1584 for performance of two plays at court that were presumably his *Campaspe* and *Sappho and Phao* (see below). The subsequent textual history of *Sappho and Phao* connects the play at every change of ownership with other plays reliably attributed to Lyly, namely, *Campaspe*, *Gallathea*, *Endymion* and *Midas*, until they and *Mother Bombie* were published together in 1632 by Blount as *Six Court Comedies* 'By the onely Rare Poet of that Time, the Wittie, Comicall, Facetiously-Quicke and vnparalleled Iohn Lilly, Master of Arts'. The Stationers' Register entry of 9 January 1627 assigning these plays to Blount refers to them as 'Sixe plays of Peter Lillyes' (*sic*; Greg, *Bibliography*, 1.36). The unmistakable imprint of Lyly's style on *Sappho and Phao*, together with its numerous echoes of *Euphues* and *Campaspe*, thus confirms an authorship that has never been in doubt.

Sappho and Phao's chronological place as the second of Lyly's plays seems no less assured. The actual date of first performance is more a matter of debate. Bond (II.310–11, 367) would prefer to identify *Campaspe* and *Sappho and Phao* as the two plays referred to in Chalmers's payment-lists, extracted from the Council Registers, in the following entry: '1st April 1582 Pd the master of the children of the Chapel for two plays on the last of December and Shrove Tuesday 20 marks, and by way of reward 20 nobles.'[11] *Campaspe* would then have appeared at court on 31 December 1581, with *Sappho and Phao* following on Shrove Tuesday, 27 February, in 1582. Since performance at Blackfriars must have preceded court performance in each case, Bond proposes that *Campaspe* was composed rather hurriedly in

the latter part of 1580, in the wake of the successful completion of
Euphues to which it is so obviously indebted, and that it may even
have been under way in 1579. Albert Feuillerat is in general agreement.[12] Bond's reasons for wishing an early date for *Sappho and Phao*
have to do chiefly with a proposed topical allegory: if the Duke
d'Alençon is to be identified with Phao as the wooer of Sappho (i.e.,
Queen Elizabeth), the play's ending with Phao's departure from
Syracuse must refer to Alençon's departure from England—an event
that occurred on 6 February 1582. Bond is obliged to admit, however, that the play could not have been written and performed at
Blackfriars during the scant three-week interval between 6 February
and 27 February, the supposed date of performance at court. Instead,
he speculates that the play was begun a good deal earlier, in 1581,
'at the time when the end of Alençon's suit was already foreseen or
surmised' (II.367), and that even the rehearsals and preliminary
performances at Blackfriars may have anticipated the actual departure of Alençon from the English court. Bond's hypothetical chrono-
logy further leads him to suppose that the writing of *Campaspe*
delayed the completion of *Euphues and His England*—a suggestion
that, as Hunter shows in his Introduction to *Campaspe* above, is
based on inconclusive evidence. The hypothesis of a date in 1581 for
the composition of *Sappho and Phao* would not only give Lyly the
benefit of prescience but would also give his play the unusual accolade
of being confirmed by historical event during the course of the play's
composition and performance.

The unlikelihood of such a scenario is only one difficulty with a
date of performance in early 1582. The title page of Q1 advertises
Sappho and Phao as performed before the queen 'by her Majesty's
Children, and the Boys of Paul's', not the Children of the Chapel
alone as in the 1 April 1582 payment list. *Campaspe*'s title page names
the same combined troupe. This large combination of the Chapel
Children and the Children of Paul's did not perform at court until
1583–4. William Hunnis, Master of the Children of the Chapel Royal
in London and lessee of the Blackfrairs Theatre after the death of
Richard Farrant (Master of the Children of the Chapel Royal at
Windsor) in 1580, transferred the lease to Henry Evans only after
many delays occasioned by a recalcitrant landlord (see Hunter's
Introduction to *Campaspe*). The death of Sebastian Westcote, Master
of the Children of Paul's, in 1582 was apparently another factor that
led to the temporary merger of the two boys' companies. Evans's
partners in leasing the Blackfriars theatre included William Hunnis,

John Lyly and the Earl of Oxford, and it was the last whose name appeared on payment lists for performances of the combined troupe.[13] As Hunter argues, Lyly was not in a position to gain control of the Blackfriars Theatre and a large troupe of boy actors before the middle of 1583. A payment of £10 was made to Lyly on 25 November 1584 for a play before the queen 'on shrovetuesdaie at nighte' by the Earl of Oxford's company; this entry appeared on the same warrant as that for a play 'vpon newyeresdaie at nighte' also by 'the Erle of Oxford his seruantes', with payment to 'John Lilie'.[14]

It seems most likely, then, that the title pages of *Campaspe* and *Sappho and Phao* seek to capitalise on the very recent court performances of 1 January 1584 and Shrove Tuesday, 3 March 1584. Performance at Blackfriars would not have preceded court performance by very long, for these supposed 'rehearsals' could not be allowed to deprive the queen of seeing the plays while they were still fresh and much talked about.

3. SOURCES AND TRADITIONS

Lyly's choice of legend for his second play represents both a continuity and a departure from his manner of proceeding in *Campaspe*. He turns once again to a historical and partly legendary figure of classical antiquity, one whose greatness might serve as a compliment to Queen Elizabeth, and, more particularly, one whose self-mastery in an affair of the heart might flatter Elizabeth as the Virgin Queen among her adoring courtiers. The choice of a woman as his central figure gives Lyly an obvious advantage in psychology over his portrayal of Alexander; no matter how fond Elizabeth may have been of comparing herself to Alexander, Caesar and other male rulers of the past, the portrait of a woman ruler triumphing over erotic passion gains in immediacy and relevance to the occasion of court performance.[15]

Alexander's encounter with Apelles and Campaspe was well known, and the names of these three figures occur with notable frequency in *Euphues*; whether or not Lyly actually began writing *Campaspe* while he was still at work on *Euphues*, as Bond speculates, he certainly was aware of this story. Sappho's love for Phao or Phaon, on the other hand, is a relatively obscure legend, one that appears nowhere amidst the vast eclectic learning of *Euphues*. It is as though Lyly consciously sought out a narrative suited to his purposes, one that would improve on his *Campaspe* by centring on a regal woman who must grapple with an unfortunate passion. If this is so, the initial conception of the play is one of analogy, even allegory: the fable is chosen less for its intrinsic significance than for its potential application.

Lyly seems unaware of, or uninterested in, much of the historical information that we possess today about Sappho. *The Oxford Companion to Classical Literature* and the *Dictionary of Greek and Roman Biography and Mythography*[16] report that she was born at Mitylene, or perhaps Eressos, on the island of Lesbos in the eastern Aegean, probably in the seventh century B.C. She was of good parentage, and was a contemporary of the poet Alcaeus. Forced to leave Lesbos, perhaps because of political difficulties, she may have gone to Sicily and died there. Apparently she married and had a daughter, Cleis. Among her brothers was Charaxus, whom she reproached for his involvement with an Egyptian courtesan named Doricha or Rhodopis. Sappho gathered together a group of women dedicated to music and poetry, or perhaps to the worship of Aphrodite. Her own literary production included nine books of odes, epithalamia, elegies and hymns, of which one complete ode and various fragments survive. They are in a variety of metres, including the so-called Sapphic. Some appear to celebrate a passionate love for other women. Virtually none of this information makes its way into Lyly's play.

About Sappho's supposed 'Lesbianism' or 'Sapphism' in the homosexual sense, references are indeed hard to find not only in Lyly but in most writers before A. C. Swinburne and others in the late nineteenth century. The *O.E.D.*'s earliest citation for 'Lesbian' or 'Sapphism' in the homosexual sense is in 1890. If Lyly was aware of the allegation, as he probably was in view of Ovid's reference to Sappho's attraction for young women *'non sine crimine'* (*Heroides*, XV.19) and of John Donne's 'Sapho to Philaenis' (written of course after Lyly's play), he seems to have chosen to overlook the matter as entirely unsuited to his project of flattering Queen Elizabeth.

His reticence on the subject of Sappho as a poetess is perhaps more surprising. Elizabeth, like her father, Henry VIII, nurtured her self-image as a monarch with a flair for literary pursuits, and so Lyly might have been expected to capitalise on the flattering analogy. Possibly he preferred to think of rulers as patrons rather than as dabblers, as his portrait of Alexander with Apelles suggests. But the larger answer may be simply that Lyly was not interested in what he could have learned about the historical figure of Sappho. Even for the historical association of Sappho with Sicily he seems to have been indebted to a suggestion in Ovid. Lyly was primarily attracted to the Sappho of legend and poetry.

Paradoxically, one legendary source to which he turned does not actually link Sappho and Phao, though it does give information about both. Phaon or Phao is instead linked with Aphrodite or Venus. This legend may have been influenced in turn by the story of Aphrodite and Adonis; indeed, Karl Otfried Müller argues that 'Phaon' or 'Phaethon' is simply another name for Adonis.[17] At any rate, Lyly found the story of the encounter between Venus and Phaon in the *Varia Historia* of Aelian or Claudius Aelianus (fl. *c*. A.D. 200). This author of *De Natura Animalium*, to whom Lyly often turned, as he did to Pliny, for abstruse lore in natural history, put together in his *Varia Historia* a compendium of broad but uncritical learning about political, literary and legendary celebrities of the classical world. Included in it is the following account of Phaon (XII.18):

> That Phaon was of a fair complexion.
> Phaon, a proper youth, excelling all other in favour and comeliness, was hidden of Venus among long lettuce [original text: lettisse] which sprung up and grew very rankly. Some hold opinion that this Phaon was a ferryman, and that he used that trade of life and exercise. So it fortuned that Venus had occasion to pass over the water, whom he, not so readily as willingly, took by the hand and received into his wherry and carried her over with as great diligence as he could for his life, not knowing all this while what she was. For which dutiful service at that instant exhibited, Venus bestowed upon him an alabaster box full of ointment for her ferryage [ferrage in Q1], wherewith Phaon, washing and scouring his skin, had not his fellow in fairness of favour and beautiful complexion alive, insomuch that the women of Mitylene were inflamed with the love of Phaon, his comeliness did so kindle their affections.[18]

Aelian adds that Phaon was afterwards taken in adultery and killed. The account makes no mention of Sappho, but is set in Mitylene. Aelian reports in his next paragraph of Sappho:

> Plato, the son of Aristo, numbereth Sappho, the versifier, and daughter of Scamandronymus, among such as were wise, learned and skilful. I hear also that there was another Sappho in Lesbos, which was a strong whore and an arrant strumpet.[19]

Aelian's reference to two Sapphos, one a poetess and one a whore, may reflect a male Athenian difficulty in coming to terms with the frankness of Sappho's lyric poetry; in many later writers, Sappho the poet is represented as a courtesan. Aelian here makes no explicit connection between his accounts of Phao and Sappho, but he does present them in such a way that Lyly would have found them in adjacent paragraphs, both figures associated with Mitylene and Lesbos.

Lyly could have encountered this story of Phao and Venus connected with that of Phao and Sappho in Palaephatus' *De fabulosis narrationibus* (*Peri Apistōn* in Greek), a widely used compilation of Greek mythography that was surely available to him.[20] As Bond says (1.157), one occasionally wonders if Lyly may not have used the succinct accounts provided by this and other convenient reference works, though he is very likely to have known Aelian and of course Ovid as well.

The legend of Sappho's love for Phao or Phaon seems to have appeared first in several lost Attic comedies,[21] but it is not until Epistle xv of Ovid's *Heroides*, 'Sappho to Phaon', that the story becomes available to Lyly in literary form. Here Lyly not only could learn the narrative details of the legendary connection between Sappho and Phao, but, more importantly, could also read an impassioned fictional account of the heroine's suffering. As is his manner, Ovid allows the woman to speak directly of her lost hopes, her fallen fortune, her fatal infatuation for a man who no longer cares for her. To avoid Sappho's love, Phaon has fled to Sicily and Mount Etna. The speaker, consumed in more than Etna's fires, takes no consolation in music or in her own poetry. No more is she moved by guilty love of the Lesbian dames as of yore. She sees herself as greater than Daphne or Ariadne in that they were not lyric poets; she believes herself worthy of comparison with her fellow islander Alcaeus, of world-wide fame, and yet has been deserted by the man she loves. She concedes her inferior stature and beauty, but pleads with Venus to help. Her life has had many sadnesses—the early loss of her parents, a brother, an infant daughter—but none so great as the loss of Phaon. Warning the maidens of Sicily to beware of the tempter now in their midst, she resolves to throw herself off the cliff at Leucadia (off the coast of Epirus). She will die while careless Phaon stays.

It was apparently common to read ll. 51-2 of this Epistle as indicating that Sappho followed Phaon to Sicily, although by no means obligatory in the text itself. Ovid's poem was translated by George Turberville in 1567, although Lyly surely must have known the original. In any event, the combination of Aelian's and Ovid's narrations gave Lyly many of the essentials of his dramatic situation: a high-born and cultivated woman protagonist torn by an unhappy love, the suggestion of a setting in Sicily (though it is Phaon alone who certainly goes there in Ovid), Venus' gift of extraordinary beauty to a ferryman with whom she has taken passage, the infatuation of other women besides Sappho with Phaon and the lack of romantic completion in the love relationship.

Lyly's changes are no less compelling. Sappho is a queen, no poetess. There is no mention of guilty love for other women. Phao is far below Sappho in station; the difference in rank between ruler and subject, a plausible deduction from Phaon's position in Aelian as ferryman used to a 'trade of life and exercise', is much emphasised in the play. Phao is not only beloved, as in the classical sources, but is himself in love, with no suggestion of the insolent masculine care-lessness so characteristic of Ovid's deserting men. As a consequence, Lyly's Sappho must learn to master her own affection for a willing Phao instead of suffering the pangs of rejection.

The symbolic contest between Sappho and Venus for the control of passionate feeling in love is new in the play; Ovid and Aelian intro-duce Venus in a conventional role only as the goddess of love and provider of physical beauty. Venus' motive in bestowing beauty on Phao as a means of entrapping Sappho in amorous longing is an in-vention of Lyly's. So is the inclusion of Cupid, of Vulcan and of the Cyclopes. Lyly adds philosophers and courtiers to the court of Sappho so that they may debate issues already aired in *Campaspe*, and in turn parodies their debate with the pert badinage of servants. Sappho's ladies-in-waiting are perhaps hinted at in Aelian's women of Mitylene and their infatuation with Phaon, but fill an expanded role in a discussion of court manners and feminine experiences in love. The ancient Sibylla to whom Phao turns for advice is derived from Ovid's *Metamorphoses* (XIV.130ff.) and perhaps from Virgil's *Aeneid* (VI.8ff.), but the inclusion of her in the present story is new, while her role as an adviser in love is indebted to medieval traditions of the court of love.[22]

Some of what Lyly added to Aelian and Ovid raises the question, pointed out to me by my colleague Janel Mueller, as to whether Lyly knew Euripides' *Hippolytus*. That play depicts the passionate suffer-ing in love of a queen, Phaedra, for her chaste stepson, Hippolytus. The intense passion is inflicted upon Phaedra by Aphrodite, who begins the play by boasting of her might amongst humanity and her determination to humble those who hold out against her, especially Hippolytus. Phaedra's situation and her symptoms anticipate those of Sappho in Lyly's play: the sudden sickness, the bitter groans, the withdrawal from company, the unwillingness to have her attendants know of her condition, the delirious raving.

Much of this is of course inherent in any literary portrayal of lovesickness, but the parallels between Lyly and Euripides are at times verbally suggestive. Compare, for example, Sappho's 'Heighho. O Mileta, help to rear me up my bed; my head lies too low. You pester me with too many clothes', etc. (III.iii.81ff.) with Phaedra's 'Lift me up! Lift my head up! All the muscles are slack and useless. . . . Take away this hat! It is too heavy to wear', etc. (ll. 198ff.).[23] Sappho is here addressing her woman, Mileta; Phaedra is addressing her nurse. Earlier in Euripides, the Chorus speaks of Phaedra as lying 'on her bed within the house, / within the house and fever wracks her' (ll. 131–3). She has eaten nothing for three days. 'Unhappy is the compound of woman's nature', the Chorus concludes (l. 161). The Chorus of palace women gathers solicitously to see the nurse bring Phaedra forth to them, much as Sappho's women gather around her, suggesting the possibility that Lyly's scenes with the court women were generated by the Euripidean prototype. Phaedra longs for 'a draught of fresh spring water' (l. 209); compare Sappho's pleading to Venus that 'my chamber have I ceiled with thy cockleshells, and dipped thy sponge into the freshest waters' (III.iii.93–5). Euripides repeatedly insists on Phaedra's unwillingness to speak of her condition (ll. 268–74, 298–310, 520, 564–5, 686–9, 710–12 and 715–22); compare Sappho at III.iii.116–22. Euripides' passage of stichomythia in which the Nurse begs Phaedra to indicate how she can be helped, building up to the name 'Hippolytus' as the answer to the mystery (ll. 325–52), is suggestive of Lyly's stichomythic dialogue between Sappho and her women in which the proposed remedy to Sappho's symptoms is 'Phao, Phao, ah Phao!' (III.iii.1–29). Hippolytus speaks in a misogynistic vein that Lyly could have found congenial to his purposes in showing the bitterness of Phao's condition.

Hippolytus is of course a tragedy, but Lyly's play too ends in a stalemate that is hardly satisfactory in terms of the normal expectations of comedy. Phaedra's resolve to resist the passion of which she is a victim and thus choose 'good name rather than life' (l. 774) resembles Sappho's self-sacrificing decision to put erotic entanglement behind her. Similarly, the ultimately triumphant and vindicating role for Artemis in Euripides' play is suggestive of the kind of victory Sappho is allowed to achieve. Artemis repudiates the hated goddess Aphrodite and offers consolation to those who practise piety; Aphrodite will have to pay for her petty vengeance.

Despite these resemblances, the case for Lyly's indebtedness to
Euripides remains inconclusive. He could have found in Seneca's
Phaedra (in the Latin text or in John Studley's translation of 1567,
called *Hippolytus*) much of what is suggestive in Euripides' play—
the suffering from passion, a stichomythic exchange with the nurse,
choric acknowledgement of Venus or Aphrodite as the cause of amorous obsession—even if at times Euripides' play is verbally closer
to Lyly and more concrete in its depiction of Aphrodite and Artemis.
Although Lyly presumably had some Greek, and although at least
seven Latin translations of Euripides' tragedies were published on the
Continent (including one at Antwerp in 1571) before 1584, we are
reminded by T. W. Baldwin[24] that even Seneca was not a usual text
in the grammar schools. For all Lyly's presumed accomplishment as
a classicist, we see him repeatedly turning to Erasmus when he might
have consulted the classical originals (see below), and we have even
less reason to be certain that he read whole texts in Greek. Sappho's
love symptoms are for the most part sufficiently generic not to require
any particular classical source.

Whether Lyly knew Sappho's 'Hymn to Aphrodite', quoted in full
by Dionysius of Halicarnassus, is more uncertain still. This is the first
of the two poems that began to be collected under Sappho's name and
printed as an addendum to sixteenth-century editions of Anacreon.
The editions, beginning in 1554 and 1556, regularly include a Latin
translation. Even if texts were available, however, Lyly shows no sign
in his play of having read the poem. The lyric depicts Sappho as a
worshipper of Aphrodite and as favoured by the serenely confident
goddess of love. Lyly's portrayal of Venus is markedly different:
Sappho deplores and eventually repudiates her enslavement to the
emotion that Venus has inflicted upon her, while Venus is the double-
dealing and vengeful goddess as in Euripides' and Seneca's plays.
The birds yoked to Aphrodite's chariot, mentioned by Lyly (see
III.iii.90–2n.), are a commonplace of Renaissance iconography.
Only Lyly's classical learning, and his interest in Cupid that might
conceivably have led him to Anacreon and to Sappho, can argue in
favour of his having known the poem.

To follow Lyly in his gathering of disparate materials is to gain a
picture not only of his extensive reading but also of his art of play
construction. His characterisations of Venus, Cupid and Vulcan, for
example, are drawn from various sources and traditions in such a way
as to refashion them for his story while at the same time playfully
capitalising on his audience's knowledge of legends about the classical

gods. His Venus is born of the foam of the sea (I.i.69), as Lyly knew
from his reading in Ovid's *Heroides* and indeed from a favourite
quotation in William Lilly and John Colet's *A Short Introduction of
[Latin] Grammar*. He seems to have drawn on Plutarch, Erasmus and
Alciati, and perhaps on Botticelli's painting of 'The Birth of Venus'
or on a description of the famous lost painting of Apelles on the same
subject, for an iconographical tradition associating Venus with the
cockleshell or scallop shell and the sponge (III.iii.93–5), one that
portrays Venus as standing with a tortoise under her foot (as she is
also described in *Euphues*, II.98, l. 21). The play alludes humorously
to the story in the *Odyssey* (VIII) of how Hephaestus captured
Aphrodite and Ares at their love-making in a net, to the delight of the
Olympian gods (I.i.73). Birds are an important part of the iconography of Venus: swans to draw her chariot, doves to signify loyal
affection, sparrows to signify lechery (II.iv.26–36, III.iii.90–2,
IV.iv.38). The peacock suggests feminine vanity as well (V.i.24).
Lyly's Venus displays all the complex states of feeling suggested in
these images, and is as much a jealous, scheming woman as she is the
goddess of love. Her motive against Sappho arises out of her character
as well as from the theme of conflict between chaste and erotic affection. The image is at once familiar in its various parts and new in its
aggregate design, allowing Lyly to manipulate convention in such a
way as to concoct for his audience a new and flattering mythology.
The goddess of love must yield sway to the Virgin Queen.

Cupid is similarly a composite of recognisable features introduced
into a new context. He is armed with bow and arrows, is presumably
winged, and refers to his own blindness as the cause of his erratic aim
(IV.i.11), though the staging does not seem to require, as in at least
one earlier play, that he be led about (see I.i.20.1 and n.). The play
refers to Cupid's love for Psyche, as told in Apuleius' *Golden Ass*
(IV.ii.15). This is the Cupid of Roman and Renaissance mythology,
not mentioned in Homer (though Hesiod does speak of him as 'fairest
of the deathless gods'), identified with the Greek Eros but now the
son of Venus rather than her companion as in early accounts. At the
same time Cupid's mischievousness is newly presented in a way that
must have interested Shakespeare (compare Puck's 'Cupid is a
knavish lad', in *A Midsummer Night's Dream*, III.ii.440), and his
changing of loyalties from Venus to Sappho is an essential part of
Lyly's updated mythology. Lyly gives Cupid a new father, Vulcan,
rather than the Mercury of mythology, perhaps in order to strengthen
Vulcan's new and unexpected role in this play.

The legends available to Lyly about Vulcan (associated with Hephaestus and known too as Mulciber) were many and varied. The more received account told of Hephaestus' having been thrown out of heaven by Jupiter for taking his mother Juno's side, and of breaking a leg as he fell on the Aegean isle of Lemnos (see the *Iliad*, I.590ff.). Elsewhere in the *Iliad*, on the other hand (e.g., XVIII.395ff.), Homer portrays him as having been lame from birth and cast out by his mother. Lyly accentuates the lameness (I.i.29–30, III.ii.60) and his cuckoldry, making Vulcan into a comic wittol husband of a beautiful and seductive wife (as suggested in the *Odyssey*, VIII). This emphasis underscores the contrast between Sappho's chaste affection and the erotic entanglement represented by Venus. The marital relationship is seldom depicted by Lyly with sympathy.

Vulcan's Cyclopes are no less eclectically portrayed. Virgil's *Aeneid* (e.g., III) offered Lyly authority for placing them in Sicily, as he does in this play, but the allusion to their 'Lemnian hammers' (IV.iv.37) recalls the Aegean location of the Cyclopes referred to in the *Iliad* (I.593). Mount Etna in Sicily was only one volcanic mountain that suggested itself as Vulcan's workshop. Lyly's stage setting for Vulcan's forge in IV.iv may owe something to the blacksmith's shop provided for Mulciber in an earlier boys' play, *Thersites* (1537), not only in the stage structure but in the mock-heroic business of providing weapons for the play's *miles gloriosus* hero. The odd marriage of classical mythology and schoolboy high jinks, so essential to Lyly's brand of comedy, is especially evident in the scenes of Vulcan, his prentice Callipho and his the other Cyclopes (who were probably played by boys even if, as has been suggested, Callisto himself was performed by an adult).

Lyly's approach to mythology and classical tradition through Ovid is evident everywhere in the play. It provides the basis for Sappho's love (*Heroides*, XV) and for Sibylla's detailed account of her being wooed by Phoebus Apollo (*Metamorphoses*, XIV). Lyly alludes familiarly to other Ovidian tales of metamorphosis, including (implicitly at least) Apollo and Daphne, Io and the gadfly, Adonis, Jupiter and Danae, and other of Jupiter's amorous encounters. Several times he recalls the story of Theseus in Daedalus' labyrinth. Other mythographers and encyclopaedists may have given him details about stories such as that of Jason and Medea (III.iv.62–3). Lyly must have had Ovid's *Ars Amatoria* and to some extent the *Remedia Amoris* in mind when he wrote Sibylla's advice to Phao on the practical arts of wooing (II.iv.61–82 and 85–134; see also III.i.19–20). Scattered indebtednesses to Virgil's *Aeneid* are apparent in the prophecies of Sibylla, in the description of Vulcan's Cyclopes, in an allusion to the feathered goddess Fortune (II.i.119), and perhaps in a reference to the wooden horse of Troy, though some of this information was also standard knowledge. Indebtedness to Homer is not always ascertainable, since many stories were available elsewhere, but Lyly does in any event refer to Homeric traditions about Vulcan, Penelope, Ulysses and jealous Juno, among others. He seems to have turned to Plautus' *Pseudolus* for the name of Callipho—it does not appear among those of the Cyclopes given in the *Aeneid*, VIII.425—and to have learned much from Plautus (as well as from Nicholas Udall) about the characterisation of clever servants.

Pliny and Aelian, and especially Erasmus's and John Heywood's collections of adages and proverbs that made extensive use of such earlier authorities, served Lyly in another important way, as repositories of the fabulous lore so essential to his Euphuistic comparisons. The range of reference is impressive. Bees are a favourite image. Deprived of their sting, they make no honey; dying with honey, they are buried in harmony; cloyed with honey, they feed on wax; full of honey, they prick most deeply. Honey itself rankles when it is eaten for pleasure. The famous honey of Hybla is associated with Sicily, where the action of the play is set. Other animal legends from proverb lore concern the bear, wasps that feed on serpents to make their stings more venomous, the halcyon and its fabulous nest, serpents that feed on fennel, and the aegisthus bird that never sleeps for fear of its hen. The choice of images thus far has much to do with stings, venom and aggression, though the fish called garus is able to heal all sickness so long as it is not named while it is being applied. Here Lyly is indebted to Erasmus's mistranslation from Pliny: see III.iii.38–9n.

Herbs warn against fading beauty, like the polion, whose leaves are white in the morning but blue before night, or counsel the advantages of age, like cotonea, which is sweetest when it is eldest. Minerals are noted for their exotic qualities, such as the crysocoll, a liquid running through veins of gold. Peoples inhabit far-off and unknown worlds, like the Micanyans who are born bald or the Arabians who, being stuffed with perfumes, burn hemlock, a rank poison.

Lyly's interest in exotic lore is not limited to Pliny, Aelian, Heywood and Erasmus. Elizabethan books on natural history, such as *Batman upon Bartholome* (1582), or, as it was earlier titled, *Bartholomaeus de Proprietatibus Rerum* (first published in Latin in Basle about 1470, published by Winkyn de Worde about 1495 in an English translation by John of Trevisa, d. 1402, and then published by Thomas Berthelet in 1535), as well as later works that reflect traditions Lyly knew, such as Edward Topsell's *The History of Four-Footed Beasts and Serpents* (1607, revised and enlarged in 1658, taken principally from the *Historiae Animalium* of Conrad Gesner), and Thomas Muffet's *The Theatre of Insects* (1634, republished in 1658), mingled observable fact with fanciful legend in a way that is notably characteristic of Lyly's style.

Thus we hear of griffins, the phoenix, turtledoves, eagles that build their nests in the sun and bite wormwood and are never struck by lightning, croaking ravens, shrieking owls, swallows, the stock-dove, the wood-quest, ants with wings, caterpillars, flies that die on honeysuckle and become poison to bees, molehills, coneys, the lamb and the fox, hemlock, cedar, juniper, oaks and acorns, myrtle, water boughs, the medlar, cammocks or crooked trees, fig trees, olive trees that are never struck by lightning, mandragola, heartsease, lettuce, nettles and roses, lunary, bugloss (a medicinal herb), another herb that is saltier the further it grows from the sea, sparks and flames, eclipses, and stones that are hardened by hammering. For the legend of the 'fly tarantula' whose venom nothing can expel but music (IV.iii.74–6), Lyly may have turned to Sir Thomas Hoby's translation of *The Courtier*, 1569; for his description of abeston (asbestos) as never cooling once it is heated, Lyly may have consulted *Bartholomaeus de Proprietatibus Rerum* or Solinus. In some cases Lyly appears to invent his own legendary natural history, especially (as Bond observes) in the wake of a citation from Erasmus or Pliny; thus his abstruse accounts of salurus, asolis, Syrian mud, Lydian steele, anyta and perillus are dressed in seeming authority but seem in fact to have no other source than the literary type to which all such fabulous citations belong.

Lyly's eclectic delight in the learning of his age extends, like that of Robert Burton after him, into fields other than natural history. He uses the language of Renaissance faculty psychology when he diagnoses gall as the source of anger (III.iii.145–6) or ascribes sleeplessness and feverishness in love to a dryness of the brain (III.iv.52; III.ii.16–21). The four elements of earth, air, fire and water are essential to an understanding of medicine and diet (III.ii.23–6; III.iii.105–6). Lyly's dream lore explores the full range of Elizabethan attitudes towards dreaming as physiologically induced, symbolic or prognosticatory (IV.iii.49–51). Lyly's many songs, and a passing reference to the vibrating of sympathetic strings (IV.iii.83–5), bespeak his acquaintance with music. He shares with his audience an implicit knowledge of the various ages of the world, of gold, silver, bronze, and iron or lead (I.iii.37).

This sort of pleasure in eclectic wisdom inevitably draws Lyly to the proverb, not simply as a source of natural lore as already noted but also for its sententious wit. He cultivates this interest with his usual free-ranging and idiosyncratic erudition, relying to be sure on conventional proverbial utterance but also turning to authorities like Erasmus and John Heywood. His favourite collection is Erasmus's *Adagia*, but he also finds sustenance in the *Similia* or *Parabolae*. For some of his proverbial lore he must also have known Erasmus's own sources in Pliny, Plutarch and the like. Heywood's *Proverbs* were certainly available to him. Whether derived from books or not, Lyly's proverbs capitalise on the same antithetical wit and moral appeal to authority that are to be found in his allusions to natural history.

One other source is so pervasive in Lyly that it is not always easy to identify: the author's experience with academic life, at the university and in his own dramaturgic relationship with the children of Oxford's company. Continuing his dialogue between university and court begun in *Euphues* (Athens and Naples) and in *Campaspe* (the philosophers, and especially Diogenes, versus the officers who serve Alexander), Lyly devotes considerable attention in *Sappho and Phao* to the debate between Pandion the scholar and Trachinus the courtier, as well as to a parody of that same debate among their pages and Callipho, one of the Cyclopes. The choice of Syracuse as the play's setting is partly owing to Ovid's *Heroides* and to Virgil's *Aeneid*, as we have seen, but a more essential reason may well be that Syracuse was known as an ancient centre of learning and aristocratic patronage of the arts. The names of Plato and Pindar were associated with Syracuse, and Richard Edwards's *Damon and Pythias* (1565?), even while offering an unflattering portrait of the tyranny for which Syracuse was also known (Dionysius, Hiero), introduced Syracuse into courtly boys' drama as a classical setting for a dialogue between scholars and rulers. Syracuse is thus a natural extension of Athens in *Campaspe*, with philosophers and kings in debate with one another, as in Edwards's play. Athens is often explicitly or implicitly at hand in *Sappho and Phao*. The Blackfriars Prologue appeals to the theatres of Athens and Rome for authority in banishing apish actions and immodesty from the stage, and in I.ii we learn that Pandion has just arrived in Syracuse from Athens. 'In Athens you have but tombs, we in court the bodies,' Trachinus admonishes his scholarly friend (I.ii.20).

In *Euphues*, Athens is transparently a substituted name for the

English universities, especially in the satire directed against decadent living among academics. In *Sappho and Phao* the laughter is more genial and the target more general. Vices and virtues at court and university are antithetically equal, as later in Touchstone's debate with Corin about court versus country (*As You Like It*, III.ii). The iniquity of flatterers is set off against the pedantry and otherworldliness of scholars, just as, in Criticus' and Molus' below-stairs version of the same debate, a square die in a page's pocket is avowed to be as decent as a square cap on a graduate's head (I.iii.14–15). Lyly jokes wryly about the spareness of Molus' 'commons in Athens' as compared with the luxurious 'diet in court' (I.iii.2), from the point of view of one who had known both. Lyly not only draws on the contrast he had experienced between Oxford and London, investing some of his own perspective in the character of Pandion,[25] but also capitalises on the details of Latin grammar and rhetoric for some of his best humorous effects. His pages continually indulge in the chop-logic of syllogism with which Lyly was unavoidably familiar through his own education and perhaps his experience with the boy actors. Scholars are 'only plodders at *ergo*, whose wits are clapped up with our books' (I.iii.16–18), and so Molus undertakes with splendid comic ineptitude to construct and deny arguments, to prove through syllogism, to affirm conclusions and deny antecedents (II.iii; III.ii). That Callipho, the simple blacksmith of Vulcan, is able to 'refel' Molus at his own game offers its own comment on what Lyly had learned at school.

4. ALLEGORY

Lyly plainly intended his dramatic portrait of Sappho as a compliment to Queen Elizabeth, before whom the play was presented at court; although the play has other interests as well, Lyly's dramatic retelling of his many sources keeps this overriding consideration in mind. May he not then have used contemporary history as his most important source, relating through allegory an actual courtship in which Elizabeth triumphed over the entanglements of love? Sappho's obscure dream (IV.iii), like that of Cynthia in *Endymion*, seems to beg its audience to discern topical application; Sibylla enigmatically warns Phao against courtly aspiration and intrigue (II.1.140–57) in terms that seem to go beyond Phao's own situation; the observations of Trachinus and Pandion about a princely tree attacked by blasts, worms and caterpillars (I.ii.37–53) are plainly critical of flattery and suspicion in the courts of princes; and the play's Epilogue expresses concern lest the auditors, entangled in a 'labyrinth of conceits', might misconstrue what they have seen through 'rash oversights'.

Historical criticism has indeed proposed an answer for these apparent puzzles: if Sappho is Elizabeth, then Phao must be the Duc d'Alençon, younger brother of the Duc d'Anjou who had wooed Elizabeth before. Alençon's suit, seriously renewed in 1578 at the instigation of Catherine de' Medici, served as the focus of delicate and prolonged negotiations between France and England. These negotiations were clearly designed by Elizabeth as a counterweight to her struggles with Philip of Spain, with whom also she had entertained the possibility of marriage. Whether serious or not in personal terms, the proposed match with Alençon had the status of state business and was much talked about at court. Alençon, the little 'Monsieur', was far from handsome, but Elizabeth had deigned to say in 1579 that 'she had never seen a man who pleased her so well, never one whom she could so willingly make her husband'.[26] Nothing came of it, and on 6 February 1582 Alençon left England for good to assume the nominal sovereignty of the United Provinces in the Netherlands offered him by the Prince of Orange. He died on 9 June 1584, after an unsuccessful military attempt on the liberties of Antwerp in June of 1583.[27]

To Bond, following up on Fleay's suggestion,[28] the identification with Alençon explains a number of the play's most arresting features: the cautions of Prologue and Epilogue against overinterpretation; Sappho's dream; Sibylla's warning to Phao against ambition, which is 'appropriate only to Alençon's career at Court, and is not fulfilled in the play';[29] Trachinus' and Pandion's animadversions against worms and caterpillars attacking a princely tree; Sibylla's closing observation to Phao that 'destiny calleth thee as well from Sicily as from love', in which there is presumably an allusion to Alençon's installation as Duke of Brabant and his oath of allegiance as sovereign of the United Provinces;[30] Lyly's suppression of what he learned from his sources (especially Ovid) about Sappho's poetic fame, her shortness of stature and her dark features; conversely Lyly's emphatic portrayal of Sappho as a queen surrounded by her court; and of course the story of Phao's invitation to court, Sappho's struggle with her emotions, and her conclusive victory over eros. The reading has been endorsed by Felix Schelling, Albert Feuillerat, Tucker Brooke, Evelyn May Albright and others.[31] Frederick Boas wonders if the play does not serve the interests of one of Elizabeth's English suitors, such as Leicester, and Gertrude Reese similarly proposes that Lyly is expressing resentment of a French match and joy at Alençon's departure.[32] Bond speculates that Catherine de' Medici may stand behind the figure of Sibylla, and supposes it likely that an original once existed for the witty Mileta and her flirtatiousness with Phao. Fleay, as we have seen, identifies Pandion with Lyly himself.[33]

Despite this unanimity of opinion among many historical critics, and the absence of any rival topical interpretation, the Alençon claim seems impossible. A topical theory of dating has to suppose a court performance on 27 February in 1582, a scant three weeks after Alençon's departure from England, and must therefore argue that writing, theatrical preparation, and perhaps even performances at Blackfriars took place while the affair of Alençon had not yet ended (see 'Date', above). If Lyly's intent was to capitalise on feelings against the proposed French match, he has made Phao surprisingly sympathetic.[34] Whatever Elizabeth may have said about Alençon, Phao's gift of extraordinary beauty would seem oddly and even ludicrously out of place in view of Alençon's ugliness. No historical person has been proposed for Venus as Sappho's rival, whereas for an audience interested in guessing at the meaning of a *roman à clef* this sort of rivalry would be a prime matter of titillation.

Most tellingly, perhaps, the portrait of Sappho in love is hardly flattering if applied to any particular incident. Sappho must compensate for Phao's reticence by a barely disguised hinting at her own passionate feeling (III.iv.42–88). With her women she is moody, restless, demanding; in soliloquy and song she is frantic and desperate (III.iii). Even though Sappho eventually conquers love's tyranny, like Alexander, the suggestion that Elizabeth went through this kind of lovesickness for Alençon would be tactless and inappropriate. Nor could England's queen be supposed to have suffered clinically thus for any of her other wooers, English or otherwise. Elizabeth's reluctance to accept advice on the marriage question, and indeed her readiness to interrupt or abruptly leave any sermon or other utterances deemed offensive, were well enough known to deter even her most intrepid critics, let alone those like Lyly who sought her support.[35]

If on the other hand we view Lyly's play as an allegory of love, these difficulties begin to disappear. Lyly's alteration of his sources requires nothing more topical than to say, as we must, that Sappho is intended to flatter Elizabeth. The portrait is scarcely more personal than that of Alexander in *Campaspe*. A monarch, adored by her subjects and drawn briefly into a strong affection for one of them, chooses singleness of life as best befitting her responsibilities to the entire kingdom. Sappho is portrayed as queen rather than as poet to accentuate her royal function, and the enhancement of her beauty as compared with Ovid's portrait is part of the conventional and outrageous flattery Elizabeth came to expect everywhere. Phao is beautiful to make him worthy of love by so excellent a queen. Phao's ultimate destiny, that of worshipping Sappho from a distance, 'my loyalty unspotted though unrewarded' (V.iii.22), justly portrays the kind of acquiescing and self-abnegating loyalty Elizabeth encouraged in those who served her; it is the kind of Platonic love between grateful subject and graceful ruler we find again in Endymion's selfless service to Cynthia. As in *Endymion*, the political nature of the allegory of love acts to discourage rather than to encourage particular claims on Elizabeth's affection. Lyly's portrait centres on Elizabeth but is generic.

The role of Venus in *Sappho and Phao*, for which the proposed historical equation offers no key, is essential to an understanding of the play's allegory of love. Venus' role is complex, perhaps even inconsistent: she acts at times like an emotional woman, at times like the classical deity, at times like the allegorical figure of the Queen of Love. Nevertheless, as Bernard Huppé argues, the allegorical meaning of her unsuccessful attempt to ensnare Sappho is clear enough: it is 'the story of the conquest by a great queen of the urgings of passionate love, her steadfast refusal to accept anything but true spiritual love, a marriage of true minds'.[36] As in all allegories, Venus is a fictional representation of an idea or emotion, not an external foe who may be blamed for failure but a distillation of the power of love as it operates in the human heart. The allegorist invents visible things to express immaterial fact.[37] If Sappho were to be conquered by Venus, the meaning would be that Sappho has succumbed to her own passion.

Lyly's portrayal of Venus embodies the misogynistic proposition, often stated in the play, that any woman will yield in time, and that if Phao uses the arts of seduction set forth in Ovid's *Ars Amatoria* and urged on him by Sibylla he is sure to succeed. Yet Phao is in no way Sappho's equal; if she were to accept his love, she would be succumbing passionately to outward beauty only. Clearly she must hold to the ideal of a marriage of true minds and must therefore heroically resolve not to yield; it would shame her to 'embrace one so mean' (IV.i.18–19). Her incomparable superiority to Venus is in affirming a virtue without which true love is impossible.[38] The affirmation is crucial for Lyly, not merely as flattery to Elizabeth but more broadly as a way of idealising love and womanhood, of countering the seductive image of woman (and of man's basely passionate nature as well) with a spiritualised vision of woman as deserving of man's worship.

Lyly's problem as allegorical dramatist was to devise forms of expression in drama through which he might convey the complex emotions of love. Drama relies on external and visible behaviour; love is pre-eminently internal and intimate. Lyly did of course have numerous models for the application of allegory to the experience of love. He knew the medieval and Renaissance traditions of allegorising Ovid, as in Arthur Golding's Preface to his sixteenth-century translation of *Metamorphoses*, where Phaeton is equated with 'the nature of blind ambition', Daphne with 'the mirror of chastity', and the like. For Golding, the pagan deities (including Venus and Cupid) are not gods but rather symbols of 'Some further things and purposes by those devices meant'.[39] Lyly knew pageants, royal entries and other public entertainments that ceaselessly glorified the Tudor monarchy in the person of Arthur or apostrophised Elizabeth as Truth or Astraea.[40] Allegorical poems like *Le Chasteau d'Amour* created elaborate external forms for the vicissitudes of courtship, and morality drama brought such figures as Contrition and Lust-in-Liking onstage to externalise the states of mind of the protagonist. The popular literary genre of dream allegory gave Lyly a precedent and model not only for his symbolic dreams but also for his conceiving the whole of *Sappho and Phao* as though it were Queen Elizabeth's own dream allegory: 'I on knee for all, entreat that your Highness imagine yourself to be in a deep dream that, staying the conclusion, in your rising your Majesty vouchsafe but to say, "And so you awaked"' (Prologue at Court).[41] Still, the devices of allegory available to Lyly in this manifold tradition were more proficient in symbolising conflict between rival ideologies than in capturing the feeling of what it is like to be in love. As Robert Y. Turner rightly insists, English comedy did not really dramatise love in any psychological sense before Lyly began writing plays.[42]

Given the kinds of allegory he knew, what means were at Lyly's disposal to express through outward gesture and dialogue what the heart feels? The available solutions, according to Turner, were not quite satisfactory; characters might simply assert their significance in the conventional language of allegory, or conversely the action might take on a momentum of its own essentially devoid of inward illumination. The latter danger is evident in comedies of romantic adventure in the 1570s, such as *Clyomon and Clamydes* or *Common Conditions*, with their tales of separation and hair's-breadth escape. Lyly's art is seemingly closer to the former model, that of didactic allegorical instruction, as when, in *Sappho and Phao*, the court ladies suggest through their various dreams their varying and typical attitudes towards romantic love (IV.iii), or when Venus explains to Cupid the allegorical significance of six arrows made in Vulcan's forge (V.i). Sibylla uses all the Ovidian commonplaces of advice in love when she warns Phao against ambition or coaches him in the rules of courtly wooing and gamesmanship. Yet Lyly's use of schematic dialogue of this kind, more literary than dramatic, is seemingly part of a conscious strategy on his part to go beyond such traditional allegory; he presents to us the highly formal and emblematic world of allegorical representation that he knew so well in order that we can measure by contrast the real innovation of his more successful love dialogue.

In other words, even while *Sappho and Phao* remains a love allegory in which characters like Venus and Cupid abstractly represent states of mind in the play's central figures, this comedy manages for the first time on the English stage to crystallise into outward gestures what is felt deeply within, in the experience of love.[43] It does so, as Turner explains, by exploring tension, misunderstandings and the limiting qualities of ambiguous language. When Sappho and Phao meet, the social barrier between them causes them to speak enigmatically, partly from fear and partly from a sensitivity to love's delicacy. The tension between unfavourable circumstance and the lovers' unspoken desire 'creates dialogue in which each assertion is tentative and each response quivering'; though love is never mentioned directly, their conversation both poignantly and wittily 'captures an unmistakable sense of what it is like to be in love' (Turner, p. 279). We as audience understand more than the lovers can communicate to one another and are thus privileged by a kind of dramatic irony or discrepant awareness that at once detaches our feelings through knowledge of the situation and intensifies our perception of poignancy in a love that is so nearly successful and yet so impossible.

The tension between desire and prohibition generates as well a series of dramatic situations in which the limitations of language express the predicament of love. Sappho and Phao, unable to speak of love directly, must turn to the language of medicine and sickness, or speak in parables of Jason and Medea, or pun on the word *yew* (you); among her women, Sappho's talk of her discomfort repeatedly suggests hidden meaning (III.iv; III.iii). Inhibited from saying what they feel, the lovers 'dramatize by their oblique expressions both their trapped situation and the desire to break out of it' (Turner, pp. 279, 287).

That Lyly is able to convey this insight into love through stage action and dialogue, while still retaining in his play the symbolic language of formal love allegory and the conventional allegorical mode of externalised personification, is an index of the play's innovation. It is well summed up in G. Wilson Knight's tribute to Lyly as one who, with love as his whole theme, is as aware as is Spenser of its complexities, yet 'is more aware than Spenser of its inward contradictions'.[44] The interplay of innovation and convention is also suggested in Paul Olsen's comparison of Lyly and Jonson as dramatists writing for a court 'consistently interested in that art which builds its meaning from the materials of traditional emblems and allegories'.[45]

With this perspective on Lyly's reshaping of allegorical tradition, we are perhaps in a position to measure the import of dreams and other enigmatic statements in the play that seem to invite topical interpretation. Sappho's dream (IV.iii) pictures a stock-dove nesting in a tall cedar only to lose its feathers and fall to the ground, while ants and caterpillars attack the tree and strip away many of its leaves. The dreamer pities both, and takes heart at the bird's attempt to fly up again; the dreamer in fact wishes that the tree might bow to assist the bird, but wakens before this can happen. In this dream ants and caterpillars certainly suggest parasitism and factionalism at court, as do the drones or beetles creeping under the wings of the princely eagle in Cynthia's dream in *Endymion* (V.i), and Lyly's audience might well posit a criticism of those who competed for Elizabeth's favour while preying upon the commonwealth like the 'caterpillars' of *Richard II*.[46]

Such an identification militates against any interpretation that seeks to align Lyly with any particular claim to Elizabeth's favour. On the other hand, the dream is generally consistent with the love allegory in that it invites sympathy for a royal figure drawn to the love of a commoner and expresses an emotional wish that such a union were possible while insisting finally on its impossibility. Phao, like the stock-dove, is beautiful, but his very beauty is disfigured by an unwarranted ambition; his rising again is possible only when he learns, like Endymion, to worship platonically from afar. On a dramatic level the dream is expressive of Sappho's own flickering hope and final resolution; like other allegories in the play, it provides a language of indirection through which she may safely externalise inner conflict.

In a similar way, Sibylla's warnings to Phao against ambition (II.i.140ff.) have a topical cast without requiring any more detailed hypothesis than a love allegory shaped for the queen's benefit. The imagery is close to that in Sappho's dream, for Phao is cautioned not to keep company with ants that have wings. He is to avoid talk of eclipses of the sun and other such omens of royal catastrophe. He is to gaze upward in worship rather than downward in envy, and is to avoid the ambitious gesture of pointing above him. Naturally he is to expect hatred if he is favoured by a prince's affection. These prophetic utterances do exceed the nature of Phao's own thoughts at the moment he hears them, for he is not yet in love with Sappho or moved by any desire to leave his life as a ferryman. The generic character of the advice certainly invites allegorical interpretation, but not to the extent of invoking Alençon's suit, since, like Sappho's dream, the delphic wisdom has application to all princes, including Elizabeth and any or all of her courtiers. The advice is dramatically expressive of Phao's emotional situation even if he is unaware of the applicability, for the audience knows already of Venus' designs on him.

So too with delphic passages elsewhere in the play. The disapproval of Trachinus and Pandion for 'blasts and water boughs, worms and caterpillars' brought by eastern wind to attack the princely tree (I.ii) is unambiguously about flattery and deception at court, but is justified by the debate of courtier and philosopher over the merits of their respective ways of life. Phao's call to destiny at the end of the play is in keeping with Sibylla's penchant for prophetic statement and with our sense that Phao, like Endymion, is no ordinary courtier but rather the embodiment of those who will continue to worship Elizabeth even as they carry out in far-flung realms her royal commands. Even Tucker Brooke, while accepting the outline of the Alençon reading, wisely concludes as follows: 'Altogether, it seems clear that the story of the play, instead of reflecting in detail the real incidents of contemporary history, is rather a tissue of harmlessly imaginary pictures shot through with idealized references to such actual happenings as the poet might feel to be wholly devoid of offence to his royal auditress.'[47]

5. THE COMEDY OF COURTSHIP

Along with their achievement of being the first comedies in English
to evoke, beneath externally allegorised action, a deeply felt inner
emotion of love, Lyly's comedies are also the first English plays in
which love itself provides the mainspring of the comedy. In this latter
regard, *Sappho and Phao* has a particular claim to priority, since even
more than *Campaspe* it gives us a courtly world in which love is, as
Marco Mincoff says, 'at once something highly serious and extremely
frivolous'.[48] Love is the 'centre of existence' both for the wooers
themselves and for the courtiers who amuse themselves with gossip
about the emotional entanglements of great persons (p. 16). Mincoff's point is that in Lyly 'the mere fact of being in love almost is
treated as a comic situation', as indeed it is for Ovid in his *Ars
Amatoria*. Lyly's theme is the way in which love 'cuts across our little
plans and makes fools of us' (p. 15). Love is also for him an elaborate
game, something to occupy the time of a leisured but narrowly
circumscribed world at court in which the attentions paid to women
are an essential part of the courtier's self-image.

This 'love-game comedy', as David Stevenson terms it, is first
developed by Lyly in the ritualistic love-encounters of *Euphues*,
where we find the customary lovesickness, the stark contrast between
exalted Petrarchan ideals and sexual desire, the self-abasement and
betrayal, the witty duels between lovers and their ladies, the amorous
skirmishes expressed in sophisticated banter.[49] *Sappho and Phao*
makes considerable use of this tradition. Phao is nearly speechless at
his first sight of Sappho; both he and Sappho suffer the physical
anguish of lovers. Sibylla advises Phao in Ovidian fashion that love is
to be 'governed by art', that 'women desire nothing more than to have
their servants officious', that he must 'be prodigal in praises and
promises', and that he would be well advised to 'look pale and learn
to be lean, that whoso seeth thee may say the gentleman is in love'
(II.iv.61–113). The chief love relationship in *Sappho and Phao* is set
in comic perspective by our awareness of the elaborate rules supposed
to govern courtship.

At the same time, Lyly constantly undercuts the artifice of such
courtly codes by the refreshingly irreverent insights of those who find
love amusing. Sappho's lady-in-waiting, Mileta, professes to 'laugh
at that you all call love, and judge it only a word called love'
(I.iv.16–17). To her it is 'good sport' to see men vacuously falling
back on what they call good manners, 'having nothing in their

mouths but "Sweet mistress", wearing our hands out with courtly kissings when their wits fail in courtly discourses—now ruffling their hairs, now setting their ruffs, then gazing with their eyes, then sighing with a privy wring by the hand, thinking us like to be wooed by signs and ceremonies' (I.iv.38–45). She makes a blatant attempt to woo Phao (III.iv) and is understandably affronted when he adopts a chivalrous line with her. Sappho's other ladies-in-waiting all have their different experiences and attitudes in the relations of the sexes. The play offers us multiple points of view about the game of love, distancing us from it, encouraging an Ovidian comic view of its folly by means of a diverse perspective. Shakespeare's *As You Like It*, with its various views on love propounded by Orlando, Rosalind, Touchstone, Jaques and the rest, uses a similar dramatic technique.

The multiple perspective serves chiefly, through contrast, as a means of our understanding the love relationship of Sappho and Phao. They are not coy and flirtatious, like Mileta, nor driven to cynicism by hard experience like Sibylla (or Euphues). Any love affair of a monarch, reflecting as it does on Elizabeth, is necessarily of a higher order. Nonetheless their love affair is essentially comic too in Mincoff's terms; even without strutting, preening and coquetry, the comedy of their love 'lies mainly in the desperate earnestness with which the lovers pursue what is mostly a very unsuitable affair. They are at bottom only playing a game, though compelled to it by Cupid, and they are as miserable over it as any tragic hero' (p. 19). Their conversation of 'misunderstood innuendos' is enriched and complicated in comic fashion by the fact that both are 'too self-absorbed to grasp the other's meaning' (p. 18). Sappho, sustained throughout her tribulations by her dignity as queen, sees at last (though only when hit by Cupid's leaden shaft) what is ridiculous in her own behaviour. Lyly's comedy of courtship, then, points to its own solution: if erotic love is ridiculous, it must be renounced by those who cannot afford to be ridiculous and who cannot also find perfect equality in love. The ending not only flatters Elizabeth but more broadly expresses a judgement about love that is inherent in Lyly's conception of its frivolous and yet serious nature.

Comedy of this delicate sort represents a departure from the farce and slapstick characteristic of much earlier English comedy. Lyly's awareness of innovation is evident in his Blackfriars Prologue, where he speaks of an intent to 'move inward delight, not outward lightness, and to breed (if it might be) soft smiling, not loud laughing, knowing it to the wise to be as great pleasure to hear counsel mixed with wit as to the foolish to have sport mingled with rudeness' (quoted in Mincoff, p. 17). Lyly allies himself with those who banished 'apish actions' and 'immodest words' from the Roman and Greek stages, and promises in his own art to be 'far from unseemly speeches to make your ears glow'. An appeal to a sophisticated courtly audience combines here with veneration for classical art and humanistic ideals to produce a kind of literary manifesto. It proclaims what Hunter, employing a phrase of George Meredith's, terms 'high comedy',[50] fulfilling as it does Sir Philip Sidney's wish to see in England a 'right comedy' free of scurrility and doltishness fit only for loud laughter.

Indeed, *Sappho and Phao* nicely illustrates the marriage of 'delight' and 'laughter' called for in *The Defence of Poesy* (1595), one in which laughter is mixed with 'delightful teaching'. Sidney offers the subject of Hercules in woman's attire and spinning at Omphale's command-ment as an example of what can breed delight and laughter together, 'for the representing of so strange a power in love procures delight, and the scornfulness of the action stirreth laughter'.[51] Lyly is surely aiming at a similar effect (Mincoff, p. 17). By poking fun at love in all its delightful follies, by inviting smiles at the familiar martyrdom of lovers and the scorn of witty court ladies while insisting at the same time on love's idealism, Lyly moves towards a more rarefied and elegant comedy than the English stage had known, one that (in Mincoff's terms) 'raises a sigh, half sympathetic, half acquiescent, over human nature itself' (p. 17). To this comedy of courtship Shakespeare is particularly indebted, even though his independence of courtly rules and his freer acceptance of courtship as a prelude to marriage enables him to move well beyond his predecessors (Lyly among them) towards comic resolutions that are satisfactory in purely human terms.

The failure of *Sappho and Phao* to acclaim sexual love or to resolve the difficulties of its protagonists in celebratory marriage, so typical of Lylyan comedy, raises questions of attitude on the part of the dramatist and his courtly audience that go well beyond the particular need to flatter Elizabeth. Mary Beth Rose examines the issue in the context of Elizabethan attitudes towards marriage.[52] For the upper classes in particular, marriage was the basis of property settlement and alliance between powerful families, and in such a case sexual love was not only an improper basis of union but also all too apt to be in conflict with overriding economic and dynastic considerations. Although the Renaissance saw conjugal loyalty and affection replace celibacy as the more socially sanctioned pattern of sexual conduct, erotic love was still often viewed as essentially incompatible with marriage. Neoplatonism, associated in the English mind with Petrarchism, encouraged (as did Christianity) a mistrust of erotic desire as incommensurate with higher idealism in love. Attempts to reconcile these divergent impulses were at times notably successful, as in Spenser's *Four Hymns* and Donne's 'The Extasie', but the conflict remained. It took the form of a polarising consciousness in which women were alternately idealised and debased.

Lyly's art represents, for Rose, an encounter between 'the dualizing, idealizing Petrarchan sensibility to which he was heir' and a newer, more pragmatic view of marriage to which Shakespeare had greater access. The polarising consciousness is everywhere apparent in the idealising raptures men make about women in *Euphues* and the blatant misogyny to which the men eventually succumb. With worship or lust as the sole alternatives available, Lyly's protagonist in *Euphues* can see love only as a compulsive, impersonal and ridiculous passion. In these same terms, *Sappho and Phao* is dominated by an uneasy mixture of cynical statements about the availability of women and idealisation of the play's central figure. The conflict of Venus and Sappho is rooted in this polarising antipathy. Small wonder then that the play ends in a victory over base desire by a woman who thereby earns the everlasting Platonic devotion of her male worshipper. However powerful and unavoidable sexual desire may be, it can form no part of the play's resolution. Only with the wider acknowledgement of moral prestige in love and marriage, and greater acceptance of a kind of equality in the marital relationship (though still within the limits of a patriarchal structure), is English drama capable of the romantic comedy produced by Shakespeare in the 1590s.[53] If one is tempted to conclude, with Hereward Price, that 'Lyly does not like women',[54] the reasons may have something to do with Lyly's courtly world and its ambivalent view of sex and marriage.

6. THE LANGUAGE OF PLAY

Lyly was once regarded as a writer whose 'Dresden china style of antiquated compliment',[55] no matter how prettily turned and no matter how influential in the development of English prose in the 1580s and '90s, was ornament divorced from substance and so unvaried in its exotic mannerisms as to be unsuited for true dramatic dialogue. His imagery, in the view of Frederic Ives Carpenter, is 'entirely ornamental', is 'adventitious, not a part of the thought', and

is 'largely imitative of foreign models'.[56] The distinguishing features
of Euphuism—its isocolon (the even balancing of parallel clauses of
equal length), its paramoion (the even balancing in parallel clauses of
recurrent sounds), its parison (the even balancing in parallel clauses
of grammatical parts of speech), its use of alliteration (similar sound
at the beginning of parallel words or phrases) and *similiter cadens*
(similarity at the end), its word-repetitions and polyptoton (the repetition of one stem with different inflectional endings), its use of
analogy from fabulous natural history, its apostrophes and set pieces
of declamation—were widely regarded as 'figures of sound' rather
than 'figures of thought'.[57]

To accentuate this seeming contrast between style and substance
is to miss the importance of antithetical structure in Lyly's way of
thinking and in his play construction. As Jonas Barish points out,
parison is not simply a figure of sound, though it is frequently paired
with sound effects; the arrangement of grammatical parts of speech
in parallel phrases is a syntactic procedure implying its own logical
structure.[58] Parison is antithetical in its expression and in its content,
and, as Albert Feuillerat observes, Lyly is unable to conceive his
ideas other than through the encounter of two opposing things; he
makes associations in terms of antithetical contrasts.[59] Lyly's antitheses, according to Barish, either define one thing by its opposite,
or hold two possibilities in equilibrium, or assert the paradoxical co-
existence of contending properties in a single phenomenon. Each kind
of antithesis has its consequences; especially in the third or paradoxical kind of antithesis, we see that like engenders unlike and that inner
self-contradiction is an essential condition of human nature.

This self-contradiction regularly takes the form of antagonism
between substance and appearance: 'the more absolute of its kind a
thing may appear to be, the more certain it is that somewhere within
it lies its own antithesis, its anti-self' (Barish, p. 22). The correspondences and the antipathies are ranged side by side in Lyly so as to
unveil 'the contradictions in nature, the infinite inconsistency of the
world' (p. 23). Lyly's examples from fabulous natural history are
always applied to human conduct, enabling us, as G. Wilson Knight
puts it, 'to read the human mind in terms of the living physical
universe'.[60] Human feelings and the universe alike display contradiction. At the same time Lyly's antithetical thought is deeply logical,
seeking to show the composite nature of experience as well as its contradictory nature, and using the debate as its most characteristic
structural device.[61]

The merger of antithetical style and thought, so admirably suited
to the long declamations of *Euphues*, is no less expressive of dramatic
conflict in *Sappho and Phao*. The characters are arranged in a series
of overlapping antithetical pairs: Vulcan and Venus, Venus and Sappho, Sappho and Phao, Cupid in relation to all these, Phao and Mileta,
Trachinus and Pandion, Criticus and Molus, Molus and Callipho.
Each of these pairings gives rise to verbal antitheses employing all the
sound-repeating devices of Euphuism, as for instance when Venus
says of her unlikely liaison with Vulcan: 'It is no less unseemly than
unwholesome for Venus, who is most honoured in princes' courts, to
sojourn with Vulcan in a smith's forge, where bellows blow instead
of sighs, dark smokes rise for sweet perfumes, and for the panting
of loving hearts is only heard the beating of steeled hammers'
(I.i.21–6).

In the soliloquies of Phao and Sappho, similarly, the mind at debate
with itself generates for every claim a counterclaim. Phao rehearses
the arguments against his ambition even in the midst of his longing
for Sappho (II.iv). The queen expresses her dilemma in a series of
natural analogies: the sun shines all day only to dip its head in the
ocean, certain herbs are saltier the further they grow from the sea, and
the like (III.iii). The logic of antithesis provides both lovers with a
means of gaining perspective on the inherent contradiction in their
behaviour and hence of attempting to control that behaviour. It provides the audience with sympathy and distance through which the
inevitability of the play's unromantic conclusion can be grasped.

One way to measure the pervasive presence of antithesis in the
content as well as in the form of *Sappho and Phao* is to consider the
many topics that are more or less formally debated, either in soliloquy
or, more often, between rival speakers. The topics are at once numerous and interrelated. The focus of Phao's deliberations when
we first meet him is the contrast between riches and the simple life,
between ambition and contentment with one's lot (I.i; II.i). This
debate takes on particularity in the contrast of court and countryside,
or the pen (with which to write love sonnets) and the oar (V.iii.12–13).
A related antithesis pits the court versus the university, good manners
versus learning, and the enjoyment of power and influence versus the
poverty of scholars; these matters are seriously discussed by Trachinus and Pandion (I.ii) and more lightheartedly by their pages,
Criticus and Molus (I.iii; II.iii; III.ii). The pages also have fun with
the supposed merits and demerits of logical reasoning, in a *jeu d'esprit*
that seems irrelevant to the play until one considers what has already

been said here about the importance of logic in coming to terms with contradictory thought.

The play's etiquette-book survey of the correct way for men and women to behave in love is a debate with major implications for the central figures. Should Phao follow Sibylla's Ovidian advice and play the cynical game of courtship for all it is worth? Will all women eventually succumb to male stratagems? May women take the initiative in wooing? Is chaste affection superior to erotic love? What is the nature of sovereignty, the right relation of sovereign to subject, the suitable place of love in the sovereign's life? The antithetical pairing of Venus and Sappho is, in these terms, a stating of alternative positions about the essential nature of women (especially royal women) and hence of men's relationship to women. Other debates in the play stem from those already mentioned: the relationship of spiritual to physical sickness (III.iii), the nature of dreams (IV.iii), the right use of clothes or of making of oaths by one in love (I.iv), the right way to conduct a duel (II.iii), the use or abuse of cosmetics (II.i), proper and improper table manners (III.ii). The emphasis on manners is not, as it frequently seems, merely superficial, in that the antithetical possibilities offer particular means of evaluating the major choices available to the play's central characters.

Word-play in Lyly is highly antithetical, and as such offers yet another opportunity for the characters to explore the inherent contradictions they face. 'Thou art a *ferry*man, Phao, yet a *free* man,' Phao begins the play, expressing in the similarity of sound the paradox of servitude to labour and freedom from ambition. 'Thou *farest* delicately if thou have a *fare* to buy anything.' As Geoffrey Tillotson demonstrates, *Sappho and Phao* is (like all of Lyly's writing) remarkably self-conscious about words and their meanings.[62] 'Thou dost not flatter thyself, Phao, thou art fair,' says Phao to himself after receiving Venus' gift of beauty. 'Fair? I fear me "fair" be a word too foul for a face so passing fair' (II.i.6–8). Ismena similarly looks askance at verbal signs and what they signify: 'I laugh at that you all call love, and judge it only a word called love' (I.iv.16–17).

The scepticism is understandable in a play that deals so often, and with such evident cynicism, in the rhetoric of persuasion. Sibylla plies Phao with Ovidian advice on the uses of language and gesture to woo a lady (II.i, iv), Cupid counsels Venus to beg of Vulcan the arrows that can turn Sappho's heart to disdain, and Venus uses her most flattering wiles to obtain her will from Vulcan, who knows well enough that he is being manipulated: 'Because you have made mine eyes drunk with fair looks, you will set mine ears on edge with sweet words' (IV.iv.21–3). The central proposition tested in this play, that all women or men can sooner or later be seduced, is essentially a proposition about language. It is answered at last by Sappho's persuasive wooing of Cupid to the cause of virtue, and by the dramatist's own metaphors of disentanglement of meaning in his Epilogue, but not before the power of language to do good has been called into question.

As a consequence of this testing of the validity of language, words often contain within them the paradoxes and contradictions characteristic of the Lylyan style as a whole; despite their seeming absoluteness, words too reveal an inner antithesis or anti-self. Words are repeated often in *Sappho and Phao*, and almost invariably with a change of meaning suggestive of the contrast between physical substance and a hidden inner truth. Sappho in bed has no recourse to expression other than to play on the medical terms being used by her anxious ladies-in-waiting (III.iii). When they urge her to have more bedclothes and 'sweat it out', that is, sweat out the fever, she replies that her best ease is to 'sigh it out'. *Disease* to them means 'illness' and to her 'absence of ease', *desire* is both 'request' and 'passionate craving', *feel* is 'perceive physically' and 'experience mentally', *burning* means 'feverish' and 'inflamed with passion'. The entire extended dialogue up to l. 24 is a tour de force of such changes and witty demonstrations of the author's verbal pyrotechnics, and yet it is also a poignant way of showing Sappho's frustrated ability only to hint at what may not be openly said. The technique is strikingly anticipatory of Shakespeare's use of double entendre to reflect conflict that cannot be stated openly, as when Juliet parries her mother's invective against Romeo with double-edged comments—'Would none but I might venge my cousin's death', III.iv.86—or when Hamlet similarly answers his uncle and mother: 'Ay, madam, it is common' (I.ii.74).

Other characters in *Sappho and Phao* make similar use of wordplay. Mileta and Pandion employ medical parlance in their verbal encounter at III.i: *cold* means variously 'a respiratory illness', 'the opposite of heat', and (as an adjective) 'dispirited', while *physic* means 'medical knowledge' or 'a purge'. *Male-content* is used as a form of 'malcontent' to make explicit the contrast with 'female content'. The witty word games and logical demonstrations of the pages often turn absurdly on word definitions: 'Thou art a smith, therefore thou art a smith.' Language seems in fact to be capable of proving anything: 'as sure as he is a smith', says Criticus to Callipho, 'thou art a devil'

(II.iii.87–94). Word-play is an essential element not simply of Lyly's style but of his antithetical vision of the hard search for truth.

Along with this seriousness of word-play, we do of course find distinctively playful aspects in Lyly's language. Euphuism can in fact be viewed as a kind of game, even if, as Jocelyn Powell argues, it is no less essential for being so. Recreation has its own function, one that depends on its being, in Johan Huizinga's terms, 'different from ordinary life'.[63] Games mattered in Renaissance courtly life. Castiglione's *The Courtier* views expertise in games as an important accomplishment for its ideal type; Sir John Davies's *Orchestra* offers courtly dance as an expression of patterned movement and order in the very cosmos as well as at court. Lyly's plays, says Powell, 'organise into an elaborate aesthetic game the exploratory, recreational activities of the court for which they were written' (p. 156). The debate, of which Lyly makes such extensive use, was a well-established game of court entertainment related to mummings and other seasonal festivities. Court revels lent themselves to repartee and other game-playing with words in order to express both temporary release from social constraint and eventual acceptance of form.

Lyly's acquaintance with this tradition of courtly pastime is evident everywhere in his writing. The atmosphere of purposeful play in his drama enhances stylistic novelty, exuberance, inventiveness and a witty facility for seeing similitude in things apparently different (such as Sappho of Lesbos and Queen Elizabeth of England). Fancy and learning are deployed around a frame of logic, encouraging a play of sound and of meaning in a way that is distinctively self-aware. Allegory and its witty similitudes invite playful cross-reference of idea to fact through which manifold possibilities of meaning emerge, and urge us to welcome his play world and acrobatics of the mind in all their extravagant fantasy.[64]

Lyly's playfulness with language is illustrative of what Joel Altman calls the 'Tudor play of mind'. Lyly's is a style of inquiry and analysis, through which he 'examines experience as a dialectical rhetorician, always holding any given perception up to the light of other possibilities'.[65] Altman sees the method as originating in the *quaestio* or hypothesised question argued from both sides (*in utramque partem*), a technique that is common in sixteenth-century fiction and notably so in *Euphues*. Although Altman does not analyse *Sappho and Phao*, we can see that the hypothesised question constitutes the basic scenic unit of this play, as it does in *Campaspe* and *Gallathea*, and that flytings, amorous play of wit, and commentary on the main action are the substance of the connecting scenes. Elizabethan courtiers were familiar from their schooling with hypothetical situations posed to train the mind in thinking pluralistically and problematically about characters and ideas. What would it be like if a female sovereign were to fall in love with a male commoner? As in *Campaspe*, concerned as it is with a similar hypothetical situation, the play invites the audience 'to weigh the alternative meanings and values discovered through analysis, and to reassemble the distinctive—if sometimes antithetical—qualities perceived into some kind of harmonious order' (p. 201). In this way 'the play functions . . . as an exercise in invention', which in Ciceronian rhetorical tradition 'was considered the most important of the five skills of the orator, since it supplied matter for discourse' (p. 50).

The allegory of *Sappho and Phao* provides an advantage, less evident in *Campaspe*, of exploring the question in greater vividness and with more demands on the audience's inventive faculty. A play designed to 'stimulate the wit to new inferences and more complex perceptions' (pp. 201–2) must of necessity use its images and analogies functionally, not ornamentally, in order to reveal duality and paradox inherent in the natural world and in human relationship to that world. Allegory itself is a form of wit, compelling the audience by its enigmas and dense correspondences (as Erasmus put it) 'to investigate certain things, and learn'.[66] Lyly's plot, says Altman, arising from a *quaestio*, 'is often really a pair of *theses* argued copiously, now through one order of the cosmos, now through another, until the whole universe seems caught up in the strife' (p. 206). Such an interpretation finds meaning not only in Lyly's use of allegory but also in the bringing together of mortals and immortals in one play, the range of social differentiation, the shifts in style from argumentative to lyric to bantering to chop-logic, the duality in which most characters are both objectively dramatic and emblematic, and the omnipresence of paradox. Along with the obvious flattery of Elizabeth, the play's inquiring mode yields a subtle critique of court life in which general harmony is achieved only at the expense of real personal loss.

7. DRAMATURGY AND STAGING

Antithesis is the key not only to Lyly's style and ideas but also to his use of the physical stage. The characters in *Sappho and Phao* who are so often arranged in overlapping pairs—Vulcan and Venus, Venus and Sappho, Sappho and Phao, Trachinus and Pandion, and the like—are presented verbally and visually as opposing numbers in a debate, a confrontation, a choice. Cupid must choose, for instance, between Sappho and Venus, and when he does so the resolution of the play's critical debate is signalled by Cupid's gesture of sitting in Sappho's lap. The topics of the play—the nature of sovereignty and the sovereign's relation to commoners, chaste versus erotic affection, court versus university, and the like—are given theatrical embodiment in the form of symmetrically opposed alternatives. Lyly's pluralistic exploration of a question from both sides is a principle of dramaturgy and staging as well as of philosophical debate.

Lyly's antithetical stage is in part a product of the theatrical resources he had at hand and in part of staging traditions in medieval and Tudor England. As Hunter has said, Lyly almost certainly designed his productions at Blackfrairs with the requirements of Whitehall and other royal palaces in mind, since court performance was the ultimate goal. His theatre at Blackfriars probably measured forty-six by twenty-six or twenty-seven feet, while the space available to him in the Great Chamber or Tudor Banqueting Hall at Whitehall was not much greater, once room had been set aside for the queen's chair of state and its dais.[67] The stages of this period, both in London and at the universities, public and private, normally provided means for paired entrances and stage houses that were conducive to alternating actions. Whether *Sappho and Phao* was set at the lower end of the hall in front of the hall screen, as traditionally assumed, has been cast in doubt by the recent investigations of Alan Nelson and others, but in any case the stage itself may have had Blackfriars' full width of twenty-six or twenty-seven feet and been as deep as thirteen and a half to fifteen feet.[68] The audience may have numbered somewhere between 120 and 400.[69] Stage 'houses', 'made of canvas, framed, fashioned, and painted accordingly, as might best serve their several purposes',[70] were readily available for the play's fixed locations, and probably two doors were in use (although the evidence on this is scanty). Like *Campaspe*, *Sappho and Phao* requires no space for acting 'above' and no trap-door. Since these two plays were acted close together in time at Blackfriars and at court, their staging requirements are, not surprisingly, similar. The only other surviving play text that may represent conditions of performance at the first Blackfriars theatre (according to Irwin Smith, though he offers no evidence), is George Peele's *The Arraignment of Paris* (Chapel Children, 1581–4), in which case the acting area must have been raised, since the text does refer to a trap-door.[71]

Lyly's task of accommodating his performances at Blackfriars to the requirements of production at court was eased by a relationship that had long existed between English drama, even of the most popular sort, and the great halls of the aristocracy. Plays as diverse as *Mankind* (*c.* :71), *Fulgens and Lucres* (*c.* 1497) and *Cambyses* (*c.* 1558–69) might be taken into Tudor banqueting halls, whether or not designed in the first instance for performance there.[72] In such a great hall the actors might perform on the floor itself or on a slightly raised stage located in the midst of the hall or possibly at its lower end, where the façade or screen provided entrance doors (often two) and a gallery above sometimes used by musicians. The most noble spectators occupied the dais at the upper end of the hall, while guests ranged themselves at tables along the two sides of the room. All Farrant needed to do, when he made his theatre at Blackfriars by removing partitions added to a hall that had provided the Dominicans with their refectory, was to regard this space as essentially like that of a great hall to which 'houses' could be added, as they often were in early performances at court (*Thersites*, 1537, and *Godly Queen Hester*, 1527–9, for example), and 'degrees' or scaffolded seating at the sides of the hall in place of tables and benches. Lyly continued what Farrant had begun. The use of boy actors in such a space was a familiar practice, for boy choristers often performed at court. All in all, then, the so-called first Blackfriars theatre must have looked very like a Tudor great hall fitted out for theatrical entertainment.[73]

This continuity of acting tradition linking the Blackfriars stage to the Tudor great hall is especially significant in terms of dramaturgy and modes of staging. Medieval and Tudor drama tended to be presentational and typological. Instead of painted scenery and verisimilar perspectives through which scenes could be realistically located and then changed behind a curtain, this staging used 'houses' or 'mansions' or '*sedes*' or '*domus*' that were simultaneously visible and located amidst a neutral playing area (or *platea*) where space and time were highly flexible. Medieval religious drama offers a remarkable versatility of this sort.

The cycles were generally acted out of doors rather than in great halls, to be sure, but the presentational vocabulary of medieval drama found its way into Tudor entertainments. *Wit and Science* (1531–47), for example, features *Mons Parnassus*, to which the student hero must aspire, and the den of the dragon Tediousness with whom he must do battle, both locations presumably represented by stage 'houses' for performance in a great hall, and signifying in visual terms the secular polarities (equivalent to heaven and hell) of Wit's unsteady pilgrimage. The staging of *Thersites* must include a forge, not unlike that of Vulcan in *Sappho and Phao*, and another door to represent Thersites' fearsome enemy, the snail. The 'houses' of Tudor plays are as symmetrically and antiphonally arranged as their characters. Even when Tudor drama approximates, in its insular and anachronistic way, the staging of classical comedy (or at least what it understood that staging to be), the effect is likely to be no less antithetical and emblematic. *Gammer Gurton's Needle* (*c*. 1552–63), for example, achieves unity of place in its tiny Cambridgeshire village with houses facing on to a street, but the typical English result is an opposition between two households and two views of country life with the hapless curate Dr Rat trafficking back and forth.

As Best has argued, Lyly's comedies regularly seem to require two opposing 'houses' that are present throughout the action even though they may at times be curtained or otherwise unemployed.[74] Lyly's stage was probably not large enough to accommodate more than two stage 'houses' with ease, and a symmetrical binary opposition was suited in any case to his antithetical mode. *Campaspe* requires Apelles' studio and Dionysus' tub, aptly chosen, as Hunter shows, to represent antithetical values of emotion and reason, acceptance and denial, art and philosophy. Alexander moves freely in stage space if (as seems likely) his palace is not a stage structure, enabling him to position himself in relation to the contrastive worlds around him. The studio is described as a 'shop', the tub as a 'cabin'. *Gallathea* presents us with the sacrificial tree on one side and perhaps a balancing group of trees on the other. In *Endymion* we are aware throughout much of the play of Endymion's lunary bank and Corsites' castle, along with a well where Eumenides finds a remedy for Endymion. And so with the rest. *Mother Bombie* adapts the classical device of dwellings on a street, and may require more doors than are commonly needed in Lyly, but even in this relatively late play the location of Mother Bombie herself is much like that of Sibylla in *Sappho and Phao* and the Temple of Cupid in *Love's Metamorphosis*.

Lyly's symbolic presentational staging, then, invites symmetrical opposition. In *Sappho and Phao* the 'houses' must represent the cave of Sibylla on the one hand and the bedchamber of Sappho on the other. Vulcan's forge may well also require a *domus*, though its single and late use in the play (IV.iv) is such as to raise the possibility that it occupied the same structure as Sibylla's cave. The suggestion of a *periaktos*, or vertically rotating prism with different scenes on each face as a means of scene-changing, seems unlikely here at such a comparatively early date,[75] but the play allows time for some other device of scene-changing to be used. (The action at the forge in IV.iv is followed by two scenes located at court, presumably on the open stage, before Sibylla's cave is again required in V.iii.) On the other hand, Venus' opening dialogue in I.i.21ff. about the indignity of her sojourning with Vulcan in his forge would be given added point if she emerged with Cupid from a stage structure or entrance visibly suggestive of that forge, and the silent presence throughout the play of such a location would enhance the play's symbolic contrasts.

In any event, the number of fixed locations is less important than the meaning of the contrast. Phao's neutral space, at the ferry and in the environs of Syracuse, is visually understood in relation to those places he must visit or from which Venus will obtain the arrows of Vulcan. The weight of Sibylla's advice is present by visual implication throughout much of the play even when she is concealed from view. Sappho's presence in her bedchamber, even when she is curtained off from view, is felt in conversations and actions for which her final decision will provide a conclusive answer. As with medieval and Tudor drama generally, the stage of *Sappho and Phao* is a composite and flexible world in which the presence of gods and mortals, aristocrats and commoners is spatially enhanced by a sense of multiple perspectives simultaneously perceived and compared.

Around and in front of these stage 'houses' lies the neutral acting space where most of the play takes place. Indeed, even at Sibylla's cave and at Sappho's bedchamber much of the action presumably takes place on the open stage rather than in the structure used to represent cave or bedchamber; Phao can remain in the open acting area as he converses with Sibylla at the mouth of her cave, and those who attend on or visit Sappho in her bedchamber need only be in the immediate vicinity. The stage structure is her curtained bed, not the entire bedchamber. 'Houses' were designed not to contain whole scenes but to present symbolic structures and major stage properties.

Accordingly, the open stage displays at once a degree of specificity and of flexibility that is well suited to both the play's classical content and its native English freedom of literary form. The stage represents Syracuse and its environs, just as it stood for Athens in *Campaspe*, and again as in that play many of the scenes require little of our localising imagination other than to suppose we are in public spaces where contrasting groups of people and of gods alternately appear.

We begin, obviously, at Phao's ferry, where Venus and Cupid engage his services to cross over to Syracuse. Trachinus and Pandion are still near the water in I.ii, and so are their servants in I.iii; Syracuse, whither they are all bent, can be reached by land (I.ii.75–6, II.ii.14) as well as by water. The court ladies in I.iv need not be imagined in a different location, though their scene is so imprecisely located that they may also be imagined at court. No properties are required for Act I, though Phao may have an oar to identify his craft. Act I thus takes place in an open location onstage identified as being either in the vicinity of the ferry or, without scenic differentiation, at court.

The visits to the stage 'houses' make plain the flexible sense of distance that this stage can achieve. In II.i Phao speaks with Sibylla at the mouth of her cave, but then without exit (II.ii) encounters Sappho and company at his ferry. Perhaps he takes a few steps from the cave to indicate presentationally a brief journey. As before, we learn that it is possible to reach Syracuse by ferry or by land. Scene iii, though it clearly follows II.ii without interruption at the ferry, is, like I.iv, a conversation that requires no location and seems generally appropriate to the court. The imagined location remains in this generalised setting, near the ferry and the court (with a second visit to Sibylla's cave in II.iv), until the end of III.ii.

Sappho's bedchamber, the play's second stage 'house', dominates the action from III.iii to the end of IV.iii. In III.iii Sappho is discovered in her bed, presumably by means of a curtain drawn back from the stage structure she occupies.[76] She stays here a long time, being curtained off from view while she sleeps and is then revealed again as appropriate to the action. Her ladies meantime attend her, leave her to her soliloquising, answer her calls for assistance and go on errands. Mileta brings Phao to visit the sick Sappho. Venus and Cupid also visit her, encountering Phao as he is about to leave. Venus and Cupid depart at the end of IV.ii for Vulcan's forge while Sappho, discovered once more in bed, recounts her dream and hears those of her ladies (IV.iii). Throughout this sequence, III.iii-IV.iii, the action remains uninterruptedly located at Sappho's bedchamber, either by her visible presence in bed or by her assumed presence behind the bed-curtains.

This sustained action centred upon Sappho's bedchamber is followed by another sequence from IV.iv to the end of V.i at the mouth of Vulcan's forge. Whether or not this location requires the same stage house as that used for Sibylla's cave, as has been speculated in this Introduction, it uses stage space in much the same way, and thus parallels the action of III.iii-IV.iii around Sappho's bedchamber. Vulcan emerges from his forge to greet his wife, Venus, who has come to ask him for six new arrow heads. He calls into the forge for his Cyclopes, who join him onstage and sing as they produce the desired arrows. Vulcan and his Cyclopes return into the forge, leaving Venus to send Cupid off to court in order to shoot his arrows at Sappho and Phao, among others. Venus then retires into the forge herself, having exited into this symbolic stage 'house' much as Sappho closed the scene at IV.iii.107.1 by the drawing of her bed-curtains.

The bare stage at the start of V.ii thus introduces the climactic scene of Sappho's triumph over Venus and of Cupid's vowing of his services to a new queen of love. In this final appearance at court, Sappho is no longer in bed; she is control of herself. She is evidently enthroned (perhaps on a throne that is brought onstage at this point) so that Cupid can crawl into her lap, and she closes this scene of very regal behaviour by commanding Mileta to 'shut the door'. A stage door serves for her final triumphant exit, leaving the last short scene to a dispirited Phao and Sibylla at the mouth of Sibylla's cave. No structure is needed to signify Sappho's palace, just as it is not needed for Alexander's palace in *Campaspe*.

In all, then, the neutral stage of *Sappho and Phao* foreshortens distance between imagined locations, shows journeys back and forth between them presentationally, and achieves a kind of unity of place by means of this imagined proximity. Stage structures in this space are symbolically important and are imagined to be occupied by unseen persons even when they are not involved in action and dialogue.

The links between scenes call for continuous action in a significantly large number of instances, and reinforce the impression of a flexible stage location in which journeys need not call for a break in the action. On no less than three occasions, at I.iii, II.iii and III.ii, comic servants remain onstage after their masters' departure to comment on what has been said in the previous scene. At II.ii, Phao remains onstage after his first interview with Sibylla and is encountered by Sappho and others. From III.iii to IV.iii inclusive, the play presents a continuous sequence at Sappho's bedchamber, and IV.iv to V.i provides another continuous action at Vulcan's forge. Continuous action bridges the transitions of act divisions at IV.i and V.i. Although, as we shall see, the play follows a classical five-act structure in its exposition, complication and dénouement, in terms of staging it can be described as a sequence of actions grouped around symbolic locations, at the ferry (and, more vaguely, near the court), at Sibylla's cave, at Sappho's bedchamber, at Vulcan's forge and

climactically at Sappho's rejuvenated court (for which no stage house
is necessary).

The time sense of this play is handled with a similar flexibility and
impression of unity. Some passage of time would seem necessary for
the court ladies to observe Phao's new beauty and to suffer his
disdain, for Phao to visit Sibylla twice, for Sappho to fall lovesick and
her ladies to seek a remedy (Sappho orders that Phao be brought to
her with medicines 'tomorrow', III.iii.76), and for Sappho to gain
control of her passions. At the end of V.i Venus retires into Vulcan's
forge to await the results of Cupid's use of his new arrows. Many
scene intervals are continuous in space and time, however, even
across act divisions, as we have seen, providing a sense of continuity
in time that is incommensurate with the logical demands of the story.
Stage time and narrative time run on separate but concurrent tracks,
as they do, for example, in Shakespeare's *Othello*.[77]

Lyly uses the Terentian formula for comedy in his five-act structure, much as he did in *Campaspe* and even in *Euphues*.[78] In the
protasis or introductory material of Acts I and II, the major characters
are introduced and their situation established as laid out in Lyly's
sources: Phao is made beautiful by Venus, Sappho and Phao meet and
fall unsuitably in love, Phao consults Sibylla and hears prophecies of
what will ensue. The *epitasis* or complication of Act III, that part of
the play when the plot thickens, revolves around Sappho's determination to resist her affliction while Phao dares to hope for her; when
they meet at her bedside, their conversation reveals how much they
are at cross-purposes. The *summa epitasis* or crisis of the complication
is reached when Venus discovers that she too is smitten with love for
Phao (III.iv–IV.ii) and that she will have to appeal to Vulcan for
new arrows. In the *catastrophe* or dénouement of Act V, Venus and
Sappho confront one another and Venus loses. The comic resolution
of the catastrophe is appropriately the point at which the play offers
itself most openly as a flattering portrayal of Elizabeth and her victory
over carnal affection.

To make such a Terentian analysis is, however, to describe only the
central action of the play. Unless we are content with Baldwin to
dismiss the rest as mere padding, we must see that Lyly is structurally
interested in more than the Terentian outline. The unhappy love
affair of Sappho and Phao is undoubtedly a single action that moves
from complication to resolution, bringing with it the comic equiva-
lents of recognition and reversal, but the play as a whole finds unity
through other and more recognisably native English means. The

rhythmic alteration from seriousness to buffoonery, for example, establishes itself with a clarity of pattern able to give added significance to the act division. In each of the first three acts, the jesting pages come before us in the wake of their courtly or philosophical masters. Although their wit combats do not make up a subplot, their encounter with Callipho adds complication and leads to a contest of syllogistic proofs that is resolved at last in laughter and song. Trachinus and Pandion rhythmically reappear in much the same way, as do the ladies of the court.

The dramatic rhythm of *Sappho and Phao* is produced also by the recurrent varieties of scenes: soliloquy, dialogue, large scenes of symmetrical tableau, rapid-fire exchange of wit. Lyly differentiates his groups of characters by their dramatic manner, and thereby creates a complementary play of mood. Powell identifies four main moods in Act I: the lyrical (Phao's monologue and dialogue with Venus), the didactic (scholar and courtier), the farcical (the pages' parody of their masters) and the mannered (the ladies' conversation), beneath all of which we detect a streak of mockery.[79] Our interest is enhanced by the variety, the pattern, the interplay. The songs are not entertaining distraction but an essential part of this rhythmic diversity of mood and stage picture.

As Best and several others have observed, the result of Lyly's style and patterned rhythm is a static drama.[80] The love story of Sappho and Phao does move through climax to resolution, but it is only one element of the play. Lacking a concluding marriage, it really goes nowhere and its result is largely adumbrated by its beginning. We come to this play with wrong expectations if we look for dramatic action. Instead we find the exploration of paradoxical situations that are suspended in time, tableau-like. In this stasis we are given time to explore complex states of mind. The result is the very opposite of narrative drama: it is a conversation piece, discursive in form, focusing upon a static concept and all the various possibilities inherent in it. Debate and play of language flourish in such a world of extended stillness. We are invited to walk in a labyrinth of conceits by the self-aware artist.

Like *Campaspe*, *Sappho and Phao* was written for Oxford's company of boy choristers, and displays many of the features of such productions already described by Hunter: speeches that encourage self-consciously formal acting and technique of delivery, juvenile wit combat, coolness and impersonality of mannered prose, and the like. We find few roles for soldiers or men of action in this play; the few

men are old like Pandion (boys took delight in aping older men), or
are witty pages of the boys' own age and educational experience, or
are handsomely young and innocent about love like Phao. Women's
parts abound, especially saucy young ladies of the court.

The play seems ideally constructed for its probable size of troupe.
Hunter observes that in *Campaspe* twenty-nine roles are reduced to
the capacities of fourteen or so actors by doubling; *Sappho and Phao*
has seventeen speaking roles (plus silent Cyclopes), and technically
could be acted by fourteen actors if the company were to double
Sibylla with Eugenua or Ismena and Trachinus and Pandion with
Canope and Favilla. Quite possibly in fact no doubling was used at
all. The reduction is minimal, would involve the actors in several
changes back and forth, and is not typical of doubling patterns in
Tudor drama. The combined troupe of the Chapel Children and
Paul's Boys that constituted Oxford's company must have had a fairly
generous capacity. The point about Eugenua, Ismena, Canope and
Favilla, the only bit parts lending themselves to doubling, is that they
seem perfectly suited to the talents of the least experienced boy actors
of whom every large juvenile acting company would have had its share
(Iras in *Antony and Cleopatra* is just such a part for the least experienced boy in Shakespeare's company). And whereas, in Hunter's
reckoning, some eighteen of *Campaspe*'s twenty-nine roles appear on
stage only once, *Sappho and Phao* brings back all of its characters for
repeated appearances. Why Lyly composed *Campaspe* with so many
sequential bit parts is unclear, but it was a method better suited to the
adult players and he soon put it aside for the more characteristic form
of coterie drama in which relatively large casts are not significantly
doubled.[81]

Sappho and Phao has no stage history other than the court performance on Shrove Tuesday in 1584 and the presumed performances
at Blackfriars before that date. It was by no means unappreciated
when it appeared; the First Quarto of 1584 was evidently successful
enough to require a second printing, and a third quarto appeared in
1591, even if the success was perhaps modest compared with that of
Campaspe. After 1591, to be sure, *Sappho and Phao* shared with other
Lyly plays the rapid eclipse of fortune that brought Lyly's career to
an untimely halt. Reavley Gair surmises that Lyly failed to please
even his first audiences by his exclusion of loud laughter and his
complex, allusive allegorical style,[82] but the discovery of a second
quarto in 1584 must cast serious doubt on that conclusion.

More recently, the play has often been ignored, condescended to, or dismissed as 'distinctly among Lyly's poorer plays'.[83] Against such a judgement, fortunately, the perceptive studies incorporated in the present Introduction cumulatively argue for a play of first historical importance and of an artistic excellence demanding only that we approach the play on its own terms. Philip Edwards too has recently described *Sappho and Phao* as perhaps Lyly's greatest dramatic achievement, one in which Lyly perfectly captures the truth, necessity and bitterness of a conflictual relationship between a queen and her court: the queen must 'always suffer because she is human enough to love and princely enough to conquer love', while her courtiers (including Lyly himself) must flatter and dissemble in their sad perception of a world in which, because of 'the necessity of the state', things must be for individual subjects 'what they lamentably are'. The relationship which is 'for the good of both' 'cannot be other than it is, yet can hardly be endured'.[84] Mincoff is right when he urges against the repeated anthologising of *Endymion* in our drama collections, good though *Endymion* undoubtedly is, and proposes that '*Gallathea* or *Sappho* would better give the total effect of Lyly's comedy.'[85] Since the date of Mincoff's essay, *Gallathea* has in fact been anthologised by Russell Fraser and Norman Rabkin, and *Campaspe* was the Lylyan text long available in J. Q. Adams's *Chief Pre-Shakespearean Dramas*. *Sappho and Phao*'s day is yet to come.

NOTES

1. 3 vols. (Oxford, 1902).
2. *Studies in Bibliography*, XLII (1989), 187–99.
3. W. W. Greg, *A Bibliography of the English Printed Drama to the Restoration*, 4 vols. (London 1939–59), 1.6.
4. Bond, II.362; *A Short-Title Catalogue of Books Printed in England, Scotland, and Ireland ... 1475–1640*, first compiled by A. W. Pollard and G. R. Redgrave, 1st ed. (London, 1926); 2nd ed., rev., enl. (1976 and 1986), II.126.
5. Greg, *A Bibliography*, I.160–1.
6. W. W. Greg, 'Bibliography—An Apologia'. *Collected Papers*, ed. J. C. Maxwell (Oxford, 1966), p. 263.
7. G. K. Hunter, *John Lyly: The Humanist as Courtier* (London, 1962), pp. 367–72; see also M. R. Best, 'A Note on the Songs in Lyly's Plays', *N.&Q.* CCX, n.s. XII (1965), 93–4, who agrees with Hunter.
8. W. W. Greg, 'The Authorship of the Songs in Lyly's Plays', *M.L.R.*, I (1905), 43–54, and John Robert Moore, The Songs in Lyly's Plays', *P.M.L.A.*, XLII (1927), 623–40.
9. *The Dramatic Works of John Lilly (The Euphuist)*, ed. F. W. Fairholt, 2 vols. (London, 1858), I.153–214.

10. Carter A. Daniel, *The Plays of John Lyly* (Lewisburg, London and Toronto, 1988).
11. Bond, II.310, cites James Boswell the younger, ed., *The Plays and Poems of William Shakespeare, with the Corrections and Illustrations of Various Commentators, Comprehending a Life of the Poet and an Enlarged History of the Stage, by the late Edmond Malone*, (London, 1821), III.423–5.
12. Albert Feuillerat, *John Lyly* (Cambridge, 1910); reissued (New York, 1968), pp. 107ff.
13. Michael Shapiro, *Children of the Revels: The Boy Companies of Shakespeare's Time and Their Plays* (New York, 1977), pp. 16–17.
14. Mary S. Steele, *Plays and Masques at Court, 1558–1642* (New Haven, 1926), pp. 89–90; C. W. Wallace, *The Evolution of the English Drama up to Shakespeare* (Berlin, 1912), p. 224.
15. Hunter, *John Lyly*, p. 167.
16. Sir Paul Harvey, ed., *The Oxford Companion to Classical Literature* (Oxford, 1937), pp. 381–2, and Sir William Smith, ed., *Dictionary of Greek and Roman Biography and Mythography*, 3 vols. (London, 1890), III.707–11.
17. Karl Otfried Müller, *A History of the Literature of Ancient Greece*, 3 vols. (rpt. Port Washington, N. Y., 1958), I.231.
18. The translation, here modernised, is that of Abraham Fleming, *A Register of Histories, Containing Martial Exploits of Worthy Warriors . . . Written in Greek by Aelianus, a Roman, and Delivered in English . . . by Abraham Fleming* (London, 1576), pp. 125–6.
19. Trans. Abraham Fleming (1576), p. 126.
20. Palaephatus, *De fabulosis narrationibus*, published with the *Fabularum Liber* attributed to C. Julius Hyginus (Basel, 1535), ed. Stephen Orgel (New York, 1976). For the Greek text see *Peri Apistōn, Mythographi Graeci*, III, fasc. 2, ed. Nicolaus Festa, Leipzig, 1902), p. 69.
21. Müller, *A History of the Literature of Ancient Greece*, I.231.
22. See William Allan Neilson, *The Origins and Sources of the Court of Love* (Boston, 1899); rpt. (New York, 1967), pp. 31, 33, and 134–5.
23. Trans. David Grene in *The Complete Greek Tragedies*, ed. David Grene and Richmond Lattimore (Chicago, 1955).
24. T. W. Baldwin, *William Shakspere's Small Latine & Lesse Greeke*, 2 vols. (Urbana, 1944), I.3.
25. Frederick Gard Fleay, *A Biographical Chronicle of the English Drama* (London, 1891), II.40, equates Pandion with Lyly too simplistically.
26. Bond, II.366, cites James Anthony Froude, *History of England from the Fall of Wolsey to the Death of Elizabeth*, 12 vols. (New York, 1881), XI.155. For more recent accounts see J. B. Black, *The Reign of Elizabeth, 1558–1603* (1964), pp. 348ff; Wallace T. MacCaffrey, *Queen Elizabeth and the Making of Policy*, 1572–1588 (Princeton, 1981), pp. 276ff.; J. E. Neale, *Queen Elizabeth* (London, 1934), pp. 237–56; and Lacey Baldwin Smith, *Elizabeth Tudor: Portrait of a Queen* (London, 1976), pp. 181ff.
27. Bond, II.366.
28. Fleay, *Biographical Chronicle*, II.40.
29. Bond, II.558.
30. *Ibid.*, II.564.
31. Felix Schelling, *Elizabethan Drama, 1558–1642* (Boston, 1908), I.127,

pp. 108–18; Feuillerat, *Lyly*, pp. 108–18; C. F. Tucker Brooke, *The Tudor Drama* (Boston, 1911), p. 175; Evelyn May Albright, *Dramatic Publication in England, 1580–1640* (New York, 1927), p. 110.

32. F. S. Boas, *Queen Elizabeth in Drama, and Related Studies* (London, 1950); Boas, *University Drama in the Tudor Age* (Oxford, 1914), pp. 20–1; Gertrude Reese, 'The Question of the Succession in Elizabethan Drama', *University of Texas Studies in English*, XXII (1942), 75.

33. Bond, II.367; Fleay, *Biographical Chronicle*, II.40.

34. David Bevington, 'John Lyly and Queen Elizabeth: Royal Flattery in *Campaspe* and *Sapho and Phao*', *Renaissance Papers 1966* (1967), 57–67; Bevington, *Tudor Drama and Politics* (Cambridge, Mass., 1968), p. 65.

35. Examples of Elizabeth's interruption of or abrupt departure from performances she considered offensive are to be found, among other places, in the *Calendar of Letters and State Letters and Papers Relating to English Affairs, Preserved Principally in the Archives of Simances [Spanish]*, vol. I, Elizabeth, 1558–67, ed. Martin A. S. Hume (London, 1892), p. 375, and are recorded in Boas, *University Drama*, p. 383, and in Hunter, *Lyly*, pp. 148–9. See also Alan F. Herr, *The Elizabethan Sermon* (Phildelphia, 1940), pp. 37–8ff. Even less likely is the notion that Elizabeth would have accepted this play as an allegory of Lyly's own hopes for royal patronage, as proposed by T. W. Baldwin, *William Shakspere's Five-Act Structure* (Urbana, Ill, 1947), pp. 409ff.

36. Bernard F. Huppé, 'Allegory of Love in Lyly's Court Comedies', *E.L.H.*, XIV (1947), 93–113.

37. C. S. Lewis, *The Allegory of Love* (Oxford, 1948), pp. 44–8.

38. Huppé, 'Allegory of Love'.

39. Arthur Golding, trans., *The XV. Bookes of P. Ovidius Naso, Entytuled Metamorphosis* (London, 1567), 'The Preface to the Reader', l. 58.

40. Alice Venezky, *Pageantry on the Shakespearean Stage* (New York, 1951), p. 145; Gordon Kipling, *The Triumphs of Honour: Burgundian Origins of the Elizabethan Renaissance* (The Hague: for the Thomas Browne Institute, 1977).

41. Huppé, 'Allegory of Love', p. 99.

42. Robert Y. Turner, 'Some Dialogues of Love in Lyly's Comedies', *E.L.H.*, XXIX (1962), 276–88.

43. Turner, 'Some Dialogues', p. 276.

44. G. Wilson Knight, 'John Lyly', *R.E.S.*, XV (1939), 146–63; rpt. in Max Bluestone and Norman Rabkin, eds., *Shakespeare's Contemporaries*, 2nd ed. (Englewood Cliffs, N. J., 1970), pp. 12–22.

45. Paul Olson, '*A Midsummer Night's Dream* and the Meaning of Court Marriage', *E.L.H.*, XXIV (1957), 95–119.

46. Hunter, *John Lyly*, pp. 174–6.

47. Brooke, *The Tudor Drama*, p. 176.

48. Marco Mincoff, 'Shakespeare and Lyly', *Shakespeare Survey*, XIV (1961), 15–24, esp. p. 16.

49. David Lloyd Stevenson, 'Lyly's Quarreling Lovers', *The Love-Game Comedy* (New York, 1966), pp. 148–73.

50. Hunter, *John Lyly*, pp. 250–2.

51. Albert Feuillerat, ed., *The Complete Works of Sir Philip Sidney*, 4 vols. (Cambridge, 1912–26), III.40ff.

52. Mary Beth Rose, 'Moral Conceptions of Sexual Love in Elizabethan Comedy', *Renaissance Drama*, n.s., XV (1984), 1–29, and *The Expense of Spirit: Love and Sexuality in English Renaissance Drama* (Ithaca, N. Y., 1988), pp. 12–42.
53. Rose, *Ibid.* See also David Bevington, '"Jack Hath Not Jill": Failed Courtship in Lyly and Shakespeare', *Shakespeare Survey*, XLII (1990), 1–13.
54. Hereward T. Price, 'Shakespeare and His Young Contemporaries', *P.Q.*, XLI (1962), 37–57.
55. John Addington Symonds, *Shakspere's Predecessors* (London, 1884; London, 1920; rpt. New York, 1967), p. 418.
56. Frederic Ives Carpenter, *Metaphor and Simile in the Minor Elizabethan Drama* (Chicago, 1895), p. 15.
57. See Morris William Croll and Harry Clemons, eds., *'Euphues: The Anatomy of Wit' and 'Euphues and His England'* (London, 1916), pp. xv–xvi. The distinction between figures of sound and of thought is that of George Puttenham, *The Art of English Poesie* (1589), Book III, chap. 3.
58. Jonas Barish, 'The Prose Style of John Lyly', *E.L.H.*, XXIII (1956), 14–35.
59. Feuillerat, *John Lyly*, p. 412.
60. Knight, 'John Lyly', p. 147.
61. Barish, 'The Prose Style of John Lyly', pp. 25–8; Walter N. King, 'John Lyly and Elizabethan Rhetoric', *S.P.*, LII (1955), 149–61.
62. Geoffrey Tillotson, 'The Prose of Lyly's Comedies', *Essays on Criticism and Research* (Cambridge, 1942; rpt. 1967), pp. 17–30.
63. Jocelyn Powell, 'John Lyly and the Language of Play', *Elizabethan Theatre*, ed. John Russell Brown and Bernard Harris, Stratford-upon-Avon Studies IX (London, 1966), pp. 147–67; Johan Huizinga, *Homo Ludens* (Basel, 1944), trans. R. F. C. Hill (London, 1949).
64. Powell, 'John Lyly and the Language of Play', p. 166.
65. Joel B. Altman, 'Quaestiones Copiosae: Pastoral and Courtly in John Lyly', *The Tudor Play of Mind* (Berkeley, 1978), pp. 196–228.
66. Erasmus, I.19, quoted by Altman, *Ibid.*, p. 206.
67. Hunter, Introduction to *Campaspe* in this volume, pp. 27ff.
68. Alan H. Nelson, ed., *Cambridge*, Records of Early English Drama, 2 vols. (Toronto, 1989), pp. 715–19; Nelson, 'Hall Screens and Elizabethan Playhouses: Counter-evidence from Cambridge', to be published soon by John Astington; and John Orrell, 'The Theatre at Christ Church, Oxford, in 1605', *Shakespeare Survey*, XXXV (1982), 129–40, take issue with those who argue for the derivation of the tiring house façade from the hall screen, such as Glynne Wickham, *Early English Stages* (London, 1966–81) and Richard Hosley, 'The Origins of the Shakespearian Playhouse', *Shakespeare 400*, ed. James G. McManaway (New York, 1964), 29–39. On the other hand, solid evidence does exist of at least occasional performance at the lower end of the hall, as Nelson freely admits; see *Dudley Carleton to John Chamberlain, 1603–1624: Jacobean Letters*, ed. Maurice Lee, Jr. (New Brunswick, 1972), letter dated 15 January 1604, pp. 53–5. On the dimensions of the Blackfriars' theatre, see Irwin Smith, *Shakespeare's Blackfriars Playhouse: Its History and Its Design* (New York, 1964); and Hunter, Introduction to *Campaspe*, pp. 27ff.

69. Shapiro, *Children of the Revels*, p. 35.
70. *Documents Relating to the Office of the Revels in the Time of Queen Elizabeth*, ed. Albert Feuillerat (Louvain, 1908), p. 145, quoted by Michael R. Best, 'The Staging and Production of the Plays of John Lyly', *Theatre Research*, IX (1968), 104–17. See also E. K. Chambers, *The Elizabethan Stage*, 4 vols. (Oxford, 1923), I, chap. 7 and III, chap. 19.
71. Shapiro, *Children of the Revels*, p. 35.
72. Richard Southern, *The Staging of Plays before Shakespeare* (London and New York, 1973).
73. Shapiro, *Children of the Revels*, p. 36.
74. Best, 'The Staging and Production of the Plays of John Lyly', *Theatre Research*, IX (1968), 104–17.
75. Best, 'The Staging and Production of the Plays of John Lyly', pp. 107–9, and Hunter, Introduction to *Campaspe*, n. 45.
76. In *The Woman in the Moon*, I.i.56, 'They draw the curtains from before Nature's shop' to reveal several images, one of which is Pandora. An analogous staging is to be found in a boys' play of 1601–03, George Chapman's *Sir Giles Goosecap*. The lovesick hero, Clarence, confined to his bed, '*draws the curtains and sits within them*', and is then visited by Eugenia with her attendants; she '*draws the curtains*' disclosing him, swears fidelity to him, and '*draws the curtains, concealing Clarence, herself, and her attendants*'. Some seventy-five lines later she draws the curtains back and announces to the public her new relationship.
77. Mable Buland, *The Presentation of Time in the Elizabethan Drama* (New York, 1912), pp. 214–15; Bond, II.368.
78. Baldwin, *William Shakspere's Five-Act Structure* pp. 493–543; Hunter, Introduction to *Campaspe*, p. 25.
79. Powell, 'John Lyly and the Language of Play', pp. 157–8.
80. Best, 'Lyly's Static Drama', *Renaissance Drama*, n.s., I (1968), 75–86.
81. Bevington, *From 'Mankind' to Marlowe* (Cambridge, Mass., 1962), pp. 28–9; Peter Saccio, *The Court Comedies of John Lyly: A Study in Allegorical Dramaturgy* (Princeton, 1969), p. 96.
82. Reavley Gair, *The Children of Paul's: The Story of a Theatre Company, 1553–1608* (Cambridge, 1982), p. 103.
83. Saccio, *The Court Comedies of John Lyly*, p. 98.
84. Philip Edwards, *Threshold of a Nation: A Study in English and Irish Drama* (Cambridge, 1979), pp. 49–53.
85. Mincoff, 'Shakespeare and Lyly', p. 24.

SAPPHO AND PHAO

[CHARACTERS IN THE DRAMA,
IN ORDER OF APPEARANCE

PHAO, *a young ferryman.*
VENUS.
CUPID.
TRACHINUS, *a courtier.*
PANDION, *a philosopher and scholar.*   5
CRITICUS, *page to Trachinus.*
MOLUS, *page to Pandion.*
MILETA,
LAMIA,
FAVILLA,   } *ladies of Sappho's court.*   10
ISMENA,
CANOPE,
EUGENUA,
SIBYLLA, *an aged soothsayer.*
SAPPHO, *Princess of Syracuse.*   15

CHARACTERS IN THE DRAMA, IN ORDER OF APPEARANCE] Such a list was first
supplied by Fairholt and was followed by Bond. Daniel arranges the names in
order of appearance. The present list follows that arrangement but adds to the
list the other Cyclopes.

TRACHINUS] an inhabitant of Trachin, a town in Thessaly. Ovid,
Metamorphoses, XI.351, calls Ceyx *Trachinius heros.*
PANDION] The name appears again in Jonson, *Cynthia's Revels.*
LAMIA] the name of a famous Athenion courtesan. Attached to this social
role, the name appears several times in Elizabethan drama.
FAVILLA] The Latin means 'fiery ash'—a name therefore appropriate to
the dreamer about fire in IV.iii. The name appears also in *Endymion*, given to
another courtly servant.
CANOPE] the name of a town in Lower Egypt, famous for its luxury
(Pliny, XXXIV.128), and hence appropriate to the dreamer about gold in IV.iii.
EUGENUA] This is the only instance in English pre-Restoration drama of
the name spelled with -ua. *Eugenia*, on the other hand, is common. (See
Thomas L. Berger and William C. Bradford, Jr., *An Index of Characters in
English Printed Drama to the Restoration*, Englewood, N.J., 1975.)
SIBYLLA] For the use of the Sibyl as an adviser in matters of love, see
William Allan Neilson, *The Origins and Sources of the Court of Love* (Boston,
1899; rept. New York, 1967), pp. 31, 33 and 134–5.
SAPPHO] Sappho is of royal birth, learned and rich (I.ii.7–9), and
presides over a court (I.ii.20, I.iii.2, etc.). The words *princess* or *queen* are not
directly applied to her, however, other than that she is to be the new queen of
love in place of Venus (V.ii.28). She is called 'a lady here in Sicily' at II.ii.3.

CALLIPHO, *one of the Cyclopes.*
VULCAN.
Other Cyclopes.

SCENE: *Syracuse*]

Lyly leaves her exact title and rank to be inferred by the courtiers of Queen Elizabeth's court.

CALLIPHO] the name of a comic character in Plautus' *Pseudolus*; see II.iii.34n. Q1 varies the spelling as *Calypho* and *Calipho*.

The Prologue at the Blackfriars

Where the bee can suck no honey, she leaveth her sting behind, and, where the bear cannot find origanum to heal his
grief, he blasteth all other leaves with his breath. We fear it is
like to fare so with us, that, seeing you cannot draw from our
labours sweet content, you leave behind you a sour mislike,   5
and with open reproach blame our good meanings because you
cannot reap your wonted mirths. Our intent was at this time to
move inward delight, not outward lightness, and to breed (if it
might be) soft smiling, not loud laughing, knowing it to the
wise to be as great pleasure to hear counsel mixed with wit as   10
to the foolish to have sport mingled with rudeness. They were
banished the theatre at Athens, and from Rome hissed, that
brought parasites on the stage with apish actions, or fools with
uncivil habits, or courtesans with immodest words. We have

1–2. *Where the bee . . . behind*] proverbial (Tilley, B207). According to
Pliny, XI.19, bees that drive their stings in deeply become drones and make no
honey. Similar images about bees recur at II.iv.34–5 and IV.iv.19–21 below.
Compare also *Euphues*, I.224, 10–11: 'the bee that hath honey in her mouth
hath a sting in her tail', and Dent, *P.L.E.D.*, B211.

2–3. *where the bear . . . breath*] Origanum's healing properties were many
and fabulous. In *Euphues*, I.208, 21–2, we are told that 'the tortoise, having
tasted the viper, sucketh origanum and is quickly revived' (taken from Pliny,
VIII.41: '*Testudo cunilae quam bubulam vocant pastu vires contra serpentes
refovet*', 'The tortoise eats cunila [a species of origanum], also called ox-grass,
to refresh its strength against the effects of snakebite'). Pliny speaks of bears in
a nearby passage. Origanum was similarly a remedy for storks having eaten
snakes, or boars suffering from blunted tusks (*O.E.D.*, citing texts from 1683
and 1398). The bear's fabled ability to *blast* or shrivel vegetation with his
breath appears in *Euphues*, II.147, 31–2, and is derived from Pliny, XI.115
(Bond, I.338 and II.554). Lyly's invented fable is thus concocted out of various
passages from Pliny.

3. *grief*] injury, suffering (*O.E.D.*, 6).

4. *like*] likely.

11. *They*] i.e., 'They . . . that brought parasites', etc. (ll. 11–13).

11–14. *They . . . words*] 'Probably amplified from Horace's brief account of
the suppression of the licence of "*vetus comoedia*" at Athens (*Ars Poetica*,
281 sqq.), and the preceding uncomplimentary reference to the wit of Plautus,
l. 270' (Bond, II.554–5; Horace, *Satires, Epistles, Ars Poetica*, ed. H. Rushton

endeavoured to be as far from unseemly speeches to make your   15
ears glow as we hope you will be from unkind reports to make
our cheeks blush. The griffin never spreadeth her wings in the
sun when she hath any sick feathers; yet have we ventured to
present our exercise before your judgements when we know
them full of weak matter, yielding rather ourselves to the cour-   20
tesy which we have ever found than to the preciseness which
we ought to fear.

19. exercise] *Q1;* exercises *Bond.*

Fairclough, 1926, pp. 473–5). Parasites and courtesans are common in Plautus'
plays, and earlier Elizabethan dramatists such as Nicholas Udall (*Ralph Roister
Doister*, Prologue) had sought to borrow from Plautus while purging his
immodest effects.

15–16. *to make . . . glow*] The ears proverbially glow, burn or tingle when
people are talking about one (Dent, *P.L.E.D.*, E14), though the point here
seems to be rather that the ears glow at hearing immodesty. Compare
Campaspe, IV.ii.4, and *Midas*, II.i.116–7.

17. *griffin*] fabulous beast usually represented as having the head and wings
of an eagle and the body and hind quarters of a lion, signifying strength and
swiftness. The legend reported here seems to be Lyly's invention, not being
warranted in Pliny, VII.2 or X.70, or Aelian, *De Natura Animalium*, IV.27,
where griffins are mentioned (Bond, II.555).

19. *our exercise*] Lyly's use elsewhere of 'our exercises' to describe his
company's dramatic activities (*Midas*, 'The Prologue in Paul's', l. 10),
Campaspe, the Epilogue at the Blackfriars, l. 5) might seem to support Bond's
emendation of Q1's 'exercise' to the plural, and the use of the plural pronoun
'them' later in the present sentence might lead to the same conclusion, but
O.E.D., 3, cites *exercise* in the sense of 'the execution of (functions)' from late
medieval usage (1393, 1432) and the word may thus embody a plural meaning.

21. *preciseness*] severity, rigorousness.

The Prologue at the Court

The Arabians, being stuffed with perfumes, burn hemlock, a rank poison; and in Hybla, being cloyed with honey, they account it dainty to feed on wax. Your Highness's eyes, whom variety hath filled with fair shows and whose ears pleasure hath possessed with rare sounds, will, we trust, at this time 5 resemble the princely eagle who, fearing to surfeit on spices, stoopeth to bite on wormwood. We present no conceits nor wars, but deceits and loves, wherein the truth may excuse the plainness, the necessity the length, the poetry the bitterness. There is no needle's point so small which hath not his compass, 10

---

10. needle's] *Q3 (needles);* needelesse *Q1.*

1–2. *The Arabians ... poison*] Bond (II.555) notes the source in Pliny, XII.38: '*Peregrinos ipsa* [Arabia] *mire odores et ad exteros petit: tanta mortalibus suarum rerum satietas est alienarumque aviditas*', 'And there is also, in Arabia, a surprising demand for imported foreign scents, so bored do people get with the things they have and so desirous of what others have', citing also in *Euphues*, I.194, 17–18, a reference to those who burn hemlock 'to smoke the bees from their hives'.
   1. *stuffed*] glutted.
   2. *Hybla*] a town and region of Sicily (not far from the Syracusa of this play) noted for its honey. Compare *Euphues*, I.221, 25, and I.314, 20, and *Endymion*, III.iv.145. It is mentioned several times by Shakespeare.
   they] i.e., the inhabitants of Hybla.
   5. *rare*] excellent.
   6. *princely eagle*] No authority has been found for this fanciful legend, but the associations of the eagle with royalty and of wormwood with bitterness are common. On the eagle, compare III.iii.87 and V.i.17 below.
   7. *conceits*] fanciful tales, trifles.
   8–9. *truth ... plainness*] Truth's tale is proverbially simple; see Dent, *P.L.E.D.*, T593. The tactful apology for presuming to speak on sensitive issues that may be related to court politics is reiterated in the Epilogue.
   9. *the bitterness*] perhaps a reference to the play's ending not with a romantic conclusion but with Phao's unhappy departure from Syracuse (V.iii.5ff.)—to which a topical interpretation might be given. See John W. Houppert, *John Lyly*, p. 74.
   10. *needle's*] Qq1–2 read 'needelesse', an error probably caused, as Bond observes (II.555) by the confusion of the ordinary unapostrophied spelling of the possessive ('needles') with the common privative suffix *-les*.
   his compass] its measurement around, girth (*O.E.D.*, sb., 7b), with a play on the idea of a needle as a mariner's magnetic navigational compass.

nor hair so slender which hath not his shadow, nor sport so
simple which hath not his show. Whatsoever we present,
whether it be tedious (which we fear) or toyish (which we
doubt), sweet or sour, absolute or imperfect, or whatsoever,
in all humbleness we all, and I on knee for all, entreat that   15
your Highness imagine yourself to be in a deep dream that,
staying the conclusion, in your rising your Majesty vouchsafe
but to say, 'And so you awaked.'

---

11. *nor hair . . . shadow*] Compare Erasmus, *Adagia*, II.836A: '*Etiam capillus
unus habet umbram suam*'.

13. *toyish*] trifling.

14. *doubt*] The antithesis of *fear* and *doubt* may suggest a meaning here of
'am uncertain about', but must also mean 'fear', 'suspect'. It would be unlike
Lyly to claim that his play is not a *jeu d'esprit*.

absolute] free from imperfection. In *Campaspe*, III.iii.7, Apelles describes
Campaspe as having 'so absolute a face'.

15. *on knee for all*] The speaker of the Prologue, perhaps Lyly, kneels to
Queen Elizabeth on behalf of his company.

17. *staying*] remaining for (*O.E.D.*, *stay*, vb.[1], 17).

18. '*And . . . awaked*'] The Prologue, by anticipating here Sappho's words
about her dream at IV.iii.26, underscores the connection between Sappho and
the royal spectator whose rising will end the play. *Sappho and Phao* is to be
Queen Elizabeth's dream, much as *A Midsummer Night's Dream* is to be the
dream of its audience.

Act I

Actus Primus, Scaena Prima.

[*Enter*] PHAO.

Phao. Thou art a ferryman, Phao, yet a free man, possessing
for riches content and for honours quiet. Thy thoughts
are no higher than thy fortunes, nor thy desires greater
than thy calling. Who climbeth, standeth on glass and
falleth on thorn. Thy heart's thirst is satisfied with thy   5
hand's thrift, and thy gentle labours in the day turn to
sweet slumbers in the night. As much doth it delight
thee to rule thine oar in a calm stream as it doth Sappho
to sway the sceptre in her brave court. Envy never
casteth her eye low, ambition pointeth always upward,   10

0.1̂.] *Bond; Phao, Venus, Cupid* / Q1. *Entering stage directions throughout are
massed at the start of each scene in the early texts.*

0.1.] Aelian, *Varia Historia*, XII.18, is Lyly's source for this scene; see
Introduction, pp. 14–15. Lyly has changed the locale from Mitylene
to Syracuse, following a suggestion in Ovid's *Heroides*, XV.11, in which Sappho
addresses her lover who has fled to Sicily. From the dialogue we understand
this scene to be placed at the ferry.

1. *free man*] with a play on *ferryman*.

2. *for riches content*] Compare the proverb, 'Contentment is great riches'
(Dent, *P.L.E.D.*, C629). Bond (II.555) urges a resemblance between Phao's
opening soliloquy and Euphues's exhortation to Philautus in *The Cooling Card*
(I.246–57), but the sentiment is conventional and widespread.

4. *Who climbeth*] He who climbs, aspires.

standeth on glass] a proverbial idea (Dent, *P.L.E.D.*, G136.1), pointing to
the fact that glass is so slippery. See Publilius Syrus, *Sententiae*, 219; '*Fortuna
vitrea est: tum cum splendet frangitur*', 'Luck is like glass—just when it glitters,
it smashes.'

6. *thrift*] industry.

gentle] honourable (with a play on 'gentle'–'sweet', ll. 6–7).

9. *sway the sceptre*] i.e., rule.

brave] fine, handsome.

9–10. *Envy . . . upward*] proverbial images of envy and ambition, later
repeated in Sibylla's warning to Phao to keep 'thine eyes upward and thy
fingers down' (II.i.155 and n.).

and revenge barketh only at stars. Thou farest delicately
if thou have a fare to buy anything. Thine angle is ready
when thine oar is idle, and as sweet is the fish which
thou gettest in the river as the fowl which other buy in
the market. Thou needest not fear poison in thy glass   15
nor treason in thy guard. The wind is thy greatest enemy, whose might is withstood with policy. O sweet life
seldom found under a golden covert, often under a
thatched cottage! But here cometh one. I will withdraw
myself aside; it may be a passenger. [*He stands aside.*]   20

              [*Enter*] VENUS [*and*] CUPID.

Venus. It is no less unseemly than unwholesome for Venus,
who is most honoured in princes' courts, to sojourn
with Vulcan in a smith's forge, where bellows blow instead of sighs, dark smokes rise for sweet perfumes,

20–20.1. *He . . . Cupid*] Bond (*subst.*); *not in* Q1. *See Collation note at 0.1.*

---

11. *barketh*] Compare the wolves barking at Cynthia in *Endymion*, V.i.120.
Vengeful feelings, like envy and ambition, are directed upward (*at stars*), at the
great.

12. *fare*] passenger's fee (with word-play on *farest*, l. 11).
angle] fishing gear.

14. *other*] others.

15. *poison*] a traditional accompaniment of greatness; compare '*venenum in
auro bibitur*', 'drunk in gold the poison is', Seneca, *Thyestes*, l. 453, trans.
Jasper Heywood, 1560, sig. B7v. See Dent, *P.L.E.D.*, P458, for other Senecan
uses.

16. *in thy guard*] Compare the death of Nero.

16–17. *The wind . . . enemy*] Compare *As You Like It*, II.i.6–11 and
II.vii.173ff.

17. *policy*] cunning (in seamanship).

17–19. *O . . . cottage*] The stoic commonplace that 'content lodges oftener in
cottages than palaces' (Dent, *P.L.E.D.*, C626) is a favourite of Seneca, as in
Hercules Furens (trans. Jasper Heywood), I. Chorus, C4, and *Hippolytus* (trans.
John Studley) 4, Chorus, L2v. Compare *Euphues*, II.46, 17–18.

18. *covert*] shelter (i.e., roof), dwelling.

20.1. *CUPID*] The text does not make clear if Cupid is to be winged and
blindfolded, but he does have his bow and arrow, and at IV.i.11 he professes to
have wounded Sappho as he did because 'I was blind'. In scene ix of *Cambyses*,
c. 1561, Venus enters 'leading out her son Cupid, blind', and has to direct the
aim of his bow; such stage business is notably lacking here. Compare the
description of Cupid in *Gallathea*, V.iii.92–3, as having wings but with no
mention of blindfolding, and conversely in *Love's Metamorphosis*, II.i.51–5,
where Cupid is described as blind, naked and winged, with bow and arrows.

22–3. *to sojourn . . . forge*] See Introduction, pp. 184–7, for the possibility

and for the panting of loving hearts is only heard the   25
beating of steeled hammers. Unhappy Venus that,
carrying fire in thine own breast, thou shouldst dwell
with fire in his forge! What doth Vulcan all day but
endeavour to be as crabbed in manners as he is crooked
in body, driving nails when he should give kisses, and   30
hammering hard armours when he should sing sweet
amours? It came by lot, not love, that I was linked with
him. He gives thee bolts, Cupid, instead of arrows,
fearing belike, jealous fool that he is, that if he should
give thee an arrow head he should make himself a broad   35
head. But come, we will to Syracusa, where thy deity
shall be shown and my disdain. I will yoke the neck that
yet never bowed, at which, if Jove repine, Jove shall
repent. Sappho shall know, be she never so fair, that
there is a Venus which can conquer, were she never so   40
fortunate.

Cupid. If Jove espy Sappho, he will devise some new shape to
entertain her.

Venus. Strike thou Sappho, let Jove devise what shape he can.

Cupid. Mother, they say she hath her thoughts in a string, that   45

(by no means certain) that Venus and Cupid enter here from a stage entrance
or structure representing Vulcan's forge, and that such a symbolic location is
visible throughout the play.

26. *steeled*] made of steel, or with the outer surface, edge or point of steel.

27. *fire*] i.e., passion (with word-play on the *fire* of Vulcan's forge, l. 28).

29–30. *crooked in body*] For various accounts of Vulcan's lameness in the
Iliad, see Introduction, p. 160. Compare *Euphues*, I.239, 21–2: 'Venus was
content to take the blacksmith with his polt foot', *Euphues*, II.88, 17 and
II.102, 14–26.

33. *bolts . . . arrows*] *Bolts* were arrows of the stouter and shorter kind, with
blunt or thickened heads, often discharged from the crossbow. Hence, as Bond
(II.555) observes, the punning opposition in 35–6 between an *arrow head* and a
broad head, i.e., one with cuckold's horns. Compare the proverbial phrase, 'a
fool's bolt is soon shot' (as in *Henry V*, III.v.122).

34. *belike*] perhaps.

35. *an arrow head*] George Hunter points out that the antithesis with *a broad
head*, ll. 35–6, seems to be secured by hearing the phrase as also 'a narrow
head'.

40. *she*] i.e., Sappho.

43. *entertain*] amuse, encounter, receive as a guest or retainer; with erotic
suggestion. Jove will disguise himself for Sappho, as he did for Leda, Europa,
Io, Danae (see IV.iii.59–66 below), etc.

45. *in a string*] on a leash, under control. Compare the proverbial phrase, 'to

she conquers affections and sendeth love up and down
upon errands. I am afraid she will yerk me if I hit her.

Venus. Peevish boy, can mortal creatures resist that which the
immortal gods cannot redress?

Cupid. The gods are amorous and therefore willing to be   50
pierced.

Venus. And she amiable and therefore must be pierced.

Cupid. I dare not.

Venus. Draw thine arrow to the head, else I will make thee
repent it at the heart. [*Phao comes forward.*] Come away,   55
and behold the ferry boy ready to conduct us. — Pretty
youth, do you keep the ferry that bendeth to Syracusa?

Phao. The ferry, fair lady, that bendeth to Syracusa.

Venus. I fear if the water should begin to swell thou wilt want
cunning to guide.   60

Phao. These waters are commonly as the passengers be, and

---

55. *Phao comes forward*] Bond (*subst.*) (*after 'conduct us' in l. 56.*)

---

have the world (fortune, love, etc.) in a string' (Dent, *P.L.E.D.*, W886), and
Euphues, II.92, 26–7: 'thou hast not love in a string, affection is not thy slave'.

46–7. *up . . . errands*] 'Fit to be sent (to send) on errands' is a proverbial idea
applied to one who is no better than a slave or menial (Dent, *P.L.E.D.*,
E180.11).

47. *yerk*] whip, lash. Compare *Pap with an Hatchet*, Bond, III.407, 14:
children who play with their food 'ought to be yerked'.

51–2. *pierced . . . pierced*] The word-play involves several meanings: (1)
moved by prayer; (2) struck by Cupid's arrows; (3) sexually penetrated.

52. *amiable*] worthy to be loved, lovely (French *aimable*).

54. *to the head*] i.e., with the arrow drawn fully back on the bowstring until
the bow is fully bent and the arrow head alongside the bow. Used again at
IV.i.6 and V.i.13.

55. *Come away*] Come along.

56–7. *Pretty youth*] Aelian, *Varia Historia* (XII.18), reports that, when he
carried Venus over the water, Phaon was rewarded with 'an alabaster box full
of ointment for her ferryage, wherewith Phaon, washing and scouring his skin,
had not his fellow in fairness of favour and beautiful complexion alive' (trans.
Abraham Fleming, 1576). Lyly gives Phao beauty from the first, though
Venus' gift makes him even more fair 'on the sudden' (I.iv.1) and thus
irresistible. Compare II.i.31–2 where Phao denies to Sibylla that he was 'born
so fair by nature'.

57. *bendeth*] directs its course (*O.E.D.*, sb., 20b). Phao's use of the word
bendeth at l. 58 may also embrace the meaning, 'bows in reverence or
submission' (*O.E.D.*, 9c), since Syracuse is the seat of Sappho's royal power.
A bow by the actor would gracefully make the point.

59. *swell*] rise in a storm.

59–60. *want cunning*] lack skill.

therefore, carrying one so fair in show, there is no cause
to fear a rough sea.

Venus. To pass the time in thy boat, canst thou devise any
pastime?   65

Phao. If the wind be with me, I can angle, or tell tales; if
against me, it will be pleasure for you to see me take
pains.

Venus. I like not fishing, yet was I born of the sea.

Phao. But he may bless fishing that caught such an one in   70
the sea.

Venus. It was not with an angle, my boy, but with a net.

Phao. So was it said that Vulcan caught Mars with Venus.

Venus. Didst thou hear so? It was some tale.

Phao. Yea, madam, and that in the boat I did mean to make   75
my tale.

Venus. It is not for a ferryman to talk of the gods' loves, but to
tell how thy father could dig and thy mother spin. But
come, let us away.

Phao. I am ready to wait.   *Exeunt.*   80

---

62. *show*] appearance.

65. *pastime*] recreation, amusement (and playing on the literal sense of *pass
the time*, l. 64).

66. *angle . . . tales*] To *angle*, or fish, has the figurative connotation of 'use
artful means to draw one's listeners out', and *tell tales* is similarly ambiguous:
(1) 'tell stories to listeners'; (2) 'tell untruths, deceive'.

67–8. *take pains*] labour to secure a good result (with a play of antithesis
between *pleasure* and *pain*).

69. *born of the sea*] Venus was said to have sprung from the foam of the sea.
See III.iii.92–5, where Sappho refers to Venus' tortoise, cockleshells and
sponge, and compare *Gallathea*, V.i.47: 'Venus was born of the sea', from
Ovid's *Heroides*, XV.213 ('*Venus orta mari*'). According to Bond, II.573, the
Ovid was quoted in Lyly's school book, *A Short Introduction of Grammar* by
William Lily or Lilly (Lyly's grandfather) and John Colet.

73. *Vulcan . . . Venus*] Homer's *Odyssey*, VIII.266–343, tells how Hephaestus
or Vulcan, by means of a net, caught his wife *in flagrante delicto* with her lover
Ares (Mars) and held them up thus to the laughter of the Olympians. In the
present scene, Venus, having introduced the idea of a net in a more innocent
context (l. 72), is not eager to hear the subject pursued. Phao does not yet
know that she is Venus, and has intended no insult.

74–6. *tale . . . tale*] mere story, falsehood . . . discourse, narrative.

78. *dig . . . spin*] i.e., Phao is a mere mortal and son of Adam. Compare the
old rhyme, 'When Adam delved and Eve span, / Who was then the
gentleman?', associated with the radicalism of Wat Tyler's insurrection (1381)
and derived seemingly from Richard Rolle of Hampole (d. *c.* 1349).

80. *wait*] serve (but invoking a paradoxical contrast of departing and
waiting).

Actus Primus, Scaena Secunda.

[*Enter*] TRACHINUS, PANDION, CRITICUS, MOLUS.

Trachinus. Pandion, since your coming from the university to
    the court, from Athens to Syracusa, how do you feel
    yourself altered, either in humour or opinion?
Pandion. Altered, Trachinus. I say no more, and shame that
    any should know so much.   5
Trachinus. Here you see as great virtue, far greater bravery,
    the action of that which you contemplate: Sappho, fair
    by nature, by birth royal, learned by education, by
    government politic, rich by peace, insomuch as it is
    hard to judge whether she be more beautiful or wise,   10
    virtuous or fortunate. Besides, do you not look on fair
    ladies instead of good letters and behold fair faces in-
    stead of fine phrases? In universities virtues and vices
    are but shadowed in colours white and black, in courts
    showed to life good and bad. There, times past are read   15

0.1. *Enter*] Bond; *not in* Q1.

1–2.] The dialogue sets the scene not far from Sappho's court in Syracuse;
see also l. 57 below, when Trachinus invites Pandion to go 'thither' to the court
with him, and ll. 75–6, in which Molus is told to 'go to Syracusa about by
land'. Compare also II.ii.13–15, in which Sappho can choose to return to her
palace by ferry or by walking 'in through the park'. The scene could thus be
near the ferry, as in scene i.
    Pandion's role as philosopher and student having come from the university
to court, able to comment on its manners and yet remain independent of royal
patronage, places him in some kind of relation to Lyly himself, as Fleay and
Bond (II.556) among others have observed, and also suggests a resemblance
both to Euphues in some of his letters and to Diogenes among other more
complacent philosophers at the court of Alexander in *Campaspe*.
    3. *humour*] 'mental disposition, mood.
    4. *I say no more*] a commonplace expression (Dent, *P.L.E.D.*, M1140–1.11)
suggesting there is indeed more to say. Used also at II.iv.109 and V.ii.83.
      6. *bravery*] splendour.
    7. *action*] practical accomplishment, as opposed to contemplation; the
distinction is based on the commonplace one between the *vita activa* and the
vita contemplativa.
    8–9. *by government politic*] judicious through self-rule and in ruling others.
    12. *good letters*] the profession of literature (*O.E.D.*, *letter*, sb., 6b).
    14. *shadowed*] indicated obscurely or in slight outline (*O.E.D.*, *shadow*, vb.,
7).
    15. *to life*] to the life, with lifelike resemblance to the original.

of in old books, times present set down by new devices,
times to come conjectured at by aim, by prophecy, or
chance; here are times in perfection, not by device, as
fables, but in execution, as truths. Believe me, Pandion,
in Athens you have but tombs, we in court the bodies,   20
you the pictures of Venus and the wise goddesses, we
the persons and the virtues. What hath a scholar found
out by study that a courtier hath not found out by
practice? Simple are you that think to see more at the
candle-snuff than the sunbeams, to sail further in a   25
little brook than in the main ocean, to make a greater
harvest by gleaning than reaping. How say you, Pandion,
is not all this true?

Pandion. Trachinus, what would you more? All true.

Trachinus. Cease then to lead thy life in a study, pinned with   30
a few boards, and endeavour to be a courtier to live in
embossed roofs.

---

32. roofs] *Q1* (rouffes).

---

16. *devices*] things artistically and fancifully conceived, as in emblematic
masques or witty conceits. The idea recurs in *device*, l. 18, where it is
associated with *fables*.

20. *Athens*] identified here with the Academy of the philosophers.

tombs] i.e., lifeless shadows and mere pictures.

24. *Simple*] Simple-minded. Compare I.iv.36.

24–5. *at the candle-snuff*] in work done studiously by the last glimmer
(snuff) of candlelight (*O.E.D.*, *candle*, 7).

27. *gleaning*] literally, the gathering of that left by the reapers in the *harvest*,
hence, gathering scraps of wisdom; with suggestion too of scraping together
the means of living in contrast to those who reap the benefits of position and
wealth. The point anticipates the joking of Molus in I.iii and subsequently
about the poverty of the scholar's life.

30. *in a study*] (1) in a room containing books, *O.E.D.*, 8b; (2) in reflective
meditation and reading; (3) in a state of mental perplexity.

30–1. *pinned . . . boards*] i.e., confined in the pinfold of the college or library
(*O.E.D.*, *pin*, vb., 10 and 11); probably with reference to the partition walls of
boards making the 'study' (compare 'Friar Bacon's study' in Oxford).
Gallathea, I.iv.20, uses the same phrase in speaking of a mariner, confined to
the planks of his vessel.

32. *embossed roofs*] Q1, 'emboste rouffes', suggests a pun on (1) carved
ceilings, such as might be covered with ornamental bosses or studs; (2)
starched and convex ruffs (Bond, II.556). *Gallathea*, V.ii.34, in which Hebe
bids farewell to princes' courts, 'whose roofs [Q1: roofes) are imbossed with
gold', supports the first of the readings here. Compare *aurea . . . tecta* in
Seneca, *Hercules Oetaeus*, l. 646, Statius, *Thebiad*, VII.56, and Jonson's 'To

Pandion. A labour intolerable for Pandion.

Trachinus. Why?

Pandion. Because it is harder to shape a life to dissemble than   35
to go forward with the liberty of truth.

Trachinus. Why, do you think in court any use to dissemble?

Pandion. Do you know in court any that mean to live?

Trachinus. You have no reason for it but an old report.

Pandion. Report hath not always a blister on her tongue.   40

Trachinus. Ay, but this is the court of Sappho, Nature's mir-
acle, which resembleth the tree salurus whose root is
fastened upon knotted steel and in whose top bud leaves
of pure gold.

Pandion. Yet hath salurus blasts and water boughs, worms   45
and caterpillars.

Trachinus. The virtue of the tree is not the cause, but the
easterly wind, which is thought commonly to bring
cankers and rottenness.

Penshurst', ll. 1-3: 'Thou art not, Penshurst, built to envious show, / Of
touch, or marble; nor canst boast a row / Of polish'd pillars, or a roof of gold.'

37–8. *Why, . . . live*] Pandion's retort derives its irony through pointing out
the obvious and unavoidable truth observed in the proverb, 'He that cannot
dissemble knows not how to live (or rule)' (Dent, *P.L.E.D.*, D386). Compare
Euphues, I.236, 19–20: 'he that cannot dissemble in love is not worthy to live',
and Pettie, *Petite Palace*, I.116: 'A settled sentence amongst you, that he which
knoweth not how to dissemble knoweth not how to live.' Cited in Tilley,
Elizabethan Proverb Lore, no. 157.

37. *in court . . . dissemble*] that any courtiers practise dissembling.

39. *for it*] for saying so.

report] idle talk; but see next note for word-play.

40. *Report . . . tongue*] proverbially, 'Report has a blister on her tongue'
(Dent, *P.L.E.D.*, R84); i.e., a blister will appear on the tongue of anyone who
tells a lie or spreads malicious rumour. Pandion ironically varies the proverb to
imply that his *report* has nothing to do with rumour or scandalous talk.
Compare *Euphues*, II.21, 5: 'my tongue would blister if I should utter them'.

42. *salurus*] This legend has no authority in Pliny or Aelian, but the tree and
its enemies resemble the cedar of Sappho's dream (IV.iii.13–17).

45. *blasts*] blights, withering.

water boughs] water-shoots or suckers growing from the tree's roots, sapping
its strength. In his Epistle Dedicatory to *Euphues* (II.5, 33), Lyly speaks of
himself as 'a water bough, no bud'.

48–9. *easterly wind . . . rottenness*] Compare Chapman, *Bussy D'Ambois*,
III.ii.389ff. (Revels edn.): 'like an eastern wind, that where it flies, / Knits nets
of caterpillars, with which you catch / The prime of all the fruits the Kingdom
yields'. (Bussy is using the metaphor in the context of court politics.) The

Pandion. Not the excellency of Sappho the occasion, but the   50
   iniquity of flatterers, who always whisper in princes'
   ears suspicion and sourness.
Trachinus. Why then you conclude with me that Sappho for
   virtue hath no co-partner.
Pandion. Yea, and with the judgement of the world that she is   55
   without comparison.
Trachinus. We will thither straight.
Pandion. I would I might return straight.
Trachinus. Why, there you may live still.
Pandion. But not still.   60
Trachinus. How like you the ladies? Are they not passing fair?
Pandion. Mine eye drinketh neither the colour of wine nor
   women.
Trachinus. Yet am I sure that in judgement you are not so
   severe but that you can be content to allow of beauty by   65
   day or by night.
Pandion. When I behold beauty before the sun, his beams dim
   beauty; when by candle, beauty obscures torchlight;
   so as no time I can judge, because at any time I cannot
   discern, being in the sun a brightness to shadow beauty   70
   and in beauty a glistering to extinguish light.
Trachinus. Scholarlike said; you flatter that which you seem to

---

origin of the idea may be in Pharaoh's dream in Genesis xli.6, where the seven
ears of corn are 'blasted with the east wind'.

57–8. *straight . . . straight*] straightway . . . unbent, free of crookedness.
Trachinus and Pandion agree on Sappho's virtues but not on the feasibility of
service at court.

59–60. *still . . . still*] continually . . . contentedly, at rest.

61. *passing*] surpassingly.

62–3. *Mine eye . . . women*] The philosopher's life has no place for wine or
women, and so he cannot judge them by their *colour*, as one appraises a wine by
its tint or a woman by her complexion (with a marked suggestion that the
colour is merely cosmetic and deceiving, *O.E.D.*, 11).

65. *allow of*] approve (*O.E.D.*, 2b).

70. *shadow*] overshadow. Pandion distinguishes as always between truth and
illusion, the first of which puts mere physical beauty in its shadow while the
other gives it an apparent advantage. The illusion of female beauty works best
by artificial light.

72–3.] i.e., in scholarly and paradoxical fashion you manage both to flatter
beauty by disqualifying yourself as judge and to put it down despite your
obvious fascination.

mislike and to disgrace that which you most wonder at.
But let us away.

Pandion. I follow. [*To Molus*] And you, sir boy, go to Syracusa   75
about by land, where you shall meet my stuff; pay for
the carriage, and convey it to my lodging.

Trachinus. I think all your stuff are bundles of paper. But now
must you learn to turn your library to a wardrobe and
see whether your rapier hang better by your side than   80
the pen did in your ear.

                    Exeunt [TRACHINUS *and* PANDION].

                 Actus Primus, Scaena Tertia.

            CRITICUS [*and*] MOLUS [*remain*].

Criticus. Molus, what odds between thy commons in Athens
and thy diet in court, a page's life and a scholar's?

---

73. to disgrace] *Q1;* seek to disgrace *Fairholt.*   75. *To Molus*] *This ed., not in
Q1; Bond inserts after 'sir boy'.*   boy] *Q2;* boyes *Q1.*   81.1.] *Bond; Exeunt Q1.*
0.1.] *Daniel, subst., Cryticus, Molus / Q1.*   2. thy diet] *Q1;* the diet *Q2.*

73. *to disgrace*] 'seem to disgrace' is understood. Fairholt's emendation,
'seek to disgrace', is probably unnecessary.

75. *sir boy*] a mock title for a diminutive page, played by a boy actor. Q2's
'boy' is seemingly a compositor's guess for Q1's 'boyes', but surely
appropriate. Pandion has only one servant.

76. *by land*] i.e., by way of the landing. Pandion's belongings have arrived
from Athens by boat.

76–8. *stuff . . . stuff*] belongings . . . rubbish.

77. *carriage*] conveyance, carrying.

79. *wardrobe*] (1) dressing room; (2) stock of wearing apparel.

0.1.] The scene continues. The two servants, having silently attended their
masters throughout I.ii, remain to offer their comment on the courtly/
academic debate just concluded. Compare II.iii.0 and III.ii.0 for similar
situations where servants remain onstage after their masters have left.

1. *odds*] difference.

commons] provisions for the academic community (originally in monastic
use).

2. *thy diet*] Q2's reading of 'the diet' is attractive at first as a way of creating
an antithesis between the academy and the court, but Molus' reply in ll. 3–4
speaks of both diets as his, one past and the other present, and so the Q1
reading seems not only more authoritative but correct. *Diet*, meaning
'provisions of food', also contains a secondary suggestion, 'meeting of estates
of a realm' (used at this time of Germany, as in the 'Diet of Worms': *O.E.D.*,

Molus. This difference: there of a little I had somewhat, here
    of a great deal nothing; there did I wear pantofles on my
    legs, here do I bear them in my hands.   5

Criticus. Thou mayst be skilled in thy logic, but not in thy
    liripoop; belike no meat can down with you unless you
    have a knife to cut it. But come among us and you shall
    see us once in a morning have a mouse at a bay.

Molus. A mouse? Unproperly spoken.   10

Criticus. Aptly understood, a mouse of beef.

Molus. I think indeed a piece of beef as big as a mouse serves
    a great company of such cats. But what else?

---

sb., 2, 5b), and punningly introduces the joke in l. 4 about eating little or
nothing.

    4. *pantofles*] slippers, indoor loose shoes for men or women. With their
embroidery in gold and silver and their corked heels, they were commonly
regarded as symbolic of decadence and pride, though at the university they
might well be plainer and more utilitarian. Compare *Endymion*, II.ii.32–4:
'because your pantables [i.e., pantofles] be higher with cork, therefore your
feet must needs be higher in the insteps'. See also *Euphues*, 1.196, 24, and
1.255, 36, where those who 'stand so on their pantofles' are exhibiting courtly
pride; see also *Euphues*, 1.202, 24, and Bond, III.507, n. 32.

    5. *bear . . . hands*] i.e., carry the pantofles for my master as a page has to do.
Gossen, *School of Abuse*, p. 30, inveighs against 'The little crackhalter that
carrieth his master's pantofles' (*O.E.D.*). See also Fairholt, 1.279, note 16 to
Endymion, for other Elizabethan references.

    7. *liripoop*] originally, the long tail of a university graduate's academic and
clerical hood, thence coming to mean a lesson or role to be learned and spoken
or acted. Criticus here seems to contrast *logic* with a more practical and
commonsense learning. Compare *Mother Bombie*, I.iii.128: 'There's a girl that
knows her liripoop,' *Pap with an Hatchet*, III.407, 30–1: 'I am not all tales, and
riddles, and rhymes, and jests, that's but my liripoop,' and 'The Entertainment of Sudley', Bond, 1.483, 6–7, in which a rustic says 'call me the cutter of
Cotswold, that looks as though he only knew his liripoop', as though it were
his ABC.

    7–8. *no meat . . . cut it*] a reference to chop-logic, and an image of
helplessness in the practical world.

    9. *a mouse at a bay*] a mouse cornered and turning to defend itself from the
baying hounds—a comically grandiose image for hunting such a small animal,
as Molus observes. *Mouse* is also a playful term for a woman (*O.E.D.*, 3a).

    11. *mouse of beef*] 'That part of the ox between the buttock and loin'
(Fairholt, 1.293). *Mouse* here means 'muscle'. Compare *mouse buttock*, 'the
fleshy piece which is cut from a round of beef' (*English Dialect Dictionary*, ed.
Joseph Wright, 1898–1905).

    13. *cats*] a term of contempt (*O.E.D.*, 2). Molus comically suspects that
these 'cats' won't have much to eat.

Criticus. For other sports, a square die in a page's pocket is as
    decent as a square cap on a graduate's head.   15
Molus. You courtiers be mad fellows. We silly souls are only
    plodders at *ergo*, whose wits are clapped up with our
    books, and so full of learning are we at home that we
    scarce know good manners when we come abroad—
    cunning in nothing but in making small things great by   20
    figures, pulling on with the sweat of our studies a great
    shoe upon a little foot, burning out one candle in seek-
    ing for another, raw worldlings in matters of substance,
    passing wranglers about shadows.
Criticus. Then is it time lost to be a scholar. We pages are   25
    politians, for look what we hear our masters talk of, we

---

14. *square die*] cube-shaped die (for gambling)—the singular of 'dice'.

15. *decent*] fitting.

16. *silly*] simple, ignorant of worldly things.

17. ergo] therefore; i.e., introducing the conclusion of a syllogism; logic in general.

18–19. *so full . . . abroad*] Bond (II.556) compares *Compaspe*, I.iii.10ff: 'seeing bookish men are so blockish and so great clerks such simple courtiers', etc., and Bacon's *The Advancement of Learning*, I.iii.8: 'learned men . . . do many times fail to observe decency and discretion in their behaviour and carriage', etc. (ed. W. A. Wright, Oxford, 1868, p. 25).

21. *figures*] (1) artificial representations, images; (2) logical or rhetorical *figures* (O.E.D., 23), especially hyperbole; (3) numbers to be multiplied.

21–2. *a great . . . foot*] a commonplace idea found in Erasmus's *Adagia*, II.566D: '*Ne supra pedem calceus* [shoe]', and II.861C: '*Herculis cothurnos aptare infanti*', 'to apply the shoes of Hercules to a child'; see Dent, *P.L.E.D.*, S366. The image contrasts a great intellectual endeavour with the insignificance of the scholar who attempts it.

22–3. *burning . . . another*] a proverbial commonplace (Dent, *P.L.E.D.*, C47) like that in ll. 21–2, suggesting futile and wasted effort. Lyly could have found it in Gosson, *School of Abuse*, p. 41.

23. *in matters of substance*] in affairs of this world; stressing the antithesis of *substance* and *shadows*, though, as Bond suggests (II.556), *substance* may bear a scholastic sense as well.

26. *politians*] '*Politien*: this word is also received from the Frenchmen, but at this day usual in court and with all good secretaries and cannot find an English word to match him. . . . *Politien* is rather a surveyor of civility than civil, and a public minister or counselor in the state.' George Puttenham, *The Art of English Poesie*, ed. Gladys D. Willcock and Alice Walker, Cambridge, 1936, p. 146, quoted in *O.E.D.* and Bond (II.556–7).

look what] whatever.

determine of; where we suspect, we undermine; and
where we mislike for some particular grudge, there we
pick quarrels for a general grief. Nothing among us but
instead of 'Good morrow,' 'What news?' We fall from   30
cogging at dice to cog with states; and so forward are
mean men in those matters that they would be cocks to
tread down others before they be chickens to rise themselves. Youths are very forward to stroke their chins
though they have no beards, and to lie as loud as he   35
that hath lived longest.

Molus. These be the golden days.

Criticus. Then be they very dark days, for I can see no gold.

Molus. You are gross-witted, master courtier.

Criticus. And you, master scholar, slender-witted.   40

---

27. *determine of*] decide, settle.

where . . . undermine] a proverbial sentiment; see Tilley, S1020 and Pettie, *Petite Palace*, II.105.

undermine] inquire secretly into, seek to undo.

28–9. *for . . . for*] on account of . . . using the pretext of.

particular grudge . . . general grief] Compare the proverb: 'One particularity concludes no generality', Tilley, P81, and Pettie, *Petite Palace*, I.138; also II.113 and 161. Criticus satirises both courtiers and their pages for using general grievances as pretexts for settling personal scores.

29. *grief*] grievance.

29–30. *Nothing . . . news*] Instead of greeting one another civilly, we inquire into the latest court gossip.

31. *cogging*] cheating.

cog with states] deal flatteringly with persons of high rank or with the political sphere (*O.E.D.*, *cog*, 5).

32. *mean men*] persons of low or middle rank.

would be cocks] Compare *Midas*, V.ii.111–12: 'to see eggs forwarder than cocks'.

33. *tread*] crush; but also the specific term for the male bird's act of copulation, as in *Euphues*, II.159, 35, and *Mother Bombie*, I.iii.54; compare *Midas*, II.ii.14, and Chaucer's 'Nun's Priest's Tale', l. 358.

rise] raise, lift up socially, politically and sexually. (*O.E.D.*'s first citation, 30b, is from 1706.)

37–8. *golden . . . gold*] See l. 41n.

39. *gross-witted*] (1) of imperfect bodily senses, unable to see well (since vision is one of the five 'wits'); (2) dull-witted, having misunderstood my meaning (as Molus explains in ll. 41–3).

40. *slender-witted*] a paradoxical word-play on *gross* and *slender*, antithetical terms despite the fact that *slender-witted* and *gross-witted* both mean 'ignorant'. Courtier-page and scholar-page are contrastingly alike.

Molus. I meant times which were prophesied golden for plenty
　　of all things, sharpness of wit, excellency in knowledge,
　　policy in government, for—
Criticus. Soft, *scholaris*, I deny your argument.
Molus. Why, it is no argument.   45
Criticus. Then I deny it because it is no argument. But let us
　　go and follow our masters.   *Exeunt.*

Actus Primus, Scaena Quarta.

[*Enter*] MILETA, LAMIA, FAVILLA,
ISMENA, CANOPE [*and*] EUGENUA.

Mileta. Is it not strange that Phao on the sudden should be
　　so fair?
Lamia. It cannot be strange, sith Venus was disposed to make
　　him fair. That cunning had been better bestowed on
　　women, which would have deserved thanks of nature.   5
Ismena. Haply she did it in spite of women, or scorn of nature.

0.1. *Enter*] Bond; not in *Q1*.   0.2. *and*] Daniel; not in *Q1*.

41. *golden*] Here and in l. 37, Molus the scholar-page alludes to the Golden
Age, a past era of plenty and a prophetically anticipated time of renewed
innocence and cultivation. Criticus (l. 38) can 'See no gold', i.e., receives no
pay and therefore accounts the present to be the 'very dark days' of the age of
iron or lead. Compare *Midas*, I.i.85–6: 'That iron world is worn out; the
golden is now come.'
　44. *scholaris*] of or belonging to a school.
　44–6. *deny . . . deny*] assert the contrary of . . . refuse to admit the existence
of. An *argument* in logic is the middle term of a syllogism; Molus' point is that
he was not using syllogistic argument, to which Criticus replies that in that
case Molus' statement is invalid.
　1–2.] The imagined location of this scene, as Bond suggests (II.557), need
not vary from that of the previous scene or scenes. The ladies have just heard
of Phao's sudden increase in physical beauty and have observed his new
behaviour (ll. 7–8), and so perhaps they are near his ferry, though they could
instead be discussing the matter at court. In any event the scenic arrangement
of the four scenes of Act I need not be visually differentiated in Lyly's theatre.
　1, 3. *strange . . . strange*] odd . . . unaccountable. Lamia's word-play relies
on the proverbial idea that the will of a god cannot be regarded as *strange*.
　5. *would . . . nature*] i.e., would have put beauty to its natural use and
thereby deserved Nature's thanks.
　6. *Haply*] Perhaps.
　in spite of] in order to spite.

Canope. Proud elf, how squeamish he is become already, using
　　　both disdainful looks and imperious words, insomuch
　　　that he galleth with ingratitude! And then, ladies, you
　　　know how it cutteth a woman to become a wooer.　　10
Eugenua. Tush, children and fools, the fairer they are, the
　　　sooner they yield. An apple will catch the one, a baby
　　　the other.
Ismena. Your lover I think be a fair fool, for you love nothing
　　　but fruits and puppets.　　15
Mileta. I laugh at that you all call love, and judge it only a
　　　word called love. Methinks liking, a curtsy, a smile,
　　　a beck, and suchlike are the very quintessence of love.
Favilla. Ay, Mileta, but were you as wise as you would be
　　　thought fair, or as fair as you think yourself wise, you　　20
　　　would be as ready to please men as you are coy to prank
　　　yourself, and as careful to be accounted amorous as you

17. curtsy] *Q1* (curtesie).

---

7. *squeamish*] reserved, distant (*O.E.D.*, 6).

9. *ingratitude*] i.e., (1) indifference to women's attentiveness, for which a
man ought always to be grateful; (2) disagreeableness, unfriendliness (*O.E.D.*,
2).

10. *cutteth*] distresses (*O.E.D.*, 5).

11–12. *children . . . yield*] Children, fools, and fairness or beauty are often
linked in proverbial statement (compare Dent, *P.L.E.D.*, C327.11 and
F530.11), though the witty formulation here may be original.

12–13. *An apple . . . other*] Compare the proverbial formula: 'Won (lost)
with an apple (egg) and lost (won) with a nut (the shell)' (Dent, *P.L.E.D.*,
A295, citing *Euphues*, 1.206, 33–4: 'If he perceive thee to be won with a nut,
he will imagine that thou wilt be lost with an apple'). *Baby* suggests 'doll'; see
l. 15n.

14. *a fair fool*] i.e., a fool for sure (playing on *fairer*, handsomer, in l. 11).

15. *puppets*] dolls. Any man in love with Eugenua, retorts Ismena, would
have to be simple and childish. (*Fruits* and *puppets* play scornfully upon *apple*
and *baby* in l. 12.)

16–17. *only . . . love*] a common formulation: 'X is but a word' (see Dent,
P.L.E.D., W781.11), and *Campaspe*, V.iv.39.

17. *liking*] sexual desire (*O.E.D.*, 2b).

curtsy] *Q1*'s 'curtesie' can be rendered *curtsy* or *courtesy* in modernised
spelling; the two forms overlap considerably as to meaning, and suggest a
feminine gesture of respect and greeting, courteous behaviour, show of
ceremonious self-deprecation, etc.

18. *beck*] gesture of salutation or respect, curtsy, nod (*O.E.D.*, sb., 2, 3).

21–2. *as you . . . yourself*] as you are now disdainful of dressing yourself up,
making ostentatious show (*O.E.D.*, *prank*, vb.[4], 2).

are willing to be thought discreet.

Mileta. No, no, men are good souls (poor souls) who never
    inquire but with their eyes, loving to father the cradle   25
    though they but mother the child. Give me their gifts,
    not their virtues; a grain of their gold weigheth down
    a pound of their wit; a dram of 'give me' is heavier than
    an ounce of 'hear me'. Believe me, ladies, 'give' is a
    pretty thing.   30

Ismena. I cannot but oftentimes smile to myself to hear men
    call us weak vessels when they prove themselves broken-
    hearted, us frail when their thoughts cannot hang
    together, studying with words to flatter and with bribes
    to allure when we commonly wish their tongues in their   35
    purses, they speak so simply, and their offers in their
    bellies, they do it so peevishly.

---

24. *good souls (poor souls)*] The word-play catches the paradox: men are a
good enough sort but poor miserable wretches.

24–6. *who . . . child*] The gist of Mileta's witty put-down of men is that they
are importunate wooers but too absorbed in mere appearances and possessions.
As Bond (II.557) suggests, the phrase sounds proverbial.

28–9. *a dram . . . 'hear me'*] proverbial (Tilley, A14). Bond (II.557 and
III.521) cites Lodge's *Rosalynde* (ed. Israel Gollancz, London, 1907, p. 137),
and compares Ovid's *Amores*, I.viii.62: '*Crede mihi, res est ingeniosa dare*',
'Believe me, giving calls for genius', quoted in *Midas*, I.i.83.

32–3. *weak . . . frail*] a commonplace observation based on 1 Peter iii.7, as
in Shakespeare's *Romeo and Juliet*, I.i.15–16: 'women, being the weaker
vessels . . .' (see Dent, *P.L.E.D.*, W655, *Euphues*, 1.223, ll. 15–16, Pettie,
Petite Palace, II.83, and *Hamlet*, I.ii.146: 'Frailty, thy name is woman'; Dent,
P.L.E.D., W700.1). Lyly here places these misogynistic sentiments in an
ironic context.

broken-hearted] In the context of Ismena's whole speech, this seems to mean
'perjured, having broken the heart's vow'; see next note.

33–4. *their thoughts . . . together*] i.e., men are inconstant. Bond (II.557)
compares *Gallathea*, IV.ii.37–8: 'It [a love knot] was made of a man's thought,
which will never hang together.'

34. *studying*] industriously applying themselves to acquiring the skill.

35–6. *wish . . . purses*] To put or have one's tongue in one's purse is a
proverbial commonplace found, e.g., in John Heywood's *Witty and Witless*, *c.*
1530, p. 201 (Dent, *P.L.E.D.*, T399). Men woo so inanely, Ismena suggests,
that it might be better if their tongues were pursed up and their money allowed
to speak for them.

simply] simple-mindedly.

36–7. *their offers . . . bellies*] i.e., it would be better if men were to eat their
words, be silent. Compare Dent, *P.L.E.D.*, B299: 'I wish it were in your belly

Mileta. It is good sport to see them want matter, for then fall
they to good manners, having nothing in their mouths
but 'Sweet mistress', wearing our hands out with courtly   40
kissings when their wits fail in courtly discourses—
now ruffling their hairs, now setting their ruffs, then
gazing with their eyes, then sighing with a privy wring
by the hand, thinking us like to be wooed by signs and
ceremonies.   45
Eugenua. Yet we, when we swear with our mouths we are not
in love, then we sigh from the heart and pine in love.
Canope. We are mad wenches, if men mark our words; for
when I say I would none cared for love more than I,
what mean I but I would none loved but I? Where we   50
cry 'Away', do we not presently say 'Go to'? And when
men strive for kisses, we exclaim 'Let us alone!' as
though we would fall to that ourselves.
Favilla. Nay, then, Canope, it is time to go and behold Phao.

(for me)', a colloquial way of retorting to some irritating insult or circumstance, and *1 Henry IV*, III.iii.49: 'I wish my face were in your belly.'

38–41.] Bond compares Rosalind's advice to Orlando in *As You Like It*,
IV.i.69–71: 'Nay, you were better speak first, and when you were gravelled
for lack of matter, you might take the occasion to kiss.' To *want matter* is to
lack anything to say to the purpose.

42. *setting their ruffs*] i.e., putting their starched neck ruffs in order by
arranging the pleats.

43. *privy*] secret, intimate.

44. *like*] likely.

49–50. *when . . . loved but I*] i.e., when I seem to say that I wish others
would be like me and regard love lightly, what do I really mean but that I
wish I outdid all others in being loved? (Canope illustrates her point that
women's responses to men's wooing often have an ostensible and a hidden
meaning.)

51. *Go to*] an expression of remonstrance, or a protest that in this case has
the force of a flirtatious denial, especially since the phrase can also mean, 'get
to work, come on' (*O.E.D.*, *go*, 91 a and b).

52. *Let us alone*] (1) Leave us in solitude; (2) Leave that to us, i.e., trust us to
fall to kissing on our own initiative (*O.E.D.*, *let*, vb.[1], 18a and d). *As though* is
similarly ambiguous; it can suggest that the women are reluctant or eager to
fall a-kissing.

54. *behold*] (1) see; (2) consider (*O.E.D.*, 6). Ismena takes the word in its
physical sense, but the ladies are too refined to go and stare at a handsome
young man. The word *and* is thus playfully ambiguous: (1) conjunction; (2) in
order to.

Ismena. Where?   55
Favilla. In your head, Ismena, nowhere else. But let us keep
    on our way.
Ismena. Wisely.   *Exeunt.*

Act II

Actus Secundus, Scaena Prima.

[*Enter*] PHAO, [*now very handsome, with a small mirror*];
SIBYLLA [*sitting in the mouth of her cave*].

Phao. Phao, thy mean fortune causeth thee to use an oar, and
thy sudden beauty a glass; by the one is seen thy need,
in the other thy pride. O Venus, in thinking thou hast
blessed me thou hast cursed me, adding to a poor estate
a proud heart and to a disdained man a disdaining mind.　　5
Thou dost not flatter thyself, Phao, thou art fair. Fair?
I fear me 'fair' be a word too foul for a face so passing
fair. But what availeth beauty? Hadst thou all things
thou wouldst wish, thou mightst die tomorrow, and,
didst thou want all things thou desirest, thou shalt live　　10
till thou diest. Tush, Phao, there is grown more pride

0.1–2.] *This ed*; Phao, Sybilla / *Q1*; Enter Phao with a small mirror; Sybilla *sitting in her Cave / Bond.*

0.1.] The location is before the mouth of Sibylla's cave, at night (ll. 15–20).
Sibylla is either visible at the mouth of her cave at the beginning of the scene or
appears there by l. 14 when Phao sees her. Bond (II.365) mentions a show
presented to Queen Elizabeth at Woodstock, 1575, and printed by George
Gascoigne as *The Tale of Hemetes the Hermit* (1577), in English, Latin, Italian
and French, containing 'the grott of Sibylla' to which ladies and knights resort
to learn the future (in John W. Cunliffe, ed., *The Complete Works of George
Gascoigne*, 2 vols., 1907, II.481). The sense of space is fluid on Lyly's stage;
without a break in the action Phao is encountered in the next scene by Sappho
at the ferry.

with a small mirror] If Phao carries an oar as well, he bears with him the
tokens of his neediness and his pride (ll. 1–3). One or more stools are also
required; see l. 23. For other uses of Sibylla as an adviser in love, see notes on
Characters in the Drama.

4–5. *poor . . . proud*] 'Poor and proud' is a commonplace paradox (Dent,
P.L.E.D., P474).

7–8. *I fear . . . passing fair*] Compare Marlowe, *1 Tamburlaine*, V.I.136
(Revels edn.): 'Fair is too foul an epithet for thee.'

7. *passing*] surpassingly.

10. *want*] lack.

10–11. *thou shalt . . . diest*] a proverbial idea (Dent, *P.L.E.D.*, L385).

223

in thy mind than favour in thy face. Blush, foolish boy,
to think on thine own thoughts; cease complaints, and
crave counsel. And lo! Behold Sibylla in the mouth of
her cave. I will salute her.—Lady, I fear me I am out of   15
my way, and so benighted withal that I am compelled
to ask your direction.

Sibylla. Fair youth, if you will be advised by me you shall for
this time seek none other inn than my cave, for that it is
no less perilous to travel by night than uncomfortable.   20

Phao. Your courtesy offered hath prevented what my necessity
was to entreat.

Sibylla. Come near. Take a stool and sit down. Now, for that
these winter nights are long, and that children delight
in nothing more than to hear old wives' tales, we will   25
beguile the time with some story. And, though you
behold wrinkles and furrows in my tawny face, yet may
you haply find wisdom and counsel in my white hairs.

Phao. Lady, nothing can content me better than a tale, neither
is there anything more necessary for me than counsel.   30

Sibylla. Were you born so fair by nature?

Phao. No, made so fair by Venus.

Sibylla. For what cause?

Phao. I fear me for some curse.

Sibylla. Why, do you love and cannot obtain?   35

Phao. No, I may obtain but cannot love.

Sibylla. Take heed of that, my child.

Phao. I cannot choose, good madam.

---

28. haply] *Q1* (happily).

---

12. *favour*] attractiveness.
19. *for that*] since (also in l. 23).
21. *prevented*] anticipated.
23. *Come near*] On staging, compare Sibylla's 'Come in' at II.iv.48 and n.
25. *old wives' tales*] a conventional formulation (Dent, *P.L.E.D.*, W388).
Compare *Euphues*, II.116, 26–7: 'into what blind and gross errors in old time
we were led, thinking every old wife's [Q: wiues] tale to be a truth'.
31–2.] Compare I.i.56–7 and n., where Venus calls Phao 'Pretty youth'
even before she has changed his appearance.
36.] Phao may be thinking of the ladies of Sappho's court; see I.iv.7–10
above. Again at ll. 131–2, he protests that 'to yield to love is the only thing I
hate'. Clearly he does not fall in love with Sappho until II.ii, though Sibylla's
advice that follows in this present scene (ll. 140ff.) does seem directed against
the ambition that will take the form of Phao's loving the queen.

Sibylla. Then hearken to my tale, which I hope shall be as a
    straight thread to lead you out of those crooked conceits   40
    and place you in the plain path of love.
Phao. I attend.
Sibylla. When I was young as you now are—I speak it without
    boasting—I was beautiful; for Phoebus in his godhead
    sought to get my maidenhead. But I, fond wench,   45
    receiving a benefit from above, began to wax squeamish
    beneath, not unlike to asolis, which being made green
    by heavenly drops shrinketh into the ground when
    there fall showers, or the Syrian mud, which being
    made white chalk by the sun never ceaseth rolling till   50
    it lie in the shadow. He to sweet prayers added great
    promises; I, either desirous to make trial of his power or
    willing to prolong mine own life, caught up my handful
    of sand, consenting to his suit if I might live as many
    years as there were grains. Phoebus—for what cannot   55
    gods do, and what for love will they not do?—granted
    my petition. And then—I sigh and blush to tell the
    rest—I recalled my promise.

---

40. *straight . . . conceits*] Sibylla will offer Phao a thread like that of Theseus,
by which he found his way through Daedalus' labyrinth. The image appears
again in the Epilogue, where it is a metaphor for dramatic interpretation.

43–89.] Sibylla's story, told in Ovid's *Metamorphoses*, XIV.130ff., is
reminiscent also of many other Ovidian tales of pursuit by the gods and
metamorphoses of the pursued, such as that of Phoebus Apollo and Daphne.
The Sibyl tells of Apollo's promise and of her forgetting to ask for enduring
youth when she asked for as many years of life as there were grains in her
handful of sand. Ovid's *Fasti*, l. 461, refers to the similar myth, found also in
Hesiod's *Theogony* (984) and elsewhere, of Tithonus, husband of Aurora or
Eos, goddess of the dawn, to whom Aurora granted immortality but without
his specifying that he remain young; he withered into a grasshopper.

45. *fond*] foolish.

47. *beneath*] here on earth.

47–51. *asolis . . . shadow*] These legends are not in Pliny, nor is asolis
identified (Bond, II.557).

53–4. *caught up . . . sand*] As Bond (II.366) notes, the details here are
particularly close to Ovid, *Metamorphoses*, XIV.132–44.

53. *my handful*] a handful.

58. *recalled*] revoked, took back. The earliest citation for this meaning in
O.E.D., recall, vb., 5, is from 1588. The context of the following lines seems
to demand this meaning rather than simply 'remembered', for which *O.E.D.*'s
earliest date (3) is 1611. The Sibyl's refusal is found in Ovid's *Metamorphoses*,
XIV.142ff., lending support to the meaning proposed here.

Phao. Was not the god angry to see you unkind?

Sibylla. Angry, my boy, which was the cause that I was   60
unfortunate.

Phao. What revenge for such rigour used the gods?

Sibylla. None but suffering us to live and know we are no gods.

Phao. I pray, tell on.

Sibylla. I will. Having received long life by Phoebus and rare   65
beauty by nature, I thought all the year would have
been May, that fresh colours would always continue,
that time and fortune could not wear out what gods and
nature had wrought up—not once imagining that white
and red should return to black and yellow; that the   70
juniper, the longer it grew, the crookeder it waxed;
or that in a face without blemish there should come
wrinkles without number. I did as you do, go with my
glass, ravished with the pride of mine own beauty; and
you shall do as I do, loathe to see a glass, disdaining   75
deformity. There was none that heard of my fault but
shunned my favour, insomuch as I stooped for age before I tasted of youth—sure to be long lived, uncertain
to be beloved. Gentlemen that used to sigh from their
hearts for my sweet love began to point with their fingers   80
at my withered face, and laughed to see the eyes out
of which fire seemed to sparkle to be succoured, being
old, with spectacles. This causeth me to withdraw myself to a solitary cave, where I must lead six hundred
years in no less pensiveness of crabbed age than grief   85

---

64. *Phao.*] *Q3; Sapho. Q1.*   70. red] *Q1* (read).   that] *This ed.; not in Q1.*
75. loathe] *Q1* (loath).   82. succoured] *Q1* (suckered).

---

59. *unkind*] ungenerous, undutiful, offering resistance (*O.E.D.*, 3b and e).

62. *rigour*] i.e., Sibylla's hard-heartedness toward Phoebus (*O.E.D.*, 5b, for
which *O.E.D.*'s earliest citation is from 1597).

65ff.] Compare Euphues's exhortations against pride of beauty (Bond, I.203
and II.557).

70. *return*] i.e., return in the biblical sense of 'dust thou art, and to dust thou
shalt return' (the Burial Service, from Ecclesiastes ix).

75. *loathe*] The word, spelled 'loath' in Q1, is ambiguously *loathe*, feel
aversion, or *loath*, reluctant. The parallelism suggests that the verbal meaning
is primary.

77. *favour*] countenance.

84–5. *six hundred years*] The Cumean Sibyl who speaks to Aeneas has lived

of remembered youth. Only this comfort: that, being ceased to be fair, I study to be wise, wishing to be
thought a grave matron since I cannot return to be a
young maid.

Phao. Is it not possible to die before you become so old?   90

Sibylla. No more possible than to return as you are, to be so
young.

Phao. Could not you settle your fancy upon any, or would not
destiny suffer it?

Sibylla. Women willingly ascribe that to fortune which wit-   95
tingly was committed by frowardness.

Phao. What will you have me do?

Sibylla. Take heed you do not as I did. Make not too much of
fading beauty, which is fair in the cradle and foul in the
grave, resembling polion, whose leaves are white in the   100
morning and blue before night, or anyta, which, being
a sweet flower at the rising of the sun, becometh a weed
if it be not plucked before the setting. Fair faces have
no fruits if they have no witnesses. When you shall
behold over this tender flesh a tough skin, your eyes   105
which were wont to glance on others' faces to be sunk so

---

700 years and has 300 more to endure. Ovid's Sibyl too has lived seven
centuries, and must still behold '*ter centum messes, ter centum musta*', '300
harvest-times, 300 vintages'. Lyly perhaps added these figures together,
instead of regarding them as in apposition, with harvest time and vintage
describing the same seasonal event.

96. *frowardness*] perversity.

100. *polion*] Pliny, XXI.21, lists '*poliom herbam inclutam Musaei et Hesiodi
laudibus ad omnia utilem praedicantium superque cetera ad famam etiam ac
dignitates, prorsusque miram, si modo (ut tradunt) folia eius mane candida, meridie
purpurea, sole occidente coerulea aspiciuntur*', 'polion, a herb praised by Musaeus
and Hesiod, who pronounce it useful for all things and above all for winning
fame and honor—indeed, a remarkable herb, if in fact it is true, as they assert,
that its leaves are white to the eye in the morning, bright red at midday and sea
blue at sundown'. As Bond notes (II.557 and III.563-4), Lyly's description of
'Salamints' as white in the morning, red at noon and purple in the evening
(*Love's Metamorphosis*, I.ii.4-5) is similarly founded on the Pliny passage.

101. *anyta*] 'Lyly, as often, caps the marvel just borrowed from Pliny with
one invented by himself' (Bond, II.557).

103-4. *Fair . . . witnesses*] Ovid, *Ars Amatoria*, III.398: '*Fructus abest, facies
cum bona teste caret*', 'Naught is gained when a comely face has none to see it.'
(This and other Ovidian parallels, especially in this scene and in II.iv, are
pointed out by Mustard.)

hollow that you can scarce look out of your own head,
and when all your teeth shall wag as fast as your tongue,
then will you repent the time which you cannot recall
and be enforced to bear what most you blame. Lose not   110
the pleasant time of your youth, than the which there is
nothing swifter, nothing sweeter. Beauty is a slippery
good which decreaseth whilst it is increasing, resembling
the medlar, which in the moment of his full ripeness is
known to be in a rottenness. Whiles you look in the   115
glass, it waxeth old with time; if on the sun, parched
with heat; if on the wind, blasted with cold. A great care
to keep it, a short space to enjoy it, a sudden time to lose
it. Be not coy when you are courted. Fortune's wings
are made of Time's feathers, which stay not whilst one   120
may measure them. Be affable and courteous in youth,
that you may be honoured in age. Roses that lose their
colours keep their savours, and, plucked from the stalk,
are put to the still. Cotonea, because it boweth when the
sun riseth, is sweetest when it is oldest, and children   125

---

110. Lose] *Q1* (Loose; *also at l. 118, etc.*).

110. *blame*] censure, find fault with.

112-13. *Beauty ... increasing*] Ovid, *Ars Amatoria*, II.113-14: '*Forma
bonum fragile est, quantumque accedit ad annos / Fit minor et spatio carpitur ipse
suo*', 'Beauty is a fragile blessing, one that decreases with time and is consumed
by its own years.'

114-15. *the medlar ... rottenness*] Medlars, eaten when decayed to a soft
pulpy state, were proverbial types of beauty's decay, no sooner ripe than rotten
(Dent, *P.L.E.D.*, M863). The asociation with feminine beauty is often
genital, as in Shakespeare's *Romeo and Juliet*, II.i.37-9. Compare *Endymion*,
III.iii.101-2, where medlars are coupled with 'lady longings'.

116. *it*] i.e., beauty.

119-20. *Fortune's wings ... feathers*] a proverbial phrase, though Dent
(*P.L.E.D.*, T342.11) gives no citation in this form prior to Lyly's play. Virgil
says of Rumour (Fama) that 'every feather on her body is a waking eye
beneath' (*Aeneid*, IV.179-90), and Chaucer's Fame has as many eyes 'As
fetheres upon foules be' (*Hous of Fame*, l. 1382).

122-3. *Roses ... savours*] Compare *Euphues*, I.203, 15-16 (Bond,
II.557).

124. *still*] distillery for making perfume. Compare *Euphues*, I.234, 16-
17, where the damask rose is said to be 'sweeter in the still than on the stalk',
and *Midas*, II.i.110-12: 'endeavour all to be wise and virtuous, that when, like
roses, you shall fall from the stalk, you may be gathered and put to the still'.

124-5. *Cotonea ... oldest*] Pliny, XXI.18: '*quaedam vetustate odoratiora, ut
cotonea*', 'some have more scent when they are old, like the cotonea' (Mustard).

which in their tender years sow courtesy shall in their
declining states reap pity. Be not proud of beauty's
painting, whose colours consume themselves because
they are beauty's painting.

Phao. I am driven by your counsel into divers conceits, neither   130
knowing how to stand or where to fall; but to yield to
love is the only thing I hate.

Sibylla. I commit you to Fortune, who is like to play such
pranks with you as your tender years can scarce bear
nor your green wits understand. But repair unto me   135
often, and, if I cannot remove the effects, yet I will
manifest the causes.

Phao. I go, ready to return for advice before I am resolved to
adventure.

Sibylla. Yet hearken two words. Thou shalt get friendship by   140
dissembling, love by hatred; unless thou perish, thou
shalt perish; in digging for a stone, thou shalt reach a
star; thou shalt be hated most because thou art loved
most; thy death shall be feared and wished. So much
for prophecy, which nothing can prevent. And this for   145
counsel, which thou mayst follow. Keep not company

---

130. divers] *Q1* (diuerse).   136. I will] *Q1;* will I *Q3.*   140. hearken] *Q2;*
yearken *Q1.*   two words] *Q1;* to my words Blount.

W. S. Jones, ed. *Pliny,* 1951, identifies *cotonea* as the quince. The detail of
bowing to the rising sun appears to be Lyly's addition.

127. *pity*] compassion, sympathy.

128–9. *painting . . . painting*] adornment with natural colour . . . cosmetic
artifice. Compare the complaints against cosmetics in *Euphues,* I.254, 30ff.,
and II.201, 15–18.

130–1. *I am . . . fall*] Phao's puzzlement is understandable: Sibylla seems to
advise him to seize pleasure while he is young and handsome, but also to
eschew pride in beauty and to live courteously while he is young so that he may
be honoured in his old age.

132. *only thing I hate*] See l. 36 and n. Sibylla's advice at this point is directed
against the dangers of aspiration at court and the resentments that would be
sure to result from the as yet unacknowledged love between Sappho and Phao.

141–2. *perish . . . perish*] Fairholt (I.293) questions the accuracy of the text
here, but, as Bond (II.557) points out, repetition of words in differing senses is
a familiar rhetorical figure often used by Lyly. Sibylla's advice is paradoxical:
unless Phao enters into the courtly world of dissembling, where he will be
much envied, he will fail in his quest.

142–3. *in digging . . . star*] i.e., you will rise paradoxically, both prospering
and incurring envy.

with ants that have wings, nor talk with any near the
hill of a mole; where thou smellest the sweetness of
serpents' breath, beware thou touch no part of the
body. Be not merry among those that put bugloss in   150
their wine and sugar in thine. If any talk of the eclipse
of the sun, say thou never sawest it. Nourish no coneys
in thy vaults nor swallows in thine eaves. Sow next thy

---

148. mole; where] *Q3;* mowle, where *Q1.*

---

147. *ants . . . wings*] Winged ants are here seen as proverbial types of self-
harming aspiration in seeking to rise above the element (earth) to which they
are 'naturally' assigned; compare IV.iii.106–7 below and *Campaspe,* IV.ii.15–
16. Lyly's citations are the earliest given by Dent (*P.L.E.D.,* A256).

148. *hill of a mole*] a type of subversion, of underground working; also, a
type of insignificance, as conventionally contrasted with a mountain. Sibylla's
advice seemingly is to eschew unwarranted aspiration (the winged ant) and
secretive intrigue, or making too much of one's tiny merit (the molehill). Bond
(II.558) speculates that the molehill could conceal eavesdroppers intent upon
factionalism—compare 'The Entertainment at Sudeley', I.478, 16—but the
emphasis there is more on the mole's blindness, which may be present here
also.

148–50. *where . . . body*] Sibylla warns against treachery masquerading
guilefully as smooth talk. Usually, as in Pliny (VIII.23; compare *Euphues,*
I.202, 19–20), it is the *panther's* sweet breath that beguiles the intended victim.
But compare *Macbeth,* I.v.67: 'Look like the innocent flower, / But be the
serpent under it.'

150–1. *bugloss . . . sugar*] Bugloss is a medicinal herb; Lady Would-Be
prescribes it for Volpone in his feigned illness along with a pharmacopoeia of
other nostrums (*Volpone,* III.iv.61). It is similar to borage, 'formerly much
esteemed as a cordial, and . . . still largely used in making cool tankard, claret
cup, etc.' (*O.E.D., borage*). Adding sugar is a cheap way of adulterating wine;
compare Falstaff in *1 Henry IV,* I.ii.111 and II.iv.465. Phao is warned against
the company of those who would improve their own wine while adulterating
his. Compare *Euphues,* II.51, 17–19: 'the throwing of bugloss into wine,
which increaseth in him that drinketh it a desire of lust, though it mitigate the
force of drunkenness'.

151. *eclipse*] a portent of disaster, such as the death of princes, about which
wise courtiers are circumspectly silent.

152–3. *coneys in thy vaults*] i.e., parasites or flatterers in your household.
The description in *Coriolanus* of those who suddenly will turn up 'out of their
burrows like coneys after rain' to share in Coriolanus' rediscovered good
fortune (IV.v.221–1) suggests a meaning very close to that of the swallows in
the eaves (see next note). *Vaults* are cellars.

153. *swallows in thine eaves*] Swallows, like false friends, proverbially fly
away upon the approach of winter (Dent, *P.L.E.D.,* S1026, citing Erasmus's
Adagia, II.22A, *C.W.E.,* XXXI.44–5: '*Hirundinem sub eodem tecto ne habeas*',
'Permit no swallow under your eaves'). Compare *Euphues,* I.234, 17–20 and
Pap with an Hatchet, III.403, 9–12.

vines mandrage, and ever keep thine ears open and thy
mouth shut, thine eyes upward and thy fingers down.   155
So shalt thou do better than otherwise, though never so
well as I wish.

Phao. Alas, madam, your prophecy threateneth miseries and
your counsel warneth impossibilities.

Sibylla. Farewell. I can answer no more.   *Exit [into cave].*   160

Actus Secundus, Scaena Secunda.

PHAO [*remains*; *enter to him*] SAPPHO,
TRACHINUS, PANDION, CRITICUS [*and*] MOLUS.

Phao. Unhappy Phao!—But soft, what gallant troop is this?
[*To Criticus*] What gentlewoman is this?

Criticus. Sappho, a lady here in Sicily.

Sappho. [*To Trachinus*] What fair boy is that?

Trachinus. Phao, the ferryman of Syracusa.   5

Phao. [*To Criticus*] I never saw one more brave. Be all ladies of
such majesty?

Criticus. No, this is she that all wonder at and worship.

---

160. *into cave*] Bond; *not in* Q1.   0.1–2.] *Bond (subst.); Phao, Sapho,
Trachinus, Pandion, Criticus, Molus / Q1.   2. To Criticus*] *This ed.; not in Q1.
4. To Trachinus*] *This ed.; not in Q1.   6. To Criticus*] *This ed.; not in Q1.

---

154. *mandrage*] mandrake or mandragora. Compare *Euphues*, II.224, 27–9:
'They that fear their vines will make too sharp wine must not cut the arms but
graft next to them mandrage, which causeth the grape to be more pleasant.'
The application is perhaps that one can calm intemperate speech in others by
using gentle words, or calm one's own intemperance by reflection.

154–5. *keep . . . shut*] proverbial wisdom, of which this is an early citation
(Dent, *P.L.E.D.*, M1254.11).

155. *thine eyes . . . down*] a proverbial warning against ambition that recalls
Phao's opening soliloquy: 'Envy never casteth her eye low, ambition pointeth
always upward' (I.i.9–10 above; see Donald Edge, 'Ambition's Finger',
American Notes and Queries, XVI, 1977, 19–21). Compare *Campaspe*,
III.v.41–2: 'stars are to be looked at, not reached at', and Dent, *P.L.E.D.*,
S825, with comparable passages in *Euphues*, II.46, 29 and II.204, 7–9.

159. *warneth*] puts one on guard against; urges (*O.E.D.*, vb.¹, 2, 6).

0.1.] The scene is continuous, with Phao remaining onstage and being
encountered at his ferry. See II.i.0 and n. From this location Sappho can
choose to return to her palace in Syracuse by ferry or 'in through the park' (ll.
14–15); compare I.ii.75–6, where Molus can similarly go about to Syracuse by
land.

3. *lady*] On this reference to Sappho as 'a lady' rather than queen or
princess, see 'Characters in the Drama', notes.

6. *brave*] handsome, finely dressed.

Sappho. [*To Trachinus*] I have seldom seen a sweeter face. Be
    all ferrymen of that fairness?   10
Trachinus. No, madam, this is he that Venus determined
    among men to make the fairest.
Sappho. Seeing I am only come forth to take the air, I will
    cross the ferry, and so the fields, then going in through
    the park; I think the walk will be pleasant.   15
Trachinus. You will much delight in the flattering green,
    which now beginneth to be in his glory.
Sappho. [*To Phao*] Sir boy, will ye undertake to carry us over
    the water?
                                         [*Phao is silent.*]
    Are you dumb? Can you not speak?   20
Phao. Madam, I crave pardon. I am spurblind; I could scarce
    see.
Sappho. It is pity in so good a face there should be an evil eye.
Phao. I would in my face there were never an eye.
Sappho. Thou canst never be rich in a trade of life of all the   25
    basest.
Phao. Yet content, madam, which is a kind of life of all the
    best.

---

9. *To Trachinus*] *This ed.; not in Q1.*   18. *To Phao*] *This ed.; not in Q1.*   19.1.
This ed.; not in Q1.

    9–10. *Be all . . . fairness*] a remark designed to raise laughter in an audience
with any experience of Thames watermen.
    14. *then*] The Q1 spelling, 'then', can be modernised 'then' or 'than', and
possibly Sappho means 'rather than' instead of the temporal sense; see
O.E.D., than, conj., 3, for instances of *than* used with ellipsis of the preceding
comparative to mean 'rather than'.
    15. *park*] In this period the word referred only to a legally designated tract of
land enclosed to preserve beasts of chase (*O.E.D.,* 1).
    16. *flattering*] charming, pleasing, promising (though for 'promising' *O.E.D.*
gives a first date of 1633).
    21. *spurblind*] apparently an alternative spelling of *purblind*, originally
meaning 'totally blind' but later 'partially blind, dim-sighted'. Phao, stricken
with love, speaks as one who has blinded himself by gazing at the 'sun' of
majesty, far above his reach.
    23. *an evil eye*] (1) defective eyesight; (2) an eye capable of inflicting injury
by a look. Sappho's hidden meaning is that she too has been wounded.
    24.] Phao wishes he had never seen Sappho, since he has been stricken
through the eyes with love for her, and wishes also to harm no one, especially
Sappho.
    27. *content*] See I.i.2, 17–19 and nn.

Sappho. Wilt thou forsake thy ferry and follow the court as
    a page?   30
Phao. As it pleaseth Fortune, madam, to whom I am a
    prentice.
Sappho. Come, let us go.
Trachinus. Will you go, Pandion?
Pandion. Yea.   35

            Exeunt [all except Criticus and Molus].

        Actus Secundus, Scaena Tertia.

     MOLUS *[and]* CRITICUS *[remain].*

Molus. Criticus comes in good time; I shall not be alone.
    —What news, Criticus?
Criticus. I taught you that lesson, to ask 'What news', and this
    is the news: tomorrow there shall be a desperate fray
    between two, made at all weapons, from the brown bill   5
    to the bodkin.

35.1.] *This ed.; Exeunt Q1; Exeunt all but Criticus / Daniel.*   0.1.] *This ed.;
Molus, Cryticus, Calypho / Q1; Enter Molus and Criticus, meeting / Bond; Enter
Molus to Criticus / Daniel.*

    0.1.] The scene continues. Despite the first line of dialogue, which might
seem to suggest that Criticus is just arriving, a more plausible interpretation is
that the two servants remain onstage. Alternatively, Molus, who does not
speak in II.ii though he is named in the opening stage direction of that scene,
may in fact enter now, at the end of II.ii, whereupon he is encountered by
Criticus, who detaches himself from the exiting group and comes across to join
him. Compare I.ii–I.iii and III.i–III.ii, where the servants are similarly
present in the first scene and then stay behind to comment on court and
academic life from their below-stairs point of view. The scene headings in Q1
merely list the names of speaking characters in the ensuing scene without
indicating when they enter, and '*Exeunt*' is often used (as at the end of I.ii) to
indicate the departure of most but not all persons onstage. Molus' first speech
may then mean, 'Criticus' being here is timely; I shall not be alone.'
    3. *I . . . lesson*] At I.iii.29–30, Criticus derided courtiers for greeting one
another with inquiries about the latest court gossip. Molus seems to have
caught the mannerism.
    5. *made . . . weapons*] using every means to win one's contest (*O.E.D.*,
weapon, 2b; compare *prize*, sb.², b).
    brown bill] weapon with a long brown handle (either rusty or painted brown)
with axe-like head, used by constables of the watch. Compare *Endymion*,
IV.ii.13, where the Constable sings to his companions, 'Come, my brown
bills, we'll roar.'
    6. *bodkin*] dagger; also pin, needle.

Molus. Now thou talkest of frays, I pray thee, what is that
    whereof they talk so commonly in court—valour, the
    stab, the pistol—for the which every man that dareth is
    so much honoured?   10
Criticus. O Molus, beware of valour. He that can look big and
    wear his dagger pommel lower than the point, that lieth
    at a good ward and can hit a button with a thrust, and
    will into the field, man to man, for a bout or two, he,
    Molus, is a shrewd fellow and shall be well followed.   15
Molus. What is the end?
Criticus. Danger or death.
Molus. If it be but death that bringeth all this commendation,
    I account him as valiant that is killed with a surfeit as
    with a sword.   20
Criticus. How so?
Molus. If I venture upon a full stomach to eat a rasher on the

---

8. *valour*] Bond (II.558) compares *Campaspe*, V.iii.11–12, when Laïs speaks
of 'a new-found term called *valiant*, a word which breedeth more quarrels
than the sense can commendation'. Satirical comment on latest fashions in
quarrelling is common in Renaissance drama, as for example in Mercutio's
diatribe against Tybalt in *Romeo and Juliet*, II.iv.19–35, and Touchstone's
mocking catalogue of the seven causes of quarrelling in *As You Like It*,
V.iv.49–102.

9. *the pistol*] the act of shooting with a pistol. *O.E.D.* cites *pistol* as a verb in
1607 but gives no citation for the meaning proposed here.

11. *valour*] Compare *Troilus and Cressida*, I.iii.176.

look big] look threatening, bluster.

12. *wear . . . point*] an aggressive fashion of wearing the knob-end and hilt of
the sword and dagger lower than its sharp end, so that the weapon is thrust
visibly outward from the body and is ready to be drawn quickly from its
sheath.

12–13. *lieth . . . ward*] stands in a good defensive posture, parries well.
Compare *1 Henry IV*, II.iv.191–2: 'Thou knowest my old ward. Here I
lay.'

13. *can . . . button*] Compare Mercutio on Tybalt: 'The very butcher of a silk
button, a duelist, a duelist' (*Romeo and Juliet*, II.iv.23–4).

15. *be well followed*] have many followers, admirers.

16. *the end*] the end of it all, the conclusion.

18. *that . . . commendation*] that all this business of courtly honour comes to.

19–20. Compare *Compaspe*, I.ii.82–3, and Hunter's note on the various
versions of this proverb ('*Plures occidit crapula quam gladius*', 'surfeit kills more
than the sword') taken from Ecclesiasticus xxxvii.34.

22–3. *rasher . . . coals*] broiled slice of bacon or ham. Compare Nashe,
Dedication to *The Unfortunate Traveller*, ed. McKerrow, II.208.

coals, a carbonado, drink a carouse, swallow all things
that may procure sickness or death, am not I as valiant
to die so in an house as the other in a field? Methinks   25
that epicures are as desperate as soldiers, and cooks
provide as good weapons as cutlers.

Criticus. O valiant knight!

Molus. I will die for it; what greater valour?

Criticus. Scholars' fight, who rather seek to choke their   30
stomachs than see their blood.

Molus. I will stand upon this point; if it be valour to dare die,
he is valiant howsoever he dieth.

Criticus. Well, of this hereafter. But here cometh Callipho; we
will have some sport.   35

[*Enter*] CALLIPHO.

Callipho. [*To himself*] My mistress I think hath got a gadfly,
never at home and yet none can tell where abroad. My
master was a wise man when he matched with such a
woman. When she comes in, we must put out the fire
because of the smoke, hang up our hammers because of   40
the noise, and do no work but watch what she wanteth.
She is fair, but by my troth I doubt of her honesty. I

35.1] *Bond; not in Q1.*   36. *To himself*] *This ed.; not in Q1.*

---

23. *carbonado*] meat scored across and grilled on the coals.
carouse] full draught of liquor, cupful drunk straight down as a toast.
26. *desperate*] reckless.
27. *cutlers*] those who make and deal in knives. The surfeiting dishes served
up by cooks can be as fatal as knives, says Molus.
30. *Scholars' fight*] i.e., that is how scholars fight.
30–1. *choke their stomachs*] (1) cram their stomachs full; (2) suppress
'stomach', i.e., valour and quarrelsomeness.
34. *of this*] more of this.
Callipho] 'The name Calypho, not among those of the Cyclopes given in
Virgil, *Aen.* viii.425 "*Brontesque Steropesque et nudus membra Pyracmon*"
["Brontes and Steropes and Pyracmon with bared limbs"], is borrowed by
Lyly from a comic character (Callipho) in Plautus' *Pseudolus*' (Bond, II.554).
36. *gadfly*] Jealous Juno sent a gadfly to plague Io, driving her restlessly here
and there. Venus is 'gadding' about.
37–8. *My master*] i.e., Vulcan.
41. *watch*] look out for.
42. *honesty*] chastity.

must seek her that I fear Mars hath found.

Criticus. Whom dost thou seek?

Callipho. I have found those I seek not.   45

Molus. I hope you have found those which are honest.

Callipho. It may be, but I seek no such.

Molus. Criticus, you shall see me by learning to prove Callipho
  to be the devil.

Criticus. Let us see. But I pray thee prove it better than thou   50
  didst thyself to be valiant.

Molus. Callipho, I will prove thee to be the devil.

Callipho. Then will I swear thee to be a god.

Molus. The devil is black.

Callipho. What care I?   55

Molus. Thou art black.

Callipho. What care you?

Molus. Therefore thou art the devil.

Callipho. I deny that.

Molus. It is the conclusion. Thou must not deny it.   60

Callipho. In spite of all conclusions, I will deny it.

Criticus. Molus, the smith holds you hard.

---

43. *that*] whom.

45–6. *found . . . found*] come across by chance . . . discovered the quality of,
came to the knowledge of.

46. *honest*] truth-telling, upright (but playing on *honesty*, chastity, in l. 42;
Criticus and Molus have overheard Callipho's opening speech).

47.] Callipho disclaims the mission of Diogenes, to look for an honest man
(see *Campaspe*, II.i). He is in search of Venus, whose 'honesty' he doubts
(Bond, ii.558).

48. *by learning*] i.e., by scholarly and rhetorical method.

50–1. *prove . . . valiant*] See ll. 22–7.

56–9.] Dent (*P.L.E.D.*, D297) cites this passage as his earliest instance for
the proverb, 'Though I am black I am not the devil.' Compare George Peele's
The Old Wife's Tale (or *The Old Wives' Tale*), D4, l. 621 (*c.* 1590), ed. Frank S.
Hook, in *Dramatic Works*, gen, ed. C. T. Prouty, 1970, p. 405.

60. *conclusion*] In logic, the *conclusion* is the last of the three propositions
forming a syllogism, being deduced from the two former terms or premises.
Logically, says Molus, one cannot *deny* the final proposition; it follows as a
necessary consequence. (In fact, Molus' syllogism is transparently and
comically defective, since not *all* black creatures are the devil.)

61. *In . . . conclusions*] no matter what you say. Callipho uses Molus' terms
of logic in non-technical senses; he can *deny* not by attacking the syllogism but
by stating simply that the conclusion is not true.

62. *the smith . . . hard*] i.e., Callipho presses you hard, refuses to give in.

Molus. Thou seest he hath no reason.

Criticus. Try him again.

Molus. [*To Callipho*] I will reason with thee now from a place.   65

Callipho. I mean to answer you in no other place.

Molus. Like master, like man.

Callipho. It may be.

Molus. But thy master hath horns.

Callipho. And so mayst thou.   70

Molus. Therefore thou hast horns, and ergo a devil.

Callipho. Be they all devils have horns?

Molus. All men that have horns are.

Callipho. Then are there more devils on earth than in hell.

Molus. But what dost thou answer?   75

Callipho. I deny that.

Molus. What?

Callipho. Whatsoever it is that shall prove me a devil. But
            hearest thou, scholar, I am a plain fellow and can
            fashion nothing but with the hammer. What wilt thou   80
            say if I prove thee a smith?

Molus. Then will I say thou art a scholar.

---

65. *To Callipho*] *This ed.; not in Q1.*   74. more] *Q1* (moe).

---

63. *no reason*] no reasoning powers or skill in logic, hence no 'reasonable'
answer.

65.] a logical phrase, meaning 'I will ground my argument on a commonplace, or proverb, or well-known passage.' Compare *Euphues*, I.299, 21: 'in
schools . . . one being urged with a place in Aristotle' (Bond, II.558), referring
to the ten categories or predicaments classifying all manners in which asser-
tions may be made of the subject (*O.E.D.*, *category*, 1).

66. *in . . . place*] i.e., here and now. (Callipho again changes a logical term
into a common meaning.)

67.] proverbial (Dent, *P.L.E.D.*, M723), offered here as the first premise of
a syllogism.

69. *horns*] Vulcan has horns because Venus has cuckolded him (with Mars).

70.] i.e., being a male, you too may be cuckolded some day.

72.] Callipho undermines Molus' 'logic' by questioning the universality of
the predication.

74. *more*] Q1's 'moe' has a separate entry (*mo*) in the *O.E.D.* and its own
linguistic history, but by the 1580s the distinction between *mo* and *more* had
disappeared to such an extent that the difference is often scribal or compositorial or at least inconsistent.

75.] i.e., how do you refute my conclusion that you are a devil?

76. *deny*] See l. 61 and n.

Criticus. Prove it, Callipho, and I will give thee a good
    colaphum.

Callipho. I will prove it, or else.   85

Criticus. Or else what?

Callipho. Or else I will not prove it. Thou art a smith, there-
    fore thou art a smith. The conclusion, you say, must not
    be denied, and therefore it is true, thou art a smith.

Molus. Ay, but I deny your antecedent.   90

Callipho. Ay, but you shall not.—Have I not touched him,
    Criticus?

Criticus. You have both done learnedly, for, as sure as he is
    a smith, thou art a devil.

Callipho. And then he a devil, because a smith, for that it was   95
    his reason to make me a devil, being a smith.

Molus. There is no reasoning with these mechanical dolts,
    whose wits are in their hands, not in their heads.

Criticus. Be not choleric, you are wise; but let us take up this
    matter with a song.   100

Callipho. I am content; my voice is as good as my reason.

Molus. Then shall we have sweet music. But come, I will not
    break off.

Song

---

84. colaphum] a blow or cuff (Greek *kolaphos*, Latin *colaphus*), an
appropriate word for its closeness of sound and sense to *Callipho* and his
hammer. Callipho evidently supposes he is being offered a prize.

88–9. *The conclusion . . . denied*] Callipho tries to defeat Molus by his own
rule of logic stated at l. 60; see note.

90. *antecedent*] Molus' logical counter-attack is to point out that a syllogism
is defective if one of its premises does not hold, but in doing so he simply
affirms that he is not a smith and thereby employs Callipho's simple stratagem
at l. 61. Hence the seeming force of Callipho's 'Ay, but you shall not' in l. 91.

93–4. *as sure . . . devil*] i.e., one argument is as worthless as the other.

95–6.] Callipho again turns Molus' argument against him: if a smith is a
devil, as Molus has argued, and if Molus is a smith, as Criticus has apparently
just agreed, then Molus is a devil; that was how he reasoned when he called me
a devil merely for being a smith.

97. *mechanical*] engaged in manual labour; of the artisan class.

99. *Be not . . . wise*] You would both be wise not to become angry.

99–100. *take . . . matter*] amicably conclude this dispute (*O.E.D.*, take,
90u). Compare *As You Like It*, V.iv.104: 'I knew when some justices could not
take up a quarrel.'

103.1–16. *Song*] This is a model instance of the 'three-man song' discussed
in *Campaspe*, I.ii.94ff. See Appendix on 'The Songs'.

Criticus.	Merry knaves are we three-a.	
Molus.	When our songs do agree-a.	105
Callipho.	O now I well see-a,	
	What anon we shall be-a.	
Criticus.	If we ply thus our singing,	
Molus.	Pots then must be flinging,	
Callipho.	If the drink be but stinging.	110
Molus.	I shall forget the rules of grammar.	
Callipho.	And I the pit-a-pat of my hammer.	
Chorus.	To th' tap-house then let's gang, and roar,	
	Call hard, 'tis rare to vamp a score,	
	Draw dry the tub, be it old or new,	115
	And part not till the ground look blue.	

Exeunt.

Actus Secundus, Scaena Quarta.

[*Enter*] PHAO.

Phao. What unacquainted thoughts are these, Phao, far unfit
    for thy thoughts, unmeet for thy birth, thy fortune, thy

104–16. *Criticus.* Merry ... blue] *Blount; not in* Q1.   0.1.] *Bond; Phao,*
Sybilla / Q1.

---

110. *stinging*] pungent; that goads or stimulates (*O.E.D.*, 3); hence, the
strong ale called *stingo*.

113. *tap-house*] ale-house or tap-room.

gang] go.

114.] call out loudly (for drink); it is a rare (enjoyable) thing to furbish up
and add to the score (?). An uncertain line. *O.E.D.* under *vamp*, vb. 1b,
glosses 'to mend or repair with or as with patches; to furnish up, renovate, or
restore', citing this passage, but definition 2, 'to put together ... out of old
materials', may be as germane. On *score*, see *O.E.D.*, sb. 11, 'innkeeper's bill
or reckoning'.

115. *tub*] i.e., barrel.

116.] Dent (*P.L.E.D.*, G466.11) cites this passage as his earliest instance of
a drinkers' vow to keep drinking as long as he is able, found also in Marston's
What You Will, in the penultimate speech of the play: 'drink till the ground
look blue'.

0.1.] As in II.i, Phao is before the mouth of Sibylla's cave, into which she
exited at the end of II.i. No change of scene is necessary, since in II.i and II.ii
the mouth of the cave and the ferry are sufficiently adjacent in Lyly's theatrical
space for the actor to make his way from one to the other without exiting and
re-entering.

1. *unacquainted*] unfamiliar, strange. The word recurs at IV.ii.17 and in
Gallathea, III.iv.58, *Endymion*, V.iii.62 and *Love's Metamorphosis*, I.ii.145.

years, for Phao? Unhappy, canst thou not be content to
behold the sun, but thou must covet to build thy nest in
the sun? Doth Sappho bewitch thee whom all the ladies   5
in Sicily could not woo? Yea, poor Phao, the greatness
of thy mind is far above the beauty of thy face, and the
hardness of thy fortune beyond the bitterness of thy
words. Die, Phao, Phao, die, for there is no hope if thou
be wise nor safety if thou be fortunate. Ah, Phao, the   10
more thou seekest to suppress those mounting affections, they soar the loftier, and the more thou wrestlest
with them, the stronger they wax—not unlike unto a
ball which, the harder it is thrown against the earth, the
higher it boundeth into the air; or our Sicilian stone,   15
which groweth hardest by hammering. O divine love,
and therefore divine because love, whose deity no conceit can compass and therefore no authority can con-

---

3–5. *canst . . . sun*] In *Euphues*, II.41, 33–6, Euphues describes 'the foolish
eagle that, seeing the sun, coveteth to build her nest in the sun' and compares
it to 'fond youth which, viewing the glory and gorgeousness of the court,
longeth to know the secrets of the court'. See also *Euphues*, I.231, 11–12, and
Dent, *P.L.E.D.*, E2.11.

5. *whom*] refers to Phao.

6. *woo*] move or invite by alluring means (*O.E.D.*, 4).

greatness] hubris.

9–10. *for . . . fortunate*] i.e., you will lose either way, either wisely
renouncing all hopes or placing yourself in danger of resentment if you
succeed.

10–12. *the more . . . loftier*] Fire proverbially burns most fiercely when kept
close (Dent, *P.L.E.D.*, F265). Compare *Euphues*, II.73, 20–1: 'Love . . .
which if you cover in a close chest will burn every place before it burst the
lock'.

12. *wrestlest*] possibly a reference to Hercules and Antaeus.

15–16. *Sicilian . . . hammering*] Compare *Euphues*, I.204, 17–18: 'the stone
of Sicilia, the which the more it is beaten the harder it is'. Mustard offers a
tentative comparison to Propertius, I.16, 29: '*Sit silice et saxo patientior illa
Sicano*', 'then would she be more stubborn than flint or Sicanian [i.e., Sicilian]
rock', where, as Mustard observes, 'the reference is about as obscure as
Lyly's'. Many of the Sicanian people migrated to Sicily, and Propertius may
well be referring (as other writers did in using the word 'Sicanian') to Etna. See
also Dent, *P.L.E.D.*, I96, for proverbial use, and Pettie, *Petite Palace*, II.133.

16–17. *O divine love . . . because love*] For the rhetorical form, compare
Campaspe, III.v.13–14, and other instances noted there, as well as IV.ii.7–8
below.

17–18. *conceit*] apprehension, understanding.

18. *compass*] comprehend fully. Compare the Prologue at the Court, l. 10.

strain, as miraculous in working as mighty, and no
more to be suppressed than comprehended! How now,   20
Phao, whither art thou carried, committing idolatry
with that god whom thou hast cause to blaspheme? O
Sappho, fair Sappho! Peace, miserable wretch, enjoy
thy care in covert, wear willow in thy hat and bays in
thy heart. Lead a lamb in thy hand and a fox in thy   25
head, a dove on the back of thy hand and a sparrow
in the palm. Gold boileth best when it bubbleth least,
water runneth smoothest where it is deepest. Let thy
love hang at thy heart's bottom, not at the tongue's
brim. Things untold are undone; there can be no greater   30
comfort than to know much, nor any less labour than to
say nothing. But ah, thy beauty, Sappho, thy beauty!
Beginnest thou to blab? Ay, blab it, Phao, as long as

---

22. *that ... blaspheme*] i.e., a false god (Love) whom it is idolatrous to
worship and who should instead be blasphemed. The rejection of idolatry
metaphorically uses the language of Reformation anti-Catholic polemicism.

24. *in covert*] in secret, under a disguise.

willow] a conventional symbol of grief for unrequited love or the loss of a
mate, here figuratively thought of by Phao as a misleading outward sign. This
is the first citation given in *O.E.D.* (sb., 1d) and Dent (*P.L.E.D.*, W403).

bays] leaves or sprigs of the laurel or bay tree, woven into a wreath or garland
to reward a conqueror or poet (*O.E.D.*, sb.¹, 3), here expressing Phao's
inward exaltation of 'poetry and passion' (Bond, II.559).

25. *lamb ... fox*] The lamb is proverbially meek and innocent while the fox
is cunning. Phao's advice to himself is to be outwardly ingenuous and inwardly
crafty.

26. *dove ... sparrow*] In the antithetical pairing of these two birds associated
with Venus, the dove hints at gently loyal affection worthy of open display (as
one might carry a favourite bird) while the sparrow signifies lecherous and
hidden desires. Venus' doves and sparrows are mentioned again at III.iii.91–2;
see also IV.iv.39. Turtledoves and sparrows are contrasted in terms of 'truth'
or steadfastness and 'desires' in *Mother Bombie*, I.iii.121–2; and in *Euphues*,
II.98, 23, Venus' pigeons denote 'piety'.

28. *water ... deepest*] a proverb (Dent, *P.L.E.D.*, W123) signifying that
truest feelings or passions are least concerned with outward demonstration. An
early citation appears in *Euphues*, II.65, 23–4.

29. *bottom*] deepest recess, inmost part (*O.E.D.*, 6).

30. *undone*] i.e., as though not done at all, leading to no bad consequences.

33. *thou*] said to himself.

blab] Phao's first meaning is that he is about to betray his secret love, but he
then comforts himself with the reflection that *blab* can inadvertently also mean
'to chatter, babble', as a fond lover might do in praise of his mistress's beauty.
See *O.E.D.*, vb.¹, 1 and 3.

thou blabbest her beauty. Bees that die with honey are
buried with harmony. Swans that end their lives with   35
songs are covered when they are dead with flowers, and
they that till their latter gasp commend beauty shall be
ever honoured with benefits. In these extremities I will
go to none other oracle than Sibylla, whose old years
have not been idle in these young attempts, and whose   40
sound advice may mitigate, though the heavens cannot remove, my miseries. O Sappho, sweet Sappho,
Sappho!—Sibylla?

SIBYLLA [*appears at the mouth of her cave*].

Sibylla. Who is there?
Phao. One not worthy to be one.   45
Sibylla. Fair Phao?
Phao. Unfortunate Phao.
Sibylla. Come in.
Phao. So I will, and quit thy tale of Phoebus with one whose

43.1.] *Bond; not in Q1.*   49. quit] *Q1* (quite).

34–5. *Bees . . . harmony*] *Bartholomew* (Berthelet), XVIII.xii, pp. cccxvi–
cccxvii^v, notes: 'Bein [bees] that make honey slayeth the males that grieve
them, and evil kings, that rule them not aright, but only eat too much
honey. . . . And bees be pleased with harmony and melody of sound of song.'
Lyly applies this love to the idea of graceful praise of beauty.

35. *Swans*] Swans were sacred to Apollo and Venus, and hence appropriate
to poetry and love. *Euphues* (II.98, 22) speaks of swans as drawing Venus'
chariot. The idea that swans sing immediately before their death is at least as
old as Chaucer, *Anelida and Arcite*, ll. 346–7. See *O.E.D.*, 2b, and Dent,
P.L.E.D., S1028. Honouring the dead with flowers is of course also
conventional, though its inclusion here as part of the mythology of the swan is
a typical Lylyan invention.

37. *latter*] last (*O.E.D.*, 3).

40. *these young attempts*] i.e., these uncertain undertakings in love by
youthful wooers.

45. *to be one*] i.e., to be alive, to exist.

48. *Come in*] It is probably not necessary that Phao actually enter the stage
structure or door representing Sibylla's cave; instead, the two may confer at
the mouth of the cave, understood to represent its interior. Compare Sibylla's
'Come near' at II.i.23.

49. *quit*] requite, repay (*O.E.D.*, 10).

thy tale of Phoebus] Sibylla's tale in II.i of her affair with Phoebus (Ovid,
Metamorphoses, XIV.130ff.), parallels Phao's love for Sappho in the contrast
between presumptuous human daring and godlike rank.

one] (1) a tale; (2) a godlike person.

brightness darkeneth Phoebus. I love Sappho, Sibylla,   50
Sappho, ah, Sappho, Sibylla!

Sibylla. A short tale, Phao, and a sorrowful. It asketh pity
rather than counsel.

Phao. So it is, Sibylla. Yet in those firm years methinketh
there should harbour such experience as may defer,   55
though not take away, my destiny.

Sibylla. It is hard to cure that by words which cannot be eased
by herbs, and yet, if thou wilt take advice, be attentive.

Phao. I have brought mine ears of purpose, and will hang at
your mouth till you have finished your discourse.   60

Sibylla. Love, fair child, is to be governed by art, as thy boat
by an oar; for fancy, though it cometh by hazard, is
ruled by wisdom. If my precepts may persuade—and I
pray thee let them persuade—I would wish thee first to
be diligent, for that women desire nothing more than   65
to have their servants officious. Be always in sight, but

---

52. *A short tale . . . sorrowful*] a set phrase. Compare Polonius's 'a short tale
to make', *Hamlet*, II.ii.146.

53. *counsel*] advice.

54. *firm*] possessing the stability and wisdom of age.

56. *though*] even though.

57–8. *It . . . herbs*] Mustard cites Ovid, *Heroides*, v.149: '*Me miseram, quod
amor non est medicabilis herbis*', 'How wretched I am, alas, that love cannot be
cured by herbs', and *Metamorphoses*, 1.523: '*Ei mihi, quod nullis amor est
sanabilis herbis*', 'Woe is me, that love cannot be cured by any herbs.'

59. *of purpose*] on purpose.

59–60. *hang . . . mouth*] This is Dent's earliest citation (*P.L.E.D.*,
H129.11) of a commonplace metaphor, to hang at or on someone's lips, tongue
or mouth.

61–2. *Love . . . oar*] Ovid, *Ars Amatoria*, 1.3: '*Arte citae veloque rates remoque
moventur, | Arte leves currus; arte regendus Amor*', 'Swift ships are made to move
by skill with sail and oar, and quick chariots are made to move by skill; let love
be guided also by skill' (cited by Mustard, who similarly cites Ovid in the notes
throughout this scene). As Bond (II.559) observes, the advice from Sibylla to
young Phao in ll. 61–82 resembles the counsel of old Psellus to Philautus in
Euphues, in which the young man is urged to practise the art of love with
diligence and with confidence that 'women yield when they are courted' by
flattery and promises (II.119, 24–5). See also Euphues's own precepts, I.255.

62. *fancy*] love.

by hazard] by chance.

65. *for that*] because.

66. *officious*] dutiful (*officiosus*), attentive.

never slothful. Flatter—I mean lie; little things catch
light minds, and fancy is a worm that feedeth first upon
fennel. Imagine with thyself all are to be won, otherwise
mine advice were as unnecessary as thy labour. It is   70
unpossible for the brittle metal of women to withstand
the flattering attempts of men. Only this: let them be
asked; their sex requireth no less, their modesties are to
be allowed so much. Be prodigal in praises and promises; beauty must have a trumpet, and pride a gift.   75
Peacocks never spread their feathers but when they are
flattered, and gods are seldom pleased if they be not

---

71. metal] *Q1* (mettall).   73. requireth no less] *Q2* (requireth no lesse);
requirrerh no losse *Q1*.

67–8. *little . . . minds*] Ovid, *Ars Amatoria*, 1.159: '*Parva leves capiunt
animos*', 'Trifles take hold of frivolous minds.' On proverbial use, see Dent,
P.L.E.D., T189 and Pettie, *Petite Palace*, II.33.

69. *fennel*] The proverbial association of fennel with flattery appears in
Hamlet, IV.v.80. See Dent, *P.L.E.D.*, F188. *Bartholomew* (Berthelet),
XVII.lxx, p. cclxiii, connects fennel with worms or serpents: 'It is said that
serpents taste thereof and done away the age of their years. . . . Serpents,
[Isidore] saith, maketh this fennel noble.' This is based on Pliny, XX.95, who
reports as follows: '*Feniculum nobilitavere serpentes gustatu, ut diximus, senectam
exuendo oculorumque aciem suco eius reficiendo*', 'As we have said [VIII.98],
serpents have made fennel famous, tasting it to cast off their old skin and using
its juice to improve their eyesight.' Compare also the *Bee* poem in Bond,
III.496.

Imagine . . . won] Ovid, *Ars Amatoria*, 1.269–70: '*Prima tuae menti veniat
fiducia, cunctas / Posse capi*', 'First let this assurance come to your mind, that all
women can be taken.' Compare Dent, *P.L.E.D.*, W681, 'all women may be
won', and *Euphues*, 1.203, 33–4, 'women are to be won with every wind'. See
also *Euphues*, 1.206, 27, and 1.211, 22.

71. *metal*] the 'stuff' of which a person is made, with reference to character.
Identical in meaning to *mettle*, a variant spelling used indiscriminately in all
senses (*O.E.D.*, *metal*, sb., 1f and *mettle* 1).

73. *less*] The Q2 reading ('lesse') is clearly a justified correction of Q1's
'losse', and is probably the intelligent emendation of the Q2 compositor.

76–8. *Peacocks . . . bribed*] Ovid, *Ars Amatoria*, 1.627–8: '*Laudatas ostendit
avis Iunonia pinnas; / Si tacitus spectes, illa recondit opes*', 'The bird of Juno
displays her plumes when they are praised; if you gaze silently, she conceals
her riches', and III.654: '*Placatur donis Iuppiter ipse datis*', 'Jupiter himself is
placated when gifts are offered.' Peacocks are symbolic of pride, as at V.i.24
and n.; compare Erasmus, *Parabolae*, 1.614A (*C.W.E.*, XXIII.255), '*Pavo non
explicat penas nisi laudatas*', 'The peacock does not unfurl her plumes unless
they are praised.'

bribed. There is none so foul that thinketh not herself
fair. In commending thou canst lose no labour, for of
everyone thou shalt be believed. O simple women, that   80
are brought rather to believe what their ears hear of
flattering men than what their eyes see in true glasses!

Phao. You digress only to make me believe that women do so
lightly believe.

Sibylla. Then to the purpose. Choose such times to break thy   85
suit as thy lady is pleasant. The wooden horse entered
Troy when the soldiers were quaffing, and Penelope,
forsooth, whom fables make so coy, among the pots
wrung her wooers by the fists when she loured on their
faces. Grapes are mind-glasses. Venus worketh in Bac-   90
chus' press and bloweth fire upon his liquor. When

78–80. *There . . . believed*] Ovid, *Ars Amatoria*, 1.613–14: '*Nec credi labor
est. Sibi quaeque videtur amanda; / Pessima sit, nulli non sua forma placet*', 'Nor is
it hard to be believed. Every woman sees herself as lovable; no matter how bad
she may look, not a one fails to be pleased by her own appearance.'

78. *foul*] ugly, the opposite of *fair* (l. 79).

79–80. *of everyone*] by every women.

82. *glasses*] mirrors.

83–4. *believe . . . believe*] hold it as true . . . give credence too easily, allow
themselves to be persuaded.

85–7. *Choose . . . quaffing*] Ovid, *Ars Amatoria*, 1.357–64: '*Illa leget tempus
. . . Pectora dum gaudent, nec sunt adstricta dolore, / Ipsa patent. . . . Tum, cum
tristis erat, defensa est Ilios armis: / Militis gravidum laeta recepit equum*', 'She will
pick a time . . . When hearts rejoice and are not constricted by grief, then they
lie open. . . . Ilium, when it was sad, was defended by its army; when it
rejoiced, it took in the horse heavy with soldiers.'

85. *break*] commence (*O.E.D.*, 24).

86. *pleasant*] good-humoured. The context suggests 'after drinking'.

87–90. *Penelope . . . faces*] Even Penelope, whom ancient poets portray as
modestly retiring, greeted her wooers when she had drunk enough, pressing
their hands secretly while she showed a frowning countenance to the world.

90. *Grapes are mind-glasses*] Compare *Euphues*, II.83, 7–8, 'Wine is the glass
of the mind', and 1.279, 13–15, 'Wine therefore is to be refrained which is
termed to be the glass of the mind.' Bond (II.559) cites Aeschylus, Fragment
393 (Augustus Nauck, ed., *Tragicorum Graecorum Fragmenta*, 2nd edn.,
Lipsiae, 1859, p. 114). Dent, *P.L.E.D.*, W481, cites from Erasmus's *Adagia*,
II.267E: '*Vinum hominis prodens arguit ingenium*', 'Wine shows the natural bent
of man.' Compare the proverbial *In vino veritas*.

91. *press*] wine press.

91–3. *When . . . incredible*] Ovid, *Ars Amatoria*, 1.467–8: '*Sit tibi credibilis
sermo consuetaque verba, / Blanda tamen*', 'Let your speech be credible and your
words familiar, yet coaxing too.'

thou talkest with her, let thy speech be pleasant but not
incredible. Choose such words as may—as many may—
melt her mind. Honey rankleth when it is eaten for
pleasure, and fair words wound when they are heard for   95
love. Write, and persist in writing; they read more than
is written to them, and write less than they think. In
conceit study to be pleasant, in attire brave but not too
curious. When she smileth, laugh outright; if rise, stand
up; if sit, lie down. Lose all thy time to keep time with   100
her. Can you sing, show your cunning; can you dance,
use your legs; can you play upon any instrument, practise your fingers to please her fancy; seek out qualities.
If she seem at the first cruel, be not discouraged. I tell

---

92. *pleasant*] amusing.

93. *incredible*] i.e., exaggerated, arch, too much.

94–5. *Honey . . . pleasure*] Compare *Euphues*. II.191, 18–19: 'Honey taken
excessively cloyeth the stomach though it be honey'; *Campaspe*, II.ii.86–7;
and Dent, *P.L.E.D.*, H560.

96. *Write*] Bond (II.559) quotes Psellus to Philautus in *Euphues*, II.119,
12–16: 'There is nothing that more pierceth the heart of a beautiful lady than
writing, where thou mayst so set down thy passions and her perfection as she
shall have cause to think well of thee and better of herself.' Much of Sibylla's
advice to Phao also anticipates that of Cupid to Ramis in *Love's Metamorphosis*,
IV.i.115ff.

96–7. *they read . . . think*] i.e., women read more into what is written to
them than the words will actually justify, and conversely only hint at what they
think in their replies. Compare Ovid, *Ars Amatoria*, II.396: '*plus multae, quam
sibi missa, legunt*', 'many read more than is written to them'.

98. *conceit*] fanciful or witty sentiment or expression (*O.E.D.*, 8).

98–9. *in attire . . . curious*] Compare Ovid, *Ars Amatoria*, I.505ff.: '*Sed tibi
nec ferro placeat torquere capillos, / Nec tua mordaci pumice crura teras*', 'But do
not indulge in curling your hair with the curling iron, or in scraping your legs
with the biting pumice-stone.'

98. *brave*] handsome, splendid.

99. *curious*] elaborate, fastidious.

99–100. *if rise . . . lie down*] Ovid, *Ars Amatoria*, I.503: '*Cum surgit, surges;
donec sedet illa, sedebis.*'

100. *Lose*] Consume, waste (*O.E.D.*, 6).

keep time] keep pace, be in harmony.

101–2. *Can you sing . . . legs*] Ovid, *Ars Amatoria*, I.595ff.: '*Si vox est, canta;
si mollia bracchia, salta.*' The parallel continues.

101. *Can you*] If you can, know how to.

103. *qualities*] skills, capacities, attainments. Compare *Campaspe*, V.i.3–4:
'*Diogenes.* What can thy sons do? *Sylvius.* You shall see their qualities.—
Dance, sirrah!' (*O.E.D.*'s first citation for this meaning.)

thee a strange thing: women strive because they would   105
be overcome. Force they call it, but such a welcome
force they account it that continually they study to be
enforced. To fair words join sweet kisses, which, if they
gently receive, I say no more, they will gently receive.
But be not pinned always on her sleeves; strangers have   110
green rushes when daily guests are not worth a rush.
Look pale and learn to be lean, that whoso seeth thee
may say the gentleman is in love. Use no sorcery to

105–8. *women . . . kisses*] Ovid, *Ars Amatoria*, 1.666–73: '*Pugnando vinci se
tamen illa volet.* . . . *Vim licet appelles; grata est vis ista puellis*', 'And yet she will
wish to be overcome in the struggle. . . . You may use force; it is pleasure to
girls', and 1.663: '*Quis sapiens blandis non misceat oscula verbis?*', 'What wise
person will fail to mingle kisses with words?'

107. *study*] make it their aim (*O.E.D.*, 4).

108. *To fair . . . kisses*] Compare Dent, *P.L.E.D.*, K107: 'After kissing
comes more kindness.'

109. *I say no more*] used here to avoid obscenity. See I.ii.4 and n.

110. *be not pinned . . . sleeves*] i.e., do not pin your hopes on her, do not place
too entire or openly professed a trust in her and let her take your service for
granted (*O.E.D.*, *pin*, vb., 4b). The image is literal: a lady might wear a lover's
favour on her sleeve, as in *Love's Labour's Lost*, V.ii.455. Dent, *P.L.E.D.*,
F32 gives Lyly's as the earliest instance of this proverbial phrase. Compare
Euphues, 1.249, 5–6: 'Alas, fond fool, art thou so pinned to their sleeves that
thou regardest more their babble than thine own bliss?'

110–11. *strangers . . . rush*] Camilla greets Euphues (*Euphues*, II.161, 16–17),
as follows: 'I am sorry, Euphues, that we have no green rushes, considering
you have been so great a stranger.' *O.E.D.* (1d) and Dent (*P.L.E.D.*, R213)
cite Heywood, *Proverbs*, II.iii, sig. F4v: 'Green rushes for this stranger.' See
also 'The Entertainment at Harefield', unconvincingly attributed to Lyly in
Bond, 1.491, 18. Rushes, often sweet-smelling when crushed, were strewn on
the floors of rooms. Lyly also plays in *not worth a rush* on the meaning 'a type of
something of no value or importance' (*O.E.D.*, 2a). See Dent, *P.L.E.D.*, S918
and Euphues's reply to Camilla, Bond, II.161, 30–1: 'Fair lady, it were
unseemly to strew green rushes for his coming whose company is not worth a
straw.'

112–13. *Look . . . love*] Ovid, *Ars Amatoria*, 1.729–38: '*Palleat omnis amans:
hic est color aptus amanti.* . . . *Arguat et macies animum.* . . . *Ut qui te videat,
dicere possit "amas"*,' 'Let every wooer be pale: this is the colour suited to the
wooer. . . . Let emaciation also show your state of mind . . . so that whoever
sees you may say, "You're in love." '

112. *lean*] Compare *As You Like It*, III.II.352: 'A lean cheek'.

113–17. *Use . . . enchanted*] Ovid, *Ars Amatoria*, II.99–124: '*Fallitur,
Haemonias siquis decurrit ad artes.* . . . *Non formosus erat, sed erat facundus
Ulixes, / Et tamen aequoreas torsit amore deas*', 'Whoever avails himself of the
Haemonian arts [so named for a district of Thessaly famed for magic] is

hasten thy success; wit is a witch; Ulysses was not fair
but wise, not cunning in charms but sweet in speech,   115
whose filed tongue made those enamoured that sought
to have him enchanted. Be not coy; bear, soothe, swear,
die to please thy lady. These are rules for poor lovers;
to others I am no mistress. He hath wit enough that
can give enough. Dumb men are eloquent if they be   120
liberal. Believe me, great gifts are little gods. When thy
mistress doth bend her brow, do not thou bend thy fist.
Cammocks must be bowed with sleight, not strength;
water to be trained with pipes, not stopped with sluices;
fire to be quenched with dust, not with swords. If thou   125

---

124. water to be] *Q1;* water [is] to be *Bond.*

---

deceived. . . . Ulysses was not handsome but he was eloquent, and notwith-
standing he enflamed with love [two] sea goddesses.' Partly quoted by Nashe,
Unfortunate Traveller, ed. McKerrow, II.299.

116. *filed*] polished, smooth. 'To file one's tongue' is a conventional
metaphor (Dent, *P.L.E.D.,* T400.2.)

117. *him enchanted*] enchanted him (referring to Circe's attempt to enchant
Odysseus).

bear] i.e., bear with her, accept whatever she does (*O.E.D.,* vb., 15, 17).

soothe] assent flatteringly to all she says, cajole, humour (*O.E.D.,* 5). Bond
(II.559) cites *Euphues,* 1.262, 15: 'What my mother saith my father sootheth.'

118–21. *These . . . liberal*] Ovid, *Ars Amatoria,* II.161–3: '*Non ego divitibus
venio praeceptor amandi: / Nil opus est illi, qui dabit, arte mea; / Secum habet
ingenium, qui, cum libet, "Accipe" dicit*', 'I do not come offering instruction in
love to those who are rich; he who will give is not in need of my art; he who
says "Accept" whenever he pleases has wit enough of his own.'

119–20. *He . . . enough*] a form of the proverb, 'He is wise that is rich'
(Dent, *P.L.E.D.,* W534).

121. *great . . . gods*] Dent (*P.L.E.D.,* G111.11) gives this as the first of two
citations of a phrase that sounds proverbial but may be original with Lyly.
Compare also Dent, *P.L.E.D.,* W704: 'Women are tempted by gifts.'

122. *bend her brow*] frown.

bend thy fist] i.e., make a threatening or defiant gesture.

123. *Cammocks*] Bond (II.559) quotes *Endymion,* III.i.36–7: 'timely . . .
crooks that tree that will be a cammock', suggesting that Lyly has in mind both
a crooked staff (*O.E.D.,* sb.[2]) and a plant or tree (*O.E.D.,* sb.[1]) that might be
trained into pleasingly crooked shapes. Compare *Euphues,* II.23, 21–2,
'crooked trees prove good cammocks', II.169, 23, and *Mother Bombie,*
I.iii.108.

124. *water to be*] i.e., water must be, is to be.

125. *fire . . . swords*] proverbial, as in Sir Thomas Elyot's *The Education or
Bringing up of Children, Translated out of Plutarch* (*c.* 1535), sig. F2: 'Cut not

have a rival, be patient. Art must wind him out, not
malice; time, not might; her change, and thy constancy.
Whatsoever she weareth, swear it becomes her. In thy
love be secret. Venus' coffers, though they be hollow,
never sound, and when they seem emptiest they are　　130
fullest. Old fool that I am, to do thee good I begin to
dote and counsel that which I would have concealed.
Thus, Phao, have I given thee certain regards, no rules,
only to set thee in the way, not to bring thee home.

---

the fire with weapon; do not imitate a man in his fury.' Bond observes (II.559)
that the wording of this proverb in Plutarch's *The Education of Children*
(*Moralia*, I.17, pp. 58–60), as derived from Pythagoras, '*Pur sidēro mē
skaleuein*', etc., is misrendered by Lyly in his *Euphues and His Ephoebus* (I.281,
18–19) as follows: 'Not to bring fire to a slaughter—that is, we must not
provoke any that is furious with words.' George Pettie uses the proverb in his
translation of Stephen Guazzo's *The Civil Conversation*, 1581, p. 41, in the
1586 edition; cited by Tilley, *Elizabethan Proverb Lore*, no. 135, along with
other citations, including Erasmus, *Adagia*, II.17C, '*Ignem ne gladio fodito*',
'Do not stir the fire with a sword' (*C.W.E.*, XXXI.36–7).

125–6. *If . . . patient*] Ovid, *Ars Amatoria*, II.539–40: '*Rivalem patienter
habe: victoria tecum / Stabit*', 'Endure a rival patiently; victory will be yours'—a
passage quoted by Lyly in *Love's Metamorphosis*, I.i.38 and I.ii.36.

126. *wind him out*] draw him out, expose him (*O.E.D.*, *wind*, vb.[1], 11d).

127. *her change*] i.e., her change of mind about whom to love.

128. *Whatsoever . . . becomes her*] Ovid, *Ars Amatoria*, II.297–8, '*Sive erit in
Tyriis, Tyrios laudabis amictus: / Sive erit in Cois, Coa decere puta*', 'If she is
dressed in Tyrian fashion, praise her Tyrian gown; if in Coan, then esteem the
Coan fashion attractive.'

128–30. *In . . . sound*] Ovid, *Ars Amatoria*, II.389: '*Ludite, sed furto celetur
culpa modesto*', 'Enjoy your sport, but let the fault be concealed by modest
stealth', and II.607–10: '*Praecipue Cytherea iubet sua sacra taceri. . . . Condita si
non sunt Veneris mysteria cistis, / Nec cava vesanis ictibus aera sonant*', 'More than
anything else, Cytherea [Venus] commands that her rites be held secret. . . .
Even if Venus' mysteries are not concealed in chests, nor does hollow bronze
resound to fierce blows.'

129. *hollow*] (1) empty of money, since love is traditionally impoverished;
(2) capable of resounding hollowly and loudly.

130. *never sound*] The word-play in l. 129 continues: (1) are unsound,
without substance; (2) never resound.

132. *dote*] act foolishly or weak-mindedly; also, be infatuatedly fond.

counsel . . . concealed] Sibylla regrets that, having fallen under the spell of
Phao's charm, she has given away women's secrets in the war of the sexes.

133. *regards*] views or considerations of a question or problem (*O.E.D.*, 6).

134. *set . . . way*] start you on your way.

home] to the point aimed at.

Phao. Ah, Sibylla, I pray go on, that I may glut myself in this   135
     science.
Sibylla. Thou shalt not surfeit, Phao, whilst I diet thee. Flies
     that die on the honeysuckle become poison to bees. A
     little in love is a great deal.
Phao. But all that can be said not enough.   140
Sibylla. White silver draweth black lines, and sweet words will
     breed sharp torments.
Phao. What shall become of me?
Sibylla. Go dare.   [*Exit into cave.*]
Phao. I go. Phao, thou canst but die, and then as good die   145
     with great desires as pine in base fortunes.   *Exit.*

---

144. *Exit into cave*] Bond; not in *Q1*.   146. *Exit*] *Q1*; *Exeunt* / Daniel.

135. *glut*] Compare Marlowe, *Doctor Faustus*, Prologue, l. 24, 'Glutted now
with learning's golden gifts', and scene i, l. 78, 'How am I glutted with conceit
of this!'
   136. *science*] knowledge acquired by study, mastery.
   137–8. *Flies . . . bees*] This proverbial-sounding lore may be Lyly's own.
   141. *White . . . lines*] proverbial, derived from Pliny, XXXIII.31, 98: '*Lineas
ex argento nigras praeduci plerique mirantur*', 'It is a source of wonder to most
people that silver produces black lines' (Mustard). Dent, *P.L.E.D.*, S459,
cites Erasmus's *Parabolae* I.602A (*C.W.E.*, XXIII.229): '*Argentum cum sit
candidum, nigras tamen ducit lineas, ut stannum*', 'Though silver is white, it
nonetheless draws black lines, as if it were lead.' Compare *Euphues*, II.167,
6–7: 'not unlike unto silver which, being white, draweth black lines'.

Act III

Actus Tertius, Scaena Prima.

[*Enter*] TRACHINUS, PANDION, MILETA, ISMENA,
[CRITICUS *and* MOLUS].

Trachinus. Sappho is fallen suddenly sick; I cannot guess the
cause.

Mileta. Some cold, belike, or else a woman's qualm.

Pandion. A strange nature of cold, to drive one into such an
heat.   5

Mileta. Your physic, sir, I think be of the second
sort, else would you not judge it rare that hot fevers are
engendered by cold causes.

Pandion. Indeed, lady, I have no more physic than will purge
choler, and that, if it please you, I will practise upon   10
you. It is good for women that be waspish.

0.1–2.] *Daniel; Trachinus, Pandion, Mileta, Ismena, Eugenua / Q1; Enter
Trachinus, Pandion Mileta, Ismena, and later Eugunua / Bond.*

0.1.] No change of scene is necessary. Trachinus speaks of walking 'into the
fields' and 'the open air' (l. 44); they are somewhere at or near the court.
Criticus and Molus, pages to Trachinus and Pandion, are not named in the
grouping of characters' names at the head of the scene because they have no
speaker's parts, but are referred to at l. 46 as though present. The situation is
like that in I.ii–I.iii and II.ii–II.iii, where the pages silently attend their
masters and then remain behind after their masters' departure to provide a
comic view of the courtly/academic debate. See I.iii.0.1n. and II.iii.0.1n.

3–8. *cold*] In the repartee of Mileta and Pandion, *cold* is given three
meanings: (1) a respiratory illness; (2) the opposite of *heat*; (3) 'without power
to move or influence', *O.E.D.*, 11; compare *The Merchant of Venice*, II.vii.73,
'Your suit is cold.'

3. *qualm*] a feeling of weakness, usually sudden.

6. *physic*] medical knowledge.

second] i.e., inferior, perhaps referring to Paracelsan (homeopathic)
medicine as against the Galenic.

9. *physic*] Pandion plays on Mileta's word *physic* in l. 6 by comically
threatening to give her a purge or cathartic (*O.E.D.*, *physic*, 4b) for her
waspishness. *Choler* or angry behaviour was conventionally attributed to an
excess of bile (choler), a hot and dry humour.

251

Ismena. Faith, sir, no, you are best purge your own melan-
   choly. Belike you are a male-content.
Pandion. It is true, and are not you a female content?
Trachinus. Soft, I am not content that a male and female con-   15
   tent should go together.
Mileta. Ismena is disposed to be merry.
Ismena. No, it is Pandion would fain seem wise.
Trachinus. You shall not fall out, for pigeons after biting fall to
   billing, and open jars make the closest jests.   20

                    [*Enter*] EUGENUA.

Eugenua. Mileta, Ismena, Mileta! Come away, my lady is in
   a swoon.
Mileta. Ay me!
Ismena. Come, let us make haste.
              [*Exeunt* EUGENUA, MILETA *and* ISMENA.]
Trachinus. I am sorry for Sappho, because she will take no   25

20.1.] *Bond; not in Q1.*   24.1.] *Bond (subst.); not in Q1.*

─────────────────────────────────

   12. *you are best*] you would do best to.
   13. *male-content*] a pun on *malcontent*, often spelled with an added 'e' (Bond,
II.559). *Melancholy* was considered the product of black bile, a cold and moist
humour.
   14. *female content*] Pandion may mean 'contentious female', using *content* in
the now obsolete sense of 'contention, dispute' (*O.E.D.*, sb.³), or else he
simply coins a female equivalent of *male*-content.
   15–16.] Trachinus continues the word-play: 'I am not satisfied or willing
that such a man and woman should be coupled.' He is possibly making a
grammatical jest as well, objecting to the coupling of what appears to be a
masculine form (male-content) with a coined feminine equivalent.
   17–18. *merry . . . wise*] More antithesis of female and male temperament in
this war of words between the sexes.
   19. *fall out*] quarrel.
   19–20. *pigeons . . . billing*] Mustard and Dent (*P.L.E.D.*, D574.11) quote
Ovid, *Ars Amatoria*, II.465–6: '*Quae modo pugnarunt, iungunt sua rostra
columbae, / Quarum blanditias verbaque murmur habet*', 'The doves who recently
fought now join bill to bill; their cooing expresses words of blandishment.' See
also *Euphues*, II.105, 4–5, and the proverb '*Amantium irae amoris redintegratio
est*', 'The falling out of lovers is the renewing of love' (Terence, *Andria*,
III.iii.23).
   20. *open . . . jests*] Frank and unrestrained quarrels often lead to intimate
merriment. (The word-play derives from the antithesis of *open* and *close*.)

physic, like you, Pandion, who, being sick of the sullens, will seek no friend.

Pandion. Of men we learn to speak, of gods to hold our peace.
Silence shall digest what folly hath swallowed, and
wisdom wean what fancy hath nursed.   30

Trachinus. Is it not love?

Pandion. If it were, what then?

Trachinus. Nothing but that I hope it be not.

Pandion. Why, in courts there is nothing more common. And
as to be bald among the Micanyans it was accounted   35
no shame, because they were all bald, so to be in love
among courtiers it is no discredit, for that they are all
in love.

Trachinus. Why, what do you think of our ladies?

Pandion. As of the Seres' wool, which, being whitest and   40
softest, fretteth soonest and deepest.

---

30. wean] *Q2* (weane)*;* weaue *Q1.*

---

26. *physic*] medicine.

26–7. *sick of the sullens*] sulky and ill-humoured; a set phrase (Dent,
P.L.E.D., S964).

28. *hold our peace*] Bond suggests (II.559) that Pandion must have guessed
Sappho's secret passion from her behaviour in II.ii, though his response here
makes sense in terms of his own philosophical temperament. Trachinus'
question at l. 31 and the following discussion up to l. 45 can similarly apply to
Sappho or more generally to philosophers and courtiers, and to Pandion in
particular.

30. *wean*] i.e., train to good habits and remove childish desire. This Q2
correction ('weane') of Q1's 'weaue' is clearly defensible and is probably the
intelligent guesswork of the Q2 compositor.

35–8.] This passage is an echo, as Bond notes (II.560), of *Euphues*, II.139,
4–5, where the Micanyans are described as 'all born bald'. The ultimate source
is Pliny, XI.47, who, speaking of the inhabitants of the island of Myconos in
the Aegean, says (a propos of hair): '*quippe Myconii carentes eo gignuntur*', 'in
fact the people of Myconos are born devoid of it'. Lyly probably derived it
from Erasmus, *Parabolae* (*C.W.E.*, XXIII.262).

40. *Seres' wool*] Euphues (*Euphues*, II.152, 22–3) speaks of 'the softness of
wool, which the Seres send'. Bond (III.505) cites Virgil's *Georgics*, II.121 as the
probable source: '*velleraque ut foliis depectant tenuia Seres*', 'and how the Seres
comb their fine fleeces from leaves'. 'Seres' is the name of a people anciently
living in eastern Asia, probably China, reputedly the original home of silk;
hence, 'Seres' wool' is silk, obtained, as Virgil suggests, from mulberry leaves.

41. *fretteth*] wears, frays.

Trachinus. I will not tempt you in your deep melancholy, lest
    you seem sour to those which are so sweet. But come,
    let us walk a little into the fields; it may be the open air
    will disclose your close conceits.   45
Pandion. I will go with you; but send our pages away.
                            Exeunt [all but Servants].

Actus Tertius, Scaena Secunda.

CRITICUS, MOLUS [*remain*].

Criticus. What brown study art thou in, Molus? No mirth?
    No life?
Molus. I am, in the depth of my learning, driven to a muse
    how this Lent I shall scamble in the court, that was
    wont to fast so oft in the university.   5
Criticus. Thy belly is thy god.
Molus. Then is he a deaf god.
Criticus. Why?
Molus. For *venter non habet aures.* But thy back is thy god.

46.1.] *Daniel (subst.); Exeunt Q1.*   0.1.] *Daniel, subst.; Criticus, Molus,*
Calipho / Q1; Enter Cryticus, Molus, afterwards Calypho / Bond.

---

    43. *those . . . sweet*] i.e., the ladies. (Trachinus is twitting Pandion for being
secretly interested in women, despite his professions of being above it all.)
    45. *close conceits*] private thoughts. In ll. 28ff. above, Pandion has shown
himself unwilling to comment on Sappho's sickness.
    0.1.] The pages of Trachinus and Pandion have no speaking parts in the
previous scene, but Pandion's closing proposal to 'send our pages away' seems
to indicate their silent presence as they attend their masters. There is no
change of scene from III.i to III.ii and the action seems to be continuous.
Certainly the debate in III.ii mimics that between the courtier and the
philosopher.
    1. *brown study*] a conventional phrase for mental abstraction (Dent,
P.L.E.D., S945), as in *Euphues*, 1.224, 36.
    3. *muse*] fit of profound meditation.
    4. *this Lent*] The title page announces that the play was performed before
Queen Elizabeth 'on Shrove Tuesday', the evening immediately preceding Ash
Wednesday and the start of Lent.
    scamble] make shift, scramble. Compare *scambling*, IV.iii.7.
    9. venter non habet aures] 'The belly has no ears', is deaf to all pleadings
and will not be satisfied by mere words. Dent (*P.L.E.D.*, B286) and Bond
(II.560) cite Erasmus's *Adagia*, II.659E, in which the saying is attributed to
Plutarch.
    thy back . . . god] i.e., like your courtier master, you worship splendid

Criticus. Then is it a blind god.   10
Molus. How prove you that?
Criticus. Easy. *Nemo videt manticae quod in tergo est.*
Molus. Then would the satchel that hangs at your god, *id est*,
　　your back, were full of meat to stuff my god, *hoc est*,
　　my belly.   15
Criticus. Excellent. But how canst thou study, when thy mind
　　is only in the kitchen?
Molus. Doth not the horse travail best that sleepest with his
　　head in the manger?
Criticus. Yes, what then?   20
Molus. Good wits will apply. But what cheer is there here this
　　Lent?
Criticus. Fish.
Molus. I can eat none. It is wind.

---

18. travail] *Q1* (trauaile).

---

apparel. Bond (II.560) compares this with Diogenes' diatribes against the
Athenians in *Campaspe*, IV.i.34–5: 'back-gods in the morning with pride, in
the evening belly-gods with gluttony'. Compare *Euphues*, II.121, 19–20:
'Another [lover] layeth all his living on his back, judging that women are
wedded to bravery.'

12. Nemo . . . est] No one sees the satchel or wallet at his own back.
Another of Erasmus's *Adagia*, II.256C, Dent, *P.L.E.D.*, W20). According to
Bond (II.560), *A Short Introduction of [Latin] Grammer*, sig H viii, quotes the
poems of Catullus, XXII.21: '*Sed non videmus manticae quod in tergo est*', 'But we
do not see what is contained in the satchel that hangs at our own back.' The
proverb means 'that we do not see ourselves as others see us', and alludes to the
fable of Aesop to the effect that 'a man carries other people's faults in a bag in
front, and his own in a bag slung behind'. The proud courtier is not aware of
his own vanity. Compare *Troilus and Cressida*, III.iii.145: 'Time hath, my lord,
a wallet at his back.'

13. id est] i.e., that is. Criticus' back is his god in the sense that he spends all
his wealth on finery, says Molus.

14. hoc est] this is.

16–17. *thy mind . . . kitchen*] Compare *Campaspe*, I.ii.79, '*semper animus
meus est in patinis*', 'my thoughts are always in the stewpan', and Hunter's note.

18. *travail*] The Q1 reading, 'trauaile', can mean both 'labour' and 'travel'.

21. *Good . . . apply*] i.e., clever people give to the proverb or truism a
specific application, make sense out of obscure sayings. 'An old jesting phrase,
used as a sarcasm' (Fairholt, 1.294–5).

24–6. *wind, fire*] i.e., two of the four elements. Molus sharpens his quarrel
against such Lenten fare as fish and eggs by describing their presumed capacity
to increase certain bodily humours such as choler or bile (hot and dry) and
thereby interfere with good health and even temperament.

Criticus. Eggs.   25
Molus. I must eat none. They are fire.
Criticus. Cheese.
Molus. It is against the old verse, *Caseus est nequam.*
Criticus. Yea, but it digesteth all things except itself.
Molus. Yea, but if a man hath nothing else to eat, what shall   30
    it digest?
Criticus. You are disposed to jest. But if your silken throat can
    swallow no packthread, you must pick your teeth and
    play with your trencher.
Molus. So shall I not incur the fulsome and unmannerly sin of   35
    surfeiting. But here cometh Callipho.

[*Enter*] CALLIPHO.

Criticus. What news?
Callipho. Since my being here, I have sweat like a dog to prove
    my master a devil; he brought such reasons to refel me
    as, I promise you, I shall like the better of his wit as   40
    long as I am with him.

36.1.] *Bond; not in Q1.*

28. Caseus est nequam] 'Cheese is nothing.' Mustard cites the old verse,
'*Caseus est nequam, qui digerit omnia sequam*', existing in an English version:
'Cheese it is a peevish elf; / It digests all things but itself.'
    29. it digesteth . . . itself] i.e., cheese aids digestion. See previous note and
Dent, *P.L.E.D.*, C269, citing Erasmus's *Parabolae*; see Walther, 1.278–81,
and especially item 2439, citing as its source the *Carmina Proverbialium*, Basel,
1576.
    32–3. if . . . packthread] In *Euphues*, II.227, 2–3, the speaker urges that
maidens not be so daintily mouthed 'that their silken throats should swallow
no packthread' (Dent, *P.L.E.D.*, P8.11, Bond, II.560). Packthread, or stout
twine used to tie up bundles, is coarser than silk. A silken esophagus too
narrow and delicate for packthread would make for a very dainty appetite.
    33–4. pick . . . trencher] i.e., behave like one whose plate has been emptied.
    36.1.] If Venus and Cupid enter earlier (I.i.20.1) from a stage entrance or
structure representing Vulcan's forge, Callipho may also do so here. See
Introduction, pp. 184–7.
    38. Since . . . here] i.e., since Callipho's encounter with the pages in II.iii,
when Molus undertook to prove Callipho to be a devil for being black like
his master Vulcan. Callipho has been attempting to practise on Vulcan the
syllogisms Molus practised on him.
    39. refel] refute.
    40. promise] assure.

Molus. How?

Callipho. Thus: I always arguing that he had horns and there-
    fore a devil, he said, 'Fool, they are things like horns,
    but no horns. For once in the senate of gods being   45
    holden a solemn session, in the midst of their talk I put
    in my sentence, which was so indifferent that they all
    concluded it might as well have been left out as put in,
    and so placed on each side of my head things like horns
    and called me a parenthesis.' Now, my masters, this   50
    may be true, for I have seen it myself about divers
    sentences.

Molus. It is true, and the same time did Mars make a full
    point, that Vulcan's head was made a parenthesis.

Criticus. This shall go with me; I trust in Syracusa to give one   55
    or other a parenthesis.

Molus. Is Venus yet come home?

Callipho. No, but were I Vulcan, I would by the gods—

Criticus. What wouldst thou?

Callipho. Nothing, but as Vulcan halt by the gods.   60

Criticus. I thought you would have hardly entreated Venus.

44–5. *horns, but no horns*] Vulcan refutes Callipho's syllogism by denying his
antecedent, as Molus did to Callipho (II.iii.90).

46. *solemn*] ceremonial, imposing.

47. *sentence*] judgement, opinion; but with a pun on the grammatical
meaning, 'a grammatically complete expression of a single thought', leading
forward to the jesting comparison of parentheses to horns in ll. 49–50.

indifferent] immaterial (*O.E.D.*, 10b).

50. *parenthesis*] The joke is repeated in John Day's *Law Tricks* (1604–7), sig.
EI: 'Vulcan with his parentheses' (*Works*, ed. A. H. Bullen, 1891, Act III,
p. 41).

masters] sirs.

52. *sentences*] (1) grammatically complete units (2) wise sayings, often
marked out by parentheses.

53–4. *make ... point*] come to a full stop, conclude (continuing the
grammatical metaphor, with however a ribald suggestion of Mars' success in
winning Venus' love—the means by which Vulcan's head was crowned with
cuckold's horns).

54. *that*] so that.

55. *This ... me*] i.e., I'll remember this, make use of it.

55–6. *give ... parenthesis*] i.e., cuckold some husband or other.

60. *halt*] Vulcan's lameness is symbolic of his impotence with Venus. *Halt*
suggests a schoolboy's grammatical joke as well: Callipho has halted in his
previous speech (see Bond, II.560), and lamely changes his imprecation '*halt by
the gods*' into a phrase of direction, 'limp past the gods'.

Callipho. Nay, Venus is easily entreated. But let that go by.
Criticus. What?
Callipho. That which maketh so many parentheses.
Molus. I must go by too, or else my master will not go by me,   65
    but meet me full with his fist. Therefore, if we shall
    sing, give me my part quickly, for if I tarry long I shall
    cry my part woefully.

Song

Omnes.	Arm, arm, the foe comes on apace.	
Callipho.	What's that red nose and sulphury face?	70
Molus.	'Tis the hot leader.	
Criticus.	What's his name?	
Molus.	Bacchus, a captain of plump fame.	

    A goat the beast on which he rides;
    Fat grunting swine run by his sides;
    His standard-bearer fears no knocks,   75
    For he's a drunken butter-box
    Who, when i'th' red field thus he revels,

---

64. parentheses] *This ed.; Parenthesis Q1.*   69–96. *Omnes . . . die] Blount; not in Q1.*

---

    62. *easily*] Callipho's answer plays on *hardly* in l. 61; Criticus meant 'harshly', but Callipho uses *easily* as antithetical to 'with difficulty', meaning that Venus is all too available to entreaty. *Hardly* then may also suggest 'with erection'.

    let . . . by] Callipho avoids speaking too explicitly about Venus' morals. Compare Mistress Quickly's 'but let that pass', *Merry Wives*, I.iv.15.

    64. *That . . . parentheses*] i.e., cuckolding.

    65. *go by . . . go by*] Molus plays upon Callipho's *go by* in l. 62, meaning to set aside the matter without further notice, in a further sense: I must depart, or else my master will not pass me by, will not let me avoid him.

    68. *cry my part*] bewail my lot (*O.E.D., part,* 7b), but punning also on *part,* musical part in their song (*O.E.D.,* 10), in l. 67.

    71. *the hot leader*] the fiery captain of *the foe* (l. 69).

    76. *a drunken butter-box*] 'A satirical term for a Dutchman, all of whom were popularly believed to be great drinkers, and inordinately fond of butter' (Fairholt, I.295). Bond (II.560) notes that among the 'characters' added to Sir Thomas Overbury's 'A Wife' in the 1614 edition is 'A Drunken Dutchman resident in England' who 'stinks of butter'. (See *The 'Conceited Newes' of Sir Thomas Overbury and His Friends,* ed. James E. Savage, Scholars' Facsimile, 1968, p. 173.) The dialect in l. 78 is meant to be Dutch or German.

    77. *red field*] i.e., field of battle.

	Cries out, 'ten towsan tun of tivells!'	
Callipho.	What's he so swaggers in the van?	
Molus.	O, that's a roaring Englishman,	80
	Who in deep healths does so excel,	
	From Dutch and French he bears the bell.	
Criticus.	What vict'lers follow Bacchus' camps?	
Molus.	Fools, fiddlers, panders, pimps and ramps.	
Callipho.	See, see, the battle now grows hot;	85
	Here legs fly, here goes heads to th' pot,	
	Here whores and knaves toss broken glasses,	
	Here all the soldiers look like asses.	
Criticus.	What man e'er heard such hideous noise?	
Molus.	O, that's the vintner's bawling boys.	90
	Anon, anon, the trumpets are	
	Which call them to the fearful bar.	
Callipho.	Rush in, and let's our forces try.	
Molus.	Oho, for see they fly, they fly!	
Criticus.	And so will I.	
Callipho.	And I.	
Molus.	And I.	95
Omnes.	'Tis a hot day in drink to die. *Exeunt.*	

---

78. *ten ... tivells*] Compare Marston, *The Dutch Courtesan*, 'ten tousand devils take you' (II.ii.8) and 'Ten tousant devla!' (IV.iii.43; ed. Fraser and Rabkin, *Drama of the English Renaissance*, II).

79. *van*] vanguard.

80. *roaring*] noisy, riotous, carousing.

81. *deep healths*] toasts accompanied by deep draughts, ones in which a lot of liquor is swallowed at one time.

82. *bears the bell*] takes first place, carries off the prize. A conventional phrase (Dent, *P.L.E.D.*, B275).

83. *vict'lers*] victuallers. Pronounced 'vittlers'.

84. *ramps*] bold and vulgar women, jades, whores. Compare *Cymbeline*, I.vi.134, 'mounting variable ramps'.

86. *legs fly*] (1) legs are blown off in the battle; (2) drinkers' legs collapse under them.

to th' pot] to ruin (*O.E.D.*, *pot*, 13f), with a play on the literal meaning, since the mock-epic battle here described is a drinking contest. *Pot* = tankard.

91. *Anon, anon*] i.e., I'll be with you in a minute; the pot-boys' answer to the drinkers' call for service. Compare *1 Henry IV*, II.iv.33ff. Their calls are compared in l. 92 to the last trumpet which calls sinners to the *fearful bar* of the Last Judgement (with a pun, perhaps, on the *bar* of the tavern).

Actus Tertius, Scaena Tertia.

SAPPHO [*discovered*] *in her bed*; MILETA, ISMENA, CANOPE,
EUGENUA, FAVILLA [*and*] LAMIA [*in attendance*].

Sappho. Heigh-ho! I know not which way to turn me. Ah, ah,
I faint, I die!
Mileta. Madam, I think it good you have more clothes, and
sweat it out.
Sappho. No, no, the best ease I find is to sigh it out.   5
Ismena. A strange disease, that should breed such a desire.
Sappho. A strange desire, that hath brought such a disease.
Canope. Where, lady, do you feel your most pain?
Sappho. Where nobody else can feel it, Canope.
Canope. At the heart?   10
Sappho. In the heart.
Canope. Will you have any mithridate?
Sappho. Yea, if for this disease there were any mithridate.

0.1–2.] *This ed.; Sapho in her bed, Mileta, Ismena, Canope, Eugenua, Fauilla,
Lamya / Q1.*

0.1.] *SAPPHO* discovered in her bed] Presumably the curtains are drawn
back from a stage structure or opening, revealing Sappho and her women. The
action of this scene need not be contained within such a structure, however.
Stools are provided near the bed for the ladies (ll. 53–4). On the possibility
that the stichomythia with which this scene begins is indebted to Euripides'
Hippolytus, see Introduction, pp. 156–8, and l. 82n. below.

3. *clothes*] bedclothes.

10–11. *At the heart / In the heart*] Sappho's distinction between *at* and *in*,
intended more for the audience than for her ladies, is that she suffers an
emotional disorder within, not a physical discomfort. A similar antithesis
between flesh and spirit informs her word-play in every reply she makes in
ll. 5–18: *sweat it out* and *sigh it out* (using *out* in the varying idiomatic senses of
'sweat out the fever' and 'sigh out my passion'), *disease* (meaning 'illness' and
'absence of ease'), *desire* ('request' and 'passionate craving'), *feel* ('perceive
physically' and 'experience mentally'), *burning* ('feverish' and 'inflamed with
passion'), *ague / agony* (with a playful application of the root word, *agon*, to two
differently derived words), etc. See Introduction, pp. 178–9.

13. *mithridate*] 'A composition of many ingredients regarded as a universal
antidote or preservative against poisons and infectious diseases' (*O.E.D.*),
named for Mithridates VI, King of Pontus (d. *c.* 63 B.C.) who reportedly made
successful use of such a nostrum. Canope offers Sappho a particular medicine,
but Sappho plays upon the word in its generic sense of 'antidote' or 'remedy'.
A term often appearing in *Euphues* (e.g., II.149, 37), and in *Midas*, IV.iv.47.

Mileta. Why, what disease is it, madam, that physic cannot
    cure?   15
Sappho. Only the disease, Mileta, that I have.
Mileta. Is it a burning ague?
Sappho. I think so, or a burning agony.
Eugenua. Will you have any of this syrup, to moisture your
    mouth?   20
Sappho. Would I had some local things to dry my brain!
Favilla. Madam, will you see if you can sleep?
Sappho. Sleep, Favilla? I shall then dream.
Lamia. As good dream sleeping as sigh waking.
Eugenua. Phao is cunning in all kind of simples, and it is hard   25
    if there be none to procure sleep.
Sappho. Who?
Eugenua. Phao.
Sappho. Yea, Phao, Phao, ah Phao! Let him come presently.
Mileta. Shall we draw the curtains whilst you give yourself to   30
    slumber?
Sappho. Do, but depart not. I have such starts in my sleep,
    disquieted I know not how.   *In a slumber.*
    Phao, Phao!
Ismena. What say you, madam?   35
Sappho. Nothing; but if I sleep not now, you send for Phao.
    Ah gods!
               She falleth asleep. The curtains drawn.
Mileta. There is a fish called garus that healeth all sickness, so
    as whilst it is applied one name not garus.

---

21. *local things*] (1) specific medicines, affecting a particular bodily part; a
medical term (*O.E.D.*, *local*, adj., A4a); (2) Phao, who is attached to his
locality and to his occupation of ferryman (*O.E.D.*, *local*, B. sb., 1).
   dry my brain] (1) remedy the imbalance of humours caused by excessive heat;
(2) check the flow of imagination.
   25. *cunning*] skilled.
   simples] medical properties of a single ingredient; with a play of antithesis
between *cunning* and *simple* that is continued in the next scene, ll. 1–4.
   25–6. *it is . . . sleep*] it's hard to imagine that not one of his medicines can
induce sleep.
   26. *procure sleep*] i.e., by administering a soporific; but to Sappho the idea is
of one who can end her restless craving. See ll. 135–9.
   38–9. *a fish . . . garus*] This bit of 'natural history' provides a good proof of
Lyly's reliance on Erasmus rather than Pliny. In the Toronto translation of the

Eugenua. An evil medicine for us women, for, if we should be   40
    forbidden to name garus, we should chat nothing but
    'garus'.
Canope. Well said, Eugenua, you know yourself.
Eugenua. Yea, Canope, and that I am one of your sex.
Ismena. I have heard of an herb called lunary that, being   45
    bound to the pulses of the sick, causeth nothing but
    dreams of weddings and dances.
Favilla. I think, Ismena, that herb be at thy pulses now, for
    thou art ever talking of matches and merriments.
Canope. It is an unlucky sign in the chamber of the sick to talk   50
    of marriages, for my mother said it foreshoweth death.
Mileta. It is very evil to Canope to sit at the bed's feet, and
    foretelleth danger. Therefore, remove your stool and
    sit by me.
Lamia. Sure it is some cold she hath taken.   55
Ismena. If one were burnt, I think we women would say he
    died of a cold.
Favilla. It may be some conceit.
Mileta. Then is there no fear, for yet did I never hear of a
    woman that died of a conceit.   60
Eugenua. I mistrust her not, for that the owl hath not shrieked

---

Parabolae (*C.W.E.*, XXIII.231, I.602E in the *Opera Omnia*), R. A. B. Mynors
points out that *garum* is, according to Pliny, 'a familiar Roman sauce' that
'heals fresh burns'. Erasmus, however, 'appears to have read him [Pliny]
hastily, and inferred a feminine form *garus*, which is itself burnt to make the
remedy'. Lyly follows Erasmus word for word.

    so as . . . garus] i.e., Sappho should not mention Phao if Phao is to heal her.
    so as] so long as.

    40–2.] Compare the saying, 'A woman does that which is forbidden her'
(Dent, *P.L.E.D.*, W650).

    45. *herb called lunary*] the fern moonwort or a similar plant, purportedly
with many magical qualities; compare *Gallathea*, III.i.20. In *Euphues*, II.172,
18, lunary is credited with bringing forth its leaves during the waxing of the
moon and shedding them in the waning. In England, lunary is still known as
'honesty', and was once thought to make locks fly open. Endymion sleeps on a
bank of lunary.

    56–7.] Ismena's jest is that the diagnosis of 'a cold' is ridiculously over-
applied to all illnesses.

    58. *conceit*] fanciful notion, i.e., a psychosomatic complaint.

    61. *I mistrust her not*] I do not fear for her.

at the window or the night-raven croaked, both being
fatal.

Favilla. You are all superstitious, for these be but fancies of
doting age, who, by chance observing it in some, have   65
set it down as a religion for all.

Mileta. Favilla, thou art but a girl. I would not have a weasel
cry, nor desire to see a glass, nor an old wife come into
my chamber, for then, though I lingered in my disease,
I should never escape it.   70

Sappho. Ah, who is there? [*The bed-curtains are drawn back.*]
What sudden affrights be these? Methought Phao came
with simples to make me sleep. Did nobody name Phao
before I began to slumber?

Mileta. Yes, we told you of him.   75

Sappho. Let him be here tomorrow.

Mileta. He shall. Will you have a little broth to comfort you?

Sappho. I can relish nothing.

Mileta. Yet a little you must take to sustain nature.

Sappho. I cannot, Mileta, I will not. O, which way shall I lie? 80
What shall I do? Heigh-ho. O Mileta, help to rear me
up my bed; my head lies too low. You pester me with

---

62. croaked] *Q2* (croked); crooked *Q1*.   71. *The bed-curtains . . . back*] *Bond*
(*subst.*); *not in Q1.*   82. bed] *Q2*; bead *Q1*; head *Daniel*.

---

62. *croaked*] *Q2*'s correction ('croked') of *Q1*'s 'crooked' is clearly right and
sufficiently self-explanatory following 'night-raven' for it to be attributed in all
probability to the Q2 compositor.

63. *fatal*] ominous (*O.E.D.*, 4c). On the ominous uses of owls, night ravens,
etc., compare *3 Henry VI*, V.vi.44ff., *Macbeth*, II.ii.3, *Much Ado*, II.iii.81,
etc.

67–8. *weasel, glass, old wife*] connected with various superstitions of bad
luck, as are also the owl and the raven. Edward Topsell's *The History of Four-
Footed Beasts and Serpents* (1607, rpt. and enl. 1658, Vol.I, *Of Four-footed
Beasts*, p. 565) reports that the weasel is called 'an unhappy, unfortunate, and
unlucky beast among hunters, for they hold opinion here in England that, if
they meet with a weasel in the morning, they shall not speed well that day'. It
can be dangerous to see one's reflection or break a mirror, and old women
(*wives*) may be witches.

82. *bed*] *Q2*'s emendation seems sensible. *Q1*'s *bead* is an unusual form for
bed (not listed in *O.E.D.*), and might be a printer's error for *head*, a reading to
which *Q1*'s punctuation ('reare me vp, my bead, my head') lends some
plausibility, and Daniel adopts this reading; but it is more likely that the Q1
compositor, memorising his line, was influenced by *head* later in the line. On

too many clothes. Fie, you keep the chamber too hot.
Avoid it! It may be I shall steal a nap when all are gone.
Mileta. We will.   85

[*Exeunt all the* Ladies.]

Sappho. (*Sola*) Ah, impatient disease of love, and goddess of
love thrice unpitiful! The eagle is never stricken with
thunder, nor the olive with lightning, and may great
ladies be plagued with love? O Venus, have I not strewed
thine altars with sweet roses, kept thy swans in clear   90
rivers, fed thy sparrows with ripe corn, and harboured
thy doves in fair houses? Thy tortoise have I nourished

85.1.] *Bond; not in* Q1; *They withdraw, leaving Sappho alone* / *Daniel.*   89.
strewed] *Q1* (strawed).

Lyly's possible indebtedness to Euripides' *Hippolytus* or to Seneca's *Phaedra*
in depicting Sappho's irritability in lovesickness, her reticence in confiding in
her women, etc., see Introduction, pp. 156–8.

   84. *Avoid it*] Leave the chamber.

   87–8. *The eagle . . . thunder*] Pliny, II.56: '*sicut nec e volucribus aquilam, quae
ob hoc armigera huius teli fingitur*', 'just as it [lightning] does not strike the eagle
among birds, which is why the eagle is portrayed as armed with a thunderbolt
as its weapon'. See also Pliny, X.3ff. (Mustard).

   88. *olive*] As a sacred tree, associated with peace, the olive might be thought
to be protected by the gods.

   89. *strewed*] *O.E.D.* supplies separate entries for 'straw' (Q1 reads
'strawed') and 'strew', but by the 1580s the meanings were identical and usage
often interchangeable.

   90–2. *swans, sparrows, doves*] On the association of these birds with Venus,
compare II.iv.26 and 35, IV.iv.39, and nn. In *Euphues*, II.98, 21–2, white
swans draw the chariot of Venus 'as the cognizance of Vesta'.

   92–4. *Thy tortoise . . . cockleshells*] As Bond (III.539) and Croll and Clemons
(p. 309) note, 'the cockle and the tortoise' are cited in *Mother Bombie*, I.iii.123,
as appropriate 'among fishes' to Venus, and in *Euphues*, II.98,21, Venus is
portrayed 'with a tortoise under her foot, as slow to harms'. Bond (II.512) and
Croll and Clemons (p. 309) cite Plutarch, 'Coniugalia Praecepta', 'Advice to
Bride and Groom' (*Moralia*, II.297ff., para. 32, repeated in 75) as mentioning a
statue by Phidias in which Aphrodite has one foot on the tortoise 'to admonish
women to home-keeping and quietness'. Croll and Clemons further cite
Erasmus, *Christiani Matrimonii Institutio* (V.695D), from Erasmus's *Adagia*,
II.555B, '*Veteres ita Venerem fingebant, ut pedibus testudinem premeret: id
innuentes, matrem familias ab aedibus nusquam opertere discedere*', 'The ancients
use to fashion Venus pressing a tortoise underfoot, thus signifying that the
mother of the family ought not to leave the home under any circumstances',
and, most pertinently, Alciati's *Emblems*, 100; see, for example, *Clarissimi Viri
d. Andreae Alciati Emblematum Libillus* (Paris, 1542), pp. 222–3, where a
naked Venus, surrounded by doves, stands with one foot on a tortoise, while

under my fig tree, my chamber have I ceiled with thy
cockleshells, and dipped thy sponge into the freshest
waters. Didst thou nurse me in my swaddling clouts   95
with wholesome herbs that I might perish in my flower-
ing years by fancy? I perceive, but too late I perceive,
and yet not too late because at last, that strains are
caught as well by stooping too low as reaching too high,
that eyes are bleared as soon with vapours that come   100
from the earth as with beams that proceed from the sun.
Love lodgeth sometimes in caves; and thou, Phoebus,
that in the pride of thy heat shinest all day in our horizon, at night dippest thy head in the ocean. Resist it,

---

103. heat] *Q1* (heate); hearte *Q2*.

the commentary, citing Phidias' statue, draws a moral conclusion similar to
that in Plutarch and Erasmus. The cockle or scallop shell is beneath Venus'
feet in Botticelli's picture (Uffizi gallery, Florence) of the Birth of Venus
arising from the sea, painted in the mid 1480s. Possibly there is an allusion to
the lost painting by Apelles, 'Venus Anadyomene', on the same subject,
especially since Apelles is prominent in *Campaspe* and is frequently cited in
Euphues. In the post-*Iliad* Homeric hymns, Venus is reported to have sprung
from the foam of the sea near Cytherea (sometimes interpreted as the sperm of
her father Zeus) and thus to have acquired her name Aphrodite or 'foam-risen'
(Greek *aphros*, foam). See I.i.69 above.

93. *fig tree*] Figs have long been considered aphrodisiac because of their
resemblance to the female sexual anatomy. Compare Charmian's remark in
Antony and Cleopatra, I.ii.34–5: 'I love long life better than figs.' The myrtle
tree is more usually associated with Venus.

ceiled] lined the ceilings or walls of.

94. *sponge*] Compare *Euphues*, II.98, 6–7, in a passage contiguous to those
cited in ll. 90–2 and 92–4nn.: 'Protagenes portrayed Venus with a sponge
sprinkled with sweet water, but if once she wrung it, it would drop blood.'
Croll and Clemons propose that this apparent invention by Lyly may have
been suggested by Pliny's account, xxv.36, of an incident in which the painter
Protagenes 'succeeded by chance in representing the foam at his dog's mouth
by throwing his sponge, full of white paint, at the canvas on which he had
made so many vain attempts'. See *Euphues*, II.135, 31. At II.184, 7–8, the
sponge is a symbol of dissembling in that it 'is full of water, yet is it not seen'.

95. *swaddling clouts*] swaddling clothes.

97. *fancy*] love.

98. *at last*] finally. Sappho's paradox is that 'last' is not necessarily 'too late'.
strains] injuries brought about by stretching or reaching too far.

103. *heat*] The Q2 reading ('hearte') is possible, but Q1's 'heate' makes good
sense in the passage; though 'pride of thy heart' is the more expected phrase,
'pride of thy heat' is sufficiently arresting for it to have well been intended.

Sappho, whilst it is yet tender. Of acorns comes oaks,   105
of drops floods, of sparks flames, of atomies elements.
But, alas, it fareth with me as with wasps who, feeding
on serpents, make their stings more venomous; for,
glutting myself on the face of Phao, I have made my
desire more desperate. Into the nest of an halcyon no   110
bird can enter but the halcyon, and into the heart of
so great a lady can any creep but a great lord? There is
an herb not unlike unto my love which, the further it
groweth from the sea, the salter it is; and my desires,
the more they swerve from reason, the more seem they   115
reasonable. When Phao cometh, what then? Wilt thou
open thy love? Yea. No, Sappho! But, staring in his
face till thine eyes dazzle and thy spirits faint, die before his face. Then this shall be written on thy tomb,

---

'Heate' would be an easy misprint for 'hearte', but the reverse is also true, or
the Q2 reading may simply be guesswork on the part of the Q2 compositor.

103–4. *horizon*] i.e., the region of the sky bounded by the horizon
(*O.E.D.*, 2b).

104–5. *Resist . . . tender*] i.e., resist love while it is still new and flexible
enough to be bent in another direction. Compare Ovid, *Remedia Amoris*, 81:
'*Opprime, dum nova sunt subiti mala semina morbi*', 'Crush, while they are still
new, the baleful seeds of sudden disease' (Mustard). On proverbial use, see
Dent, *P.L.E.D.*, A22, D617 and S714.

105. *comes*] a singular verb following a singular nominative concept: from
the planting of acorns comes oaks.

106. *elements*] i.e., earth, air, fire and water.

107–8. *wasps . . . venomous*] Bond (II.561) cites Pliny, XI.116: '*Vespae
serpente avide vescuntur, quo alimento mortiferos ictus faciunt*', 'Wasps devour a
snake greedily, and by so doing make their sting fatal.' Thomas Muffett
similarly reports of wasps in *Theatre of Insects* (1634), pp. 921–6, that 'They
feed on flesh of serpents and then they sting mortally.'

110–11. *Into . . . halcyon*] From Aelian, *De Natura Animalium*, IX.17. Pliny,
X.47, says of the halcyon or kingfisher that '*nidi earum admirationem habent
pilae figura paulum eminenti ore perquem angusto, grandium spongearum simili-
tudine*', 'their nests are admired for their shape, that of a ball slightly projecting
with a very narrow mouth, resembling very large sponges' (see also Bond,
II.561).

112–4. *There . . . is*] This bit of lore is unidentified and may be invented.

116. *reasonable*] i.e., speciously plausible.

117. *open*] reveal, declare (*O.E.D.*, vb., 9b).

staring] gazing steadily.

that, though thy love were greater than wisdom could   120
endure, yet thine honour was such as love could not
violate.—Mileta!

[*Enter* MILETA *and* ISMENA.]

Mileta. I come.

Sappho. It will not be. I can take no rest, which way soever
    I turn.   125

Mileta. A strange malady.

Sappho. Mileta, if thou wilt, a martyrdom. But give me my
    lute, and I will see if in song I can beguile mine own
    eyes.

Mileta. Here, madam.   [*She gives a lute to Sappho.*]   130

Sappho. Have you sent for Phao?

Mileta. Yea.

Sappho. And to bring simples that will procure sleep?

Mileta. No.

Sappho. Foolish wench, what should the boy do here if he   135
    bring not remedies with him? You think belike I could
    sleep if I did but see him. Let him not come at all. Yes,
    let him come. No, it is no matter. Yet will I try; let him
    come. Do you hear?

Mileta. Yea, madam, it shall be done. [*She moves away from*   140
    the bed.] Peace, no noise; she beginneth to fall asleep.
    I will go to Phao.

Ismena. Go speedily, for if she wake and find you not here she

---

122.1.] *Bond (subst.); not in* Q1.   130. *She gives . . . Sappho*] *This ed.; not in*
Q1.   140–1. *She moves . . . bed*] *This ed.; not in* Q1; *She comes from the recess /*
Bond.

124. *It will not be*] a conventional phrase of impatience; compare 'Will it not
be?' (Dent, *P.L.E.D.*, B112.2).

127. *martyrdom*] intense suffering, more than a simple *malady*, and with
further suggestion (hidden from Mileta) of heroic self-sacrifice in the religion
of love.

137. *sleep . . . him*] Compare the word-play at ll. 5–6 and nn.; here, as there,
the emotional and amorous meaning is apparent to the audience but is hidden
from Mileta by the irony of double entendre. Sappho wishes Mileta to hear
only a rebuke for supposing that a medical attendant could be any possible use
without his medicines.

will be angry. Sick folks are testy, who, though they eat
nothing, yet they feed on gall.   145

[*Exit* MILETA: ISMENA *retires.*]

The Song

Sappho. O cruel Love! On thee I lay
          My curse, which shall strike blind the day:
          Never may sleep with velvet hand
          Charm thine eyes with sacred wand;
          Thy gaolers shall be hopes and fears,   150
          Thy prison-mates, groans, sighs and tears;
          Thy play to wear out weary times,
          Fantastic passions, vows and rhymes;
          Thy bread be frowns, thy drink be gall,
          Such as when you Phao call   155
          The bed thou liest on by despair;
          Thy sleep, fond dreams; thy dreams, long care;
          Hope, like thy fool, at thy bed's head
          Mock thee till madness strike thee dead,

145.1.] *Bond (subst.); not in Q1.*   146–61. *Sappho. O cruel . . . dies.*] *Blount;
not in Q1.*   159. Mock] *Bond (Mocke); Mockes Blount.*

---

145. *gall*] bile, the secretion of the liver, associated in humours theory with
asperity; or of the gall-bladder, hence bitter and rancorous.

145.1 ISMENA *retires*] Ismena should not be understood to hear Sappho's
song, since it is a private confession of love. Yet she indicates her intention of
remaining while Mileta goes after Phao, and Ismena is in attendance when
Sappho is again discovered in bed in the next scene (III.iv.37.1–2).

145.2 *The Song*] The boy playing Sappho accompanies himself on the lute.
The song is printed in Blount's *Six Court Comedies* (1632), as here, in
continuous, non-strophic verse. But it falls easily into four quatrains, the final
quatrain expressing its finality by a change of metre. See Appendix on 'The
Songs'.

147. *strike . . . day*] i.e., cast all into darkness.

152. *Thy play*] your pastime (shall be).

155–6. *Such . . . despair*] as when you despairingly call your bed 'Phao'.
Sappho wishes that Love, like herself, may bitterly suffer the sleepless
torments of one unhappily in love. Bond (II.561) compares *Tottel's Miscellany*
(ed. Edward Arber, Westminster, 1897, p. 236): 'And tells her pillow all the
tale / How thou hast done her woe and bale.'

157. *fond*] foolish, idle.

158. *like thy fool*] Love is personified as a great lady with a fool in her
retinue.

As, Phao, thou dost me with thy proud eyes;   160
In thee poor Sappho lives, for thee she dies.
                      [The bed-curtains close.]

        Actus Tertius, Scaena Quarta.

      [Enter] MILETA *[and]* PHAO.

Mileta. I would either your cunning, Phao, or your fortune
    might by simples provoke my lady to some slumber.
Phao. My simples are in operation as my simplicity is, which,
    if they do little good, assuredly they can do no harm.
Mileta. Were I sick, the very sight of thy fair face would drive   5
    me into a sound sleep.
Phao. Indeed, gentlewomen are so drowsy in their desires that
    they can scarce hold up their eyes for love.
Mileta. I mean, the delight of beauty would so bind my senses
    as I should be quickly rocked into a deep rest.   10
Phao. You women have an excuse for an advantage, which

161.1.] *Bond (subst.); not in Q1.* 0. Tertius] *Q2;* terius *Q1.* Quarta]
Fairholt; prima *Q1.* 0.1.] *Bond; Mileta, Phao, Ismena, Sapho, Venus / Q1.*
9. bind] *Q1* (binde); blinde *Q2.*

---

160. *As*] Just as.

   0.1.] The scene appears to be continuous, although the staging situation is
not like others (e.g., I.iii, II.ii, II.iii, III.ii) in which characters remain onstage
at the start of a new scene; Mileta must exit at III.iii.145.1 and return now at
III.iv.0.1 with Phao, as she was bid, to the vicinity of Sappho's curtained bed.
It is the bed that creates the sense of a continuous scene; Ismena, though
presumably not visible, is understood to be still in attendance. See l. 37.1–2.

   1–3. *cunning, simples, simplicity*] The antithetical word-play is continued
from l. 25 in the previous scene, to which Mileta now adds the commonplace
antithesis of *cunning* and *fortune*, skill and luck.

   8. *scarce . . . eyes*] Phao alludes to women's langourous glances and flirtatious
lowering of their eyelids as tokens of desire, but he also interprets Mileta's
speech in a self-effacing way as meaning that his looks would simply put
gentlewomen to sleep.

   9. *bind*] Q2's emendation ('blinde') of Q1's 'binde' is possible, since beauty
is perceived by the eyes. If so, it represents the commonsense correction of an
easy misprint. However, 'binde' can also be defended as meaning to bind up or
fetter the senses, as with babies in swaddling bands, rocked asleep (l. 10), and
it is the reading of the authoritative quarto.

   11–13.] i.e., You women must be allowed to take the advantage in debate or
repartee, though the excuse (of presumed feminine weakness) is thereby

must be allowed because only to you women it was
allotted.

Mileta. Phao, thou art passing fair, and able to draw a chaste
eye not only to glance but to gaze on thee. Thy young   15
years, thy quick wit, thy staid desires are of force to
control those which should command.

Phao. Lady, I forgot to commend you first, and, lest I should
have overslipped to praise you at all, you have brought
in my beauty, which is simple, that in courtesy I might   20
remember yours, which is singular.

Mileta. You mistake of purpose, or misconster of malice.

Phao. I am as far from malice as you from love, and to mistake
of purpose were to mislike of peevishness.

Mileta. As far as I from love? Why, think you me so dull I   25

---

turned to your benefit. *It*, in l. 12, refers perhaps to both the excuse and the
advantage: women are paradoxically given both frailty and the ability to turn
that frailty to their own use.

14. *passing*] surpassingly.

16. *staid*] steadfast, lacking in caprice.

16–17. *of force . . . command*] strong enough to enforce the affections of
those persons who should command affection in you. The observation applies
to Sappho, but at present it points to the inversion of sexual roles in which
Mileta, as a woman who should normally command the affection of her servant
in love, has so yielded to desire as to take the initiative in commending his
beauty.

17. *control*] overmaster.

18–21.] Phao acknowledges that courtesy should have required him to
speak first in commendation of the lady.

20. *simple*] plain, unadorned. (Recalling the word-play on *simples* and
simplicity in ll. 2–3.)

21. *singular*] unique, without peer. The word-play on *singular* and *simple*
(ll. 20–1) relies on a common meaning: sole, mere, pure, single.

22.] Mileta suggests that she is either deliberately misunderstood or, worse
still, accused of having praised Phao only to fish for a compliment. The
spelling of *misconster* [misconstrue] is kept for the sake of *similiter cadens* and
assonance.

23–4. *to mistake . . . peevishness*] to misunderstand on purpose would be to
take offence foolishly and peevishly. As Bond (II.561) observes, *peevishness*
seemingly means 'folly' and the like, but may here employ something of its
modern sense. Compare I.i.48 and I.iv.37 above; also *Endymion*, I.i.19 and
Midas, V.iii.72. Or Phao may equate 'mistake of purpose' with his own
supposed insensitivity and 'mislike of peevishness' with Mileta's response; in
the equivalent construction, to mistake on purpose would be as bad as to
mislike out of spitefulness and perversity.

25. *As . . . love*] Phao meant only that he was far from presuming Mileta to

cannot love, or so spiteful I will not?

Phao. Neither, lady. But how should men imagine women can
love, when in their mouths there is nothing rifer than
'in faith, I do not love'?

Mileta. Why, will you have women's love in their tongues?   30

Phao. Yea, else do I think there is none in their hearts.

Mileta. Why?

Phao. Because there was never anything in the bottom of a
woman's heart that cometh not to her tongue's end.

Mileta. You are too young to cheapen love.   35

Phao. Yet old enough to talk with market folks.

Mileta. Well, let us in.

[*The bed-curtains are drawn back and* SAPPHO *is discovered in bed,
with* ISMENA *in attendance. Phao and Mileta approach.*]

Ismena. [*To Sappho*] Phao is come.

Sappho. Who? Phao? Phao—let him come near. But who sent
for him?   40

Mileta. You, madam.

Sappho. I am loath to take any medicines, yet must I rather
than pine in these maladies. Phao, you may make me
sleep, if you will.

[*Exeunt* MILETA *and* ISMENA.]

Phao. If I can I must, if you will.   45

---

28. than] *Q1* (then).   36. *Phao*] *Q3*; *Sapho* / *Q1*.   37.1–2.] *This ed.; not in
Q1; The curtains are drawn back* / Bond; *They come to Sapho and Ismene* / Daniel.
38. *To Sappho*] *This ed.; not in Q1*.   44.1.] Bond; *not in Q1*.

---

be in love with him, but she interprets his phrase to mean she is incapable of all
love.

28. *rifer*] more frequently employed.

33–4.] 'To have (it) at one's tongue's end' is a conventional metaphor
(Dent, *P.L.E.D.*, T413). See also Dent, *P.L.E.D.*, S196, 'Trust no secret
with a woman', and compare Hotspur to his wife Kate in *1 Henry IV*,
II.iii.107–10.

35–6.] Phao's misogynistic remarks about women, says Mileta, *cheapen* love
in the sense of 'chaffer, haggle', and with perhaps a hint of 'lower in
estimation'—a meaning not attested to in the *O.E.D.* until 1654. Phao, in
reply, insists on the commercial sense of 'bargain, offer a price for'.

37. *let us in*] let us go in.

44.1. Exeunt *MILETA* and *ISMENA*] Perhaps they retire within the
structure representing Sappho's bedchamber, where they are 'discovered' at
IV.iii.0.1 in attendance on Sappho.

Sappho. What herbs have you brought, Phao?

Phao. Such as will make you sleep, madam, though they
    cannot make me slumber.

Sappho. Why, how can you cure me when you cannot remedy
    yourself?   50

Phao. Yes, madam, the causes are contrary. For it is only a
    dryness in your brains that keepeth you from rest.
    But—

Sappho. But what?

Phao. Nothing, but mine is not so.   55

Sappho. Nay, then I despair of help if our disease be not all
    one.

Phao. I would our diseases were all one.

Sappho. It goes hard with the patient when the physician is
    desperate.   60

Phao. Yet Medea made the everwaking dragon to snort when

---

51. *causes*] cases.

52. *a dryness . . . brains*] a feverishness, associated (as Bond notes, II.561–2),
with sleeplessness in Robert Burton's *Anatomy of Melancholy*, Part I, Sect. 2,
Memb. 2. Subsec. 7: 'But, as I have said, waking overmuch is both a symptom
and an ordinary cause [of melancholy]. It causeth dryness of the brain, frenzy,
dotage . . . as Lemnius hath it.' Sappho seems to make an opposite diagnosis of
her condition at III.iii.21, when she asks for something to 'dry my brain',
but even the presumed experts disagreed on such matters.

54. *But what*] Sappho's interrupting betokens her eagerness to hear what
causes Phao's sleeplessness.

55. *mine is not so*] Phao cannot presume other than that Sappho's symptoms
are merely physical, his emotional.

56–7.] (1) if you cannot cure the disease you yourself have (which you are in
best position to understand), how can I expect you to cure mine? (Compare
ll. 49–50); (2) my case is desperate if you are not in love also. (The second of
these meanings is apparent to the audience but hidden from Phao.)

all one] (1) one and the same; (2) all together (*O.E.D.*, *all*, adv., 5a and b).

59. *goes hard*] On the possibility of erotic suggestion, see III.ii.62 and
III.iii.25–6 and nn.

60. *desperate*] i.e., with no hope of accomplishing a cure. (But with a
meaning that also applies to Phao, of which Sappho can hardly be conscious:
'desperately in love'.) Compare Publilius Syrus, '*Crudelem medicum intemperans
aeger facit*', 'The intemperate patient makes the physician cruel' (*Sententiae*,
no. 104, pp. 28–9).

61. *Medea . . . dragon*] With a sweet magical song Medea charmed to sleep
the fearsome serpent guarding the golden fleece. (*Fabularum Liber*, Basel,
1535, compiled by Jacobus Micyllus and attributed, almost certainly erro-
neously, to C. Julius Hyginus; ed. Stephen Orgel, 1976, xxi–xxvii.) In Ovid,

she, poor soul, could not wink.

Sappho. Medea was in love, and nothing could cause her rest
　　but Jason.

Phao. Indeed, I know no herb to make lovers sleep but hearts- 　65
　　ease, which, because it groweth so high, I cannot reach,
　　for—

Sappho. For whom?

Phao. For such as love.

Sappho. It groweth very low, and I can never stoop to it, that— 　70

Phao. That what?

Sappho. That I may gather it. But why do you sigh so, Phao?

Phao. It is mine use, madam.

Sappho. It will do you harm, and me too, for I never hear one
　　sigh but I must sigh also. 　　　　　　　　　　　　　　　75

Phao. It were best then that your ladyship give me leave to be
　　gone, for I can but sigh.

Sappho. Nay, stay; for, now I begin to sigh, I shall not leave
　　though you be gone. But what do you think best for
　　your sighing to take it away? 　　　　　　　　　　　　80

Phao. Yew, madam.

Sappho. Me?

Metamorphoses, VII.196, Medea uses magical herbs. Perhaps the implication is
that Phao offers to sing.

　　snort] snore, as in *Euphues*, II.213, 11–12: 'while they themselves either
dally in sin or snort in sleep'.

　　62. *wink*] close the eyes. Phao suggests that Medea was too busy and
endangered to sleep, but Sappho in the next speech attributes the sleeplessness
to love melancholy (such as she knows herself to suffer).

　　65–6. *heartsease*] (1) in the sixteenth century, applied to both the pansy and
the wallflower (*O.E.D.*); (2) peace of mind.

　　66. *it groweth so high*] The wallflower, growing wild on walls, on rocks and in
quarries, might be high to reach and thus symbolic of the aspiration Phao must
conquer in himself.

　　70. *It groweth very low*] The pansy grows low to the ground and hence may
symbolise the stooping that Sappho must avoid.

　　73. *mine use*] my custom.

　　74. *harm*] Sappho refers to the theory of sighs stealing blood from the heart,
as in *Hamlet*, IV.vii.121, *A Midsummer Night's Dream*, III.ii.97, etc.

　　76–8. *leave ... leave*] permission ... leave off, cease. The antithesis is
intensified by the repetition of 'to be gone', 'though you be gone'.

　　81. *Yew*] Lyly's spelling is perhaps his way of indicating for the reader a
double entendre that in the theatre would probably seem more witty and less
forced than on the printed page. Webster uses the pun in Vittoria's dream in
The White Devil, I.ii.230ff. (Revels edn.).

Phao. No, madam, yew of the tree.

Sappho. Then will I love yew the better. And indeed I think it
   would make me sleep too; therefore, all other simples   85
   set aside, I will simply use only yew.

Phao. Do, madam, for I think nothing in the world so good
   as yew.

Sappho. Farewell for this time.

   [*Phao moves away from her bed, and its curtains close.*
   Enter] VENUS [*and* CUPID].

Venus. Is not your name Phao?   90

Phao. Phao, fair Venus, whom you made so fair.

Venus. So passing fair, O fair Phao, O sweet Phao! What wilt
   thou do for Venus?

Phao. Anything that cometh in the compass of my poor
   fortune.   95

Venus. Cupid shall teach thee to shoot, and I will instruct thee
   to dissemble.

Phao. I will learn anything but dissembling.

Venus. Why, my boy?

Phao. Because then I must learn to be a woman.   100

Venus. Thou heardest that of a man.

Phao. Men speak truth.

Venus. But truth is a she, and so always painted.

Phao. I think, a painted truth.

Venus. Well, farewell for this time, for I must visit Sappho.   105

                                              PHAO *exit.*

88.1–2.] *This ed.; not in Q1; He comes from the recess, the curtains close behind*
him, Enter Venus and Cupid / Bond; Exit Sapho. Enter Venus and Cupid / Daniel.

84–5. *it . . . sleep*] i.e., you ('yew') would make me sleep; with reference to
the yew tree, often planted in churchyards and associated with melancholy.
Compare *The White Devil*, IV.iii.120–1 (Revels edn.). Its berries were
considered poisonous and its shadow dangerous.

86, 88. *yew . . . yew*] The seeming obviousness of the word-play is eased by
the double dramatic irony: each speaker is conscious of a hidden meaning and
yet apparently oblivious of the other speaker's private awareness.

92.] It is evidently here that Venus falls in love with Phao (see IV.ii.1–2),
and perhaps some stage action here should show Cupid taking aim at his
mother or giving powerful effect to Phao's eyes.

103. *truth is a she*] Veritas is one of the four daughters of God in medieval
iconography.

103–4. *painted . . . painted*] depicted . . . feigned.

105. *farewell . . . time*] Venus' words are the same as those used by Sappho,
l. 89.

Act IV

Actus Quartus, Scaena Prima.

VENUS [and] CUPID [remain. The bed-curtains are drawn back,
discovering] SAPPHO.

Venus. Sappho, I have heard thy complaints and pitied thine
agonies.

Sappho. O Venus, my cares are only known to thee, and by
thee only came the cause. Cupid, why didst thou wound
me so deep?   5

Cupid. My mother bade me draw mine arrow to the head.

Sappho. Venus, why didst thou prove so hateful?

Venus. Cupid took a wrong shaft.

Sappho. O Cupid too unkind, to make me so kind that almost I
transgress the modesty of my kind!   10

Cupid. I was blind and could not see mine arrow.

Sappho. How came it to pass thou didst hit my heart?

Cupid. That came by the nature of the head, which, being once
let out of the bow, can find none other lighting place but
the heart.   15

Venus. Be not dismayed. Phao shall yield.

Sappho. If he yield, then shall I shame to embrace one so

0.1–2.] *This ed.; Venus, Sapho, Cupid / Q1; The curtains are drawn back. Venus,
Sapho, Cupid / Bond; Enter Sapho to Venus and Cupid / Daniel.*

0.1–2.] The scene is evidently continuous, since the stage direction 'Phao
exit' leaves Cupid and Venus onstage. Compare the transition from Act IV to
Act V. The lack of opportunity for a pause in these two instances challenges, at
least for the mid 1580s, the theory that boys' plays had musical interludes
between the acts.

1. *thy complaints*] i.e., those Sappho uttered in III.iii.89ff., invoking Venus'
aid.

3. *only known*] known only.

6. *to the head*] See I.i.54 and n.

9. *unkind*] (1) cruel; (2) unnatural.

9–10. *kind ... kind*] loving, fond ... gender and natural disposition.

14. *lighting*] alighting.

mean; if not, die because I cannot embrace one so mean.
Thus do I find no mean.

Venus. Well, I will work for thee. Farewell.   20
Sappho. Farewell, sweet Venus, and thou, Cupid, which art
sweetest in thy sharpness.

        Exit SAPPHO [*i.e., the bed-curtains close*].

Actus Quartus, Scaena Secunda.

VENUS [*and*] CUPID [*remain*].

Venus. Cupid, what hast thou done? Put thine arrows in
Phao's eyes, and wounded thy mother's heart?
Cupid. You gave him a face to allure; then why should not I
give him eyes to pierce?
Venus. O Venus, unhappy Venus, who in bestowing a benefit   5
upon a man hast brought a bane unto a goddess! What
perplexities dost thou feel? O fair Phao, and therefore
made fair to breed in me a frenzy! O would that, when I
gave thee golden locks to curl thy head, I had shackled
thee with iron locks on thy feet! And when I nursed   10
thee, Sappho, with lettuce, would it had turned to

22.1. *i.e., the bed-curtains close*] *This ed.; not in Q1.*   0.1.] *Daniel; Venus,
Cupid* / *Q1.*

18–19. *mean . . . mean . . . mean*] of low station . . . unkind in love . . .
moderation.
    22. *sharpness*] (1) with sharp-pointed arrows; (2) bitterness.
    1–2. *Put . . . heart*] Cupid has not struck Phao's eyes with his arrows, but
made arrows of Phao's eyes.
    7–8. *O fair Phao . . . frenzy*] For the rhetorical form, see II.iv.16–17 and n.
above.
    9–10. *locks . . . locks*] tresses . . . bolts and keys.
    11. *with lettuce*] Aelian, *Varia Historia*, XII.18, reports that Phaon, 'of a fair
complexion', was 'hidden of Venus among long lettuce which sprung up and
grew very rankly' (trans. Abraham Fleming, 1576; the old spelling of the word
is 'lettisse'). Pliny (XIX.38) mentions one kind of lettuce that is called in Greek
the anti-aphrodisiac (*astutida*) or eunuch's lettuce (*eunoucheion*). John Gerard's
Herbal presents a more nourishing view of lettuce: 'being taken before meat it
doth many times stir up appetite' (1633 edn., p. 308). Erasmus's note to his
Adagia, 'Similes habent labra lactucas', 'like lips, like lettuce', i.e., like has met
its like (II.386D), works on the notion of lettuce as smooth and thistle (*carduus*)
as rough, making much the same distinction that Venus makes in contrasting
the 'smooth skin' of Phao's face with the 'rough scar in my heart' (l. 13).

hemlock! Have I brought a smooth skin over thy face to
make a rough scar in my heart, and given thee a fresh
colour like the damask rose to make mine pale like the
stained turquoise? O Cupid, thy flames with Psyche   15
were but sparks, and my desires with Adonis but
dreams, in respect of these unacquainted torments.
Laugh, Juno, Venus is in love! But Juno shall not see
with whom, lest she be in love. Venus, belike, is become
stale; Sappho, forsooth, because she hath many virtues,   20
therefore she must have all the favours. Venus waxeth
old; and then she was a pretty wench, when Juno was a
young wife; now crow's foot is on her eye, and the black
ox hath trod on her foot. But were Sappho never so vir-

---

15. turquoise] *This ed.; * Turkie *Q1;* Turkis *Blount;* turquie *Daniel.*   Psyche]
Daniel; Psyches / Q1.

12. *hemlock*] a poison.
thy] i.e., Phao's.
14. *damask rose*] a rose supposed originally to have been brought from
Damascus. It is a type of perishable beauty in *Euphues,* 1.234, 16, in *Love's
Metamorphoses,* IV.i.100–1 and in Shakespeare's *Twelfth Night,* II.iv.112.
15. *turquoise*] a gem of a sky-blue to apple-green colour, here *stained* or
deprived of colour and lustre (*O.E.D., stain,* vb., 1) and hence pale. Fairholt
(1.295) notes that the turquoise was thought to have the power of foretelling
danger to any wearer by changing to a paler tint, and quotes Swan's *Speculum
Mundi*: 'The sympathising turquoise true doth tell, / By turning pale, its owner
is not well.' David Hoeniger has pointed out to me that the Q1 spelling,
'Turkie', may be a misprint for 'turkies' or 'turkis', variant spellings of
turquoise. Compare *Campaspe,* I.i.14.
Psyche] The love of Cupid for Psyche (Greek for breath, life, soul) is told in
Apuleius' *Golden Ass* (second century A.D.), Book IV. Q1's 'Psyches', though
read by Fairholt as meaning 'Psyche's', is simply an older spelling of the
proper name. Compare 'Ganymedes' for 'Ganymede' at IV.iv.31 below.
16. *Adonis*] Venus' love for this fair youth, in which the goddess of love
herself was infatuated by mortal beauty, parallels her present love for Phao.
The story, as told by Ovid, *Metamorphoses,* X.519ff., can be regarded as one of
Lyly's sources.
17. *unacquainted*] unfamiliar, strange.
18. *Laugh, Juno*] Venus' rivalry with the jealous queen of the gods is
described in the *Iliad* and elsewhere.
19. *lest . . . love*] i.e., lest Juno also fall in love with Phao.
20. *stale* (with a suggestion of 'whore').
23–4. *crow's foot . . . her foot*] These conventional signs of age (Dent,
P.L.E.D., C865 and O103) are paired also in *Euphues,* 1.203, 6–7 and in
Love's Metamorphosis, IV.1.135–7. The black ox's tread is a token of being

tuous, doth she think to contend with Venus to be as 25
amorous? Yield, Phao, but yield to me, Phao. I entreat
where I may command; command thou, where thou
shouldst entreat. In this case, Cupid, what is thy counsel? Venus must both play the lover and the dissembler,
and therefore the dissembler because the lover. 30

Cupid. You will ever be playing with arrows, like children
with knives, and then when you bleed you cry. Go to
Vulcan. Entreat by prayers, threaten with blows, woo
with kisses, ban with curses—try all means to rid these
extremities. 35

Venus. To what end?

Cupid. That he might make me new arrows, for nothing can
root out the desires of Phao but a new shaft of incon-
stancy, nor anything turn Sappho's heart but a new
arrow of disdain. And then, they disliking one the 40
other, who shall enjoy Phao but Venus?

Venus. I will follow thy counsel; for Venus, though she be in
her latter age for years, yet is she in her nonage for
affections. When Venus ceaseth to love, let Jove cease
to rule. But come, let us to Vulcan.   *Exeunt.* 45

---

32. cry. Go] *Q3* (cry: go); cry, go *Q1*.

---

worn 'either with age or care' (Robert Nares, *A Glossary*, 1822, new edns. in
1882 and 1905). Bond (i.336–7) cites Martin Marprelate's *An Epitome* (rpt.
London, 1843), p. 10: 'The black ox hath trodden on his foot; he hath had
some trial by woeful experience.' John Heywood includes this saying in his
Proverbs, p. 17.
     26–7. *I entreat ... command*] Compare *Campaspe*, II.2.117, where
Alexander, in a parallel soliloquy, declares: 'I am a king and will command.'
Bond (ii.562) compares *Richard III*, IV.iv.345: 'Say that the king, which may
command, entreats', and *Twelfth Night*, II.v.104: 'I may command where I
adore.' Compare also *Love's Labour's Lost*, IV.i.80: 'Shall I command thy love?
I may.'
     29. *play ... dissembler*] Compare III.iv.96ff. above.
     34. *ban*] curse.
     43. *latter age for years*] advanced age in respect of years.
     43–4. *nonage for affections*] youth in respect of lustful passion.

Actus Quartus, Scaena Tertia.

SAPPHO [*is discovered in bed as the bed-curtains*
are drawn back, attended by] MILETA, ISMENA,
EUGENUA, LAMIA, FAVILLA [*and*] CANOPE.

Sappho. What dreams are these, Mileta? And can there
be no truth in dreams? Yea, dreams have their truth.
Methought I saw a stock-dove or wood-quest—I know
not how to term it—that brought short straws to build
his nest in a tall cedar, where, whilst with his bill he was   5
framing his building, he lost as many feathers from
his wings as he laid straws in his nest; yet, scambling
to catch hold to harbour in the house he had made, he
suddenly fell from the bough where he stood. And then,
pitifully casting up his eyes, he cried in such terms (as I   10
imagined) as might either condemn the nature of such
a tree or the daring of such a mind. Whilst he lay quak-
ing upon the ground, and I gazing on the cedar, I might
perceive ants to breed in the rind, coveting only to
hoard, and caterpillars to cleave to the leaves, labouring   15
only to suck, which caused more leaves to fall from
the tree than there did feathers before from the dove.
Methought, Mileta, I sighed in my sleep, pitying both
the fortune of the bird and the misfortune of the tree;
but in this time quills began to bud again in the bird,   20
which made him look as though he would fly up,

---

o.1–3.] *This ed.; Sapho, Mileta, Ismena, Lamya, Fauilla, Canope / Q1; The
curtains are again drawn back. Sapho, Mileta, Ismena, Eugunua, Lamya,
Fauilla, Canope / Bond; Enter Sapho, Mileta, Ismena, Eugenua, Canope,
Lamya, and Favilla / Daniel.* 16. more] *Q1* (mo).

---

3. *stock-dove or wood-quest*] sometimes differentiated as the wild pigeon,
Columba aeneas, and the ring dove, *Columba palumbus*, though both might be
regarded as species of the wood-pigeon (*O.E.D.*). On allegorical interpretations of Sappho's dream, see Introduction, pp. 164–71.
    4. *short straws*] i.e., inadequate talent, or lack of provident foresight. Long
straws are best for nest building. Perhaps connected with the ancient lottery
method of drawing short or long straws; *O.E.D., cut*, sb., 1.
    7. *scambling*] scrambling, as also at III.ii.4.
    19. *fortune*] chance, hap; not 'good fortune', despite the antithesis of *fortune*
and *misfortune*.
    20. *quills*] feathers, as in *Gallathea*, I.i.31 and in *Endymion*, V.ii.22–3.

and then wished I that the body of the tree would
bow that he might but creep up the tree; then—and
so—Heigh-ho!

Mileta. And so what?   25

Sappho. Nothing, Mileta, but—and so I waked. But did
nobody dream but I?

Mileta. I dreamed last night—but I hope dreams are contrary
—that, holding my head over a sweet smoke, all my
hair blazed on a bright flame. Methought Ismena cast   30
water to quench it; yet the sparks fell on my bosom,
and, wiping them away with my hand, I was all in a gore
blood, till one with a few fresh flowers stanched it. And
so, stretching myself as stiff, I started; it was but a
dream.   35

Ismena. It is a sign you shall fall in love with hearing fair
words. Water signifieth counsel, flowers death. And
nothing can purge your loving humour but death.

Mileta. You are no interpreter, but an interprater, harping
always upon love till you be as blind as a harper.   40

Ismena. I remember, last night but one, I dreamed mine eye-
tooth was loose and that I thrust it out with my tongue.

Mileta. It foretelleth the loss of a friend; and I ever thought
thee so full of prattle that thou wouldst thrust out thy
best friend with thy tattling.   45

Ismena. Yea, Mileta, but it was loose before, and, if my friend

---

44–5. thy best] *This ed.;* the best *Q1.*

26. *and so I waked*] See the Prologue at the Court, l. 18n.

28. *dreams are contrary*] Compare the proverb, 'Dreams go by contraries'
(Dent, *P.L.E.D.*, D588).

32–3. *in a gore blood*] Compare *Romeo and Juliet*, III.i.56: 'all in gore
blood'.

39. *interprater*] a nonce-word invented by Lyly (this is the only example in
the *O.E.D.*) for the sake of the jingle, i.e., one who prates.

40. *as blind as a harper*] a proverbial comparison (Dent, *P.L.E.D.*, H175).

44–5. *thy best . . . tattling*] Q2's 'the best friend with the tatling' is perhaps a
flawed attempt to correct Q1's 'the best friend with thy tatling' in which the
printer mistakenly changed 'thy' instead of 'the'. Both Q1 and Q2's mistakes
are easy printing errors.

46–7. *loose . . . loose*] insecurely attached . . . sexually unrestrained. The
word-play lends sexual suggestion to *thrust, kept in*, etc., especially in the
context of a dream.

be loose, as good thrust out with plain words as kept in
with dissembling.

Eugenua. Dreams are but dotings, which come either by
things we see in the day or meats that we eat, and so the   50
common sense preferring it to be the imaginative.

Ismena. Soft philosophatrix, well seen in the secrets of art and
not seduced with the superstitions of nature!

Sappho. Ismena's tongue never lieth still; I think all her
teeth will be loose, they are so often jogged against   55
her tongue. But say on, Eugenua.

Eugenua. There is all.

Sappho. What did you dream, Canope?

Canope. I seldom dream, madam; but sithence your sickness —
I cannot tell whether with overwatching — but I have   60
had many fantastical visions. For, even now slumbering
by your bed's side, methought I was shadowed with a
cloud where, labouring to unwrap myself, I was more
entangled. But in the midst of my striving it seemed
to mizzle gold, with fair drops; I filled my lap, and,   65

---

60. overwatching] *Q2* (ouerwatching); ourwatching *Q1*.   65. mizzle] *Q1*
(mysell).

49–50. *Dreams . . . day*] Compare '*Quod vigilans voluit, somnavit dormiens*',
and Kyd, *Cornelia*, III.i.66: 'We dream by night what we by day have
thought.' Compare also the proverbial saying, 'Dreams are lies', of which the
present quotation is Dent's earliest citation (*P.L.E.D.*, D587). Lyly's speakers
variously present the whole range of Elizabethan attitudes towards dreams, as
true prognostications, as directly contrary to truth (l. 28), and as responses
induced by physiological processes. The topic had long been a favourite one;
compare Chaucer's *Hous of Fame*, 'The Nun's Priest's Tale', etc.

50. *meats*] food.

50–1. *the common sense . . . imaginative*] the common view is that dreams are
produced by the imaginative faculty.

52. *philosophatrix*] not in the *O.E.D.*; presumably in the sense of a female
philosopher.

well seen] well versed. (Said mockingly.)

57. *There is all*] That is all I have to say. (Eugenua wants no more of
Ismena's mocking.)

59. *sitthence*] ever since.

60. *overwatching*] keeping watch through the night. Q1's 'ourwatching' is
probably a misprint, corrected in Q2's 'ouerwatching', though it has been
variously interpreted as 'our watching' and as a spelling variant of 'o'erwatching'.

65. *mizzle*] rain in very fine drops, drizzle. *O.E.D.* quotes Spenser's
Shepherdes Calendar, November, l. 208: 'Now gynnes to mizzle, hye we

running to show it my fellows, it turned to dust. I
blushed, they laughed, and then I waked, being glad it
was but a dream.

Ismena. Take heed, Canope, that gold tempt not your lap, and
    then you blush for shame.   70

Canope. It is good luck to dream of gold.

Ismena. Yea, if it had continued gold.

Lamia. I dream every night, and the last night this: Methought
    that, walking in the sun, I was stung with the fly taran-
    tula, whose venom nothing can expel but the sweet con-   75
    cent of music. I tried all kind of instruments, but found
    no ease till at the last two lutes tuned in one key so glut-

---

[75–6. concent] *Q1.* (consent).

---

homeward fast.' As Bond (II.563) observes, the dream is reminiscent of Zeus'
descent to Danaë in a shower of gold; compare *Euphues*, 1.236, 12–13,
Gallathea, II.iii.90–1, *Midas*, II.i.14–15; and *Woman in the Moon*, II.i.13.
The dreams of Sappho's women express a range of feminine experiences in
love: blaze of passion, loss, seduction, bribery, marriage. (Q1's 'myself' is a
variant spelling.)

    71.] Compare *Romeo and Juliet*, I.iv.73: 'o'er lawyers' fingers, who straight
dream on fees', but contrast *The Merchant of Venice*, II.v.18–19, 'There is
some ill a-brewing towards my rest, / For I did dream of moneybags tonight',
and *Timon*, III.i.6: 'I dreamt of a silver basin and ewer tonight.'

    72.] i.e., yes, if you awakened and discovered the gold still there, rather
than having turned to dust as in your dream. (Ismena interprets the turning of
gold to dust as the shame resulting when a lady is seduced by means of gold
poured in her lap.)

    74–6. *the fly . . . music*] not among the remedies in Pliny, XXIX.27, but Bond
(II.563) cites Sir Thomas Hoby's translation of *The Courtier*, 1561 (ed. W. E.
Henley, The Tudor Translations, London, 1900, p. 36): 'in Pulia of them that
are bitten with a tarantula, about whom men occupy many instruments of
music', and Lodge's *Rosalynde*, ed. Israel Gollancz (London, 1907), p. 152.
The belief is of folk origin, but is attested to by many reputable Renaissance
physicians, including Ambroise Paré, *Works*, trans. Thomas Johnson (London,
1649), chap. xxxiii, 'Of Certain Wonderful and Extravagant ways of
Curing Diseases', p. 37, and Bk. XXI, 'Of Poisons and of . . . the Bitings and
Stings of Other Venomous Creatures', pp. 504–34; the harmony of music
could supposedly counteract madness as well as the poison of a spider's bite.
The tarantula is in fact a wood spider, not a flying creature, and its bite,
though toxic, is not extremely so.

    75–6. *concent*] harmony (*O.E.D.*); from Latin *concentus*; sometimes con-
fused with *consent*, and so spelled in Q1–2). This instance predates *O.E.D.*'s
earliest citation, 1585. Compare *Campaspe*, III.iv.109.

    77, 83. *two lutes . . . key*] An emblem of love using this image appears in
Jacob Cats, *Proteus*, 43.1. It is reprinted in Arthur Henkel and Albrecht

ted my thirsting ears that my grief presently ceased, for
joy whereof, as I was clapping my hands, your ladyship
called.   80

Mileta. It is a sign that nothing shall assuage your love but
marriage, for such is the tying of two in wedlock as is
the tuning of two lutes in one key; for, striking the
strings of the one, straws will stir upon the strings of
the other, and, in two minds linked in love, one cannot   85
be delighted but the other rejoiceth.

Favilla. Methought going by the seaside among pebbles I saw
one playing with a round stone, ever throwing it into
the water when the sun shined. I asked the name. He
said it was called abeston, which, being once hot, would   90
never be cold. He gave it me, and vanished. I, forgetting myself, delighted with the fair show, would
always show it by candlelight, pull it out in the sun,
and see how bright it would look in the fire where,
catching heat, nothing could cool it. For anger I threw   95
it against the wall, and, with the heaving up of mine
arm, I waked.

Mileta. Beware of love, Favilla, for women's hearts are such
stones, which, warmed by affection, cannot be cooled
by wisdom.   100

Favilla. I warrant you, for I never credit men's words.

Ismena. Yet be wary, for women are scorched sometimes

Schöne, eds., *Emblemata* (Stuttgart, 1967), column 1300, under the title '*zwei
Lauten deren Saiten gleichgestimmt sind*', '*Quid non sentit Amor*', and moralised
as '*Harmonie der Liebenden*'.

83–5. *striking . . . the other*] Mileta describes the phenomenon of sympathetic vibration.

90. *abeston*] an obsolete form of Greek 'asbestos', referred to in *Euphues*,
I.191, 32, and in *Mother Bombie*, I.iii.125, where its reputed property of being
once hot never to turn cold is a token of woman's constancy. Compare also
Rabelais, *Le Tiers Livre*, chap. lii, ed. M. A. Screech (Geneva, 1964, p. 350).
The abeston is here thrown into the water when the sun shines (l. 89) lest it
ignite and consume itself; Favilla's more reckless behaviour of playing with its
fire (her name means 'fiery ash') seems to Mileta a sign of consuming passion
rather than of constancy. Bond (II.563) suggests that Lyly's authority is
Bartholomew [Berthelet], XVI.xii, fol. ccxxvi^v), 'If it be once kindled it never
quencheth', rather than Pliny. Bond also cites (III.539) Solinus, *Polyhistor*
(Biponti, 1794), Cap. vii: '*Asbestos nomen est . . . qui accensus semel exstingui
nequitur*', 'Asbestos is so named because once it is lit it never goes out.'

101.] Favilla protests that she is proof against men's seductive talk.

with men's eyes, though they had rather consume than
confess.

Sappho. Cease your talking, for I would fain sleep to see if I   105
can dream whether the bird hath feathers or the ants
wings. Draw the curtain.

[*The bed-curtains close around Sappho. Her* Ladies *exeunt.*]

Actus Quartus, Scaena Quarta.

[*Enter*] VENUS [*and*] CUPID.

Venus. Come, Cupid, Vulcan's flames must quench Venus'
fires. Vulcan?

VULCAN [*appears at the mouth of his forge*].

Vulcan. Who?

Venus. Venus.

Vulcan. Ho, ho! Venus.   5

Venus. Come, sweet Vulcan, thou knowest how sweet thou
hast found Venus, who, being of all the goddesses the
most fair, hath chosen thee of all the gods the most foul;
thou must needs then confess I was most loving. Inquire
not the cause of my suit by questions, but prevent the   10
effects by courtesy. Make me six arrow heads; it is given
thee of the gods by permission to frame them to any

107.1.] *This ed.; not in Q1; The curtains close / Bond; Exeunt / Daniel.*   0.1.]
Bond; Venus, Vulcan, Cupid / Q1; Enter Venus and Cupid, and, separately,
Vulcan and Calypho / Daniel.   2.1.] *This ed.; not in Q1; Vulcan looks out of the*
Forge / Bond.

103. *consume*] allow themselves to be consumed, waste away (*O.E.D.*, 6).
106–7. *whether . . . wings*] Sappho refers to her dream at the start of this
scene.
    ants wings] See II.i.147 and n.
    0.1.] Location is before the mouth of Vulcan's forge. The stage setting is
reminiscent of the blacksmith's shop provided for Mulciber (identified with
Vulcan or Hephaestus) in *Thersites*, 1537, where 'the god of fire, / Smith unto
Jupiter' forges weapons for the play's *miles gloriosus* hero (A1v; see Bond,
II.253). *Thersites*, like *Sappho and Phao*, is a boys' play, and in both plays the
part of Vulcan or Mulciber offers opportunities for comic exaggeration of
deformity and age by young actors (or, if an adult male took such parts, for
comic contrast between youth and age).
    1–2. *Vulcan's . . . fires*] i.e., Vulcan's forge must provide the arrows to cure
Venus' lovesickness.
    10–11. *prevent the effects*] anticipate the result.

purpose I shall request them by prayer. Why lourest
thou, Vulcan? Wilt thou have a kiss? Hold up thy head;
Venus hath young thoughts and fresh affections. Roots   15
have strings when boughs have no leaves. But hearken
in thine ear, Vulcan: how sayst thou?

Vulcan.   Vulcan is a god with you when you are disposed to
flatter—a right woman, whose tongue is like a bee's
sting, which pricketh deepest when it is fullest of   20
honey. Because you have made mine eyes drunk with
fair looks, you will set mine ears on edge with sweet
words. You were wont to say that the beating of hammers made your head ache and the smoke of the forge
your eyes water, and every coal was a block in your way.   25
You weep rose-water when you ask and spit vinegar
when you have obtained. What would you now with
new arrows? Belike Mars hath a tougher skin on his
heart, or Cupid a weaker arm, or Venus a better courage. Well, Venus, there is never a smile in your face but   30
hath made a wrinkle in my forehead. Ganymede must
fill your cup, and you will pledge none but Jupiter.

---

31. Ganymede] *This ed.; Ganymedes / Q1.*

13. *I shall*] i.e., for which I shall.

15–16. *Roots . . . leaves*] i.e., roots remain alive when boughs are bare in
winter. Even in the wintry relationship of Venus and Vulcan love may be
recoverable.

16. *strings*] root filaments (*O.E.D.*, 2b).

19. *a right woman*] a common phrase. *Right* (*O.E.D.*, adj., III. 17) means
'having the true character of'.

19–21. *bee's sting . . . honey*] proverbial (Dent, *P.L.E.D.*, B211). Compare
the Prologue at the Blackfriars, ll. 1–2, and *Euphues*, 1.224, 10–11: 'The bee
that hath honey in her mouth hath a sting in her tail.' Pliny, XI.19, reports the
opinion of some observers somewhat differently, that if bees' stings are driven
in far, some of the guts follow; afterwards the bees are drones and do not make
honey (compare Bond, II.563).

26. *weep rose-water . . . spit vinegar*] a conventional antithesis, of which this
passage is an early citation in Dent (*P.L.E.D.*, R186.11).

29–30. *courage*] inclination, spirit, vigour. Perhaps, says Vulcan, Venus
needs new arrows because she has some new scheme of conquest in love.

31. *wrinkle in my forehead*] (1) wrinkle of worry; (2) cuckold's horns.
Compare III.ii.49–64 above.

31–2. *Ganymede . . . cup*] i.e., you are not content to be waited on unless by
Jupiter's own cupbearer; you insist on the best for yourself.

32. *pledge*] drink a toast to.

But I will not chide, Venus. [*Calling within.*] Come,
Cyclops! My wife must have her will. Let us do that in
earth which the gods cannot undo in heaven.　　　　　　35
Venus. Gramercy, sweet Vulcan. To your work.

[*Enter* the Cyclopes.
Venus and Cupid stand aside.]

The Song, in making of the arrows

Vulcan. My shag-hair Cyclops, come, let's ply
　　Our Lemnian hammers lustily.
　　　　By my wife's sparrows,
　　　　I swear these arrows　　　　　　　　　40
　　　　Shall singing fly
　　　Through many a wanton's eye.
　　These headed are with golden blisses,
　　These silver ones feathered with kisses,

---

33. *Calling within*] This ed.; not in Q1.　36.1–2.] This ed.; not in Q1.　37–52.
Vulcan. My . . . holiday] Blount; not in Q1.

---

34. *Cyclops*] a singular form in Greek, but Lyly uses it in a plural sense; also
at l. 37.
　My wife . . . will] Compare the proverb, 'Women will have their wills'
(Dent, *P.L.E.D.*, W723), and *The Woman in the Moon*, V.i.326.
　that] i.e., make people fall in love; perhaps remembering Publilius Syrus:
'*Amare et sapere vix deo conceditur*', 'To love and be wise at the same time is
scarcely granted to a god' (*Sententiae*, pp. 16–17). Compare *Euphues*, I.210,
5–6: 'To love and to live well is not granted to Jupiter,' and *Campaspe*,
II.ii.105.
　36.3. *in making . . . arrows*] The song's title plainly calls for pantomimic
action to accompany the singing.
　37–52.] The Song has only Vulcan's name attached to it, and 'my' in l. 39
implies a single voice, but the last two lines suggest a more concerted effect.
　38. *Lemnian*] Vulcan refers to Lemnos in the Aegean, his favourite residence
among the Sintians, according to the *Iliad* (1.593–4). For having taken the part
of Juno (or Hera), Vulcan (or Hephaestus) was thrown out of heaven by
Jupiter (or Zeus), fell nine days and was picked up, with one leg broken, by
fishermen on the island of Lemnos. Milton alludes to the legendary fall of
Mulciber on to Lemnos in *Paradise Lost*, 1.740–7. Bond notes (II.563) that the
Cyclopes are often associated with Sicily (e.g., in the *Aeneid*, III.569ff.), where
this play is located. Vulcan's workshop was traditionally thought to be under
Mount Etna on Sicily. In some other legends, however, the Cyclopes occupied
Thrace.
　39. *sparrows*] On their association with Venus and lechery, see II.iv.26 and
III.iii.90–2 above and nn.

But this of lead   45
Strikes a clown dead
When in a dance
He falls in a trance,
To see his black-brow lass not buss him,
And then whines out for death t'untruss him.   50
So, so, our work being done, let's play,
Holiday, boys, cry holiday.
                    [*Exeunt* the Cyclopes *into the forge.*]
Vulcan. [*Presenting her with the arrows*] Here, Venus, I have
    finished these arrows by art; bestow them you by wit,
    for as great advice must he use that hath them as he   55
    cunning that made them.
Venus. Vulcan, now you have done with your forge, let us
    alone with the fancy; you are as the fletcher, not the
    archer, to meddle with the arrow, not the aim.
Vulcan. I thought so; when I have done working, you have   60
    done wooing. Where is now 'sweet Vulcan'? Well, I can
    say no more but this, which is enough and as much as
    any can say: Venus is a woman.
Venus. Be not angry, Vulcan; I will love thee again when I
    have either business or nothing else to do.   65

52.1.] *This ed.; not in Q1.*   53. *Presenting . . . arrows*] *This ed.; not in Q1.*

49. *black-brow*] The word suggests a rustic, unsophisticated kind of beauty
(as in *The Winter's Tale*, II.i.8, and *Love's Labour's Lost*, IV.iii.253), an
impression reinforced by the rustic register evident in *lass* and *buss* (kiss).

50. *untruss*] i.e., undo, unburden. The word (used most commonly of
undoing one's breeches) has a comic inappropriateness to high emotions. Lyly
uses it with satiric effect in reference to Sir Thopas (the *miles gloriosus*) in
Endymion, III.iii.142–4: 'Love . . . kept such a tumbling in his body that he
was glad to untruss the points of his heart'; and so here of the 'clown' or rustic
in l. 46.

55. *advice*] prudence.

57–8. *let . . . fancy*] leave the working out of the inventive design to me and
Cupid.

58. *fletcher*] maker of arrows.

59. *meddle*] busy yourself (a term often carrying erotic connotations).

60–1. *done . . . done*] completed . . . ceased.

63. *Venus is a woman*] a conventional misogynistic sentiment (compare
Dent, *P.L.E.D.*, W637.1).

65. *business*] i.e., a matter needing your assistance, like the arrows.

Cupid. My mother will make much of you when there are no
    more men than Vulcan.

[VULCAN retires into his forge.]

67.1.] *Bond; not in* Q*1.*

66–7. *when . . . Vulcan*] Compare the proverbial jest, 'If she (he) were the
only woman (man) (in the world)', Dent, *P.L.E.D.*, W631.

Act V

Actus Quintus, Scaena Prima.

VENUS [*and*] CUPID [*remain*].

Venus. Come, Cupid, receive with thy father's instruments thy
mother's instructions [*Presenting an arrow*], for thou
must be wise in conceit if thou wilt be fortunate in execution. This arrow is feathered with the wings of aegithus,
which never sleepeth for fear of his hen; the head   5
touched with the stone perillus, which causeth mistrust

0.1.] Daniel; *Venus, Cupid* / *Q1*.   2. *Presenting an arrow*] This ed.; not in *Q1*.

0.1.] The scene is unchanged, with Cupid and Venus remaining onstage. As
Bond notes (II.563), their dialogue may be designed to suggest a movement
towards Sappho's palace, but at the scene's end Venus can exit into the forge to
await the result of Cupid's work.

1. *thy father's*] Traditionally Cupid is the son of Venus and Mercury, but
here the father is Vulcan. See I.i.20.1 and n. above.

2–44. Presenting an arrow . . . a sixth arrow] I am informed by Thomas
Hyde that Cupid seemingly does not acquire multiple arrows in antiquity other
than the golden and lead arrows mentioned in Ovid's *Metamorphoses*, I (see
ll. 39–40n. below). Such mythographers as Giraldi, Conti and Cartari do not
mention the arrows used in this present scene. In the *Roman de la Rose*
(907ff.), Dieu d'amours has two bows that correspond to Ovid's two arrows
and five arrows to go with each bow: golden arrows for beauty, simplicity,
openness, company and fair seeming, black arrows for pride, villainy, shame,
despair and new thought. Analogues link these arrows to the 'quinque lineae'
of love. Lyly does not follow this allegorical tradition of equating various
arrows with the causes of love or the psychology of enamourment. The arrows
in this scene, Hyde suggests, are probably mythographic inventions, variations
on received themes, like the play itself. See also Thomas Hyde, *The Poetic
Theology of Love: Cupid in Renaissance Literature* (Newark, Del., 1986) and
William Allan Neilson, *The Origins and Sources of the Court of Love* (Boston,
1899; rpt. New York, 1967).

3. *conceit*] conception, idea.

4–5. *aegithus . . . hen*] According to Pliny, x.9, the *aegithus* is a kind of hawk
which, when lame in one foot, is a fortunate omen for marriage contracts and
the like ('*ex his aegithum claudum altero pede prosperrimi augurii nuptialibus
negotiis et pecuariae rei*'). The description suggests Vulcan, lame and watchfully
jealous of his wife.

6. *perillus*] evidently Lyly's invention (Bond, II.564).

and jealousy. Shoot this, Cupid, at men that have fair
wives, which will make them rub the brows when they
swell in the brains. [*Presenting a second arrow*] This shaft
is headed with Lydian steel, which striketh a deep dis-   10
dain of that which we most desire; the feathers are of
turtle, but dipped in the blood of a tigress. Draw this up
close to the head at Sappho, that she may despise where
now she dotes. Good my boy, gall her on the side, that
for Phao's love she may never sigh. [*Presenting a third*   15
arrow] This arrow is feathered with the phoenix' wing,
and headed with the eagle's bill; it maketh men passionate in desires, in love constant, and wise in conveyance,
melting as it were their fancies into faith. This arrow,
sweet child, and with as great aim as thou canst, must   20
Phao be stricken withal; and cry softly to thyself in the
very loose, 'Venus!' Sweet Cupid, mistake it not; I will
make a quiver for that by itself. [*Presenting a fourth*
arrow] The fourth hath feathers of the peacock, but
glued with the gum of the myrtle tree, headed with fine   25

---

9. *Presenting a second arrow*] *This ed.; not in Q1.*   15–16. *Presenting a third*
arrow] *This ed.; not in Q1.*   22. Sweet] *Q2* (Sweete); Swite *Q1.*   it] *Q1*; me
Q2.   23–4. *Presenting a fourth arrow*] *This ed.; not in Q1.*

8. *rub the brows*] i.e., detect cuckold's horns.
9. *swell in the brains*] conceive jealous thoughts.
10. *Lydian steel*] evidently another Lylyan invention.
striketh] induces, impresses on the mind (*O.E.D.*, vb., 66).
12. *turtle*] turtledove.
13. *close to the head*] See I.i.54 and n.
14. *on the side*] in the midriff (*O.E.D.*, *side*, 1), whence come her *sighs.*
16. *phoenix'*] legendary bird thought to be consumed in flame and reborn in
its own ashes, symbol of immortality and constancy.
17. *eagle's*] The eagle is a royal bird, as in the Prologue at the Court, l. 6, and
at III.iii.87.
18. *conveyance*] clever management (of the love affair).
22. *loose*] loosing of the shaft.
it] Q2's emendation to 'me' is interesting even though Q1 can be read
intelligibly; the emendation is likely to be no more than the Q2 compositor's
guess, and is unnecessary. There is a misprint earlier in the same line in Q1
('Swite', corrected in Q2 to 'Sweete').
24. *peacock*] a type of vainglory, as for example at II.iv.76 above and in
Euphues, II.86, 26–7 and II.199, 21. The image recurs at V.ii.86–7 below.
25. *myrtle*] a tree sacred to Venus and used as an emblem of love (*O.E.D.*).

gold, and fastened with brittle chrysocoll. This shoot at
dainty and coy ladies, at amiable and young nymphs;
choose no other white but women. For this will work
liking in their minds, but not love; affability in speech,
but no faith; courtly favours, to be mistresses over　　30
many but constant to none; sighs to be fetched from
the lungs, not the heart, and tears to be wrung out with
their fingers, not their eyes; secret laughing at men's
pale looks and neat attire, open rejoicing at their own
comeliness and men's courting. Shoot this arrow among　　35
the thickest of them, whose bosoms lie open because
they would be stricken with it. And, seeing men term
women Jupiter's fools, women shall make men Venus'
fools. [*Presenting a fifth arrow*] This shaft is lead in the
head, and whose feathers are of the night-raven, a deadly　　40
and poisoned shaft which breedeth hate only against

---

39. *Presenting a fifth arrow*] This ed.; not in *QI*.

---

26. *chrysocoll*] Pliny, XXXIII.26, speaks of chrysocolla as a liquid flowing
through the veins of gold, a kind of slime that becomes hardened by the cold of
winter until it attains the hardness of pumice, hence 'brittle' ('*Chrysocolla umor
est in puteis, quos diximus, per venam auri defluens crassescente limo rigoribus
hibernis usque in duritiam pucimis*'; see Bond, II.564).

28. *white*] target, literally the white centre or bull's eye. Similarly in
Euphues, II.166, 5, and 168, 12, the beauty of women is 'the white, a fair mark
for him that draweth in Cupid's bow'. (Perhaps with a pun on *wight*, living
being.)

32–3. *with their fingers*] The finger in the eye is a conventional outward sign
of distress (Dent, *P.L.E.D.*, F229), here seen as a superficial sign only.

34. *pale . . . attire*] conventional signs of the lover.

35–6. *among the thickest*] in the very midst.

37. *would*] wish to; but with suggestion also of 'deserve to'. Such court
ladies who want to be coy flirts get what they ask for.

38. *Jupiter's fools*] i.e., often seduced by the king of the gods, and
(implicitly) by men as well.

38–9. *Venus' fools*] i.e., slaves to feminine caprice.

39–40. *lead . . . head*] Cupid's arrows of gold and lead, one causing love and
the other a negation of love, and indeed the whole concept of Cupid drawing
from his quiver different sorts of arrows, are found in Ovid, *Metamorphoses*,
1.470–1, but see also note at ll. 2–44 above. In *Cambyses*, *c.* 1561, scene ix,
Venus enters 'leading out her son Cupid, blind: he must have a bow and two
shafts, one headed with gold and the other with lead'. Venus bids her son
shoot King Cambyses with the gold-headed arrows so that the king will fall in
love with his kinswoman. (See Bond, II.253–4.)

41. *hate only*] nothing but hate.

those which sue for love. Take heed, Cupid, thou hit
not Phao with this shaft, for then shall Venus perish.
[*Presenting a sixth arrow*] This last is an old arrow but
newly mended, the arrow which hit both Sappho and   45
Phao, working only in mean minds an aspiring to supe-
riors and in high estates a stooping to inferiors; with
this, Cupid, I am galled myself, till thou have galled
Phao with the other.

Cupid. I warrant you, I will cause Phao to languish in your   50
love and Sappho to disdain his.

Venus. Go, loiter not, nor mistake your shaft.

                                  [*Exit* CUPID.]

Now, Venus, hast thou played a cunning part, though
not current. But why should Venus dispute of unlawful-
ness in love or faith in affection, being both the goddess   55
of love and affection, knowing there is as little truth
to be used in love as there is reason? No, sweet Phao,
Venus will obtain because she is Venus. Not thou, Jove,
with thunder in thy hand, shalt take him out of my
hands; I have new arrows now for my boy, and fresh   60
flames at which the gods shall tremble if they begin to
trouble me. But I will expect the event, and tarry for
Cupid at the forge.   [*Exit into the forge.*]

           Actus Quintus, Scaena Secunda.

      [*Enter*] SAPPHO, CUPID [*and*] MILETA.

Sappho. What hast thou done, Cupid?

44. *Presenting a sixth arrow*] *This ed.; not in Q1.*   47. high] *Q1* (heigh).   52.1.]
Bond; not in Q1.   63. *Exit . . . forge*] *Bond (subst); not in Q1.*   o.1.] *Daniel
(subst.); Sapho, Cupid, Mileta, Venus / Q1.*

    42. *sue*] plead, petition.
    44–5. *but newly*] only recently.
    46. *mean*] lowly.
    48. *galled . . . galled*] unquiet, distressed . . . wounded.
    49. *the other*] i.e., the third arrow above, of passionate and constant love.
    54. *current*] generally accepted, or smoothly flowing. As Venus goes on to
admit, her conduct goes against law and custom.
    dispute of] argue or debate about.
    62. *expect the event*] await the outcome.
    o.1.] We are evidently to understand that we are at Sappho's palace, though
not her bedchamber; the bed-curtains are not mentioned. Sappho must have a
throne to sit in when Cupid crawls into her lap, and the scene closes with
Sappho's order to shut the door.

Cupid. That my mother commanded, Sappho.

Sappho. Methinks I feel an alteration in my mind and as it were a withdrawing in myself of mine own affections.

Cupid. Then hath mine arrow his effect.   5

Sappho. I pray thee, tell me the cause.

Cupid. I dare not.

Sappho. Fear nothing, for if Venus fret, Sappho can frown; thou shalt be my son. Mileta, give him some sweetmeats. Speak, good Cupid, and I will give thee many   10 pretty things.

Cupid. My mother is in love with Phao. She willed me to strike you with disdain of him and him with desire of her.

Sappho. O spiteful Venus! Mileta, give him some of that. What else, Cupid?   15

Cupid. I could be even with my mother, and so I will if I shall call you mother.

Sappho. Yea, Cupid, call me anything, so I may be even with her.

Cupid. I have an arrow with which if I strike Phao it will cause   20 him to loathe only Venus.

Sappho. Sweet Cupid, strike Phao with it. Thou shalt sit in my lap; I will rock thee asleep and feed thee with all these fine knacks.

Cupid. I will about it.   *Exit* CUPID.   25

Sappho. But come quickly again.—Ah, unkind Venus, is this thy promise to Sappho? But if I get Cupid from thee,

---

4. withdrawing] *Q1;* withstanding *Q2.*

---

2. *That*] That which.

4. *withdrawing*] Q2's 'withstanding' is an interesting reading, but it has no authority and Q1's word is obviously appropriate.

in] into.

5. *his*] its.

12–13. *strike . . . of him*] Venus' orders, carried out for her own self-interested aims, have the paradoxical effect of allowing Sappho to achieve the self-mastery she has desired.

14. *some of that*] i.e., more sweetmeats (ll. 9–10).

18. *so*] provided that.

20. *an arrow*] presumably the arrow that breeds hate, given to Cupid at V.i.39.

21. *loathe only*] do nothing but loathe. Compare *hate only* in V.i.41.

24. *knacks*] dainties, delicacies (*O.E.D.*, 3b).

27. *thy promise*] given at IV.i.16–20.

I myself will be the queen of love. I will direct these
arrows with better aim and conquer mine own affections
with greater modesty. Venus' heart shall flame, and her   30
love be as common as her craft. O Mileta, time hath
disclosed that which my temperance hath kept in! But
sith I am rid of the disease, I will not be ashamed to
confess the cause. I loved Phao, Mileta—a thing unfit
for my degree, but forced by my desire.   35

Mileta. Phao?

Sappho. Phao, Mileta, of whom now Venus is enamoured.

Mileta. And do you love him still?

Sappho. No, I feel relenting thoughts, and reason not yielding
to appetite. Let Venus have him—No, she shall not   40
have him. But here comes Cupid.

[*Enter* CUPID. *He climbs onto Sappho's lap
and gives her his arrows.*]

How now, my boy, hast thou done it?

Cupid. Yea, and left Phao railing on Venus and cursing her
name, yet still sighing for Sappho and blazing her
virtues.   45

Sappho. Alas, poor Phao! Thy extreme love should not be
requited with so mean a fortune; thy fair face deserved
greater favours. I cannot love; Venus hath hardened my
heart.

[*Enter*] VENUS.

Venus. I marvel Cupid cometh not all this while. — How now,   50
in Sappho's lap?

Sappho. Yea, Venus, what say you to it, in Sappho's lap?

Venus. Sir boy, come hither.

Cupid. I will not.

Venus. What now? Will you not? Hath Sappho made you so   55
saucy?

41.1–2.] *This ed.; not in Q1; Re-enter Cupid / Bond.*   49.1.] *Bond; not in Q1.*

31. *common*] indiscriminate, frequent, sluttish.
32. *kept in*] kept hidden.
39. *relenting*] slackening, cooling (*O.E.D., relent,* 2c).
44. *still*] continually.
blazing] emblazoning, proclaiming.

Cupid. I will be Sappho's son. I have, as you commanded,
   stricken her with a deep disdain of Phao, and Phao, as
   she entreated me, with a great despite of you.

Venus. Unhappy wag, what hast thou done? I will make thee   60
   repent it, every vein in thy heart.

Sappho. Venus, be not choleric. Cupid is mine; he hath given
   me his arrows, and I will give him a new bow to shoot in.
   You are not worthy to be the lady of love, that yield so
   often to the impressions of love. Immodest Venus, that   65
   to satisfy the unbridled thoughts of thy heart trans-
   gressest so far from the stay of thine honour!—How
   sayst thou, Cupid, wilt thou be with me?

Cupid. Yes.

Sappho. Shall not I be on earth the goddess of affections?   70

Cupid. Yes.

Sappho. Shall not I rule the fancies of men and lead Venus in
   chains like a captive?

Cupid. Yes.

Sappho. It is a good boy.   75

Venus. What have we here? You the goddess of love? And you
   her son, Cupid? I will tame that proud heart, else shall
   the gods say they are not Venus' friends. And as for
   you, sir boy, I will teach you how to run away: you shall
   be stripped from top to toe, and whipped with nettles,   80
   not roses. I will set you to blow Vulcan's coals, not to
   bear Venus' quiver. I will handle you for this gear. Well,

---

62–3. *he . . . arrows*] Compare Thomas Churchyard's *A Discourse of the
Queen's Majesty's Entertainment in Suffolk and Norfolk*, etc. (often referred to as
The Norwich Entertainment), 1578, where Queen Elizabeth is made the
recipient of Cupid's bow and arrows tipped with lead or with gold (sig.
C4v–E2; reprinted in John Nichols, ed., *The Progresses and Public Procesions of
Queen Elizabeth*, 3 vols., 1788–1805).

64. *the lady of love*] the lady who rules love (*O.E.D.*, *lady*, 2). This sense
sharpens the antithesis to 'yield' in l. 64.

67. *stay*] restraint.

76–80. *What have we here, from top to toe, whipped with nettles*] commonplace expressions (Dent, *P.L.E.D.*, W280.2, T436, N135.1). Lyly's use of
'whipped with nettles' is the earliest example of this cited by Dent.

80–1. *nettles, not roses*] Compare the motto in the Prologue to *Midas*, 'Stirps
rudis urtica est: stirps generosa, rosa*', 'A person of base stock is a nettle, one of
noble birth a rose.'

82. *handle you*] treat you (badly).

gear] matter, goings on.

I say no more. But as for the new mistress of love, or
lady—I cry you mercy, I think you would be called a
goddess—you shall know what it is to usurp the name of   85
Venus. I will pull those plumes and cause you to cast
your eyes on your feet, not your feathers; your soft hair
will I turn to hard bristles, your tongue to a sting, and
those alluring eyes to unluckiness, in which, if the gods
aid me not, I will curse the gods.   90

Sappho. Venus, you are in a vein answerable to your vanity,
whose high words neither become you nor fear me. But
let this suffice: I will keep Cupid in despite of you, and
yet with the content of the gods.

Venus. Will you? Why then we shall have pretty gods in   95
heaven, when you take gods prisoners on earth. Before
I sleep, you shall both repent and find what it is but to
think unreverently of Venus. Come, Cupid, she knows
not how to use thee. Come with me, you know what I
have for you. Will you not?   100

---

83. *I say no more*] See I.ii.4 and n.

84. *cry you mercy*] beg your pardon (said with mocking politeness). Compare
Mother Bombie, IV.ii.28: 'I cry you mercy, I took you for a joint stool', the
familiar form of the phrase that turns up in *King Lear,* III.vi.52.

86. *pull those plumes*] a conventional image of stripping someone of the
symbols of dignity and rank (Dent, *P.L.E.D.,* P441.1). Compare Robert
Greene's *Friar Bacon,* c. 1589–92, ed. Daniel Seltzer, 1963, VIII.115: 'And
shall thy plumes be pulled by Venus down?'

86–7. *cause . . . feathers*] The peacock 'hath foulest feet and rivelled [i.e.,
wrinkled]. And he wondereth of the fairness of his feathers, and areareth them
up as it were a circle about his head, and then he looketh to his feet and seeth
the foulness of his feet and, like as he were ashamed, he letteth his feathers fall
suddenly and all the tail downward' (*Bartholomew* [Berthelet], XII.xxxi,
p. clxxiii'). See Dent, *P.L.E.D.,* P158. The image of the peacock occurs
earlier at II.iv.76 and V.i.24. *Feathers* and *eyes* (in the context of a reference to
the peacock) are connected by the idea of the 'eyes' in a peacock's tail.
Compare the Prologue at the Blackfriars to *Campaspe,* ll. 1–2.

89. *unluckiness*] This seems a strange antithesis for *alluring,* unless (as
George Hunter suggests) the pronunciation allows un-*looky*-ness. But Venus
may simply mean that Sappho will no longer be lucky in attracting men with
her alluring eyes. In her vengeful wish to transform Sappho into a stinging
animal, Venus resembles Circe.

92. *high*] haughty.
fear] frighten.

97. *but*] merely.

Cupid. Not I.

Venus. Well, I will be even with you both, and that shortly.

Exit.

Sappho. Cupid, fear not, I will direct thine arrows better.
Every rude ass shall not say he is in love. It is a toy made
for ladies, and I will keep it only for ladies.   105

Cupid. But what will you do for Phao?

Sappho. I will wish him fortunate. This will I do for Phao,
because I once loved Phao; for never shall it be said that
Sappho loved to hate, or that out of love she could not
be as courteous as she was in love passionate. Come,   110
Mileta, shut the door.   *Exeunt.*

Actus Quintus, Scaena Tertia.

[*Enter*] PHAO [*to*] SYBILLA [*at the mouth of her cave*].

Phao. [*To himself*] Go to Sibylla, tell the beginning of thy love
and the end of thy fortune. And lo, how happily she
sitteth in her cave. — Sibylla?

Sibylla. Phao, welcome. What news?

Phao. Venus, the goddess of love, I loathe; Cupid caused it   5
with a new shaft. Sappho disdaineth me; Venus caused
it for a new spite. O Sibylla, if Venus be unfaithful in
love, where shall one fly for truth? She useth deceit; is it
not then likely she will dispense with subtlety? And,
being careful to commit injuries, will she not be careless   10
to revenge them? I must now fall from love to labour,
and endeavour with mine oar to get a fare, not with my

0.1.] *Bond (subst.); Phao, Sybilla / Q1.*   1. *To himself*] *This ed.; not in Q1.*
Go to] *Q2;* Goe too *Q1.*

---

111. *shut the door*] Sappho's order indicates a more formal courtly scene and
ceremonial exit, through one of the stage doors, than in her bedchamber
scenes. She has recovered her full regal dignity.

2. *happily*] by good fortune, haply.

8. *truth*] faith and trust (in love).

9. *dispense with*] grant dispensation for, permit (*O.E.D.*, 15).

10. *careful*] painstaking, zealous; antithetical to *careless*, with reckless
disregard of the consequences, *O.E.D.*, 3.

10–11. *careless . . . them*] careless in revenging the injuries done her;
disregarding the hurt she does.

pen to write a fancy. Loves are but smokes which vanish
in the seeing and yet hurt whilst they are seen. A ferry,
Phao? No, the stars cannot call it a worser fortune.   15
Range rather over the world, forswear affections, entreat for death. O Sappho, thou hast Cupid in thine
arms, I in my heart; thou kissest him for sport, I must
curse him for spite. Yet will I not curse him, Sappho,
whom thou kissest. This shall be my resolution: wher-   20
ever I wander, to be as I were ever kneeling before
Sappho, my loyalty unspotted though unrewarded.
With as little malice will I go to my grave as I did lie
withal in my cradle. My life shall be spent in sighing
and wishing, the one for my bad fortune, the other for   25
Sappho's good.

Sibylla. Do so, Phao, for destiny calleth thee as well from
Sicily as from love. Other things hang over thy head,
which I must neither tell nor thou inquire. And so
farewell.   [*Exit* SIBYLLA *into her cave.*]   30

Phao. Farewell, Sibylla, and farewell, Sicily! Thoughts shall be
thy food, and in thy steps shall be printed behind thee

---

15. call it] *Q1;* call thee to *Bond.*   16. Range] *Blount;* Raung *Q1.*   30. *Exit
. . . cave*] *This ed.; not in Q1; Exit Sybilla / Daniel.*

---

13. *a fancy*] a literary invention, love sonnet.
   smokes which vanish] 'To vanish like smoke' is proverbial (Dent, *P.L.E.D.*,
S576.11).
   15. *the stars . . . fortune*] i.e., being a ferryman once again is not the *worser
fortune* (because deprived of Sappho) that my stars have allotted me. Phao has
determined not to 'endeavour with mine oar to get a fare', as he puts it in l. 12,
but to embrace a peripatetic fortune more suited to his bitterness. Bond's
emendation, 'the stars cannot call thee to a worser fortune', seems
unnecessary.
   21. *as I were*] as if I were.
   kneeling] Perhaps we are to understand that at this point the actor kneels
before Queen Elizabeth, as commonly at the end of court plays. The speaker of
the Epilogue might normally be expected to perform that function instead, but
that speech is addressed throughout to all the audience and seems designed for
Blackfriars performance. Compare the kneeling in the Prologue at the Court,
l. 14 and n.
   27. *destiny calleth thee*] On possible allegorical interpretations, see Introduction, pp. 164–71.
   32. *thy*] Phao speaks to himself.

that there was none so loyal left behind thee. Farewell,
Syracusa, unworthy to harbour faith, and, when I am
gone, unless Sappho be here, unlikely to harbour any.   35
[*Exit.*]

35.1.] *Daniel; not in Q1; Exeunt | Bond.*

The Epilogue

They that tread in a maze walk oftentimes in one path, and
at the last come out where they entered in. We fear we have
led you all this while in a labyrinth of conceits, divers times
hearing one device, and have now brought you to an end where
we first began; which wearisome travail you must impute to   5
the necessity of the history, as Theseus did his labour to the art
of the labyrinth. There is nothing causeth such giddiness as
going in a wheel, neither can there anything breed such tediousness as hearing many words uttered in a small compass. But if
you accept this dance of a fairy in a circle, we will hereafter at   10
your wills frame our fingers to all forms. And so we wish every
one of you a thread to lead you out of the doubts wherewith we
leave you intangled, that nothing be mistaken by our rash
oversights nor misconstrued by your deep insights.

---

5. travail] *Q1* (trauaile).   Q1 concludes with a colophon: '*Imprinted at London
by Tho-/*mas Dawson, for Thomas Cadman.'

---

1. *maze*] See T. W. Baldwin, *William Shakspere's Five-Act Structure*, pp.
499–500, on the Epilogue as a clue to the structure of the play.

5. *travail*] The Q1 reading, 'trauaile', supports the meanings of labour and
of travel in a labyrinth.

6. *Theseus*] Theseus slew the Minotaur of Crete with Ariadne's help, and
made his way out of Daedalus' famous labyrinth by means of a ball of golden
thread (see l. 13). Lyly invites his spectators to see themselves as like Theseus,
unravelling what apears at first to be only a maze. A favourite image: compare
II.i.40 above; *Euphues*, 1.289, 8; II.22, 21; II.52, 25–6; II.121, 18; II.156,
20–1, etc.

9. *compass*] circumscribed time and space, but with a play on the idea of a
wheel (l. 8) or *circle* (l. 10).

10. *circle*] (1) the circular dramatic structure as described; (2) the magic
circle within which the magician has conjured the dancing fairy.

11. *forms*] images, representations. The dramatist and his acting company
promise to reward an appreciative audience with further dramatic representations made to suit the audience's pleasure.

12–14. *a thread . . . insights*] The disclaimer of rash purpose by the dramatist
and warning against overinterpretation seem called for by the delicacy of
allegorical interpretations to which the play lends itself, but the idea is also
conventional.

APPENDIX
The Songs in *Campaspe* and *Sappho and Phao*

On the general question of the authorship of the songs in Lyly's plays, I do not see any reason to change the argument presented in the Appendix to my *John Lyly*, pp. 367–72. The songs were not printed in Lyly's lifetime; their first appearance was in the texts Blount printed in 1632 in his *Six Court Comedies*. The possibility that Blount derived the song texts from sources that were not authentic is thus opened up as an intriguing hypothesis. It is a hypothesis impossible to disprove; but the evidence that has been adduced to support it is equally without force. And that may be the strongest statement on this matter that can be made. What seems to be re-quired of an editor of Lyly is, instead of a fruitless speculation about authenticity, rather a handling of the songs in terms of the effect they make in their current positions; and it is to this issue that I shall devote the present appendix.

How can one describe the songs that appear in this volume? Fortunately they all conform to types that are well attested in Eliza-bethan music. Three of the songs, *Campaspe*, I.ii, *Sappho and Phao*, II.iii and III.ii—all at the ends of the scenes in which they appear—belong to the category of the popular 'three-man' or 'freeman' song. In all the cases these are songs of good life, sung in the anticipation of eating and drinking. In the *Campaspe* song the three servant boys (Granichus, Psyllus, Manes) are leaving the scene in order to eat well at Plato's expense. Each boy has one stanza, the leader (Manes) having the last one; in the course of the song the 'riddle'—which is best: wine (stanza 1), women (stanza 2), or food (stanza 3)—is ex-plored and then given its definitive answer (food). All three sing the final verse in which the primacy of food is asserted, though all three delights are celebrated.

In *Sappho and Phao* II.iii the singers are the courtly pages Criticus and Molus and the Cyclops, Callipho. Again we have singing as an anticipation of and substitute for physical enjoyment ('To th' tap-house then let's gang'), reconciling, as in the *Campaspe* example, the oppositions that have emerged most strongly in the logic-chopping of the preceding dialogue by means of a musically controlled presentation, numbering down the line, one, two, three, and concluding in a chorus. I suspect that Callipho the Cyclops, who has been the clumsy butt of the boys' nimble wit in the preceding dialogue, may have been played by an adult,[1] who would naturally supply the bass line in the choric section. The same threesome sings a second three-man song at the end of Act III, scene ii, this time in a celebration of Bacchus and his modern representatives. This is the most elaborately organised of the three-man songs in these plays: beginning and ending with the metaphor of war, it sets up a series of irregular 'stanzas' in the middle (each stanza introduced by a question to Molus) and each in turn evoking some vision of hectic drunkenness as a set of questions and answers is passed nimbly from person to person across the Hudibrastic metre.[2]

The love songs of Apelles (III.v.71ff.) and Sappho (III.iii.146ff.) mark quite a different use of the powers of these boy singers. Both of these are solo songs arising out of erotic frustration and sung in soliloquy. Apelles ends his long preceding speech by stating the impossibility of rendering his love in spoken utterance, and then he breaks into song. Sappho, bedsick with frustrated love, calls for her lute to 'see if in song I can beguile mine own eyes', dismisses her waiting women, and then sings (to her own accompaniment on the lute, one must assume). Both singers evoke their own situations, however, only at the very ends of their songs. The rest of their material is elaborately, even playfully, oblique, made up out of imagined mythological scenes organised as catalogues: Cupid and Campaspe are imagined playing at cards for kisses, and a list of the stakes set and lost is given; Love (or Cupid) is cursed with a series of pains and deprivations, and a list of these is given. The metrical forms here are regular but non-stanzaic. Music is used in these scenes, no less than in the three-man songs, to present a reconciliation of points of view that the prose dialogue can only show as antithetical. Among the servants, the reconciliation that drowns the argument is social drinking, represented by social singing; in the high-life world of individualised emotion, the imagination of an externally structured art-world is shown to have power to calm the fevered mind and reconcile it to external reality.

1. See Hunter, *John Lyly*, p. 92, n. 15.
2. Molus makes a remark here which may have a bearing on the performance of the songs. 'If we shall sing' he says, 'give me my part quickly'. This could be taken to imply that the boys used their part-books for their performances.

The two remaining songs in these plays both in their different ways integrate the music into scenes which are in some sense *about* music. In Act V, scene i of *Campaspe* Sylvius brings his performing children to Diogenes to see if he will agree to tutor them. Trico's particular talent is in singing and he demonstrates this in a song, just as his brothers have demonstrated dancing and tumbling. The song, 'What bird so sings' (ll. 35ff.), is presumably, given the context, presented as a virtuoso prize-song and it would not be surprising to learn that the bird noises were given a fairly elaborate treatment. If that were so, Diogenes' derogatory comments would fit not only with his character but also with a widespread distrust of elaborate vocalisations. It would be like Lyly to give us a highly wrought model of art together with a plausible reason for distrusting it.

In *Sappho and Phao* the most integrated of the songs has, un- usually, an authentic stage direction, printed in the quartos, relating it to the action of the play. Act IV, scene iv shows us Venus per- suading Vulcan to forge new arrows for Cupid's bow. Her seduction works, and then we see Vulcan and his Cyclopes at the forge, he singing 'the song, in making of the arrows' (ll. 36.3ff.) with (perhaps) some choral reinforcement. The context marks this out as a work- song, but the rhythmical oddity of the verse suggests something more grotesque, more appropriate to the character of the uxorious lame god. Whether or not the Cyclopes beat time with hammers on anvils cannot be said. The possibility of an early version of the Anvil Chorus is intriguing but must be suspect.

Glossarial Index to the Commentary

An asterisk indicates that the annotation supplements information relating to sense, usage or date provided by the *O.E.D.*. The form listed is usually that which appears in the text. When a gloss is repeated in the annotations, only the initial occurrence is indexed.